A MULTILINGUAL DICTIONARY OF ARTIFICIAL INTELLIGENCE

English, German, French, Spanish, Italian

OTTO VOLLNHALS

ROUTLEDGE

LONDON AND NEW YORK

First published in 1992
by Routledge
11 New Fetter Lane, London EC4P 4EE

Simultaneously published in the USA and Canada
by Routledge
a division of Routledge, Chapman and Hall, Inc.
29 West 35th Street, New York, NY 10001

Set in 9/11pt Times, 500 DPI by Quorum Technical Services Limited, Cheltenham, Gloucestershire, GL52 6XH
Printed in Great Britain by Clays Ltd, St Ives plc

British Library Cataloguing in Publication Data
A catalogue record for this book is available from the British Library.

Library of Congress Cataloging-in-Publication Data
Vollnhals, Otto.
A multilingual dictionary of artificial intelligence / Otto Vollnhals.
p. cm.
Includes index.
ISBN 0-415-07465-7 (HB)
1. Artificial intelligence—Dictionaries—Polyglot.
2. Dictionaries, Polyglot. I. Title
Q334.2.V65 1992 91-36370
006.3'03—dc20 CIP

CONTENTS

INTRODUCTION

This dictionary is the result of several years' intensive study of the specialist literature in all areas within the field of artificial intelligence. It was in the process of reading material in five languages (English, German, French, Spanish and Italian), all covering the same subject matter, that the idea arose of carrying out a systematic terminological study and establishing linguistic equivalents between the languages. The use of a laptop PC and a database program lightened the load considerably, indeed made it almost enjoyable, especially during the stage in which the word list was growing from an initially modest bilingual glossary to a fully fledged database with many thousands of entries covering five languages.

The process of refining and checking the contents of the work to attain the high level of comprehensiveness and consistency that was always the target was carried out by combing numerous indexes, detailed contents listings and vocabulary lists gleaned from specialist publications, trade fair catalogues and conference papers. The inexhaustible wealth of literature on AI held in Siemens AG's technical library at their Munich Perlach plant was also absolutely invaluable in ensuring that all the most current AI terminology was extensively covered.

The sheer number of publications that have appeared over the last few years in the field of AI is so immense that any bibliography that could be given here would be hopelessly incomplete. Rather than produce a listing so inadequate as to be useless, the decision has been taken to omit a bibliography completely.

Areas covered

EXPERT SYSTEMS
GAMES
IMAGE PROCESSING
KNOWLEDGE
LEARNING
LINGUISTICS
LOGIC
MT (MACHINE TRANSLATION)
MATHS
NEURAL NETS
NLP (NATURAL LANGUAGE PROCESSING)
PROGRAMMING
RECOGNITION
ROBOTICS
SYNTHESIS
THEORY

All the important subject areas within artificial intelligence are represented, as well as the relatively new field of neural networks. Expert systems receives the fullest attention, reflecting its present significance within the subject. Conventional robotics, on the other hand, has been pared to only the bare essentials. Terminology from tangentially related disciplines has also been included where it is important to the field of AI. Entries with no subject label are either self-explanatory (e.g. 'speech recognition') or not confined to one area (e.g. 'rule'), or they belong to the basic vocabulary of AI (e.g. 'learning'). The most significant subject area for any one entry term is given here, but that should not be taken to indicate that the term is restricted to that area.

Selection criteria

With such a rapidly developing subject as artificial intelligence it is inevitable that there are a number of different movements and schools of thought, not just at the research level but also within the sphere of development and production. This not infrequently leads to conflicting terminological usage, which a dictionary of this kind cannot hope to explore or explain. No statement on the status of the English headwords nor of their equivalent terms in the four target languages is implied by their inclusion here; their presence is simply a reflection of their occurrence in the specialist literature. Similarly, the order in which synonyms or translations are given does not imply an order of preference, nor does it imply that one term may be more standard than another. The fact that English terms are used liberally in the field of AI not just in German but also in the romance languages has also been appropriately reflected here.

Organization of material

In the main section of the dictionary, in which all five languages are presented, English has been used as the language determining the lexicographic presentation. The headwords are arranged and numbered in English alphabetical order. The other languages are accessed by means of alphabetical indexes, one for each language. In line with standard practice nowadays, strict letter-by-letter alphabetical order is followed throughout. Comments, explanations and references to synonyms and antonyms further increase the usefulness of the dictionary, especially to those people who are not themselves experts in the field of AI. The structure of the main section and of the indexes has been kept deliberately simple in order that even the casual user can be confident of obtaining maximum information quickly and easily.

Grammatical information

Grammatical information (noun, adjective, verb, etc.) is only given for the English headwords when not to do so could result in mistakes or misunderstandings. In the target languages, the gender of all nominal translations is given. In cases where the translation follows the pattern 'noun + preposition + noun' – a particularly common structure in the romance languages – the gender marking refers to the first noun, as the head of the translation, although for technical reasons it is given after the complete translation. This point should be borne in mind by the user who might otherwise be led into making mistakes.

Genders have been given throughout the main section of the dictionary but not in the indexes, which have been left as uncluttered as possible.

Cross-references

For the sake of simplicity, different symbols have been used to distinguish types of cross-reference. The ordinary 'see' or 'see also' type of cross-reference is denoted by →. Abbreviations are entered in their strict alphabetical place with a cross-reference to the full form, for example:

CWA → closed world assumption

At 'closed world assumption' the user will find the complete entry giving all the languages and including the abbreviation.

Synonyms are indicated by the = sign. In order to make synonymous relationships clear, all the synonyms are listed at the relevant main entry, for example:

if–then rule = production rule; condition–action rule

Each individual synonym also appears in its alphabetical place, cross-referred to the main entry, thus:

production rule → if–then rule

Abbreviations of synonyms of main entries are also given cross-references to the main entries, for example:

PDP = parallel distributed programming → connection science

Terms with opposite meanings are indicated by the symbol ≠, for example:

permanent knowledge ≠ temporary knowledge

Finally, the symbol ↔ invites the user to compare the term with a related term, for example:

voice chip ↔ speech-processing chip

Other features

The romance languages allow much more flexibility with the building blocks of a multi-word term than is the case in either German or English. Take for example the term 'word hypothesis generation'. In the romance languages, the precise translation will depend on whether only one hypothesis or several hypotheses are to be generated, and furthermore whether they are to be generated for only one word or for several words - 'génération de l'hypothèse du mot', 'génération des hypothèses des mots', etc. It would be impracticable, if not impossible, to list in a dictionary all the variants that might arise. If for no other reasons than the constraints of space, a dictionary must limit itself to presenting a selection only. In such cases users must apply their own knowledge of the language to find the most appropriate formulation for the particular context before them. This dictionary can only provide the building blocks, not the finished building.

Otto Vollnhals
Munich, Spring 1992

A MULTILINGUAL DICTIONARY OF ARTIFICIAL INTELLIGENCE

A

1 *E* AA
→ action aider

2 *E* AAAI
= American Association for Artificial Intelligence

3 *E* A* algorithm (LOGIC)
G A*-Algorithmus (m)
F algorithme A* (m)
S algoritmo A* (m)
I algoritmo A* (m)

4 *E* abduction (*a form of deduction*) (LOGIC)
↔ induction
G Abduktion (f)
F abduction (f)
S abducción (f)
I abduzione (f)

5 *E* abductive (*reasoning etc.*) (LOGIC)
G abduktiv
F abductif
S abductivo
I abduttivo

6 *E* abductive logic
G abduktive Logik (f)
F logique abductive (f)
S lógica abductiva (f)
I logica abduttiva (f)

7 *E* abductive reasoning (LOGIC)
G abduktives Schließen (n)
F raisonnement abductif (m)
S razonamiento abductivo (m)
I ragionamento abduttivo (m)

8 *E* ABS
→ artificial belief system

9 *E* abstract data type (PROGRAMMING)
G abstrakter Datentyp (m)
F type abstrait de données (t.a.d.) (m)
S tipo abstracto de datos (m)
I tipo astratto di dati (m)

10 *E* abstraction (LOGIC)
G Abstraktion (f)
F abstraction (f)
S abstracción (f)
I astrazione (f)

11 *E* abstraction hierarchy (KNOWLEDGE)
G Abstraktionshierarchie (f)
F hiérarchie d'abstraction (f)
S jerarquía de abstracción (f)
I gerarchia di astrazione (f)

12 *E* abstraction level (LOGIC)
= level of abstraction
G Abstraktionsebene (f); Abstraktionsniveau (n); Abstraktionsstufe (f)
F niveau d'abstraction (m)
S nivel de abstracción (m)
I livello di astrazione (m)

13 *E* abstraction rule (LOGIC)
G Abstraktionsregel (f)
F règle d'abstraction (f)
S regla de abstracción (f)
I regola di astrazione (f)

14 *E* abstraction space (EXPERT SYSTEMS)

G Abstraktionsraum (m)
F espace d'abstraction (m)
S espacio de abstracción (m)
I spazio di astrazioni (m)

15 *E* absurd (LOGIC)
G absurd
F absurde
S absurdo
I assurdo

16 *E* AC
→ applicability conditions

17 *E* accessibility relation (PROGRAMMING)
G Zugangsrelation (f)
F relation d'accessibilité (f)
S relación de accesibilidad (f)
I relazione di accessibilità (f)

18 *E* access-oriented programming
G zugriffsorientierte Programmierung (f)
F programmation orientée vers l'accès (f)
S programación orientada en el acceso (f)
I programmazione orientata all'accesso (f)

19 *E* access tools (KNOWLEDGE)
G Zugriffswerkzeuge (n pl)
F outils d'accès (m pl)
S herramientas de acceso (f pl)
I tool di accesso (m pl)

20 *E* accumulate (*knowledge etc.*)
G ansammeln; akkumulieren
F accumuler
S acumular
I accumulare

21 *E* accumulated evidence (LOGIC)
G akkumulierte Evidenz (f)
F évidence accumulée (f)
S evidencia acumulada (f)
I evidenza accumulata (f)

22 *E* accumulation (*of information etc.*) (KNOWLEDGE)
G Sammlung (f)
F accumulation (f)
S acumulación (f)
I accumulazione (f)

23 *E* achievement (*of objectives etc.*) (EXPERT SYSTEMS)
G Erreichung (f)
F aboutissement (m)
S consecución (de objetivos) (f); cumplimentación (f); cumplimiento (m)
I conseguimento (m)

24 *E* acoustic analysis (RECOGNITION)
G akustische Analyse (f)
F analyse acoustique (f)
S análisis acústico (m)
I analisi acustica (f)

25 *E* acoustic information (RECOGNITION)
G akustische Information (f); Information in akustischer Form (f)
F information acoustique (f)
S información acústica (f)
I informazione acustica (f)

26 *E* acoustic-phonetic decoding (RECOGNITION)
G akustisch-phonetische Decodierung (f)
F décodage acoustico-phonétique (DAP) (m)
S decodificación acústica y fonética (f)
I decodificazione acustica e fonetica (f)

27 *E* acoustic processor (RECOGNITION)
G Akustikprozessor (m)
F processeur acoustique (m)
S procesador acústico (PA) (m)
I processore acustico (m)

28 *E* acoustic quality (*of a speech signal*) (RECOGNITION)
G akustische Qualität (f)
F qualité acoustique (f)
S calidad acústica (f)
I qualità acustica (f)

29 *E* acquisition (*of knowledge etc.*)
G Erwerb (m); Akquisition (f)
F acquisition (f)
S adquisición (f)
I acquisizione (f)

30 *E* action[1] (EXPERT SYSTEMS)
G Aktion (f); Handlung (f)
F action (f)
S acción (f)
I azione (f)

31 *E* action[2]
→ action part[1]

32 *E* action aider (AA) (EXPERT SYSTEMS)
G aktionsunterstützendes Element (n); Aktionshilfe (f)
F support d'action (m)
S soporte de acción (m)
I supporto all'azione (m)

33 *E* action clause (LOGIC)
G Aktionsklausel (f)
F clause d'action (f)
S cláusula de acción (f)
I clausola di azione (f)

34 *E* action part[1] (*of a production rule; the 'then part' of a rule*) (EXPERT SYSTEMS)
= action
G Aktionsteil (einer Produktionsregel) (m); Aktion (Konklusion einer Produktionsregel) (f)
F action (f)
S parte de acción (f)
I parte azione (f)

35 *E* action part[2]
→ right-hand side

36 *E* action plan (EXPERT SYSTEMS)
G Aktionsplan (m)
F plan d'actions (m)
S plano de acciones (m); plano de actuación (m)
I piano delle azioni (m)

37 *E* action planning (EXPERT SYSTEMS)
G Aktionsplanung (f)
F planification d'actions (f)
S planificación de acciones (f)
I pianificazione delle azioni (f)

38 *E* action theorem (LOGIC)
G Aktionstheorem (n)
F théorème d'action (m)
S teorema de acción (m)
I teorema d'azione (m)

39 *E* activation (NEURAL NETS)
G Aktivierung (f)
F activation (f)
S activación (f)
I attivazione (f)

40 *E* activation algorithm (THEORY)
G Aktivierungsalgorithmus (m)
F algorithme d'activation (m)
S algoritmo de activación (m)
I algoritmo di attivazione (m)

41 *E* activation context (NEURAL NETS)
G Aktivierungskontext (m)
F contexte d'activation (m)
S contexto de activación (m)
I contesto di attivazione (m)

42 *E* activation cycle (NEURAL NETS)
G Aktivierungszyklus (m)
F cycle d'activation (m)
S ciclo de activación (m)
I ciclo di attivazione (m)

43 *E* activation function (NEURAL NETS)
G Aktivierungsfunktion (f)
F fonction d'activation (f)
S función de activación (f)
I funzione di attivazione (f)

44 *E* activation mechanism (PROGRAMMING)
G Aktivierungsmechanismus (m)
F mécanisme d'activation (m)
S mecanismo de activación (m)
I meccanismo di attivazione (m)

45 *E* activation model (NEURAL NETS)
G Aktivierungsmodell (n)
F modèle d'activation (m)
S patrón de activación (m)
I modello di attivazione (m)

46 *E* activation state (THEORY)
G Aktivierungszustand (m)
F état d'activation (m)
S estado de activación (m)
I stato di attivazione (m)

47 *E* activation threshold (NEURAL NETS)
G Aktivierungsschwelle (f)
F seuil d'activation (m)
S umbral de activación (m)
I soglia di attivazione (f)

48 *E* active blackboard (KNOWLEDGE)
≠ passive blackboard
G aktives Blackboard (n)
F tableau noir actif (m)
S pizarra activa (f)
I blackboard attiva (f); lavagna attiva (f)

49 *E* active image (*that can be processed interactively*)
G aktives Bild (n)
F image active (f)
S imagen activa (f)
I immagine attiva (f)

50 *E* active state (PROGRAMMING)
G aktiver Zustand (m)
F état actif (m)
S estado activo (m)
I stato attivo (m)

51 *E* active value (PROGRAMMING)
= demon
G aktiver Wert (m)
F valeur active (f)
S valor activo (m)
I valore attivo (m)

52 *E* actor (KNOWLEDGE)
G Aktor (m); Akteur (m); Handlungsträger (m)
F acteur (m)
S actor (m)
I attore (m)

53 *E* actor-based programming
G aktorenbasiertes Programmieren (n)
F programmation par acteurs (f)
S programación por actores (f)
I programmazione sulla base di attori (f)

54 *E* actor model (KNOWLEDGE)
G Aktorenmodell (n)
F modèle d'acteurs (m)
S modelo de actores (m)
I modello di attori (m)

55 *E* actual knowledge
G tatsächliches Wissen (n)
F connaissances effectives (f pl)
S conocimiento efectivo (m)
I conoscenza effettiva (f)

56 *E* actual parameter (PROGRAMMING)
G Aktualparameter (m)
F paramètre actuel (m)
S parámetro actual (m)
I parametro attuale (m)

57 *E* acyclic graph (PROGRAMMING)
G azyklischer Graph (m)

F graphe acyclique (m)
S grafo acíclico (m)
I grafo aciclico (m)

58 *E* adaptability (*of a system etc.*) (EXPERT SYSTEMS)
G Anpassungsfähigkeit (f)
F adaptabilité (f)
S adaptabilidad (f)
I adattabilità (f)

59 *E* adaptation phase (RECOGNITION)
G Anpassungsphase (f)
F phase d'adaptation (f)
S fase de adaptación (f)
I fase di adattamento (f)

60 *E* adaptation to errors (EXPERT SYSTEMS)
G Anpassung an Fehler (f); Fehleradaptation (f)
F adaptation aux erreurs (f)
S adaptación a los errores (f)
I adattamento agli sbagli (m)

61 *E* adaptive (*program, system, etc.*)
G adaptiv; anpassungsfähig
F adaptatif
S adaptativo
I adattivo

62 *E* adaptive expert system
G adaptives Expertensystem (n)
F système expert adaptatif (m)
S sistema experto adaptativo (m)
I sistema esperto adattativo (m)

63 *E* adaptive production system (EXPERT SYSTEMS)
G adaptives Produktionssystem (n)
F système de production adaptatif (m)
S sistema de producción adaptativo (m)
I sistema di produzione adattivo (m)

64 *E* adaptive resonance net (ARN) (NEURAL NETS)
G ARN-Netz (n)
F réseau à résonance adaptative (m)
S red de resonancia adaptativa (f)
I rete a risonanza adattiva (f)

65 *E* add list (LOGIC)
G Additionsliste (f)
F liste des prédicats additionnels (f)
S lista de predicados adicionales (f)
I lista di predicati da aggiungere (f)

66 *E* adjacency matrix (THEORY)
G Adjazenzmatrix (f)
F matrice d'adjacence (f)
S matriz de adyacencia (f)
I matrice di adiacenza (f)

67 *E* adjacent (*arc, node*) (THEORY)
G adjazent; benachbart
F adjacent; voisin
S adyacente
I adiacente

68 *E* admissible value (PROGRAMMING)
G zulässiger Wert (m)
F valeur admissible (f)
S valor admisible (m)
I valore amissibile (m)

69 *E* advanced architecture
G höhere Architektur (f)
F architecture avancée (f)
S arquitectura avanzada (f)
I architettura avanzata (f)

70 *E* advanced language
→ high-level language

71 *E* advanced reasoning (PROGRAMMING)
G höheres Inferieren (n)
F raisonnement évolué (m)
S razonamiento avanzado (m)
I ragionamento avanzato (m)

72 *E* advanced reasoning tool (ART) (PROGRAMMING)
G höheres Inferierinstrument (n)
F outil de raisonnement évolué (m)
S herramienta de razonamiento avanzado (f)
I strumento di ragionamento avanzato (m)

73 *E* advance knowledge
→ prior knowledge

74 *E* advisory system (EXPERT SYSTEMS)
G Beratungssystem (n)
F système de conseil (m)
S sistema de consulta (m)
I sistema di consulenza (m)

75 *E* agenda (EXPERT SYSTEMS)
= job list
G Aktionsliste (f); Agenda (f)
F agenda (m)
S agenda (f); lista ordenada de acciones (f)
I agenda (f)

76 *E* agenda-based system (EXPERT SYSTEMS)
G agendagesteuertes System (n)
F système dirigé par agenda (m)
S sistema guiado por agenda (m)
I sistema basato su agende (m)

77 *E* agent (*action-performing element*) (NLP)
G Agent (m)
F agent (m)
S agente (m)
I agente (m)

78 *E* agent–object rule (KNOWLEDGE)
G Agent–Objekt-Regel (f)
F règle agent–objet (f)
S regla agente–objeto (f)
I regola agente–oggetto (f)

79 *E* agglomerative technique (*a clustering technique*) (KNOWLEDGE)
≠ divisive technique
G agglomeratives Verfahren (n)
F technique d'agglomération (f)
S técnica de aglomeración (f)
I tecnica agglomerativa (f)

80 *E* aggregation[1] (*of knowledge etc.*)
G Aggregierung (f); Anhäufung (f)
F agrégation (f)
S agregación (f)
I aggregazione (f)

81 *E* aggregation[2] (*of an object*) (IMAGE PROCESSING)
G Aggregation (f)
F assemblage (m)
S asemblaje (m)
I assiemaggio (m); assemblaggio (m)

82 *E* AI
→ artificial intelligence

83 *E* AI applications
G KI-Anwendungen (f pl)
F applications de l'IA (f pl)
S aplicaciones de la IA (f pl)
I applicazioni di IA (f pl)

84 *E* AI architecture
G KI-Architektur (f)
F architecture IA (f)
S arquitectura de IA (f)
I architettura IA (f)

85 *E* AI conference
G KI-Konferenz (f); Konferenz über Künstliche Intelligenz (f)
F conférence sur l'IA (f)
S conferencia sobre IA (f)
I conferenza di IA (f)

86 *E* AI expert
G KI-Experte (m)
F expert en IA (m)

S experto de IA (m)
I esperto di IA (m)

87 *E* AI fields
G Bereiche der künstlichen Intelligenz (m pl); KI-Bereiche (m pl)
F secteurs de l'IA (m pl)
S campos de IA (m pl)
I campi dell'IA (m pl); aree dell'IA (f pl)

88 *E* AI lab
= AI laboratory
G KI-Labor (n)
F laboratoire d'IA (m)
S laboratorio de IA (m)
I laboratorio di IA (m); laboratorio di intelligenza artificiale (m)

89 *E* AI language
= artificial intelligence language
G KI-Sprache (f); Sprache für die künstliche Intelligenz (f)
F langage pour l'IA (m)
S lenguaje de IA (m)
I linguaggio di IA (m)

90 *E* aim
→ goal

91 *E* AI machine
→ artificial intelligence computer

92 *E* AI methods
= AI techniques
G KI-Methoden (f pl); KI-Verfahren (n pl)
F méthodes de l'intelligence artificielle (f pl); techniques IA (f pl)
S técnicas de inteligencia artificial (f pl); técnicas de IA (f pl)
I metodi di IA (m pl); tecniche di IA (f pl)

93 *E* AI network node
G KI-Netzknoten (m)
F nœud de réseau IA (m)
S nodo de redes IA (m)
I nodo in una rete IA (m)

94 *E* AIPE
→ AI programming environment

95 *E* AI products
G KI-Produkte (n pl)
F produits IA (m pl)
S productos de IA (m pl)
I prodotti di IA (m pl)

96 *E* AI programming
G KI-Programmierung (f)
F programmation en IA (f)
S programación para IA (f)
I programmazione di IA (f)

97 *E* AI programming environment (AIPE)
G KI-Programmierumgebung (f)
F environnement de programmation IA (m)
S entorno de programación IA (m)
I ambiente di programmazione di intelligenza artificiale (m)

98 *E* AI programming language
G KI-Programmiersprache (f)
F langage de programmation d'IA (m)
S lenguaje de programación para IA (m)
I linguaggio di programmazione IA (m)

99 *E* AI project
G KI-Projekt (n); AI-Projekt (n)
F projet d'intelligence artificielle (m); projet d'IA (m)
S proyecto de IA (m); proyecto sobre IA (m)
I progetto di IA (m)

100 *E* AI research
= artificial intelligence research

G KI-Forschung (f); AI-Forschung (f)
F recherche en IA (f)
S investigaciones en inteligencia artificial (f pl); investigación en IA (f); investigación sobre IA (f)
I ricerca di IA (f); ricerca in IA (f)

101 *E* AI researcher
= artificial intelligence researcher
G KI-Forscher (m)
F rechercheur d'IA (m); chercheur en IA (m)
S investigador en IA (m)
I ricercatore di IA (m); ricercatore dell'intelligenza artificiale (m)

102 *E* AISB
= Artificial Intelligence and Simulation of Behaviour

103 *E* AI software (PROGRAMMING)
G KI-Software (f)
F logiciel d'IA (m); logiciel IA (m)
S software de IA (m)
I software per l'IA (m); software di IA (m)

104 *E* AI specialist
G KI-Spezialist (m)
F spécialiste en IA (m); cogniticien (m)
S especialista en inteligencia artificial (m)
I specialista di IA (m)

105 *E* AI teaching system
→ intelligent tutoring system

106 *E* AI techniques
→ AI methods

107 *E* AI workstation
G KI-Arbeitsplatz (m)
F station de travail pour l'IA (f)
S estación de trabajo para IA (f)
I stazione di lavoro IA (f)

108 *E* AKO relation
= a kind of relation
→ is-a relation

109 *E* algorithm (MATHS)
G Algorithmus (m)
F algorithme (m)
S algoritmo (m)
I algoritmo (m)

110 *E* algorithm bank (EXPERT SYSTEMS)
G Algorithmenbank (f)
F banque d'algorithmes (f)
S banco de algoritmos (m)
I banca di algoritmi (f)

111 *E* algorithmic approach
→ algorithmic method

112 *E* algorithmic knowledge
G algorithmisches Wissen (n)
F connaissance algorithmique (f)
S conocimiento algorítmico (m)
I conoscenza algoritmica (f)

113 *E* algorithmic method (EXPERT SYSTEMS)
= algorithmic approach
G algorithmische Methode (f); Algorithmusmethode (f)
F méthode algorithmique (f)
S método algorítmico (m)
I metodo algoritmico (m); approccio algoritmico (m)

114 *E* algorithmic programming
≠ heuristic programming
G algorithmisches Programmieren (n)
F programmation algorithmique (f)
S programación algorítmica (f)
I programmazione algoritmica (f)

115 *E* algorithmic solution (EXPERT SYSTEMS)
G algorithmische Lösung (f)
F solution algorithmique (f)

S solución algorítmica (f)
I soluzione algoritmica (f)

116 E allophone (*variant of the same phoneme*) (RECOGNITION)
G Allophon (n)
F allophone (m)
S alófono (m)
I allofono (m)

117 E alpha-beta method (EXPERT SYSTEMS)
= alpha-beta pruning
G Alpha-Beta-Methode (f); Alpha-Beta-Verfahren (n); Alpha-Beta-Prozedur (f)
F procédé alpha-bêta (m)
S procedimiento alfa-beta (m); poda alfa-beta (f)
I metodo alfa-beta (m)

118 E alpha-beta pruning
→ alpha-beta method

119 E alpha cutoff (LOGIC)
G Alpha-Abschneiden (n)
F coupe alpha (f)
S poda alfa (f)
I taglio alfa (m)

120 E alpha value (LOGIC)
G Alphawert (beim Alpha-Beta-Verfahren) (m)
F valeur alpha (f)
S valor alfa (m)
I valore alfa (m)

121 E alternative (*noun*) (LOGIC)
G Alternative (f)
F alternative (f)
S alternativa (f)
I alternativa (f)

122 E AM
→ associative memory

123 E ambiguity (LINGUISTICS)
G Zweideutigkeit (f); Mehrdeutigkeit (f); Vieldeutigkeit (f); Ambiguität (f)
F ambiguïté (f)
S ambigüedad (f); equivocación (f)
I ambiguità (f)

124 E ambiguous (LINGUISTICS)
G zweideutig; mehrdeutig; vieldeutig; ambig
F ambigu
S ambiguo
I ambiguo

125 E analogical inference
→ analogical reasoning

126 E analogical knowledge representation
G analoge Wissensdarstellung (f)
F représentation analogique des connaissances (f)
S representación analógica de conocimientos (f)
I rappresentazione analogica del conoscimento (f)

127 E analogical learning
→ learning by analogy

128 E analogical problem space (EXPERT SYSTEMS)
G analoger Problemraum (m)
F espace-problème analogique (m)
S espacio problema analógico (m)
I spazio problema analogico (m)

129 E analogical reasoning (LOGIC)
= analogical inference
G analoges Schlüsseziehen (n); Analogieschluß (m); analoges Schließen (n); analoges Inferieren (n)
F raisonnement analogique (m); raisonnement par analogie (m)
S razonamiento analógico (m); razonamiento por analogía (m)
I ragionamento analogico (m)

130 *E* analogical representation (LOGIC)
≠ propositional representation
G analoge Darstellung (f)
F représentation analogique (f)
S representación analógica (f)
I rappresentazione analogica (f)

131 *E* analogy (LOGIC)
G Analogie (f)
F analogie (f)
S analogía (f)
I analogia (f)

132 *E* analogy algorithm (LOGIC)
G Analogiealgorithmus (m)
F algorithme par analogie (m)
S algoritmo por analogía (m)
I algoritmo per analogia (m)

133 *E* analyser (RECOGNITION)
G Analysator (m)
F analyseur (m)
S analizador (m)
I analizzatore (m)

134 *E* analyser (program) (NLP)
G Analyseprogramm (n)
F analyseur (programme) (m)
S programa de análisis (m)
I programma analizzatore (m)

135 *E* analysis of natural language
→ natural-language analysis

136 *E* analysis/resynthesis (SYNTHESIS)
≠ rule synthesis
G Analyse/Wiedersynthese (f)
F analyse/resynthèse (f)
S análisis/resíntesis (f)
I analisi/risintesi (f)

137 *E* analytical approximation (MATHS)
G analytische Annäherung (f)
F approximation analytique (f)
S aproximación analítica (f)
I approssimazione analitica (f)

138 *E* anaphoric reference (LINGUISTICS)
G Anapher (f)
F référence anaphorique (f); anaphore (f)
S referencia anafórica (f); anáfora (f)
I riferimento anaforico (m)

139 *E* ancestor (node) (*in semantic networks*) (KNOWLEDGE)
= antecedent (node); predecessor; parent (node)
G Vorgänger (m); Vorgängerknoten (m); Vorfahre (m)
F ancêtre (m); nœud ancêtre (m); antécédent (nœud) (m); précurseur (m)
S ascendiente (m); nodo ascendiente (m); predecesor (m); nodo predecesor (m); antecesor (m); nodo antecedente (m)
I predecessore (m); nodo precedente (m); nodo predecessore (m); nodo antenato (m)

140 *E* ancestor filter strategy (EXPERT SYSTEMS)
G Vorgänger-Filter-Strategie (f); Vorfahren-Filter-Strategie (f)
F stratégie de filtrage des ancêtres (f)
S estrategia de filtraje de ascendientes (f)
I controllo per mezzo dei predecessori (m)

141 *E* AND expansion (LOGIC)
G UND-Expansion (f)
F expansion ET (f)
S expansión AND (f)
I espansione AND (f)

142 *E* AND node (LOGIC)
↔ OR node

G UND-Knoten (m); AND-Knoten (m)
F nœud ET (m)
S nodo AND (m)
I nodo AND (m)

143 *E* AND/OR graph (*a graph with AND nodes and OR nodes*) (LOGIC)
G UND/ODER-Graph (m); AND/OR-Graph (m)
F graphe ET/OU (m)
S grafo AND/OR (m); grafo Y/O (m)
I grafo AND/OR (m)

144 *E* AND/OR search tree
→ AND/OR tree

145 *E* AND/OR tree (LOGIC)
= AND/OR search tree
G UND/ODER-Baum (m)
F arbre (de recherche) ET/OU (m)
S árbol AND/OR (m); árbol Y/O (m)
I albero AND/OR (m)

146 *E* AND/OR tree expansion (EXPERT SYSTEMS)
G Expansion eines UND/ODER-Baums (f)
F expansion d'arbre ET/OU (f)
S expansión de un árbol AND/OR (f)
I espansione dell'albero AND/OR (f)

147 *E* AND relation (LOGIC)
G UND-Beziehung (f); Konjunktion (f)
F relation ET (f)
S relación AND (f)
I rapporto congiuntivo (AND) (m)

148 *E* ANN
→ artificial neural network

149 *E* ANS
= artificial neural system
→ artificial neural network

150 *E* answering strategy (EXPERT SYSTEMS)
G Antwortstrategie (f)
F stratégie de réponse (f)
S estrategia de respuesta (f)
I strategia di risposta (f)

151 *E* antecedent[1] (*of a rule; the 'if part' of a rule*) (EXPERT SYSTEMS)
G Antezedens (n); Antezedensteil (m); Wenn-Teil (einer Regel) (m)
F antécédent (m)
S antecedente (primera proposición) (m)
I antecedente (m)

152 *E* antecedent[2] (*noun*)
→ left-hand side

153 *E* antecedent (node)
→ ancestor (node)

154 *E* antecedent conditions (EXPERT SYSTEMS)
G Voraussetzungen für das Zutreffen einer Regel (f pl)
F conditions antécédentes (f pl)
S condiciones antecedentes (f pl)
I condizioni antecedenti (f pl)

155 *E* antecedent reasoning
→ data-driven inference

156 *E* antecedent rule (EXPERT SYSTEMS)
G Antezedensregel (f)
F règle antécédente (f)
S regla antecedente (f)
I regola antecedente (f)

157 *E* anthropomorphic robot (*a human-like robot*)
G anthropomorpher Roboter (m)
F robot anthropomorphe (m)

S robot antropomorfo (m)
I robot antropomorfo (m)

158 *E* AO* algorithm (*a variation of the A* algorithm*) (LOGIC)
G AO*-Algorithmus (m)
F algorithme AO* (m)
S algoritmo AO* (m)
I algoritmo AO* (m)

159 *E* AP
→ automatic programming

160 *E* applicability conditions (AC) (EXPERT SYSTEMS)
G Anwendbarkeitsbedingungen (f pl)
F conditions d'applicabilité (f pl)
S condiciones de aplicabilidad (f pl)
I condizioni di applicabilità (f pl)

161 *E* applicable (*rule etc.*) (EXPERT SYSTEMS)
G anwendbar
F applicable
S aplicable
I applicabile

162 *E* application-dependent (PROGRAMMING)
G anwendungsabhängig
F dépendant de l'application
S dependiente de la aplicación
I dipendente dall'applicazione

163 *E* application domain (KNOWLEDGE)
= domain
G Anwendungsbereich (m); Anwendungsgebiet (n); Anwendungsfeld (n)
F domaine d'application (m)
S dominio de aplicación (m)
I dominio di applicazione (m)

164 *E* application of a rule (LOGIC)
G Anwendung einer Regel (f)
F application d'une règle (f)
S aplicación de una regla (f)
I applicazione di una regola (f)

165 *E* apply (*a rule*) (LOGIC)
G anwenden
F appliquer
S aplicar
I applicare

166 *E* approximate reasoning (EXPERT SYSTEMS)
G näherungsweises Schließen (n); approximatives Schließen (n)
F raisonnement approximatif (m)
S razonamiento aproximado (m)
I ragionamento approssimato (m)

167 *E* approximate reasoning rule (EXPERT SYSTEMS)
G näherungsweise Inferenzregel (f)
F règle de raisonnement approximatif (f)
S regla de razonamiento aproximado (f)
I regola per il ragionamento approssimato (f)

168 *E* approximation (MATHS)
G Näherung (f); Approximation (f)
F approximation (f)
S aproximación (f)
I approssimazione (f); accostamento (ad una soluzione) (f)

169 *E* approximation algorithm (MATHS)
G approximierender Algorithmus (m)
F algorithme d'approximation (m)
S algoritmo de aproximación (m)
I algoritmo di approssimazione (m)

170 *E* approximation technique (MATHS)
G Näherungsverfahren (n)
F technique d'approximation (f)
S método de aproximación (m)

I tecnica di approssimazione (f)

171 *E* AP system
→ automatic programming system

172 *E* arbitrary decision (EXPERT SYSTEMS)
G willkürliche Entscheidung (f)
F décision arbitraire (f)
S decisión arbitraria (f)
I decisione arbitraria (f)

173 *E* arbitrary rule (EXPERT SYSTEMS)
G willkürliche Regel (f)
F règle arbitraire (f)
S regla arbitraria (f)
I regola arbitraria (f)

174 *E* arc^1 (***between nodes in a graph***) (LOGIC)
= link; edge
G Kante (f); Bogen (m); Glied (n); Verbindung (f)
F arc (reliant deux nœuds) (m); arête (f)
S arco (de conexión) (m); enlace (entre nodos) (m); conexión (entre nodos) (f)
I arco (di connessione) (m); ramo (m)

175 *E* arc^2
→ link^1

176 *E* archetype (LOGIC)
G Archetyp (m)
F archétype (m)
S arquetipo (m)
I archetipo (m)

177 *E* architecture (*of a system etc.*)
G Architektur (f)
F architecture (f)
S arquitectura (f)
I architettura (f)

178 *E* area of discourse (RECOGNITION)
G Diskursbereich (m); Bereich (m)
F domaine de discours (m)
S área de discurso (f)
I dominio del discorso (m)

179 *E* area of expertise
→ domain of expertise

180 *E* argument (LOGIC)
G Argument (n)
F argument (m)
S argumento (m)
I argomento (m)

181 *E* argumentation (LOGIC)
G Argumentation (f)
F argumentation (f)
S argumentación (f)
I argomentazione (f)

182 *E* arithmetic expression (*with arithmetic operators*) (MATHS)
G arithmetischer Ausdruck (m)
F expression arithmétique (f)
S expresión aritmética (f)
I espressione aritmetica (f)

183 *E* arithmetic operator (*plus, minus, times or divide*) (MATHS)
G arithmetisches Operationssymbol (n)
F opérateur arithmétique (m)
S operador aritmético (m)
I operatore aritmetico (m)

184 *E* arity (*the number of arguments of a predicate*) (LOGIC)
G Anzahl der Argumente (eines Prädikats) (f)
F arité (nombre d'arguments) (f); poids (m)
S aridad (f)
I arità (f)

185 *E* ARN
→ adaptive resonance net

186 *E* ART
→ advanced reasoning tool

187 *E* articulator (SYNTHESIS)
G Artikulierungssystem (n)
F système d'articulation (m)
S sistema de articulación (m)
I sistema di articolazione (m)

188 *E* artificial belief system (ABS) (LOGIC)
G künstliches Überzeugungssystem (n)
F système de croyance artificielle (m)
S sistema de confianza artificial (m)
I sistema di convinzioni artificiali (m)

189 *E* artificial cognition (THEORY)
= machine cognition
G künstliche Kognition (f)
F cognition artificielle (f)
S cognición artificial (f)
I cognizione artificiale (f)

190 *E* artificial intelligence (AI)
G künstliche Intelligenz (KI) (f); artifizielle Intelligenz (AI) (f); Intellektik (f)
F intelligence artificielle (IA) (f)
S inteligencia artificial (IA) (f)
I intelligenza artificiale (IA) (f)

191 *E* artificial intelligence ...
→ AI ...

192 *E* artificial intelligence computer
= AI computer; AI machine
G KI-Rechner (m); KI-Computer (m); KI-Maschine (f)
F ordinateur pour l'intelligence artificielle (m); ordinateur IA (m); machine IA (f)
S ordenador para IA (m)
I elaboratore per IA (m); macchina IA (f)

193 *E* artificial intelligence database
= AI database
G KI-Datenbasis (f)
F base de données en intelligence artificielle (f); base de données IA (f)
S base de datos de inteligencia artificial (f)
I base di dati IA (f)

194 *E* artificial intelligence system
= AI system
G KI-System (n); AI-System (n); System mit künstlicher Intelligenz (n)
F système d'intelligence artificielle (m); système IA (m)
S sistema de inteligencia artificial (m); sistema de AI (m)
I sistema di IA (m); sistema di intelligenza artificiale (m)

195 *E* artificial neural network (ANN)
= artificial neural system (ANS)
G künstliches neuronales Netz (KNN) (n)
F réseau neuromimétique (RN) (m); réseau neuronal artificiel (m)
S red neuronal artificial (f)
I rete neuronale artificiale (f)

196 *E* artificial neural system (ANS)
→ artificial neural network

197 *E* artificial perception (THEORY)
= machine perception
G künstliche Wahrnehmung (f)
F perception artificielle (f)
S percepción artificial (f)
I percezione artificiale (f)

198 *E* artificial reason (THEORY)
G künstlicher Verstand (m)
F raison artificielle (f)
S razón artificial (f)
I ragione artificiale (f)

199 *E* artificial speech
→ synthetic speech

200 *E* artificial vision
→ computer vision

201 *E* artificial vision system
→ computer vision system

202 *E* ascending hierarchical model (KNOWLEDGE)
G Modell mit aufsteigender Hierarchie (n)
F modèle hiérarchique ascendant (m)
S modelo jerárquico ascendente (MJA) (m)
I modello gerarchico ascendente (m)

203 *E* aspect (NLP)
G Aspekt (m)
F aspect (m)
S aspecto (m)
I aspetto (m)

204 *E* aspiration search (EXPERT SYSTEMS)
G Erwartungssuche (f)
F recherche par aspiration (f)
S búsqueda orientada a expectativas (f)
I ricerca orientata a aspettative (f)

205 *E* ASR
→ automatic speech recognition

206 *E* assertion[1] (*of a fact etc.*) (LOGIC)
= claiming
G Behauptung (f)
F assertion (f)
S aserción (f)
I asserzione (f)

207 *E* assertion[2] (*of correctness etc.*) (LOGIC)
G Zusicherung (f)
F assurance (f)
S afirmación (f)
I asserzione (f)

208 *E* assertional database
→ declarative database

209 *E* assertional system
→ declarative system

210 *E* assertion list (LOGIC)
G Aussagenliste (f)
F liste des propositions (f)
S lista de proposiciones (f)
I elenco delle proposizioni (m)

211 *E* assessment of uncertainty
→ uncertainty assessment

212 *E* assignment clause (LOGIC)
G Zuweisungsklausel (f)
F clause d'assignation (f)
S cláusula de asignación (f)
I clausola di assegnazione (f)

213 *E* assignment of a value (LOGIC)
G Zuweisung eines Werts (f)
F assignation d'une valeur (f)
S asignación de un valor (f)
I assegnazione di un valore (f)

214 *E* assignment predicate (LOGIC)
G Zuweisungsprädikat (n)
F prédicat d'assignation (m)
S predicado de asignación (m)
I predicato di assegnazione (m)

215 *E* association (LOGIC)
G Assoziation (f)
F association (f)
S asociación (f)
I associazione (f)

216 *E* association list (KNOWLEDGE)
G Assoziationsliste (f)
F liste des associations (f)
S lista de asociaciones (f)
I lista delle associazioni (f)

217 *E* association model (NEURAL NETS)
G Assoziationsmodell (n)
F modèle des associations (m)

S modelo de asociaciones (m)
I modello delle associazioni (m)

218 *E* associative (*search etc.*) (LOGIC)
G assoziativ
F associatif; par association
S asociativo
I associativo

219 *E* associative memory (AM) (*other types: random or sequential*) (KNOWLEDGE)
G assoziativer Speicher (m); Assoziativspeicher (m)
F mémoire associative (f)
S memoria asociativa (f)
I memoria associativa (MA) (f)

220 *E* associative network (KNOWLEDGE)
G assoziatives Netz (n)
F réseau associatif (m)
S red asociativa (f)
I rete associativa (f)

221 *E* associative values (LOGIC)
G Assoziativwerte (m pl)
F valeurs associatives (f pl)
S valores asociativos (m pl)
I valori associativi (m pl)

222 *E* associativity (*in propositional logic*)
G Assoziativität (f)
F associativité (f)
S asociatividad (f)
I associatività (f)

223 *E* assumption
→ subsumption

224 *E* assumption-based (*system etc.*) (LOGIC)
≠ justification-based
G auf Annahmen beruhend
F basé sur suppositions
S basado en suposiciones
I basato su assunzioni

225 *E* ATMS
= assumption-based truth maintenance system

226 *E* ATN
→ augmented transition network

227 *E* ATN grammar (NLP)
= augmented transition network grammar
G ATN-Grammatik (f)
F grammaire ATN (f)
S gramática ATN (f)
I grammatica ATN (f)

228 *E* atom (*cannot be split into smaller units*) (PROGRAMMING)
G Atom (n)
F atome (m)
S átomo (m)
I atomo (m)

229 *E* atomic formula (THEORY)
G Atomformel (f)
F formule atomique (f)
S fórmula atómica (f)
I formula atomica (f)

230 *E* atom of belief (LOGIC)
G Überzeugungsatom (n)
F atome de croyance (m)
S átomo de confianza (m)
I atomo di convinzione (m)

231 *E* attached predicate (LOGIC)
G angehängtes Prädikat (n)
F prédicat attaché (m)
S predicado asignado (m)
I predicato assegnato (m)

232 *E* attached procedure (PROGRAMMING)
↔ procedural attachment
G angehängte Prozedur (f)
F procédure attachée (f)
S procedimiento asignado (m)
I procedura assegnata (f)

233 *E* attachment (PROGRAMMING)
G Auswertung (f); Attachment (n)
F attachement (m)
S asignación (f)
I assegnazione (f)

234 *E* attempt recording (EXPERT SYSTEMS)
G Aufzeichnung der Versuche (f)
F enregistrement de tentatives (m)
S registro de tentativas (m)
I traccia dei tentativi (f)

235 *E* attentional focusing
→ attention focusing

236 *E* attention focusing (RECOGNITION)
= attentional focusing
G Konzentrierung der Aufmerksamkeit (auf ein Thema) (f)
F centrage de l'attention (m)
S concentración de atención (f)
I concentrazione dell'attenzione (f)

237 *E* attribute[1] (*of an object*) (LOGIC)
G Attribut (n)
F attribut (m)
S atributo (m)
I attributo (m)

238 *E* attribute[2] (*of a frame*)
→ slot

239 *E* attribute hierarchy (LOGIC)
G Attributhierarchie (f)
F hiérarchie des attributs (f)
S jerarquía de los atributos (f)
I gerarchia degli attributi (f)

240 *E* attribute–object–value (KNOWLEDGE)
G Attribut–Objekt–Wert (m)
F attribut–objet–valeur (f)
S atributo–objeto–valor (m)
I attributo–oggetto–valore (m)

241 *E* attribute value (KNOWLEDGE)
G Attributwert (m)
F valeur d'attribut (f)
S valor de un atributo (m)
I valore dell'attributo (m)

242 *E* attribute–value pair (KNOWLEDGE)
= a–v pair
G Attribut/Wert-Paar (n)
F paire attribut–valeur (f); couple attribut–valeur (m); couple a–v (m)
S par atributo–valor (m); par A–V (m)
I coppia attributo–valore (f)

243 *E* augmented decision network (EXPERT SYSTEMS)
G erweitertes Entscheidungsnetz (n)
F réseau de décision augmenté (m)
S red de decisión aumentada (f)
I rete di decisione aumentata (f)

244 *E* augmented transition network (ATN) (NLP)
G erweitertes Übergangsnetz (n); augmentiertes Übergangsnetzwerk (n)
F réseau de transition augmenté (ATN) (m)
S red de transición aumentada (ATN) (f)
I rete di transizione aumentata (f); ATN (f); rete di transizione estesa (f)

245 *E* augmented transition network grammar
→ ATN grammar

246 *E* auto-associative memory (NEURAL NETS)
G autoassoziativer Speicher (m)
F mémoire auto-associative (f)
S memoria autoasociativa (f)
I memoria autoassociativa (f)

247 *E* autocorrelation (LOGIC)

G Autokorrelation (f)
F auto-corrélation (f)
S autocorrelación (f)
I autocorrelazione (f)

248 *E* autodocumentation (*of a system*) (EXPERT SYSTEMS)
G Selbstdokumentation (f)
F autodocumentation (f)
S autodocumentación (f)
I autodocumentazione (f)

249 *E* autoepistemic logic
G autoepistemische Logik (f)
F logique auto-épistémique (f)
S lógica auto-epistémica (f)
I logica autoepistemica (f)

250 *E* autoepistemic reasoning (LOGIC)
G autoepistemisches Schließen (n)
F raisonnement auto-épistémique (m)
S razonamiento auto-epistémico (m)
I ragionamento autoepistemico (m)

251 *E* automated decision making (EXPERT SYSTEMS)
G automatisiertes Entscheiden (n)
F prise de décisions automatisée (f)
S toma automatizada de decisiones (f)
I presa automatizzata di decisioni (f)

252 *E* automated knowledge acquisition
G automatisierte Wissensaufnahme (f); automatisierter Wissenserwerb (m)
F acquisition automatique de connaissances (f)
S adquisición de conocimientos automatizada (f)
I acquisizione automatizzata di conoscimento (f)

253 *E* automated natural language understanding
= automatic understanding of natural language
G automatisiertes Verstehen natürlicher Sprache (n)
F compréhension automatisée du langage naturel (f)
S comprensión automatizada del lenguaje natural (f)
I comprensione automatizzata del linguaggio naturale (f)

254 *E* automated theorem proving
→ automatic theorem proving

255 *E* automated vision (IMAGE PROCESSING)
G automatisiertes Sehen (n)
F vision automatisée (f)
S visión automatizada (f)
I visione automatizzata (f)

256 *E* automatic diagnosis (EXPERT SYSTEMS)
G automatische Diagnose (f)
F diagnostic automatique (m)
S diagnóstico automático (m)
I diagnosi automatica (f)

257 *E* automatic (hand)writing recognition (IMAGE PROCESSING)
G automatische (Hand)Schrifterkennung (f)
F reconnaissance automatique de l'écriture manuscrite (f)
S reconocimiento automático de escritura (m)
I riconoscimento automatico della scrittura (m)

258 *E* automatic learning
G automatisches Lernen (n)
F apprentissage automatique (m)
S aprendizaje automático (m)
I apprendimento automatico (m)

259 *E* automatic processing of natural language
G automatische Verarbeitung natürlicher Sprache (f)
F traitement automatique du langage naturel (m)
S proceso automático del lenguaje natural (m)
I elaborazione automatica del linguaggio naturale (f)

260 *E* automatic programmer
G automatisches Programmiergerät (n)
F programmeur automatique (m)
S programador automático (m)
I programmatore automatico (m)

261 *E* automatic programming (AP)
G automatisches Programmieren (AP) (n); automatisierte Programmierung (f)
F programmation automatique (f)
S programación automática (f)
I programmazione automatica (f)

262 *E* automatic programming system (EXPERT SYSTEMS)
= AP system
G automatisches Programmiersystem (n); AP-System (n)
F système de programmation automatique (m)
S sistema de programación automático (m)
I sistema di programmazione automatica (m)

263 *E* automatic reasoning (LOGIC)
G automatisches Schlüsseziehen (n)
F raisonnement automatique (m)
S razonamiento automático (m)
I ragionamento automatico (m)

264 *E* automatic speech processing (RECOGNITION)
G automatische Sprachverarbeitung (f)
F traitement automatique de la parole (m)
S procesamiento automático de la voz (m)
I processamento automatico del parlato (m)

265 *E* automatic speech recognition (ASR)
G automatische Spracherkennung (f)
F reconnaissance automatique de la parole (RAP) (f)
S reconocimiento automático del habla (RAH) (m)
I riconoscimento automatico del parlato (m)

266 *E* automatic theorem proving (EXPERT SYSTEMS)
= automated theorem proving
G automatisches Beweisen (n); automatisches Beweisführen (n); automatisches Beweisverfahren (n)
F démonstration automatique de théorèmes (f); preuve automatisée de théorèmes (f); résolution automatique de théorèmes (f)
S resolución automática de teoremas (f); demostración automática de teoremas (f)
I dimostrazione automatica di teoremi (f); risoluzione automatica di teoremi (f)

267 *E* automatic understanding (RECOGNITION)
G automatisches Verstehen (n)
F compréhension automatique (de la parole) (f)
S comprensión automática (f)
I comprensione automatica (f)

268 *E* automatic understanding of natural language
→ automated natural language understanding

269 *E* automatic voice analysis (RECOGNITION)
G automatische Stimmanalyse (f); automatische Sprachanalyse (f)
F analyse automatique de la voix (f)
S análisis automático de la voz (m)
I analisi automatica della voce (f)

270 *E* auxiliary problem space (EXPERT SYSTEMS)
G Hilfsproblemraum (m); zusätzlicher Problemraum (m)
F espace-problème auxiliaire (m)
S espacio de problema auxiliar (m)
I spazio problema ausiliario (m)

271 *E* availability heuristics (LOGIC)
G Verfügbarkeitsheuristik (f)
F heuristique de disponibilité (f)
S heurística de disponibilidad (f)
I euristica di disponibilità (f)

272 *E* avoidance of contradiction (LOGIC)
G Vermeidung von Widersprüchen (f)
F évitement de contradiction (m)
S evitación de contradicciones (f)
I l'evitare le contraddizioni (m)

273 *E* a–v pair
→ attribute–value pair

274 *E* axiom (*a statement that is assumed true*) (LOGIC)
G Axiom (n)
F axiome (m)
S axioma (m)
I assioma (m)

275 *E* axiomatic system (LOGIC)
G axiomatisches System (n); Axiomensystem (n)
F système axiomatique (m)
S sistema axiomático (m)
I sistema assiomatico (m)

B

276 *E* B
→ belief

277 *E* B* algorithm (EXPERT SYSTEMS)
G B*-Algorithmus (m)
F algorithme B* (m)
S algoritmo B* (m)
I algoritmo B* (m)

278 *E* back-and-forth search (EXPERT SYSTEMS)
G Vorwärts- und Rückwärtssuche (f)
F recherche aller-retour (f)
S búsqueda adelante y atrás (f)
I ricerca avanti e indietro (f)

279 *E* back chaining
→ backward chaining

280 *E* background knowledge
G Hintergrundwissen (n)
F connaissances d'arrière-plan (f pl)
S conocimiento de fondo (m)
I conoscenza di fondo (f)

281 *E* back prop
→ back-propagation

282 *E* back-propagation (BP; back prop) (EXPERT SYSTEMS)
= backward error propagation; error back propagation
G Fortpflanzung (von Fehlern) in Rückwärtsrichtung (f); Rückwärtspropagierung (f); Backpropagation (f)
F propagation vers l'arrière (f)
S propagación para atrás (f)
I propagazione all'indietro (di errori ecc.) (f)

283 *E* backtrack (*verb*) (EXPERT SYSTEMS)
G im Backtrackingverfahren arbeiten; zurückverfolgen; rücksetzen
F reculer; opérer un retour-arrière
S retroceder; volver atrás; volverse al último punto
I ritornare sui propri passi; risalire all'indietro; tornare indietro; procedere a ritroso; rintracciare l'ultima decisione

284 *E* backtracking (*noun*) (EXPERT SYSTEMS)
G Backtracking (n); Zurückziehungsverfahren (n); Zurückverfolgen (n); Rücksetzen (n)
F retour arrière (m); remontée (f); recul (m)
S retroceso (m); vuelta atrás (f)
I backtracking (ritorno sui propri passi) (m); ritorno sulle proprietracce (m); ritorno all'ultimo nodo (m)

285 *E* backtracking mechanism (EXPERT SYSTEMS)
G Backtrackingmechanismus (m)
F mécanisme de retour arrière (m)
S mecanismo de retroceso (m)
I meccanismo di backtracking (m)

286 *E* backtracking search (EXPERT SYSTEMS)
G Suche mit Backtracking (f)
F recherche avec retour arrière (f)
S búsqueda con vuelta atrás (f)
I ricerca con backtracking (f)

287 *E* backtracking strategy (EXPERT SYSTEMS)
G Backtrackingstrategie (f); Zurückziehungsstrategie (f)
F stratégie de retour arrière (f); stratégie de remontée (f); stratégie de recul (f)
S estrategia de retroceso (f); estrategia de vuelta atrás hasta la última decisión tomada (f)
I strategia di backtracking (f); procedura di ritorno (f)

288 *E* backward-acting rule
→ backward-chaining rule

289 *E* backward-chained (EXPERT SYSTEMS)
G rückwärtsverkettet
F chaîné vers l'arrière
S encadenado para atrás
I concatenato all'indietro

290 *E* backward chaining (EXPERT SYSTEMS)
= back chaining; top-down chaining
G Rückwärtsverkettung (f); rückwärtsverkettend (adj)
F chaînage arrière (m); chaînage en arrière (m)
S encadenamiento para atrás (m); encadenamiento hacia atrás (m)
I concatenamento a ritroso (m); retroconcatenazione (f); concatenamento all'indietro (m); concatenazione inversa (f)

291 *E* backward-chaining rule (EXPERT SYSTEMS)
= backward rule; backward-acting rule
G rückwärtswirkende Regel (f); Rückwärtsregel (f)
F règle de chaînage arrière (f)
S regla de encadenamiento hacia atrás (f)
I regola di concatenamento indietro (f)

292 *E* backward-chaining strategy (EXPERT SYSTEMS)
G Rückwärtsverkettungsstrategie (f)
F stratégie de chaînage arrière (f)
S estrategia de encadenamiento para atrás (f)
I strategia di concatenamento indietro (f)

293 *E* backward error propagation
→ back-propagation

294 *E* backward inference (LOGIC)
G Inferieren in Rückwärtsrichtung (n)
F inférence vers l'arrière (f)
S inferencia para atrás (f)
I inferenza a ritroso (f)

295 *E* backward planning (LOGIC)
G Rückwärtsplanen (n)
F planification vers l'arrière (f)
S planificación para atrás (f)
I pianificazione a ritroso (f)

296 *E* backward pruning (EXPERT SYSTEMS)
≠ forward pruning
G Abschneiden in Rückwärtsrichtung (n)
F coupe vers l'arrière (f)
S poda para atrás (f)
I potatura a ritroso (f)

297 *E* backward reasoning (EXPERT SYSTEMS)
= top-down reasoning
≠ forward reasoning
G Rückwärtsschließen (n); Rückwärtsableitung (f)
F raisonnement vers l'arrière (m)
S razonamiento para atrás (m)
I ragionamento all'indietro (m); ragionamento in backward (m); ragionamento a ritroso (m)

298 *E* backward reasoning system (EXPERT SYSTEMS)

G rückwärtsgesteuertes System (n)
F système de raisonnement vers l'arrière (m)
S sistema de razonamiento hacia atrás (m)
I sistema di ragionamento all'indietro (m)

299 *E* backward resolution (LOGIC)
G Rückwärtsresolution (f)
F résolution vers l'arrière (f)
S resolución para atrás (f)
I risoluzione a ritroso (f)

300 *E* backward rule
→ backward-chaining rule

301 *E* backward search (EXPERT SYSTEMS)
≠ forward search
G Rückwärtssuche (f); Suche in Rückwärtsrichtung (f)
F recherche vers l'arrière (f); recherche avec retour arrière (f)
S búsqueda hacia atrás (f); búsqueda por retroceso (f); búsqueda con vuelta atrás (f)
I ricerca all'indietro (f)

302 *E* balanced tree (*with search paths of equal length*) (LOGIC)
G ausgeglichener Baum (m)
F arbre équilibré (m)
S árbol balanceado (m)
I albero bilanciato (m)

303 *E* B&B search
→ branch-and-bound search

304 *E* base grammar (NLP)
G Basisgrammatik (f)
F grammaire de base (f)
S gramática de base (f)
I grammatica di base (f)

305 *E* base level
→ basic level

306 *E* base proposition (LOGIC)
G Grundaussage (f)
F proposition de base (f)
S afirmación básica (f)
I proposizione di base (f)

307 *E* basic clause (*a clause with no variables*) (LOGIC)
G Grundklausel (f)
F clause de base (f)
S cláusula de base (f)
I clausola di base (f)

308 *E* basic concept (LOGIC)
= primitive
G Grundbegriff (m)
F concept de base (m)
S concepto básico (m); primitivo (m)
I concetto di base (m)

309 *E* basic entity (LOGIC)
G Grundeinheit (f)
F entité de base (f)
S entidad básica (f)
I entità di base (f)

310 *E* basic hypothesis (LOGIC)
G Grundhypothese (f)
F hypothèse de base (f)
S hipótesis básica (de partida) (f)
I ipotesi di base (f)

311 *E* basic instance (LOGIC)
G Grundinstanz (f)
F instance de base (f)
S instancia de base (f)
I istanza di base (f)

312 *E* basic knowledge
G Basiswissen (n)
F connaissance de base (f)
S conocimiento básico (m)
I conoscenza di base (f)

313 *E* basic level
= base level
G Basisebene (f)

F niveau de base (m)
S nivel básico (m)
I livello di base (m)

314 E basic set (LOGIC)
G Basismenge (f)
F ensemble de base (m)
S conjunto de base (m)
I insieme di base (m)

315 E basic transition network (BTN) (NLP)
G Basisübergangsnetz(werk) (n)
F réseau de transition de base (m)
S red de transición básica (f)
I rete di transizione di base (f)

316 E Baum–Welch algorithm
→ forward–backward algorithm

317 E Bayesian approach (LOGIC)
= Bayesian decision method; Bayesian inference theory
G Bayessches Verfahren (n)
F approche Bayesienne (f)
S modelo bayesiano (m)
I metodo Bayesiano approssimato (m); tecnica Bayesiana (f)

318 E Bayesian decision method
→ Bayesian approach

319 E Bayesian inference theory
→ Bayesian approach

320 E Bayesian network
→ Bayes network

321 E Bayesian probability (LOGIC)
G Bayessche Wahrscheinlichkeit (f)
F probabilité Bayesienne (f)
S probabilidad bayesiana (f)
I probabilità Bayesiana (f)

322 E Bayes network (LOGIC)
= Bayesian network
G Bayessches Netz (n)
F réseau de Bayes (m)
S red de Bayes (f)
I rete di Bayes (f)

323 E Bayes theorem (LOGIC)
G Bayessche Wahrscheinlichkeitstheorie (f); Satz von Bayes (m)
F théorème de Bayes (m); formule de Bayes (f)
S regla de Bayes (f); teoría bayesiana (f)
I teorema di Bayes (m)

324 E beam (*the most promising alternatives in a search*) (EXPERT SYSTEMS)
G Beam (m)
F faisceau (de solutions) (m)
S haz (m)
I fascia (f)

325 E beam search (EXPERT SYSTEMS)
G Beam-Suche (f)
F recherche (de solutions etc.) en faisceau (f)
S búsqueda beam search (f); búsqueda en haz (f)
I ricerca tipo beam search (f)

326 E belief (B) (LOGIC)
G Glaube (m); Glauben (m); Überzeugung (f)
F croyance (f)
S confianza (f)
I convinzione (f); confidenza (f)

327 E belief logic
= logic of beliefs
G Überzeugungslogik (f)
F logique de croyances (f)
S lógica de confianzas (f)
I logica delle convinzioni (f)

328 E belief propagation (EXPERT SYSTEMS)
G Überzeugungsausbreitung (f)
F propagation de croyances (f)
S propagación de confianzas (f)

I propagazione delle convinzioni (f)

329 *E* belief revision (EXPERT SYSTEMS)
= revision of beliefs
G Überzeugungsrevision (f)
F révision de croyance (f)
S revisión de confianzas (f)
I revisione delle convinzioni (f)

330 *E* belief space (EXPERT SYSTEMS)
= view; vista
G Überzeugungsraum (m)
F espace de croyance (m)
S espacio de confianza (m)
I spazio delle convinzioni (m)

331 *E* belief system (EXPERT SYSTEMS)
G Überzeugungssystem (n)
F système de croyance(s) (m)
S sistema de confianzas (m)
I sistema di convinzioni (m)

332 *E* belief theory (LOGIC)
G Überzeugungstheorie (f)
F théorie de croyance (f)
S teoría de confianzas (f)
I teoria delle convinzioni (f)

333 *E* best candidate (*for a solution etc.*) (EXPERT SYSTEMS)
G bester Kandidat (m)
F meilleur candidat (m)
S candidato mejor (m)
I candidato migliore (m)

334 *E* best-few strategy (EXPERT SYSTEMS)
G Best-Few-Strategie (f)
F stratégie des plus prometteurs (f)
S estrategia primero los mejores (f)
I strategia best-few (f)

335 *E* best-first search (EXPERT SYSTEMS)
G Best-First-Suche (f); Bestensuche (f)
F recherche 'meilleur d'abord' (f); recherche du meilleur d'abord (f)
S búsqueda de primero el mejor (f)
I ricerca best-first (f)

336 *E* best-first strategy (EXPERT SYSTEMS)
G Best-First-Strategie (f)
F stratégie de meilleur d'abord (f)
S estrategia primero el mejor (f)
I strategia best-first (f)

337 *E* best-fit algorithm (LOGIC)
G Best-Fit-Algorithmus (m)
F algorithme d'ajustement optimal (m)
S algoritmo best-fit (m)
I algoritmo best-fit (m)

338 *E* best solution (EXPERT SYSTEMS)
G beste Lösung (f)
F solution meilleure (f)
S solución mejor (f)
I soluzione migliore (f)

339 *E* best value (PROGRAMMING)
G bestmöglicher Wert (m); Bestwert (m)
F valeur meilleure (f)
S valor mejor (m)
I valore migliore (m)

340 *E* BetaLISP (*a LISP dialect*) (PROGRAMMING)
G BetaLISP
F BetaLISP
S BetaLISP
I BetaLISP

341 *E* beta structure (PROGRAMMING)
G Betastruktur (f)
F structure bêta (f)
S estructura beta (f)
I struttura beta (f)

342 *E* beta value (*of alpha-beta method*) (LOGIC)
G Beta-Wert (m)

F valeur bêta (f)
S valor beta (m)
I valore beta (m)

343 *E* BFS
→ breadth-first search

344 *E* biconditional (LOGIC)
G mit zwei Bedingungen; bikonditional
F biconditionnel
S bicondicional
I bicondizionale

345 *E* bidirectional chaining (EXPERT SYSTEMS)
G bidirektionale Verkettung (f)
F chaînage bidirectionnel (m)
S encadenamiento bidireccional (m)
I concatenamento bidirezionale (m)

346 *E* bidirectional graph (LOGIC)
G bidirektionaler Graph (m)
F graphe bidirectionnel (m)
S grafo bidireccional (m)
I grafo bidirezionale (m)

347 *E* bidirectional inference (EXPERT SYSTEMS)
G bidirektionales Inferieren (n)
F inférence bidirectionnelle (f)
S inferencia bidireccional (f)
I inferenza bidirezionale (f)

348 *E* bidirectional search (*forward and backward*) (EXPERT SYSTEMS)
G bidirektionale Suche (f); Vor- und Rückwärtssuche (f)
F recherche bidirectionnelle (f)
S búsqueda bidireccional (f)
I ricerca bidirezionale (f)

349 *E* binary relation (LOGIC)
G binäre Relation (f)
F relation binaire (f)
S relación binaria (f)
I relazione binaria (f)

350 *E* binary resolution (LOGIC)
G binäre Auflösung (f)
F résolution binaire (f)
S resolución binaria (f)
I risoluzione binaria (f)

351 *E* binary search (LOGIC)
G binäre Suche (f)
F recherche binaire (f)
S búsqueda binaria (f)
I ricerca binaria (f)

352 *E* binary search tree (LOGIC)
G binärer Suchbaum (m)
F arbre de recherche binaire (m)
S árbol de búsqueda binario (m)
I albero di ricerca binario (m)

353 *E* binary tree (LOGIC)
G Binärbaum (m)
F arbre binaire (m)
S árbol binario (m)
I albero binario (m)

354 *E* bind (*a variable to a value*) (LOGIC)
G binden
F lier
S enlazar
I legare

355 *E* binding (*of a variable*) (LOGIC)
= variable binding
G Binden (einer Variablen) (n); Variablenbindung (f)
F liage (m)
S asignación de valores a una variable (f); enlace (m)
I legamento (m)

356 *E* blackboard (*common storage area of knowledge bases*) (EXPERT SYSTEMS)
G Blackboard (n); Wandtafel (f); Tafel (f)
F tableau noir (m); blackboard (m)
S pizarra (f); blackboard (m); tablero de representación (m)

I blackboard (f); lavagna (f)

357 *E* blackboard architecture (EXPERT SYSTEMS)
G Blackboardarchitektur (f)
F architecture de tableau noir (f); structure de blackboard (f)
S arquitectura de pizarra (f)
I architettura tipo blackboard (f)

358 *E* blackboard method (*for problem resolution*) (EXPERT SYSTEMS)
G Tafelmethode (f); Blackboardmethode (f)
F méthode du tableau noir (f)
S método de pizarra (m)
I metodo blackboard (m)

359 *E* blackboard model (EXPERT SYSTEMS)
G Wandtafelmodell (n)
F modèle de tableau noir (m); modèle de blackboard (m)
S modelo de pizarra (m)
I modello tipo blackboard (m)

360 *E* blackboard system (EXPERT SYSTEMS)
G Blackboardsystem (n)
F système de tableau noir (m)
S sistema de pizarra (m)
I sistema tipo blackboard (m)

361 *E* black box (PROGRAMMING)
G Black Box (f); Schwarzer Kasten (m)
F boîte noire (f)
S caja negra (f)
I scatola nera (f)

362 *E* blind search (LOGIC)
G blinde Suche (f)
F recherche aveugle (f)
S búsqueda ciega (f); búsqueda a ciegas (f); búsqueda desinformada (f)
I ricerca cieca (f)

363 *E* block of knowledge
→ chunk (of knowledge)

364 *E* block of rules
→ set of rules

365 *E* blocks world (THEORY)
= toy world
G Blockwelt (f); Klötzchenwelt (f)
F monde des blocs (m); univers des cubes (m); micro-monde (m)
S mundo de bloques (m); mundo de los cubos (m)
I mondo a blocchi (m)

366 *E* body of a rule (EXPERT SYSTEMS)
G Regelkörper (m); Kern einer Regel (m)
F corps d'une règle (m)
S cuerpo de una regla (m)
I corpo di una regola (m)

367 *E* body of knowledge (EXPERT SYSTEMS)
G Wissensgrundlage (f)
F base de savoir (f)
S cuerpo de conocimientos (m)
I base del sapere (f)

368 *E* Boltzmann machine (NEURAL NETS)
G Boltzmann-Maschine (f)
F machine de Boltzmann (f)
S máquina de Boltzmann (f)
I macchina di Boltzmann (f)

369 *E* Boolean constraint propagation (LOGIC)
= Waltz filtering
G Boolesche Constraint-Fortpflanzung (f)
F propagation de contraintes booléennes (f)
S propagación de restricciones booleanas (f)
I propagazione di vincoli booleani (f)

370 *E* bottom up
≠ top down
G Bottom-Up-... (von unten nach oben)
F ascendant
S hasta arriba
I dal basso verso l'alto

371 *E* bottom-up chaining
→ forward chaining

372 *E* bottom-up interpreter (PROGRAMMING)
≠ top-down interpreter
G Bottom-Up-Interpreter (m)
F interpréteur ascendant (m)
S intérprete bottom-up (m)
I interprete tipo bottom-up (m)

373 *E* bottom-up parser (NLP)
≠ top-down parser
G Bottom-Up-Parser (m)
F analyseur ascendant (m)
S analizador bottom-up (m); analizador de abajo arriba (m)
I parser tipo bottom-up (m)

374 *E* bottom-up programming
= modular programming
≠ top-down programming
G Bottom-Up-Programmierung (f)
F programmation ascendante (f)
S programación bottom-up (f); programación hasta arriba (f)
I programmazione bottom-up (f)

375 *E* bottom-up strategy (EXPERT SYSTEMS)
≠ top-down strategy
G Bottom-Up-Strategie (f)
F stratégie ascendante (f)
S estrategia bottom-up (f)
I strategia dal basso verso l'alto (f)

376 *E* boundaries[1] (*of an object*) (IMAGE PROCESSING)
= edges
G Konturen (f pl)
F bords (m pl)
S márgenes (m pl)
I margini (f pl)

377 *E* boundaries[2] (*of a search*) (EXPERT SYSTEMS)
G Grenzen (f pl)
F limites (f pl)
S fronteras (f pl)
I limiti (m pl)

378 *E* boundary description (*of an object*) (IMAGE PROCESSING)
G Randbeschreibung (f)
F description des bords (f)
S descripción de márgenes (f)
I descrizione dei margini (f)

379 *E* bounded (*search etc.*) (PROGRAMMING)
G begrenzt; eingeschränkt
F limité
S limitado
I limitato

380 *E* bound variable (LOGIC)
≠ free variable
G gebundene Variable (f)
F variable liée (f)
S variable enlazada (f)
I variabile legata (f)

381 *E* BP
→ back-propagation

382 *E* branch (*of a tree*) (LOGIC)
= interconnecting arc
G Zweig (m)
F branche d'arbre (f)
S rama (f); ramificación (f)
I ramo (m)

383 *E* branch-and-bound algorithm (LOGIC)
G Branch-and-bound-Algorithmus (m)
F algorithme de séparation et d'évaluation progressive (m)

S algoritmo de ramificación y limitación (m)
I algoritmo di ramificazione e limitazione (m)

384 *E* branch-and-bound search (LOGIC)
= B&B search
G Branch-and-bound-Suche (f)
F recherche par le plus court chemin (f)
S búsqueda de caminos más cortos (f)
I ricerca secondo il cammino più corto (f)

385 *E* branching factor (*in a search tree*) (LOGIC)
G Verzweigungsfaktor (m)
F facteur de branchement (m)
S factor de ramificación (m)
I fattore di ramificazione (m)

386 *E* branching point
→ branch point

387 *E* branch node (PROGRAMMING)
G Verzweigungsknoten (m)
F nœud de branchement (m)
S nodo de ramificación (m)
I nodo di diramazione (m)

388 *E* branch point (LOGIC)
= branching point
G Verzweigungspunkt (m); Verzweigung (f)
F point de branchement (m)
S punto de ramificación (m)
I punto di diramazione (m)

389 *E* breadth first (LOGIC)
≠ depth first
G breitenorientiert; Breite zuerst
F largeur d'abord
S de amplitud prioritaria
I dapprima in ampiezza

390 *E* breadth-first search (BFS) (EXPERT SYSTEMS)
≠ depth-first search
G Breadth-First-Suchverfahren (n); Breite-zuerst-Suche (f); Breitensuche (f); breitenorientierte Suche (f)
F recherche en largeur d'abord (f); exploration en largeur d'abord (f)
S búsqueda en amplitud (de amplitud prioritaria) (f) ; búsqueda en extensión (f); búsqueda a lo ancho (hacia lo ancho) (f)
I ricerca in ampiezza (f); metodo breadth-first (m)

391 *E* breadth-first strategy (EXPERT SYSTEMS)
G Breite-zuerst-Strategie (f); Breitenstrategie (f)
F stratégie en largeur (f)
S estrategia de búsqueda en amplitud (f)
I strategia di ricerca in larghezza (f)

392 *E* breadth of search (LOGIC)
G Suchbreite (f)
F largeur de recherche (m)
S anchura de la búsqueda (f)
I ampiezza di ricerca (f)

393 *E* brute-force method (*in problem solving*) (LOGIC)
G bedingungsloses Ausschöpfen aller Möglichkeiten (n); Gewaltmethode (f)
F méthode de la force brute (f)
S método a viva fuerza (m)
I metodo a forza viva (m)

394 *E* BTN
→ basic transition network

395 *E* building of expert systems
→ expert system building

396 *E* built-in predicate (KNOWLEDGE)
G systemdefiniertes Prädikat (n)
F prédicat implanté (m); prédicat intégré (m)
S predicado incorporado (m)
I predicato predefinito dal sistema (m)

C

397 *E* C++ (*object-oriented programming language*)
G C++
F C++
S C++
I C++

398 *E* CA
→ concept analyser

399 *E* CAI
→ computer-aided instruction

400 *E* calculus (LOGIC)
G Kalkül (n oder m)
F calcul (m)
S cálculo (m)
I calcolo (m)

401 *E* CAM
→ content-addressable memory

402 *E* candidate (*for a solution etc.*) (LOGIC)
G Kandidat (m)
F candidat (m)
S candidato (m)
I candidato (m)

403 *E* candidate elimination (EXPERT SYSTEMS)
G Ausscheiden möglicher Lösungen (n); Kandidateneliminierung (f)
F élimination de candidats (f)
S eliminación de candidatos (f); reducción de posibles candidatos (f)
I eliminazione di candidati (f)

404 *E* canned input
→ preprogrammed input

405 *E* canned response (EXPERT SYSTEMS)
G vorher abgespeicherter Antworttext (m)
F réponse préenregistrée (f)
S respuesta pregrabada (f)
I risposta preregistrata (f)

406 *E* canonical form (NLP)
G kanonische Form (f); Grundform (f)
F forme canonique (f)
S forma canónica (f)
I forma canonica (f)

407 *E* canonical representation (KNOWLEDGE)
G kanonische Darstellung (f)
F représentation canonique (f)
S representación canónica (f)
I rappresentazione canonica (f)

408 *E* CAP
→ computer-aided programming

409 *E* CAPS
→ computer-aided problem solving

410 *E* cascaded ATN (CATN) (NLP)
G kaskadiertes ATN (n)
F réseau ATN cascadé (m)
S red ATN en cascada (f)
I rete ATN in cascata (f)

411 *E* cascaded inference (LOGIC)
G kaskadierte Inferenz (f)
F inférence cascadée (f)
S inferencia en cascada (f)

I inferenza in cascata (f)

412 *E* case (LINGUISTICS)
G Fall (m); Kasus (m)
F cas (m)
S caso (m)
I caso (m)

413 *E* case analysis (EXPERT SYSTEMS)
G Fallanalyse (f); Kasusanalyse (f)
F analyse de cas (f)
S análisis de casos (m)
I analisi di casi (f)

414 *E* case-based learning
→ learning from examples

415 *E* case-based reasoning (CBR) (EXPERT SYSTEMS)
G fallbasiertes Inferieren (n); fallbasiertes Schließen (n)
F raisonnement à base de cas (m)
S razonamiento basado en casos (m)
I ragionamento basato su casi (m)

416 *E* case data (EXPERT SYSTEMS)
G Falldaten (n pl)
F données de cas (f pl)
S datos de casos (m pl)
I dati su casi (m pl)

417 *E* case data management (EXPERT SYSTEMS)
G Falldatenverwaltung (f)
F gestion de données de cas (f)
S gestión de datos de casos (f)
I gestione dei dati su casi (f)

418 *E* case data manager (EXPERT SYSTEMS)
G Falldatenverwaltungskomponente (f)
F gestionnaire pour l'archivage de cas (m)
S gestor de los datos de casos (m)
I programma di gestione dei dati su casi (m)

419 *E* case-dependent (EXPERT SYSTEMS)
G fallabhängig
F dépendant du cas
S dependiente del caso
I dipendente dal caso

420 *E* case frame (NLP)
G Kasusrahmen (m)
F cadre sémantique casuel (m)
S frame de caso (m)
I frame di caso (m); quadro del case (m)

421 *E* case grammar (KNOWLEDGE)
G Case Grammar (f); Fallgrammatik (f); Kasusgrammatik (f)
F grammaire de cas (f); grammaire casuelle (f)
S gramática de casos (f)
I grammatica a casi (f)

422 *E* case library (EXPERT SYSTEMS)
G Fallbibliothek (f)
F bibliothèque de cas (f)
S librería de casos (f)
I casistica di esempi (f)

423 *E* case marker (KNOWLEDGE)
G Fallmarkierer (m)
F marqueur de cas (m)
S marcador de caso (m)
I marcatore di caso (m)

424 *E* case-oriented (KNOWLEDGE)
G fallorientiert
F orienté cas
S orientado a casos
I orientato ai casi

425 *E* case semantics (NLP)
G Fallsemantik (f); Case-Semantik (f)
F sémantique casuelle (f)
S semántica de casos (f)
I semantica a casi (f)

426 *E* case structure (EXPERT SYSTEMS)
G Fallstruktur (f)
F structure des cas (f)
S estructura dos casos (f)
I struttura dei casi (f)

427 *E* case study (EXPERT SYSTEMS)
G Fallstudie (f)
F étude de cas (f)
S estudio de casos (m)
I studio dei casi (m); casistica (f)

428 *E* case theory (LOGIC)
G Falltheorie (f)
F théorie des cas (f)
S teoría de casos (f)
I teoria dei casi (f)

429 *E* CAT
= computer-assisted translation
→ machine-assisted translation

430 *E* categorial reasoning
→ categorical reasoning

431 *E* categorical reasoning (LOGIC)
= categorial reasoning
G kategorisches Inferieren (n)
F raisonnement catégorique (m)
S razonamiento categórico (m)
I ragionamento categorico (m)

432 *E* categorization (KNOWLEDGE)
G Kategorisierung (f)
F catégorisation (f)
S categorización (f)
I categorizzazione (f)

433 *E* category (KNOWLEDGE)
G Kategorie (f)
F catégorie (f)
S categoría (f)
I categoria (f)

434 *E* CATN
→ cascaded ATN

435 *E* causal chain (LOGIC)
G kausale Kette (f); Kausalkette (f)
F chaîne causale (f)
S cadena causal (f)
I catena causale (f)

436 *E* causal chaining (LOGIC)
G kausale Verkettung (f); Kausalverkettung (f)
F chaînage causal (m)
S encadenamiento causal (m)
I concatenamento causale (m)

437 *E* causal event (LOGIC)
G Kausalereignis (n); kausales Ereignis (n)
F événement causal (m)
S acontecimiento causal (m)
I evento causale (m)

438 *E* causal graph (CG) (LOGIC)
G Kausalgraph (m)
F graphe causal (m)
S grafo causal (m)
I grafo causale (m)

439 *E* causality (LOGIC)
G Kausalität (f)
F causalité (f)
S causalidad (f)
I causalità (f)

440 *E* causal knowledge (LOGIC)
G kausales Wissen (n)
F connaissances causales (f pl)
S conocimiento causal (m)
I conoscenza causale (f)

441 *E* causal link (LOGIC)
G kausale Verknüpfung (f)
F lien causal (m)
S enlace causal (m)
I link causale (m); legame causale (m)

442 *E* causal model (EXPERT SYSTEMS)
≠ heuristic model
G Kausalmodell (n); kausales Modell (n)

F modèle causal (m)
S modelo causal (m)
I modello causale (m)

443 *E* causal modelling (EXPERT SYSTEMS)
G Kausalmodellierung (f)
F modélisation causale (f)
S modelación causal (f)
I modellazione causale (f)

444 *E* causal net (EXPERT SYSTEMS)
G kausales Netz (n); Kausalnetz (n)
F réseau causal (m)
S red causal (f)
I rete causale (f)

445 *E* causal reasoning (LOGIC)
G kausales Inferieren (n); kausales Schließen (n)
F raisonnement causal (m)
S razonamiento causal (m)
I ragionamento causale (m)

446 *E* causal relation (LOGIC)
G Kausalrelation (f); Kausalbeziehung (f)
F relation causale (f)
S relación causal (f)
I relazione causale (f)

447 *E* cause and effect
G Ursache und Wirkung
F cause et effet
S causa–efecto
I causa e effetto

448 *E* CAV
→ computer-aided vision

449 *E* CBR
→ case-based reasoning

450 *E* CBT
= computer-based training

451 *E* CC
→ conceptual cohesiveness

452 *E* CD
→ conceptual dependency

453 *E* CD-based (*based on a system of conceptual dependency*) (KNOWLEDGE)
G CD-gestützt
F basé sur DC
S basado en DC
I basato su DC

454 *E* CD representation
→ conceptual dependency representation

455 *E* CDT
→ conceptual dependency theory

456 *E* cell (*of a neural network*)
= unit
G Zelle (f)
F cellule (f)
S célula (f)
I cellula (f)

457 *E* certain (*information etc.; truth value 100 = true or 0 = false*) (LOGIC)
G sicher
F certain
S cierto
I certo

458 *E* certainty (LOGIC)
↔ probability
G Gewißheit (f); Sicherheit (f)
F certitude (f)
S certidumbre (f); certeza (f)
I certezza (f)

459 *E* certainty-based reasoning (LOGIC)
G sicheres Schließen (n)
F raisonnement certain (m)
S razonamiento cierto (m)
I ragionamento certo (m)

460 *E* certainty factor (CF) (*a value between 0 and 100*) (LOGIC)

= confidence factor; degree of truth
G Sicherheitsfaktor (SF) (m); Konfidenzfaktor (m); Evidenzwert (m)
F facteur de certitude (m); coefficient de certitude (m); coefficient de vraisemblance (cv) (m)
S factor de certidumbre (FC) (m); factor de confianza (m)
I fattore di certezza (m); fattore di confidenza (m)

461 *E* certainty factor propagation (EXPERT SYSTEMS)
G Evidenzwertpropagierung (f)
F propagation du facteur de certitude (f)
S propagación del factor de confianza (f)
I propagazione del fattore di certezza (f)

462 *E* certainty theory
G Gewißheitstheorie (f)
F théorie de certitude (f)
S teoría de certidumbre (f)
I teoria della certezza (f)

463 *E* CF[1]
→ certainty factor

464 *E* CF[2]
→ context-free

465 *E* CFG
→ context-free grammar

466 *E* CF grammar
→ context-free grammar

467 *E* CFL
→ context-free language

468 *E* CG
→ causal graph

469 *E* CH
→ chaining

470 *E* chain (*verb*) (PROGRAMMING)
G verketten
F enchaîner
S encadenar
I concatenare

471 *E* chaining (CH) (*noun*) (PROGRAMMING)
G Kettung (f); Verkettung (f)
F enchaînement (m)
S encadenamiento (m)
I concatenamento (m); concatenazione (f)

472 *E* chaining rule (EXPERT SYSTEMS)
= chain rule
G Kettenregel (f)
F règle d'enchaînement (f)
S regla de encadenamiento (f)
I regola di concatenamento (f)

473 *E* chain rule
→ chaining rule

474 *E* character recognition (IMAGE PROCESSING)
G Zeichenerkennung (f)
F reconnaissance de caractères (f)
S reconocimiento de caracteres (m)
I riconoscimento di caratteri (m)

475 *E* chart parser (NLP)
G Tabellenparser (m)
F analyseur de tables (m)
S analizador de tablas (m)
I parser di tabelle (m); analizzatore de tabelle (m)

476 *E* chart parsing (NLP)
G Tabellenparsing (n)
F analyse de tables (f)
S parsing de tablas (m)
I parsing di tabelle (m); analisi di tabelle (f)

477 *E* chess program (GAMES)
G Schachspielprogramm (n)
F programme d'échecs (m)
S programa de ajedrez (m)
I programma per giocare a scacchi (m)

478 *E* child (*son or daughter: a node inheriting from a predecessor*) (KNOWLEDGE)
G Kind (n); Sohn (m)
F fils (m) (ou fille (f))
S hijo (m)
I figlio (m)

479 *E* child concept (KNOWLEDGE)
= subconcept; lower-level concept
≠ parent concept
G Unterbegriff (m)
F sous-concept (m)
S subconcepto (m)
I sotto-concetto (m)

480 *E* childless node (LOGIC)
G Knoten ohne Nachkommen (m)
F nœud sans fils (m)
S nodo sin hijos (m); nodo estéril (m)
I nodo senza figli (m)

481 *E* child node (LOGIC)
= daughter node
G Kindknoten (m)
F nœud fils (m)
S nodo hijo (m)
I nodo figlio (m)

482 *E* choice point (LOGIC)
= decision point
G Verzweigungspunkt (m); Entscheidungsstelle (f)
F point de décision (m)
S punto de decisión (m)
I punto di decisione (m)

483 *E* choice set (*a set of alternatives*) (LOGIC)
G Auswahlmenge (f)
F ensemble de sélection (m)
S conjunto de selección (m)
I insieme di scelta (m)

484 *E* chronological backtracking (EXPERT SYSTEMS)
≠ dependency-directed backtracking
G chronologisches Backtracking (n); chronologisches Zurückverfolgen (n)
F recul chronologique (m)
S retroceso cronológico (m)
I backtracking cronologico (m)

485 *E* chunk
→ segment

486 *E* chunk (of knowledge)
= knowledge chunk; block of knowledge; clump of knowledge
G Chunk (Informationseinheit) (m); Stück (n); 'Brocken' (m); Wissenseinheit (f)
F fragment de connaissance (m); fragment de savoir (m)
S pieza de conocimiento (f); racimo (m); unidad de conocimiento (f)
I chunk (m); elemento singolo (m)

487 *E* Church's thesis (THEORY)
G Churchsche These (f)
F thèse de Church (f)
S tesis de Church (f)
I tesi di Church (f)

488 *E* circular inference (LOGIC)
G Ringschluß (m)
F inférence circulaire (f)
S inferencia circular (f)
I inferenza circolare (f)

489 *E* circular list (*in LISP*) (PROGRAMMING)
G zirkuläre Liste (f)
F liste circulaire (f)
S lista circular (f)

I lista circolare (f)

490 *E* circular rule (EXPERT SYSTEMS)
G Zirkelregel (f)
F règle circulaire (f)
S regla circular (f)
I regola circolare (f)

491 *E* circumscription (LOGIC)
G Zirkumskription (f); Umschreibung (f)
F circonscription (f)
S circunscripción (f)
I circoscrizione (f)

492 *E* circumscription strategy (LOGIC)
G Zirkumskriptionsstrategie (f)
F stratégie de circonscription (f)
S estrategia de circunscripción (f)
I strategie di circoscrizione (f)

493 *E* CK
→ control knowledge

494 *E* CL
→ computational linguistics

495 *E* claiming (*noun*)
→ assertion[1]

496 *E* class formation (KNOWLEDGE)
G Klassenbildung (f)
F formation de classes (f)
S formación de clases (f)
I formazione di classi (f)

497 *E* class hierarchy (KNOWLEDGE)
G Klassenhierarchie (f)
F hiérarchie de classe (f)
S jerarquía de clase (f)
I gerarchia di classe (f)

498 *E* classical logic
= conventional logic; traditional logic; standard logic
G klassische Logik (f); herkömmliche Logik (f)
F logique conventionnelle (f); logique classique (f); logique standard (f)
S lógica clásica (f); lógica convencional (f)
I logica classica (f)

499 *E* classification (KNOWLEDGE)
G Klassifikation (f); Klassifizierung (f)
F classification (f)
S clasificación (f)
I classificazione (f)

500 *E* classification system (KNOWLEDGE)
G Klassifikationssystem (n)
F système de classification (m)
S sistema de clasificación (m)
I sistema di classificazione (m)

501 *E* classifier algorithm (KNOWLEDGE)
G Klassifikationsalgorithmus (m)
F algorithme de classification (m)
S algoritmo clasificador (m)
I algoritmo classificatore (m)

502 *E* class name (KNOWLEDGE)
G Klassenname (m)
F nom de classe (m)
S nombre de clase (m)
I nome di classe (m)

503 *E* class of knowledge
G Wissensart (f)
F classe de connaissance (f)
S clase de conocimiento (f)
I classe di conoscenza (f)

504 *E* class of value (LOGIC)
G Werteklasse (f)
F classe de valeur (f)
S clase de valor (f)
I classe di valore (f)

505 *E* class variable (LOGIC)
G Klassenvariable (f)

F variable de classe (f)
S variable de clase (f)
I variabile di classe (f)

506 *E* clausal form
→ clause form

507 *E* clausal representation (LOGIC)
G Klauseldarstellung (f)
F représentation clausale (f)
S representación clausal (f)
I rappresentazione sotto forma di clausola (f)

508 *E* clause¹ (LOGIC)
G Klausel (f); Klause (f); Clause (f)
F clause (f)
S cláusula (f)
I clausola (f)

509 *E* clause² (LINGUISTICS)
G Satz (m)
F phrase (f)
S frase (f)
I frase (f)

510 *E* clause form (LOGIC)
= clausal form
G Klauselform (f)
F forme clausale (f)
S forma clausal (de la lógica) (f)
I forma in clausole (f)

511 *E* clause set
→ set of clauses

512 *E* clause space (NEURAL NETS)
G Klauselraum (m)
F espace de clauses (m)
S espacio de cláusulas (m)
I spazio delle clausole (m)

513 *E* cliché (*standard procedure*) (KNOWLEDGE)
G Klischee (n)
F cliché (m)
S cliché (m)
I cliché (m)

514 *E* CLISP (*conversational LISP*) (PROGRAMMING)
G CLISP
F CLISP
S CLISP
I CLISP

515 *E* closed list (*of expanded nodes in a search tree*) (LOGIC)
G Closed-Liste (f)
F liste fermée (f)
S lista cerrada (f)
I lista chiusa (f)

516 *E* closed world assumption (CWA) (THEORY)
G Annahme der Weltabgeschlossenheit (f)
F hypothèse du monde fermé (f); hypothèse du monde clos (f)
S hipótesis del mundo cerrado (f)
I postulato del mondo chiuso (m); ipotesi del mondo chiuso (f); assunzione del mondo chiuso (f)

517 *E* CLS
→ concept learning system

518 *E* clue word (*in discourse understanding*) (RECOGNITION)
G Cluewort (für das Verstehen entscheidendes Wort) (n)
F mot clé (m)
S palabra clave (f)
I parola chiave (f)

519 *E* clump of knowledge
→ chunk (of knowledge)

520 *E* cluster (*noun*) (KNOWLEDGE)
G Cluster (m)
F groupe (m)
S agrupamiento (m)
I gruppo (m); agglomerato (m); grappolo (m)

521 *E* clustering technique (*for objects*) (KNOWLEDGE)

G Clustern (n)
F technique de groupement (f)
S técnica de agrupamiento (f)
I tecnica di raggruppamento (f)

522 E CM
→ Connection Machine

523 E coarticulation (RECOGNITION)
G Koartikulation (f)
F coarticulation (f)
S coarticulación (f)
I coarticolazione (f)

524 E code tree (PROGRAMMING)
G Codebaum (m)
F arbre de codage (m)
S árbol de códigos (m)
I albero di codici (m)

525 E coding theory
G Codierungstheorie (f)
F théorie des codes (f)
S teoría de códigos (f)
I teoria dei codici (f)

526 E cognition (*the process of knowing*)
G Kognition (f); Erkenntnis (f)
F cognition (f)
S cognición (f)
I cognizione (f)

527 E cognition theory
G Kognitionstheorie (f)
F théorie de cognition (f)
S teoría cognoscitiva (f)
I teoria cognitiva (f)

528 E cognitive (*relating to cognition*) (THEORY)
G kognitiv
F cognitif
S cognitivo; cognoscitivo
I cognitivo

529 E cognitive abilities (THEORY)
G kognitive Fähigkeiten (f pl)
F capacités cognitives (f pl)
S capacidades cognitivas (f pl)
I capacità cognitive (f)

530 E cognitive behaviour (THEORY)
G kognitives Verhalten (n)
F comportement cognitif (m)
S comportamiento cognoscitivo (m)
I comportamento cognitivo (m)

531 E cognitive compatibility (EXPERT SYSTEMS)
G kognitive Kompatibilität (f)
F compatibilité cognitive (f)
S compatibilidad cognitiva (f)
I compatibilità cognitiva (f)

532 E cognitive computer (THEORY)
G kognitiver Rechner (m)
F ordinateur cognitif (m); machine savante (f)
S ordenador cognitivo (m)
I elaboratore cognitivo (m)

533 E cognitive economy (KNOWLEDGE)
G ökonomischer Umgang mit den kognitiven Ressourcen (m)
F économie cognitive (f)
S economía cognitiva (f)
I economia cognitiva (f)

534 E cognitive level (LOGIC)
G kognitive Ebene (f)
F niveau cognitif (m)
S nivel cognoscitivo (m)
I livello cognitivo (m)

535 E cognitive method (THEORY)
G kognitive Methode (f)
F méthode cognitive (f)
S método cognoscitivo (m)
I metodo cognitivo (m)

536 E cognitive model (THEORY)
G kognitives Modell (n); Kognitionsmodell (n)
F modèle cognitif (m)
S modelo cognoscitivo (m)

I modello cognitivo (m)

537 *E* cognitive modelling (THEORY)
G kognitive Modellierung (f)
F modélisation cognitive (f)
S modelación cognoscitiva (f)
I modellazione cognitiva (f)

538 *E* cognitive process (THEORY)
G kognitiver Prozeß (m)
F procédé cognitif (m)
S proceso cognoscitivo (m)
I processo cognitivo (m)

539 *E* cognitive processing (THEORY)
G kognitive Verarbeitung (f)
F traitement cognitif (m)
S procesamiento cognoscitivo (m)
I trattamento cognitivo (m)

540 *E* cognitive processor (THEORY)
G kognitiver Prozessor (m)
F processeur cognitif (m)
S procesador cognoscitivo (m)
I processore cognitivo (m)

541 *E* cognitive psychology (THEORY)
G kognitive Psychologie (f); Kognitionspsychologie (f); Wissenspsychologie (f) (adj kognitionspsychologisch)
F psychologie cognitive (f)
S psicología cognoscitiva (f); psicología cognitiva (f)
I psicologia cognitiva (f)

542 *E* cognitive science (THEORY)
G Cognitive Science (f); kognitive Wissenschaft (f)
F sciences cognitives (f pl)
S ciencia cognitiva (f); ciencias cognoscitivas (f pl)
I scienza cognitiva (f); scienze cognitive (m)

543 *E* cognitivism (THEORY)
G Kognitivismus (m)
F cognitivisme (m)
S cognitivismo (m)
I cognitivismo (m)

544 *E* coherence relations (LOGIC)
G Kohärenzrelationen (f pl)
F relations de cohérence (f pl)
S relaciones de coherencia (f pl)
I relazioni di coerenza (f pl)

545 *E* colour vision (IMAGE PROCESSING)
G Farbsehen (n)
F vision en couleurs (f)
S visión en colores (f)
I visione a colori (f)

546 *E* combinational analysis
→ combinatorial analysis

547 *E* combination rule (of Dempster) (THEORY)
G Kombinationsregel (f)
F règle de combinaison (f)
S regla de combinación (f)
I regola di combinazione (f)

548 *E* combinatorial analysis (THEORY)
= combinational analysis
G kombinatorische Analyse (f)
F analyse combinatoire (f)
S análisis combinatorio (m)
I analisi combinatoria (f)

549 *E* combinatorial explosion (LOGIC)
G kombinatorische Explosion (f)
F explosion combinatoire (f)
S explosión combinatoria (f)
I esplosione combinatoria (f)

550 *E* combinatoric methods
→ combinatorics

551 *E* combinatorics (LOGIC)
= combinatoric methods
G Kombinatorik (f)
F méthodes combinatoires (f pl)
S métodos combinatorios (m pl)
I metodi combinatori (m pl)

552 *E* combinatory logic
G kombinatorische Logik (f)
F logique combinatoire (f)
S lógica combinatoria (f)
I logica combinatoria (f)

553 *E* combined certainty (LOGIC)
G kombinierte Sicherheit (f)
F certitude combinée (f)
S certidumbre combinada (f)
I certezza combinata (f)

554 *E* command language (PROGRAMMING)
G Kommandosprache (f)
F langage de commande (m)
S lenguaje de comando (m)
I linguaggio di comando (m)

555 *E* command recognition system (PROGRAMMING)
G Kommandoerkennungssystem (n)
F système de reconnaissance des commandes vocales (m)
S reconocimiento de comandos (m)
I riconoscimento di comandi (m)

556 *E* common knowledge
G gemeinsames Wissen (n); Gemeinschaftswissen (n)
F connaissances communes (f pl)
S conocimiento común (m)
I conoscenza comune (f)

557 *E* Common LISP (*a standardized version of LISP*) (PROGRAMMING)
G Common LISP
F Common LISP
S Common LISP
I Common LISP

558 *E* commonsense (KNOWLEDGE)
G gesunder Menschenverstand (m)
F sens commun (m); bon sens (m)
S sentido común (m)
I buon senso (m); senso comune (m)

559 *E* commonsense knowledge
= world knowledge; everyday knowledge
G Umweltwissen (n); Weltwissen (n); Alltagswissen (n); Allgemeinwissen (n)
F connaissance de sens commun (f); connaissance de bon sens (f)
S conocimiento de sentido común (m)
I conoscenza di buon senso (f); conoscenza di senso comune (f)

560 *E* commonsense reasoning (LOGIC)
G Schlußfolgern mit gesundem Menschenverstand (n)
F raisonnement de sens commun (m)
S razonamiento de sentido común (m)
I commonsense reasoning (m); ragionamento di buon senso (m)

561 *E* commonsense rule (EXPERT SYSTEMS)
G Regel des gesunden Menschenverstands (f)
F règle de sens commun (f)
S regla de sentido común (f)
I regola di buon senso (f)

562 *E* communication interface (EXPERT SYSTEMS)
G Kommunikationsschnittstelle (f)
F interface de communication (f)
S interfaz de comunicación (f)
I interfaccia di comunicazione (f)

563 *E* compiled knowledge
G gesammeltes Wissen (n); angesammeltes Wissen (n); kompiliertes Wissen (n)
F connaissance compilée (f); connaissances agrégées (f pl)
S conocimiento compilado (m)
I conoscenza compilata (f)

564 *E* complete graph (LOGIC)

G vollständiger Graph (m)
F graphe complet (m)
S grafo completo (m)
I grafo completo (m)

565 E completeness hypothesis (LOGIC)
G Vollständigkeitshypothese (f)
F hypothèse de complétude (f)
S hipótesis de integridad (f)
I ipotesi della completezza (f)

566 E completion (*of images etc.*)
G Vervollständigung (f)
F complètement (m)
S completamiento (m)
I completamento (m)

567 E complex event (EXPERT SYSTEMS)
G komplexes Ereignis (n)
F événement complex (m)
S acontecimiento complejo (m)
I evento complesso (m)

568 E complexity (*of a problem etc.*) (EXPERT SYSTEMS)
G Komplexität (f)
F complexité (f)
S complejidad (f)
I complessità (f)

569 E complex task
G komplexe Aufgabe (f)
F tâche complexe (f)
S tarea compleja (f)
I lavoro complesso (m)

570 E composite conclusion (LOGIC)
G zusammengesetzter Schluß (m)
F conclusion composite (f)
S conclusión compuesta (f)
I conclusione composta (f)

571 E composite graph (LOGIC)
G zusammengesetzter Graph (m)
F graphe composite (m)
S grafo compuesto (m)
I grafo composto (m)

572 E composite inference rule (EXPERT SYSTEMS)
G zusammengesetzte Inferenzregel (f)
F règle d'inférence composite (f)
S regla composicional de inferencia (f)
I regola di inferenza composta (f)

573 E compound clause (*clauses linked by logical operators*) (LOGIC)
↔ simple clause
G zusammengesetzte Klausel (f)
F clause composée (f)
S cláusula compuesta (f)
I clausola composta (f)

574 E compound event (EXPERT SYSTEMS)
G zusammengesetztes Ereignis (n)
F événement composé (m)
S acontecimiento compuesto (m)
I avvenimento composto (m)

575 E compound forms (LINGUISTICS)
G zusammengesetzte Formen (f pl)
F formes composées (f pl)
S formas compuestas (f pl)
I forme composte (f pl)

576 E compound goal (EXPERT SYSTEMS)
G zusammengesetztes Ziel (n)
F but composé (m)
S objetivo compuesto (m)
I obiettivo composto (m)

577 E compound proposition (LOGIC)
G zusammengesetzte Aussage (f)
F proposition composée (f)
S sentencia compuesta (f)
I proposizione composta (f)

578 E compound term (LOGIC)
G zusammengesetzter Ausdruck (m)
F terme composé (m)
S término compuesto (m)
I termine composto (m)

579 *E* comprehension of discourse
→ discourse understanding

580 *E* computational linguistics (CL)
G Computerlinguistik (f)
F linguistique computationnelle (f)
S lingüística computacional (f)
I linguistica computazionale (f)

581 *E* computational logic
G Computerlogik (f)
F logique computationnelle (f)
S lógica computacional (f)
I logica computazionale (f)

582 *E* computational vision
→ computer vision

583 *E* computer-aided instruction (CAI) (LEARNING)
G computerunterstützte Unterweisung (CUU) (f)
F enseignement assisté par ordinateur (EAO) (m)
S enseñanza asistida por ordenador (EAO) (f)
I istruzione assistita dall'elaboratore (f)

584 *E* computer-aided problem solving (CAPS) (EXPERT SYSTEMS)
G rechnerunterstütztes Problemlösen (n)
F résolution de problèmes assistée par ordinateur (f)
S resolución de problemas asistida por ordenador (f)
I risoluzione di problemi con l'assistenza dell'elaboratore (f)

585 *E* computer-aided programming (CAP)
G computerunterstütztes Programmieren (n)
F programmation assistée par ordinateur (f)
S programación asistida por ordenador (PAO) (f)
I programmazione computerizzata (f)

586 *E* computer-aided vision (CAV) (IMAGE PROCESSING)
G rechnerunterstütztes Sehen (n)
F vision assistée par ordinateur (f)
S visión asistida por ordenador (f)
I visione assistita dall'elaboratore (f)

587 *E* computer-assisted translation (CAT)
→ machine-assisted translation

588 *E* computer-based medical consultations (EXPERT SYSTEMS)
G rechnergestützte medizinische Beratung (f)
F consultation médicale assistée par ordinateur (f)
S consulta médica asistida por ordenador (f)
I consultazione medica assistita dall'elaboratore (f)

589 *E* computer chess (GAMES)
G Computerschach (n)
F échecs sur ordinateur (m pl)
S ajedrez de computador (m)
I scacchi col computer (m pl)

590 *E* computer-generated speech (SYNTHESIS)
G computererzeugte Sprache (f)
F parole générée par ordinateur (f)
S habla generada por ordenador (f)
I parlato generato da elaboratore (m)

591 *E* computer intelligence
→ machine intelligence

592 *E* computerized vision
→ computer vision

593 *E* computer learning
G Computerlernen (n)

F apprentissage par ordinateur (m)
S aprendizaje por ordenador (m)
I apprendimento dall'elaboratore (m)

594 *E* computer vision (CV) (IMAGE PROCESSING)
= artificial vision; computational vision; computerized vision
G künstliches Sehen (n); Computervision (f)
F vision par ordinateur (f); vision artificielle (f); visionique (f)
S visión artificial (VA) (f); visión por computador (f)
I visione artificiale (f)

595 *E* computer vision system (IMAGE PROCESSING)
= artificial vision system
G künstliches Sehsystem (n)
F système de vision par ordinateur (m); système de vision artificielle (m)
S sistema de visión artificial (SVA) (m)
I sistema di visione artificiale (m)

596 *E* computer voice output (SYNTHESIS)
G Computersprachausgabe (CSA) (f)
F sortie vocale par ordinateur (f)
S salida vocal de ordenador (f)
I uscita fonica dall'elaboratore (f)

597 *E* concept (KNOWLEDGE)
G Begriff (m); Konzept (n)
F concept (m)
S concepto (m)
I concetto (m)

598 *E* concept acquisition (KNOWLEDGE)
G Begriffserwerb (m)
F acquisition des concepts (f)
S adquisición de conceptos (f)
I acquisizione di concetti (f)

599 *E* concept analyser (CA) (NLP)
G Begriffsanalysator (m)
F analyseur des concepts (m)
S analizador de conceptos (m)
I analizzatore di concetti (m)

600 *E* concept-based model (KNOWLEDGE)
G begriffsbasiertes Modell (n)
F modèle conceptuel (m)
S modelo conceptual (m)
I modello sulla base di concetti (m)

601 *E* concept description (KNOWLEDGE)
G Begriffsbeschreibung (f); Konzeptbeschreibung (f)
F description du concept (f)
S descripción de conceptos (f)
I descrizione di concetti (f)

602 *E* concept-driven system (KNOWLEDGE)
G begriffsgesteuertes System (n)
F système dirigé par concepts (m)
S sistema guiado por conceptos (m)
I sistema guidato da concetti (m)

603 *E* concept formation (LOGIC)
G Begriffsbildung (f); Konzeptbildung (f)
F formation de concepts (f)
S formación de conceptos (f)
I formazione di concetti (f)

604 *E* concept hierarchy (KNOWLEDGE)
G Begriffshierarchie (f)
F hiérarchie de concepts (f)
S jerarquía de conceptos (f)
I gerarchia dei concetti (f)

605 *E* concept learning
= learning of concepts; conceptual learning
↔ learning from examples
G Lernen von Begriffen (n); begriffliches Lernen (n)

F apprentissage de concepts (m); apprentissage conceptuel (m)
S aprendizaje de conceptos (m); aprendizaje conceptual (m)
I apprendimento di concetti (m); apprendimento concettuale (m)

606 *E* concept learning system (CLS)
G Begriffslernsystem (n)
F système d'apprentissage conceptuel (m)
S sistema de aprendizaje de conceptos (m)
I sistema di apprendimento di concetti (m)

607 *E* concept prototyping (PROGRAMMING)
G Konzept-Prototyping (n)
F prototypage de concepts (m)
S prototipación de conceptos (f)
I prototipazione di concetti (f)

608 *E* concept space (EXPERT SYSTEMS)
G Konzeptraum (m)
F espace de concepts (m)
S espacio de conceptos (m)
I spazio dei concetti (m)

609 *E* concept tree (KNOWLEDGE)
G Begriffsbaum (m)
F arbre de concepts (m)
S árbol de conceptos (m)
I albero dei concetti (m)

610 *E* conceptual (KNOWLEDGE)
G begrifflich; konzeptionell
F conceptuel
S conceptual
I concettuale

611 *E* conceptual analyser
→ conceptual parser

612 *E* conceptual analysis (NLP)
G Begriffsanalyse (f)
F analyse conceptuelle (f)
S análisis conceptual (m)
I analisi concettuale (f)

613 *E* conceptual case (NLP)
G konzeptueller Kasus (m)
F cas conceptuel (m)
S caso conceptual (m)
I caso concettuale (m)

614 *E* conceptual clustering (KNOWLEDGE)
G Clustern von Begriffen (n)
F groupement de concepts (m)
S agrupamiento conceptual (m); agrupamiento de conceptos (m)
I raggruppamento concettuale (m)

615 *E* conceptual cohesiveness (CC) (KNOWLEDGE)
G begriffliche Kohärenz (f)
F cohérence conceptuelle (f)
S consistencia conceptual (f)
I coerenza concettuale (f)

616 *E* conceptual dependency (CD) (KNOWLEDGE)
G konzeptuelle Dependenz (f); Begriffsabhängigkeit (f); Conceptual Dependency (m)
F dépendance conceptuelle (DC) (f)
S dependencia conceptual (f)
I dipendenza concettuale (f)

617 *E* conceptual dependency representation (KNOWLEDGE)
= CD representation
G Darstellung mit konzeptueller Dependenz (f); CD-Darstellung (f)
F représentation en dépendance conceptuelle (f); représentation en DC (f)
S representación de dependencia conceptual (f)
I rappresentazione della dipendenza concettuale (f)

618 *E* conceptual dependency rule (EXPERT SYSTEMS)

G CD-Regel (f) (mit konzeptueller Dependenz arbeitend)
F règle de dépendance conceptuelle (f)
S regla de dependencia conceptual (f)
I regola di dipendenza concettuale (f)

619 *E* conceptual dependency structure (KNOWLEDGE)
G CD-Struktur (f)
F schéma de dépendance conceptuelle (m); schéma DC (m)
S estructura de dependencia conceptual (f)
I struttura della dipendenza concettuale (f)

620 *E* conceptual dependency theory (CDT)
G Theorie von der Conceptual Dependency (f); konzeptuelle Abhängigkeitstheorie (f)
F théorie de la dépendance conceptuelle (TDC) (f)
S teoría de dependencia conceptual (f)
I teoria della dipendenza concettuale (f)

621 *E* conceptual graph (NLP)
G Begriffsgraph (m); konzeptueller Graph (m)
F graphe conceptuel (m)
S grafo conceptual (m)
I grafo concettuale (m)

622 *E* conceptualization (KNOWLEDGE)
G Conceptualization (f); Konzeptualisierung (f)
F conceptualisation (f)
S conceptualización (f)
I concettualizzazione (f)

623 *E* conceptualize (KNOWLEDGE)
G konzeptualisieren
F conceptualiser
S conceptualizar
I concettualizzare

624 *E* conceptual knowledge
G begriffliches Wissen (n)
F connaissance conceptuelle (f)
S conocimiento conceptual (m); conocimiento sobre conceptos (m)
I conoscenza concettuale (f)

625 *E* conceptual learning
→ concept learning

626 *E* conceptual level (KNOWLEDGE)
G Begriffsebene (f)
F niveau conceptuel (m)
S nivel conceptual (m)
I livello concettuale (m)

627 *E* conceptually dependent (KNOWLEDGE)
G konzeptuell abhängig
F à dépendance conceptuelle
S de dependencia conceptual
I concettualmente dipendente

628 *E* conceptual node (LOGIC)
G Begriffsknoten (m); Konzeptknoten (m)
F nœud conceptuel (m)
S nodo conceptual (m)
I nodo concettuale (m); nodo di concetto (m)

629 *E* conceptual parser (NLP)
= conceptual analyser
G Begriffsparser (m)
F analyseur conceptuel (m)
S parser conceptual (m)
I parser concettuale (m); analizzatore concettuale (m)

630 *E* conceptual relation (KNOWLEDGE)
G Begriffsbeziehung (f); Begriffsrelation (f)
F relation entre concepts (f); relation conceptuelle (f)

S relación conceptual (f)
I relazione concettuale (f)

631 *E* conceptual representation system (KNOWLEDGE)
= meaning-based representation system
G begriffliches Darstellungssystem (n)
F système de représentation conceptuelle (m)
S sistema de representación conceptual (m)
I sistema di rappresentazione concettuale (m)

632 *E* conceptual scene (KNOWLEDGE)
G Begriffsszene (f)
F scène conceptuelle (f)
S escena conceptual (f)
I scena concettuale (f)

633 *E* conceptual structure (KNOWLEDGE)
G Begriffsstruktur (f)
F structure conceptuelle (f)
S estructura conceptual (f)
I struttura concettuale (f)

634 *E* conceptual tree (KNOWLEDGE)
G Begriffsbaum (m)
F arbre conceptuel (m)
S árbol conceptual (m)
I albero concettuale (m)

635 *E* conclusion (LOGIC)
G Schluß (m); Konklusion (f)
F conclusion (f)
S conclusión (f)
I conclusione (f)

636 *E* conclusion part (*of a rule*) (LOGIC)
= 'then' part; consequence; consequent
≠ premise part
G Dann-Teil (einer Regel) (m); Konklusionsteil (m); Sukzedens (n); Konsequenz (f); Konsequenzteil (m)
F partie de conclusion (f); conséquent (m)
S parte de conclusión (f); parte entonces (f); consecuente (m)
I parte conclusiva (f); conseguente (m)

637 *E* concrete representation (KNOWLEDGE)
G konkrete Darstellung (f)
F représentation concrète (f)
S representación concreta (f)
I rappresentazione concreta (f)

638 *E* condition (LOGIC)
G Bedingung (f)
F condition (f)
S condición (f)
I condizione (f)

639 *E* condition–action rule[1] (*situation–action rule*) (EXPERT SYSTEMS)
G Bedingungs–Handlungs-Regel (f)
F règle condition–action (f)
S regla condición–acción (f)
I regola condizione–azione (f)

640 *E* condition–action rule[2]
→ if–then rule

641 *E* conditional (LOGIC)
G bedingt
F conditionnel
S condicional
I condizionale

642 *E* conditional probability (LOGIC)
G bedingte Wahrscheinlichkeit (f)
F probabilité conditionnelle (f)
S probabilidad condicional (f)
I probabilità condizionale (f)

643 *E* condition-driven (EXPERT SYSTEMS)

G bedingungsgesteuert; bedingungsorientiert
F dirigé par conditions
S guiado por condiciones
I comandato da condizioni

644 *E* confidence (LOGIC)
G Konfidenz (f); Vertrauen (n); Zutrauen (n)
F confiance (f)
S confianza (f)
I confidenza (f)

645 *E* confidence factor
→ certainty factor

646 *E* confidence island (LOGIC)
G Konfidenzinsel (f)
F îlot de confiance (m)
S isla de confianza (f)
I isola di confidenza (f)

647 *E* confidence limit (LOGIC)
G Konfidenzgrenze (f)
F seuil de confiance (m)
S límite de confianza (m)
I limite di confidenza (m)

648 *E* confidence scale (LOGIC)
G Konfidenzskala (f)
F échelle de confiance (f)
S escala de confianza (f)
I scala di confidenza (f)

649 *E* confidence value (LOGIC)
G Konfidenzwert (m)
F valeur de confiance (f)
S valor de confianza (m)
I valore di confidenza (m)

650 *E* configuration space (EXPERT SYSTEMS)
= C space
G Konfigurationsraum (m)
F espace de configuration (m)
S espacio de configuración (m)
I spazio di configurazione (m)

651 *E* configuration system (EXPERT SYSTEMS)
G Konfigurierungssystem (n); Entwurfssystem (n); Konfigurator (m)
F système de configuration (m)
S sistema de configuración (m)
I sistema di configurazione (m)

652 *E* conflict
G Konflikt (m)
F conflit (m)
S conflicto (m)
I conflitto (m)

653 *E* conflict handling (EXPERT SYSTEMS)
G Konfliktbehandlung (f)
F gestion des conflits (f)
S gestión de conflictos (f)
I gestione dei conflitti (f)

654 *E* conflicting (*rules etc.*) (EXPERT SYSTEMS)
G konfligierend; widersprüchlich
F conflictuel
S conflictivo
I conflittuale

655 *E* conflict resolution (EXPERT SYSTEMS)
G Konfliktlösung (f); Konfliktauflösung (f)
F résolution de conflit(s) (f)
S resolución de conflictos (f)
I risoluzione di conflitti (f)

656 *E* conflict resolution strategy (EXPERT SYSTEMS)
G Konfliktlösungsstrategie (f)
F stratégie de résolution de conflits (f)
S estrategia para resolver conflictos (f)
I strategia per la risoluzione di conflitti (f)

657 *E* conflict set (EXPERT SYSTEMS)

G Konfliktmenge (f)
F ensemble de conflit (m)
S conjunto conflicto (m)
I insieme conflittuale (m)

658 *E* confluence (LOGIC)
G Konfluenz (f)
F confluence (f)
S confluencia (f)
I confluenza (f)

659 *E* confusion matrix (*a matrix of substitution errors*) (RECOGNITION)
G Konfusionsmatrix (f); Verwechslungsmatrix (f)
F matrice de confusion (f)
S matriz de confusión (f)
I matrice di confusione (f)

660 *E* conjectural reasoning (LOGIC)
G Inferieren durch Mutmaßung (n)
F raisonnement conjectural (m)
S razonamiento sobre conjeturas (m)
I ragionamento congetturale (m)

661 *E* conjecture (LOGIC)
G Mutmaßung (f); Vermutung (f)
F conjecture (f)
S conjetura (f)
I congettura (f)

662 *E* conjunction (*of conditions, involving an AND*) (LOGIC)
↔ disjunction
G Konjunktion (f)
F conjonction (f)
S conjunción (f)
I congiunzione (f)

663 *E* conjunctive rule (EXPERT SYSTEMS)
G konjunktive Regel (f)
F règle conjonctive (f)
S regla conjuntiva (f)
I regola congiuntiva (f)

664 *E* connected graph (LOGIC)
G zusammenhängender Graph (m)
F graphe connexe (m)
S grafo conectado (m)
I grafo connesso (m)

665 *E* connected speech
→ continuous speech

666 *E* connected-speech recognition
→ continuous-speech recognition
≠ isolated-words recognition
G Erkennen zusammenhängender gesprochener Sprache (n); Erkennen gebundener Rede (n)
F reconnaissance du discours continu (f); reconnaissance de la parole continue (f)
S reconocimiento del lenguaje hablado (m); reconocimiento de habla contínua (o conectada) (m)
I riconoscimento del parlato (m)

667 *E* connection graph (LOGIC)
G Konnektionsgraph (m); Klauselgraph (m)
F graphe de connexion (m)
S grafo de conexión (m)
I grafo di connessione (m)

668 *E* connectionism (THEORY)
G Konnektionismus (m)
F connexionisme (m)
S conexionismo (m)
I connessionismo (m)

669 *E* connectionist model
→ neural network model

670 *E* Connection Machine (CM) (THEORY)
G Connection Machine (f)
F machine à connexions (f)
S máquina de conexión (f)
I Connection Machine (f); macchina di connessione (f)

671 *E* connection science (THEORY)

= parallel distributed processing (PDP)
G Konnektionswissenschaft (f); verteilte Parallelverarbeitung (f); PDP
F traitement distribué parallèle (m)
S procesamiento paralelo distribuido (m)
I elaborazione parallela distribuita (f)

672 *E* connective (*noun*) (PROGRAMMING)
= connector
G Verknüpfungssymbol (n); Junktor (m)
F connecteur (m); opérateur propositionnel (m)
S conectivo (m); conector (m)
I simbolo di connessione (m); connettore (m); connettivo (m)

673 *E* connectivity (*of a system*)
G Konnektivität (f)
F connectivité (f)
S conectividad (f)
I connettività (f)

674 *E* connector
→ connective

675 *E* consequence (*of a rule*)
→ conclusion part; right-hand side

676 *E* consequent (*noun*)
→ conclusion part; right-hand side

677 *E* consequent reasoning (LOGIC)
G konsequentes Inferieren (n)
F raisonnement conséquent (m)
S razonamiento consecuente (m)
I ragionamento coerente (m)

678 *E* consistency (LOGIC)
G Konsistenz (f)
F cohérence (f)
S consistencia (f)
I coerenza (f)

679 *E* consistency check (NLP)
G Konsistenzprüfung (f)
F contrôle de la cohérence (m)
S verificación de coherencia (f)
I controllo di coerenza (m)

680 *E* consistency problem (KNOWLEDGE)
G Konsistenzproblem (n)
F problème de cohérence (m)
S problema de consistencia (m)
I problema di coerenza (m)

681 *E* consolidation
→ unification

682 *E* constrain (*a problem*) (EXPERT SYSTEMS)
G einschränken; eingrenzen
F contraindre
S limitar
I vincolare

683 *E* constrained domain
→ restricted domain

684 *E* constrained environment (EXPERT SYSTEMS)
G eingeschränkte Umgebung (f)
F environnement restreint (m)
S entorno limitado (m)
I ambiente vincolato (m)

685 *E* constraining (*adjective*) (EXPERT SYSTEMS)
G einschränkend
F contraignant
S restrictivo
I vincolante

686 *E* constraint (EXPERT SYSTEMS)
G Constraint (m); Einschränkung (f); Beschränkung (f); Randbedingung (f); Grenzwert (m)
F contrainte (f)
S restricción (f); vinculación (f)

I vincolo (che vieta certe situazioni) (m)

687 *E* constraint analysis (EXPERT SYSTEMS)
G Constraintanalyse (f); Analyse der Randbedingungen (f)
F analyse de contraintes (f)
S análisis de restricciones (m)
I analisi dei vincoli (f)

688 *E* constraint-based system (EXPERT SYSTEMS)
G constraintbasiertes System (n)
F système basé sur contraintes (m); système à base de contraintes (m)
S sistema basado en restricciones (m)
I sistema basato su vincoli (m)

689 *E* constraint generation (EXPERT SYSTEMS)
G Constraintgenerierung (f)
F génération de contraintes (f)
S generación de restricciones (f)
I generazione di vincoli (f)

690 *E* constraint network (EXPERT SYSTEMS)
G Constraintnetz (n); Beschränkungsnetz (n)
F réseau de contraintes (m)
S red de restricciones (f)
I rete di vincoli (f)

691 *E* constraint programming
G Constraint-Programmierung (f)
F programmation par contraintes (f); programmation avec contraintes (f)
S programación por restricciones (f)
I programmazione sulla base di vincoli (f)

692 *E* constraint propagation (*over the constraint network; can be constructive or destructive*) (EXPERT SYSTEMS)
G Constraintpropagierung (f)
F propagation de contraintes (f)
S propagación de restricciones (f)
I propagazione dei vincoli (f)

693 *E* constraint satisfaction (EXPERT SYSTEMS)
G Erfüllung der Constraints (Randbedingungen) (f); Beschränkungserfüllung (f)
F satisfaction des contraintes (f)
S satisfacción de restricciones (f)
I soddisfazione di vincoli (f)

694 *E* constraints list (EXPERT SYSTEMS)
= list of constraints
G Beschränkungsliste (f)
F liste de contraintes (f)
S lista de restricciones (f)
I elenco dei vincoli (m)

695 *E* constraints relaxation (EXPERT SYSTEMS)
G Lockerung der Beschränkungen (f)
F relâchement des contraintes (m)
S relajación de restricciones (f)
I rilassamento dei vincoli (m)

696 *E* consultation (EXPERT SYSTEMS)
G Konsultation (f); Beratung (f); Befragung (f)
F consultation (f)
S consulta (f)
I consultazione (f); consulenza (f)

697 *E* consultation interface (EXPERT SYSTEMS)
G Abfrageschnittstelle (f)
F interface de consultation (f)
S interfaz de consulta (f)
I interfaccia di consultazione (f)

698 *E* consultation paradigm (EXPERT SYSTEMS)
G Konsultationsparadigma (n); Beratungsparadigma (n)
F paradigme de consultation (m)
S paradigma de consulta (m)
I paradigma di consultazione (m)

699 *E* consultation program (EXPERT SYSTEMS)
G Konsultationsprogramm (n)
F programme de consultation (m)
S programa de consulta (m)
I programma di consultazione (m); programma di consulto (m)

700 *E* consultation system (EXPERT SYSTEMS)
G Befragungssystem (n)
F système de consultation (m)
S sistema de consulta (m); sistema consultor (m); sistema de consultoría (m)
I sistema consultativo (m); sistema di consultazione (m)

701 *E* consultation tool (EXPERT SYSTEMS)
G Befragungswerkzeug (n)
F outil de consultation (m)
S herramienta de consulta (f)
I tool consultativo (m); mezzo di consultazione (m)

702 *E* content-addressability (*of a storage etc.*) (PROGRAMMING)
G Inhaltsadressierbarkeit (f)
F adressabilité par contenu (f)
S direccionabilidad por el contenido (f)
I indirizzabilità del contenuto (f)

703 *E* content-addressable memory (CAM) (PROGRAMMING)
G inhaltsadressierbarer Speicher (m)
F mémoire adressable par contenu (f); mémoire adressable selon le contenu (f)
S memoria direccionable por el contenido (f)
I memoria accessibile sulla base del contenuto (f)

704 *E* content-dependent (KNOWLEDGE)
G inhaltsabhängig
F dépendant du contenu
S dependiente del contenido
I dipendente dal contenuto

705 *E* content-oriented (KNOWLEDGE)
G inhaltsorientiert
F orienté au contenu
S orientado al contenido
I orientato al contenuto

706 *E* context[1] (*of a situation etc.*) (KNOWLEDGE)
G Kontext (m); Zusammenhang (m)
F contexte (m)
S contexto (m)
I contesto (m)

707 *E* context[2] (*of a word etc.*) (LINGUISTICS)
G Kontext (m)
F contexte (m)
S contexto (m)
I contesto (m)

708 *E* context[3]
→ short-term memory buffer

709 *E* context dependence (NLP)
G Kontextabhängigkeit (f)
F dépendance du contexte (f)
S dependencia del contexto (f)
I dipendenza dal contesto (f)

710 *E* context-dependent (NLP)
≠ context-independent
G kontextabhängig
F dépendant du contexte
S dependiente del contexto

I dipendente dal contesto

711 *E* context-dependent knowledge
= relative knowledge
G kontextabhängiges Wissen (n); relatives Wissen (n)
F connaissance dépendante du contexte (f)
S conocimiento dependiente del contexto (m)
I conoscenza dipendente dal contesto (f)

712 *E* context-free (CF) (NLP)
G kontextfrei (kf)
F non-contextuel
S de contexto libre
I svincolato dal contesto

713 *E* context-free grammar (CFG) (LINGUISTICS)
= CF grammar
≠ context-sensitive grammar
G kontextfreie Grammatik (kfG) (f)
F grammaire non contextuelle (f); grammaire à contexte libre (f)
S gramática de contexto libre (f); gramática de libre contexto (f)
I grammatica context-free (f); grammatica che non tiene conto del contesto (f)

714 *E* context-free language (CFL) (LINGUISTICS)
G kontextfreie Sprache (kfS) (f)
F langage non contextuel (m); langage à contexte libre (m)
S lenguaje de contexto libre (m)
I linguaggio context-free (m); linguaggio a contesto libero (m)

715 *E* context-independent (NLP)
≠ context-dependent
G kontextunabhängig
F indépendant du contexte
S independiente del contexto
I indipendente dal contesto

716 *E* context information (NLP)
G Kontextinformation (f)
F information sur le contexte (f)
S información del contexto (f)
I informazione sul contesto (f)

717 *E* context–parameter–value triplet (KNOWLEDGE)
= CPV triplet
↔ object–attribute–value triplet
G Kontext–Parameter–Wert-Tripel (n)
F triplet contexte–paramètre–valeur (m); triplet CPV (m)
S tripla contexto–parámetro–valor (f); terna contexto–parámetro–valor (f)
I triplo contesto–parametro–valor (m)

718 *E* context-sensitive (CS) (NLP)
G kontextsensitiv
F sensitif au contexte
S de contexto sensible
I sensibile al contesto

719 *E* context-sensitive grammar (CSG) (LINGUISTICS)
= CS grammar; type 1 grammar
≠ context-free grammar
G kontextsensitive Grammatik (ksG) (f)
F grammaire sensitive au contexte (f)
S gramática sensible al contexto (f); gramática de contexto sensible (f)
I grammatica sensibile al contesto (f)

720 *E* context space (NLP)
G Kontextraum (m)
F espace de contexte (m)
S espacio de contexto (m)
I spazio di contesto (m)

721 *E* context tree (KNOWLEDGE)

G Kontextbaum (m)
F arbre de contextes (m)
S árbol de contextos (m)
I albero di contesti (m)

722 *E* contextual (KNOWLEDGE)
G Kontext...
F contextuel
S de contexto
I contestuale

723 *E* contextual meaning (NLP)
G kontextuelle Bedeutung (f); Bedeutung im Kontext (f)
F sens contextuel (m)
S significado en el contexto (m)
I significato nel contesto (m)

724 *E* continuation rule (EXPERT SYSTEMS)
G Fortsetzungsregel (f)
F règle de continuation (f)
S regla de continuación (f)
I regola di continuazione (f)

725 *E* continuous speech (*as opposed to isolated words*) (RECOGNITION)
= connected speech
↔ fluent speech
G kontinuierlich gesprochene Sprache (f); kontinuierliche Sprechsprache (f); gebundene Rede (f)
F parole(s) continue(s) (f (pl)); flot de parole continue (m); discours continu (m); flot continu de mots (m); mots enchaînés (m pl)
S discurso continuo (m); habla continua (f)
I parlato connesso (m); linguaggio parlato (m)

726 *E* continuous-speech recognition
→ connected-speech recognition
≠ isolated-words recognition
G Erkennen kontinuierlich gesprochener Sprache (n); Erkennung kontinuierlicher Sprechsprache (f)
F reconnaissance de la parole continue (f); reconnaissance (automatique) du discours continu (f)
S reconocimiento del discurso contínuo (RDC) (m)
I riconoscimento del parlato connesso (m)

727 *E* continuous-speech recognizer
→ speech recognition system

728 *E* contour tracking technique (IMAGE PROCESSING)
G Konturermittlungstechnik (f)
F technique de suivi de contour (f)
S técnica de detección de contornos (f)
I rilevamento di contorni (m)

729 *E* contradiction (LOGIC)
G Widerspruch (m); Kontradiktion (f)
F contradiction (f); antilogie (f)
S contradicción (f)
I contraddizione (f)

730 *E* contradictory (LOGIC)
G widersprüchlich
F contradictoire
S contradictorio
I contraddittorio

731 *E* control clause (PROGRAMMING)
G Steuerungsklausel (f)
F clause de contrôle (f)
S cláusula de control (f)
I clausola di controllo (f)

732 *E* control flow
→ flow of control

733 *E* control information (EXPERT SYSTEMS)
G Steuerungsinformation (f); Kontrollinformation (f)

F information de contrôle (f)
S información de control (f)
I informazione di controllo (f)

734 *E* control knowledge (CK)
G Steuerungswissen (n); Kontrollwissen (n)
F connaissance de contrôle (f)
S conocimiento de control (m)
I conoscenza di controllo (f)

735 *E* control language (PROGRAMMING)
G Steuerungssprache (f)
F langage de contrôle (m)
S lenguaje de control (m)
I linguaggio di controllo (m)

736 *E* control module (EXPERT SYSTEMS)
G Steuerungsmodul (n)
F module de contrôle (m)
S módulo de control (MC) (m)
I modulo di controllo (m)

737 *E* control paradigm (EXPERT SYSTEMS)
G Steuerparadigma (n)
F paradigme de contrôle (m)
S paradigma de control (m)
I paradigma di controllo (m)

738 *E* control rule (EXPERT SYSTEMS)
G Steuerregel (f)
F règle de contrôle (f)
S regla de control (f)
I regola di controllo (f)

739 *E* control space (EXPERT SYSTEMS)
G Steuerungsraum (m)
F espace de contrôle (m)
S espacio de control (m)
I spazio di controllo (m)

740 *E* control strategy (*for problem resolution*) (EXPERT SYSTEMS)
G Kontrollstrategie (f); Ablauf(steuerungs)strategie (f); Steuerungsstrategie (f); Abarbeitungsstrategie (f)
F stratégie de contrôle (f)
S estrategia de control (f)
I strategia di controllo (f)

741 *E* control strategy system
→ strategic expert system

742 *E* control structure (EXPERT SYSTEMS)
G Kontrollstruktur (f)
F structure de contrôle (f)
S estructura de control (f)
I struttura di controllo (f)

743 *E* conventional logic
→ classical logic

744 *E* conversation system (PROGRAMMING)
G Dialogsystem (n); dialogfähiges System (n); interaktives System (n)
F système de conversation (m)
S sistema con capacidad conversacional (m); sistema interlocutor (m)
I sistema in grado di conversare (m)

745 *E* co-occurrence (LINGUISTICS)
G Cookkurrenz (f)
F co-occurrence (f)
S co-ocurrencia (f)
I co-occorrenza (f)

746 *E* cooperative problem solving (EXPERT SYSTEMS)
G kooperative Problemlösung (f)
F résolution coopérative de problèmes (f)
S resolución cooperativa de problemas (f)
I risoluzione cooperativa di problemi (f)

747 *E* cooperative reasoning (EXPERT SYSTEMS)
G kooperatives Inferieren (n)
F raisonnement coopératif (m)
S razonamiento cooperativo (m)
I ragionamento cooperativo (m)

748 *E* coordination network (EXPERT SYSTEMS)
G Koordinierungsnetz (n)
F réseau de coordination (m)
S red de coordenación (f)
I rete di coordinamento (f)

749 *E* correlation (LOGIC)
G Korrelation (f)
F corrélation (f)
S correlación (f)
I correlazione (f)

750 *E* correspondence generation (EXPERT SYSTEMS)
G Korrespondenzerzeugung (f)
F génération de correspondance (f)
S generación de correspondencia (f)
I generazione di corrispondenza (f)

751 *E* correspondence problem (IMAGE PROCESSING)
G Übereinstimmungsproblem (n); Korrespondenzproblem (n)
F problème de correspondance (m)
S problema de correspondencia (m)
I problema di corrispondenza (m)

752 *E* counterfactuals (LOGIC)
G konträre Fakten (n pl); Tatsachen, die dagegen sprechen (f pl)
F faits contraires (m pl)
S evidencias en contra (f pl)
I controfatti (m pl); fatti contrari (m pl)

753 *E* covariant (*adjective*) (LOGIC)
G kovariant
F covariant
S covariante
I covariante

754 *E* CPV triplet
→ context–parameter–value triplet

755 *E* credibility (LOGIC)
= plausibility
G Glaubwürdigkeit (f); Plausibilität (eines Schlusses) (f)
F crédibilité (f); plausibilité (f); vraisemblance (f); véracité (f)
S credibilidad (f)
I credibilità (f)

756 *E* crisis management (EXPERT SYSTEMS)
G Krisenmanagement (n)
F gestion de crise (f)
S gestión de crisis (f)
I gestione delle crisi (f)

757 *E* criterion (*plural:* criteria)
G Kriterium (n)
F critère (m)
S criterio (m)
I criterio (m)

758 *E* critical (*system etc.; learning from failures*) (EXPERT SYSTEMS)
G kritisch
F critique
S crítico
I critico

759 *E* critical node (LOGIC)
G kritischer Knoten (m)
F nœud critique (m)
S nodo crítico (m)
I nodo critico (m)

760 *E* critical pair (LOGIC)
G kritisches Paar (n)
F paire critique (f)
S par crítico (m)
I coppia critica (f)

761 *E* cross correlation (LOGIC)
G Kreuzkorrelation (f)

F corrélation croisée (f)
S correlación cruzada (f)
I correlazione crociata (f)

762 *E* crossover (of rules) (EXPERT SYSTEMS)
G Regelkombination (f)
F combinaison de règles (f)
S combinación de reglas (f)
I crossover (m); combinazione di regole (f)

763 *E* CS
→ context-sensitive

764 *E* CSG
→ context-sensitive grammar

765 *E* CS grammar
→ context-sensitive grammar

766 *E* C space
→ configuration space

767 *E* current facts (EXPERT SYSTEMS)
G aktuelle Daten (n pl)
F faits courants (m pl)
S factos actuales (m pl)
I fatti attuali (m pl); fatti correnti (m pl)

768 *E* current knowledge (*temporary and permanent knowledge*)
G aktuelles Wissen (n)
F connaissance courante (f)
S conocimiento actual (m)
I conoscenza attuale (f)

769 *E* current object (LOGIC)
G aktuelles Objekt (n)
F objet courant (m)
S objeto corriente (m)
I oggetto corrente (m)

770 *E* current problem (EXPERT SYSTEMS)
G aktuelles Problem (n)
F problème courant (m)
S problema en curso (m)
I problema attuale (m)

771 *E* current state (EXPERT SYSTEMS)
G aktueller Zustand (m)
F état courant (m)
S estado actual (m)
I stato corrente (m)

772 *E* customized expert system
G maßgeschneidertes Expertensystem (n)
F système expert sur mesure (m)
S sistema experto a la medida (m)
I sistema esperto fatto su misura (m)

773 *E* cut
→ no-backtrack facility

774 *E* cutoff
→ pruning

775 *E* cut operator (*for pruning subtrees*) (PROGRAMMING)
G Cut-Operator (m)
F opérateur de coupe (m)
S operador de corte (m)
I operatore di taglio (m)

776 *E* CV
→ computer vision

777 *E* CWA
→ closed world assumption

778 *E* cyclic graph (PROGRAMMING)
G zyklischer Graph (m)
F graphe cyclique (m)
S grafo cíclico (m)
I grafo ciclico (m)

D

779 *E* dag
→ directed acyclic graph

780 *E* data abstraction (PROGRAMMING)
G Datenabstraktion (f)
F abstraction des données (f)
S abstracción de datos (f)
I astrazione di dati (f)

781 *E* data-directed
→ data-driven

782 *E* data-directed interpreter (PROGRAMMING)
G datengesteuerter Interpreter (m)
F interpréteur guidé par les données (m)
S intérprete dirigido por los datos (m)
I interprete guidato dai dati (m)

783 *E* data-directed reasoning
→ data-driven inference

784 *E* data-directed search (EXPERT SYSTEMS)
G datengesteuerte Suche (f)
F recherche guidée par les données (f)
S búsqueda guiada por los datos (f)
I ricerca guidata dai dati (f)

785 *E* data-driven (EXPERT SYSTEMS)
= data-directed
≠ goal-driven
G datengesteuert; datengetrieben
F guidé par les données; dirigé par les données
S guiado por (los) datos; dirigido por los datos
I guidato dai dati

786 *E* data-driven inference (LOGIC)
= data-directed reasoning; antecedent reasoning
↔ goal-directed inference
G datengesteuertes Inferieren (n); datengetriebene Inferenz (f)
F inférence guidée par les données (f)
S inferencia guiada por datos (f)
I inferenza guidata dai dati (f)

787 *E* data-driven system (EXPERT SYSTEMS)
≠ model-driven system
G datengesteuertes System (n); datengetriebenes System (n)
F système guidé par les données (m)
S sistema impulsado por datos (m)
I sistema data-driven (m); sistema guidato dai dati (che gli vengono forniti) (m)

788 *E* data-oriented (PROGRAMMING)
G datenorientiert
F orienté données
S orientado a los datos
I orientato ai dati

789 *E* daughter node[1] (LOGIC)
G Tochterknoten (m)
F nœud sœur (m)
S nodo hija (m)
I nodo figlia (m)

790 *E* daughter node[2]
→ child node

791 *E* daughters (*descendants of the same node*) (LOGIC)
G Töchter (f pl)

F sœurs (f pl)
S hijas (f pl)
I figlie (f pl)

792 E DCA
→ domain-closure assumption

793 E dcu
→ discourse constituent unit

794 E DDM
→ dynamic discourse model

795 E decision
G Entscheidung (f)
F décision (f)
S decisión (f)
I decisione (f)

796 E decision aid
→ decision support

797 E decision aid system
→ decision-support system

798 E decision analysis (EXPERT SYSTEMS)
G Entscheidungsanalyse (f)
F analyse de la décision (f)
S análisis de la decisión (m)
I analisi della decisione (f)

799 E decision building (EXPERT SYSTEMS)
G Entscheidungsbildung (f)
F formation des décisions (f)
S formación de decisiones (f)
I formazione delle decisioni (f)

800 E decision criterion (EXPERT SYSTEMS)
G Entscheidungskriterium (n)
F critère de décision (m)
S criterio de decisión (m)
I criterio di decisione (m)

801 E decision graph (LOGIC)
G Entscheidungsgraph (m)
F graphe de décision (m)
S grafo de decisión (m)
I grafo di decisione (m)

802 E decision making
→ decision taking

803 E decision model (EXPERT SYSTEMS)
G Entscheidungsmodell (n)
F modèle décisionnel (m)
S modelo de decisión (m)
I modello di decisione (m)

804 E decision pattern (EXPERT SYSTEMS)
G Entscheidungsmuster (n)
F modèle de décision (m)
S patrón de decisión (m)
I pattern decisionale (m)

805 E decision point (*in a network etc.*)
→ choice point

806 E decision procedure (EXPERT SYSTEMS)
G Entscheidungsvorgang (m)
F procédure de décision (f)
S procedimiento de decisión (m)
I procedura di decisione (f)

807 E decision process (EXPERT SYSTEMS)
G Entscheidungsprozeß (m)
F procédé de décision (m)
S proceso de decisión (m)
I processo di decisione (m); processo decisionale (m)

808 E decision rule (EXPERT SYSTEMS)
G Entscheidungsregel (f)
F règle de décision(s) (f)
S regla de decisión (f)
I regola di decisione (f)

809 E decision strategy (EXPERT SYSTEMS)
G Entscheidungsstrategie (f)

F stratégie de décision (f); stratégie décisionnelle (f)
S estrategia de decisión (f)
I strategia di decisione (f)

810 *E* decision support (EXPERT SYSTEMS)
= decision aid
G Entscheidungsunterstützung (f); Entscheidungshilfe (f)
F aide à la décision (f); aide à la prise de décisions (f)
S ayuda a la decisión (f)
I supporto alla decisione (m); aiuto alla decisione (m)

811 *E* decision-support system (DSS) (EXPERT SYSTEMS)
= decision aid system
G Entscheidungshilfesystem (n); Decision-Support-System (n); entscheidungsunterstützendes System (n)
F décisionnel (m) (logiciel d'aide à la décision); système d'aide à la décision (SAD) (m)
S sistema de ayuda a la decisión (m)
I sistema di sostegno della decisione (m); sistema di supporto alle decisioni (m)

812 *E* decision table (DETAB) (EXPERT SYSTEMS)
G Entscheidungstabelle (f)
F table de décision (f)
S tabla de decisión (f)
I tavola di decisione (f)

813 *E* decision taking (EXPERT SYSTEMS)
= decision making
G Treffen von Entscheidungen (n)
F prise de décisions (f)
S toma de decisiones (f)
I presa di decisioni (f)

814 *E* decision theory (THEORY)
G Entscheidungstheorie (f)
F théorie des décisions (f); théorie de la décision (f)
S teoría de decisiones (f)
I teoria delle decisioni (f)

815 *E* decision tree (DT) (EXPERT SYSTEMS)
G Entscheidungsbaum (m)
F arbre de décision (m); arbre décisionnel (m)
S árbol de decisiones (m)
I albero delle decisioni (m); albero decisionale (m)

816 *E* decision variable (EXPERT SYSTEMS)
G Entscheidungsvariable (f)
F variable de décision (f)
S variable de decisión (f)
I variabile di decisione (f)

817 *E* declarative (*adjective*) (KNOWLEDGE)
≠ procedural
G deklarativ
F déclaratif
S declarativo
I dichiarativo

818 *E* declarative database (PROGRAMMING)
= assertional database
G deklarative Datenbasis (f)
F base de données déclarative (f); base de données assertionnelle (f)
S base de datos declarativa (f)
I base di dati dichiarativa (f)

819 *E* declarative knowledge
≠ procedural knowledge
G deklaratives Wissen (n)
F connaissance déclarative (f); connaissance assertionnelle (f)
S conocimiento declarativo (m)
I conoscenza dichiarativa (f)

820 *E* declarative language (PROGRAMMING)
G deklarative Sprache (f)
F langage déclaratif (m)
S lenguaje declarativo (m)
I linguaggio dichiarativo (m)

821 *E* declarative programming
≠ procedural programming
G deklaratives Programmieren (n)
F programmation déclarative (f)
S programación declarativa (f)
I programmazione dichiarativa (f)

822 *E* declarative representation (KNOWLEDGE)
≠ procedural representation
G deklarative Repräsentation (f)
F représentation déclarative (f)
S representación declarativa (f); método declarativo de representación (m)
I rappresentazione dichiarativa (f)

823 *E* declarative semantics (PROGRAMMING)
≠ procedural semantics
G deklarative Semantik (f)
F sémantique déclarative (f)
S semántica declarativa (f)
I semantica dichiarativa (f)

824 *E* declarative structure (PROGRAMMING)
G deklarative Struktur (f)
F structure déclarative (f)
S estructura declarativa (f)
I struttura dichiarativa (f)

825 *E* declarative system (KNOWLEDGE)
= assertional system
≠ taxonomic system
G deklaratives System (n)
F système déclaratif (m); système assertionnel (m)
S sistema declarativo (m)
I sistema dichiarativo (m)

826 *E* decomposition *(of a problem etc.)* (EXPERT SYSTEMS)
G Zerlegung (f)
F décomposition (f)
S descomposición (f)
I scomposizione (f)

827 *E* decomposition metalanguage (NLP)
G Dekompositions-Metasprache (f)
F métalangage de subdivision (m)
S metalenguaje de descomposición (m)
I metalinguaggio di scomposizione (m)

828 *E* deduce (LOGIC)
G deduzieren
F déduire
S deducir; realizar deducciones
I dedurre

829 *E* deduction (LOGIC)
G Deduktion (f); Ableitung (f) (von Schlüssen etc.); Herleitung (f)
F déduction (f)
S deducción (f)
I deduzione (f)

830 *E* deduction chain (LOGIC)
G Deduktionskette (f)
F chaîne de déduction (f)
S cadena de deducción (f)
I catena deduttiva (f)

831 *E* deduction-driven (EXPERT SYSTEMS)
G deduktionsgesteuert
F guidé par déductions
S guiado por deducciones
I guidato da deduzioni

832 *E* deduction engine (EXPERT SYSTEMS)
G Deduktionskomponente (f)
F moteur de déduction (m)
S módulo de deducción (m)

I macchina di deduzione (f); meccanismo deduttivo (m)

833 *E* deduction rule (LOGIC)
G Ableitungsregel (f)
F règle de déduction (f); règle déductive (f)
S regla deductiva (f)
I regola deduttiva (f)

834 *E* deduction system (LOGIC)
G Deduktionssystem (n)
F système de déduction (m)
S sistema de deducción (m)
I sistema di deduzione (m)

835 *E* deduction tree (LOGIC)
G Deduktionsbaum (m)
F arbre de déduction (m)
S árbol de deducción (m)
I albero di deduzione (m)

836 *E* deductive (LOGIC)
G deduktiv; ableitend
F déductif
S deductivo
I deduttivo

837 *E* deductive inference (LOGIC)
G deduktiver Schluß (m)
F inférence déductive (f)
S inferencia deductiva (f)
I inferenza deduttiva (f)

838 *E* deductive inference rule (LOGIC)
G deduktive Inferenzregel (f)
F règle d'inférence déductive (f)
S regla de inferencia deductiva (f)
I regola di inferenza deduttiva (f)

839 *E* deductive knowledge acquisition
G deduktiver Wissenserwerb (m)
F acquisition déductive de connaissances (f)
S adquisición de conocimiento deductivo (f)
I acquisizione di conoscenza deduttiva (f)

840 *E* deductive learning
= learning by deduction
G deduktives Lernen (n)
F apprentissage déductif (m)
S aprendizaje deductivo (m)
I apprendimento deduttivo (m)

841 *E* deductive logic
G deduktive Logik (f)
F logique déductive (f)
S lógica deductiva (f)
I logica deduttiva (f)

842 *E* deductive machine (LOGIC)
G deduktive Maschine (f)
F machine déductive (f)
S máquina deductiva (f)
I macchina deduttiva (f)

843 *E* deductive method (of reasoning) (LOGIC)
= deductive reasoning method
G deduktiver Schlußprozeß (m)
F méthode déductive (f)
S método deductivo (m)
I metodo deduttivo (m)

844 *E* deductive power (EXPERT SYSTEMS)
G Deduktionsleistung (f)
F puissance déductive (f)
S potencia deductiva (f)
I potenza deduttiva (f)

845 *E* deductive reasoning (LOGIC)
= reasoning by deduction
G deduktives Inferieren (n); deduktives Schließen (n)
F raisonnement déductif (m)
S razonamiento deductivo (m)
I ragionamento deduttivo (m)

846 *E* deductive reasoning method
→ deductive method (of reasoning)

847 *E* deductive system (EXPERT SYSTEMS)
G deduktives System (n)

F système déductif (m)
S sistema deductivo (m)
I sistema deduttivo (m)

848 *E* deepening (*of a search*) (EXPERT SYSTEMS)
G Vertiefung (f)
F approfondissement (m)
S profundización (f)
I approfondimento (m)

849 *E* deep knowledge
↔ experiential knowledge
≠ surface knowledge
G Tiefenwissen (n)
F connaissances profondes (f pl)
S conocimiento profundo (m)
I conoscenza profonda (f)

850 *E* deep knowledge system (EXPERT SYSTEMS)
G System mit Tiefenwissen (n)
F système basé sur les connaissances profondes (m)
S sistema de conocimientos profundos (m)
I sistema di conoscenza profonda (m)

851 *E* deep structure (*of a language*) (NLP)
G Tiefenstruktur (f)
F structure en profondeur (f)
S estructura de profundidad (f)
I struttura in profondità (f)

852 *E* default
→ default value

853 *E* default assignment (PROGRAMMING)
G Defaultzuweisung (f); Standardzuweisung (f)
F affectation par défaut (f)
S asignación por defecto (f)
I assegnazione per difetto (f)

854 *E* default conclusion (LOGIC)
G Defaultschluß (m)
F conclusion par défaut (f)
S conclusión por defecto (f)
I conclusione di default (f); conclusione da difetto (f)

855 *E* default reasoning (LOGIC)
= reasoning by default
G Default Reasoning (m); Ermangelungsschließen (n); Schließen anhand von Standardvorgaben (n)
F raisonnement par défaut (m)
S razonamiento por defecto (m)
I ragionamento per default (m); ragionamento da difetto (m)

856 *E* default rule (EXPERT SYSTEMS)
G Default-Regel (f)
F règle de défaut (f); règle par défaut (f)
S regla por defecto (f)
I regola per difetto (f)

857 *E* default value (PROGRAMMING)
= default
G Default-Wert (m); Voreinstellung (f); Standardwert (f)
F valeur par défaut (f); valeur de défaut (f); valeur implicite (f)
S valor por defecto (m); valor por omisión (m)
I valore di default (m); valore di difetto (m)

858 *E* degree
→ depth^2

859 *E* degree of abstraction (LOGIC)
G Abstraktionsgrad (m)
F degré d'abstraction (m)
S grado de abstracción (m)
I grado di astrazione (m)

860 *E* degree of certainty (LOGIC)
G Sicherheitsgrad (m)
F degré de certitude (m)

S grado de certeza (m); grado de certidumbre (m); nivel de certeza (m)
I grado di certezza (m)

861 *E* degree of confidence (LOGIC)
G Konfidenzgrad (m); Vertrauensgrad (m)
F degré de confiance (m); degré de certitude (m)
S grado de confianza (m)
I grado di confidenza (m)

862 *E* degree of credibility (LOGIC)
G Glaubwürdigkeitsgrad (m)
F degré de crédibilité (m)
S grado de creencia (m); grado de credibilidad (m)
I grado di credibilità (m)

863 *E* degree of experience (KNOWLEDGE)
G Maß an Erfahrung (n)
F degré d'expérience (m)
S grado de experiencia (m)
I grado di esperienza (m)

864 *E* degree of freedom (DOF)
G Freiheitsgrad (m)
F degré de liberté (m)
S grado de libertad (m)
I grado di libertà (m)

865 *E* degree of intelligence
→ intelligence level

866 *E* degree of match (IMAGE PROCESSING)
G Grad der Übereinstimmung (m)
F degré de correspondance (m)
S grado de correspondencia (m)
I grado di corrispondenza (m)

867 *E* degree of reliability (LOGIC)
G Zuverlässigkeitsgrad (m)
F degré de fiabilité (m)
S grado de fiabilidad (m)
I grado di affidabilità (m)

868 *E* degree of truth[1] (LOGIC)
G Wahrheitsgrad (m)
F degré de vérité (m)
S grado de verdad (m)
I grado di verità (m)

869 *E* degree of truth[2]
→ certainty factor

870 *E* degree of uncertainty (LOGIC)
G Unsicherheitsgrad (m)
F degré d'incertitude (m)
S grado de incertidumbre (m)
I grado di incertezza (m)

871 *E* delayed evaluation
→ lazy evaluation

872 *E* deletion strategy (*elimination of redundant clauses*) (LOGIC)
G Deletionsstrategie (f)
F stratégie de suppression (f)
S estrategia de supresión (f)
I strategia di soppressione (f)

873 *E* delta rule (THEORY)
= least mean squares rule; Widrow–Hoff rule
G Deltaregel (f); Regel mit Lehrer (f)
F règle delta (f)
S regla delta (f)
I regola delta (f)

874 *E* demo model (EXPERT SYSTEMS)
G Demonstrationsmodell (n)
F modèle de démonstration (m); démonstrateur (m)
S modelo para demostración (m)
I modello per dimostrazioni (m)

875 *E* demon[1] (*a process started automatically*) (PROGRAMMING)
G Dämon (m); Dämonprozedur (f)
F démon (m)
S demon (m)
I demone (m)

876 *E* demon[2]
→ active value

877 *E* demonstration prototype (EXPERT SYSTEMS)
G Demonstrationsprototyp (m)
F prototype de démonstration (m)
S prototipo de demostración (m)
I prototipo di dimostrazione (m)

878 *E* De Morgan's law (THEORY)
G De Morgansches Gesetz (n)
F loi de De Morgan (f)
S ley de De Morgan (f)
I legge di De Morgan (f)

879 *E* dependency (LOGIC)
G Abhängigkeit (f)
F dépendance (f)
S dependencia (f)
I dipendenza (f)

880 *E* dependency-directed (*system etc.*) (EXPERT SYSTEMS)
G abhängigkeitsgesteuert
F dirigé par les dépendances
S dirigido por dependencias
I comandato dalle dipendenze

881 *E* dependency-directed backtracking (EXPERT SYSTEMS)
≠ chronological backtracking
G abhängigkeitsgesteuertes Backtracking (n); intelligentes Backtracking (n)
F retour arrière dirigé par les dépendances (m)
S vuelta atrás dirigida por dependencias (f)
I backtracking comandato dalle dipendenze (m)

882 *E* depth[1] (*of a node*) (LOGIC)
G Tiefe (eines Knotens) (f); Stufe (eines Knotens) (f)
F profondeur (d'un nœud) (f)
S profundidad (f)
I profondità (di un nodo) (f)

883 *E* depth[2] (*of a tree; number of hierarchical levels*) (LOGIC)
= degree
G Tiefe (eines Baums) (f); Ordnung (eines Baums) (f)
F profondeur (d'un arbre) (f)
S profundidad (f)
I profondità (di un albero) (f)

884 *E* depth[3] (*of a search*) (EXPERT SYSTEMS)
G Penetranz (f); Tiefe (einer Suche) (f)
F profondeur (d'une recherche) (f)
S límite de profundidad (m)
I profondità (f)

885 *E* depth bound[1] (EXPERT SYSTEMS)
G Suchtiefe (f); Tiefenschranke (f)
F limite de profondeur (f)
S límite de profundidad (m)
I limite di profondità (m)

886 *E* depth bound[2]
→ maximum search depth

887 *E* depth first (EXPERT SYSTEMS)
≠ breadth first
G tiefenorientiert
F en profondeur d'abord
S por profundidad primaria
I dapprima in profondità

888 *E* depth-first iterative deepening (DFID) (EXPERT SYSTEMS)
G iterative Tiefensuche (f)
F profondissement itératif en profondeur d'abord (m)
S profundización iterativa por profundidad primaria (f)
I approfondimento iterativo dapprima in profondità (m)

889 *E* depth-first search (DFS) (EXPERT SYSTEMS)
≠ breadth-first search
G Depth-First-Suchverfahren (n); Depth-First-Suche (f);

Tiefensuche (f); tiefenorientiertes Suchverfahren (n)
F recherche en profondeur d'abord (f); exploration en profondeur d'abord (f)
S búsqueda en profundidad (por profundidad prioritaria) (f); búsqueda hacia el fondo (f)
I ricerca in profondità (f); metodo depth-first (m)

890 *E* depth of knowledge
→ knowledge depth

891 *E* depth ratio (IMAGE PROCESSING)
G Tiefenverhältnis (n)
F coefficient de profondité (m)
S coeficiente de profundidad (m)
I coefficiente di profondità (m)

892 *E* depth structure (KNOWLEDGE)
G Tiefenstruktur (f)
F structure profonde (f)
S estructura profunda (f)
I struttura profonda (f)

893 *E* derivation (LOGIC)
G Ableitung (f)
F dérivation (f)
S derivación (f)
I derivazione (f)

894 *E* derivation tree (LOGIC)
G Ableitungsbaum (m)
F arbre de dérivation (m)
S árbol de derivación (m)
I albero di derivazione (m)

895 *E* derive (LOGIC)
G ableiten
F dériver
S derivar
I derivare

896 *E* descendant (LOGIC)
= successor
G Nachfolger (m); Nachkomme (m); Abkömmling (m)
F descendant (m); successeur (m)
S descendiente (m); sucesor (m)
I discendente (m); successore (m)

897 *E* descendant node (LOGIC)
= successor node
G Nachfolgerknoten (m); Nachfolgeknoten (m)
F nœud descendant (m)
S nodo descendiente (m); nodo sucesor (m)
I nodo discendente (m)

898 *E* descending hierarchical model (KNOWLEDGE)
G Modell mit absteigender Hierarchie (n)
F modèle hiérarchique descendant (m)
S modelo jerárquico descendente (MJD) (m)
I gerarchia discendente (f)

899 *E* description space (EXPERT SYSTEMS)
G Beschreibungsraum (m)
F espace de description (m)
S espacio de descripción (m)
I spazio delle descrizioni (m)

900 *E* descriptive clause (LOGIC)
G deskriptive Klausel (f); beschreibende Klausel (f)
F clause descriptive (f)
S cláusula descriptiva (f)
I clausola descrittiva (f)

901 *E* descriptive learning
G deskriptives Lernen (n); Lernen durch Beschreiben (n)
F apprentissage descriptif (m)
S aprendizaje por descripción (m)
I apprendimento per descrizione (m)

902 *E* desired object (IMAGE PROCESSING)
G Zielobjekt (n)

F objet recherché (m); objet désiré (m); objet visé (m)
S objeto deseado (m)
I oggetto desiderato (m)

903 E desired state (EXPERT SYSTEMS)
G gewünschter Zustand (m); Sollzustand (m)
F état désiré (m)
S estado deseado (m)
I stato desiderato (m)

904 E DET
→ determiner

905 E DETAB
→ decision table

906 E determination interval (EXPERT SYSTEMS)
G Determinationsintervall (n)
F intervalle de détermination (m)
S intervalo de determinación (m)
I intervallo di determinazione (m)

907 E determiner (DET) (LOGIC)
G Determinierer (m)
F déterminant (m)
S determinante (m)
I determinante (m)

908 E determinism (THEORY)
G Determinismus (m)
F déterminisme (m)
S determinismo (m)
I determinismo (m)

909 E deterministic (*adjective*) (THEORY)
G deterministisch
F déterministe
S determinista
I deterministico

910 E deterministic parser (NLP)
G deterministischer Parser (m)
F analyseur déterministe (m)
S parser determinista (m)
I parser deterministico (m)

911 E deterministic parsing (NLP)
G deterministisches Parsing (n)
F analyse déterministe (f)
S parsing determinista (f); análisis sintáctico determinista (m)
I parsing deterministico (m)

912 E development environment (PROGRAMMING)
G Entwicklungsumgebung (f)
F environnement de développement (m)
S entorno de desarrollo (m)
I ambiente di sviluppo (m)

913 E development of expert systems
→ expert system development

914 E development support system (PROGRAMMING)
G Entwicklungsunterstützungs-system (n)
F système de soutien de développement (m)
S sistema de soporte de desarrollo (m)
I sistema di aiuto allo sviluppo (m)

915 E development system (PROGRAMMING)
G Entwicklungssystem (n)
F système de développement (m)
S sistema de desarrollo (m)
I sistema di sviluppo (m)

916 E development tool (PROGRAMMING)
G Entwicklungswerkzeug (n)
F outil de développement (m)
S herramienta de desarrollo (f)
I tool di sviluppo (m)

917 E deviant logics
→ non-classical logic

918 *E* DFID
→ depth-first iterative deepening

919 *E* DFS
→ depth-first search

920 *E* diagnosis system (EXPERT SYSTEMS)
G Diagnosesystem (n)
F système de diagnostic(s) (m)
S sistema de diagnóstico (m)
I sistema di diagnosi (m)

921 *E* diagnostic expert system
G Diagnoseexpertensystem (n)
F système expert diagnosticien (m); système expert d'aide au diagnostic (m)
S sistema experto diagnóstico (m)
I sistema esperto diagnostico (m)

922 *E* diagnostic reasoning (EXPERT SYSTEMS)
G diagnostisches Schlüsseziehen (n)
F raisonnement diagnostique (m)
S razonamiento diagnóstico (m)
I ragionamento diagnostico (m)

923 *E* dialogue (PROGRAMMING)
G Dialog (m)
F dialogue (m)
S diálogo (m)
I dialogo (m)

924 *E* dialogue-based (EXPERT SYSTEMS)
G auf Dialog basierend
F basé sur dialogue
S basado en diálogos
I basato su dialogo

925 *E* dialogue control (PROGRAMMING)
G Dialogsteuerung (f)
F gestion du dialogue (f)
S gestión de diálogo (f)
I controllo del dialogo (m)

926 *E* dialogue module (EXPERT SYSTEMS)
G Dialogkomponente (f)
F composante dialogue (f)
S módulo de diálogo (m)
I modulo per il dialogo (m)

927 *E* dialogue-oriented (EXPERT SYSTEMS)
G dialogorientiert
F orienté dialogue
S orientado al diálogo
I orientato al dialogo; consultativo

928 *E* dialogue pattern (RECOGNITION)
G Dialogmuster (n)
F modèle de dialogue (m)
S patrón de diálogo (m)
I pattern di dialogo (m); modello di dialogo (m)

929 *E* dialogue understanding (RECOGNITION)
G Dialogverstehen (n)
F compréhension de dialogues (f)
S comprensión de diálogos (f)
I comprensione di dialoghi (f)

930 *E* difference information (EXPERT SYSTEMS)
G Differenzinformation (f)
F information sur les différences (f)
S información de diferencia (f)
I informazione sulla differenza (f)

931 *E* difference list (EXPERT SYSTEMS)
G Differenzliste (f)
F liste de différence (f)
S lista de diferencia (f)
I lista di differenza (f)

932 *E* difference reduction (EXPERT SYSTEMS)
G Differenzreduzierung (f)
F réduction des différences (f)
S reducción de diferencia (f)
I riduzione della differenza (f)

933 *E* difference table (EXPERT SYSTEMS)
G Differenztabelle (f)
F table de différence (f)
S tabla de diferencia (f)
I tabelle di differenza (f pl)

934 *E* differential model (THEORY)
G Differentialmodell (n)
F modèle différentiel (m)
S modelo diferencial (m)
I modello differenziale (m)

935 *E* directed acyclic graph (dag) (LOGIC)
G gerichteter azyklischer Graph (m); schleifenloser Graph (m)
F graphe acyclique orienté (m)
S grafo acíclico orientado (m)
I grafo aciclico orientato (m)

936 *E* directed arc (LOGIC)
= oriented edge
G gerichtete Kante (f)
F arc orienté (m)
S arco orientado (m)
I arco orientato (m)

937 *E* directed graph (LOGIC)
= oriented graph
G gerichteter Graph (m); Digraph (m)
F graphe dirigé (m)
S grafo dirigido (m)
I grafo orientato (m)

938 *E* direction of flow (PROGRAMMING)
G Flußrichtung (f)
F direction de flux (f)
S sentido de flujo (m)
I verso del flusso (m); direzione del flusso (f)

939 *E* disambiguate (NLP)
G disambiguieren
F désambiguïser
S desambiguar
I disambiguare

940 *E* disambiguation (NLP)
G Disambiguierung (f)
F désambiguïsation (f)
S desambiguación (f)
I disambiguazione (f)

941 *E* disbelief (LOGIC)
G Unglaube (m); Zweifel (m)
F doute (m)
S duda (f)
I dubbio (m)

942 *E* discourse (RECOGNITION)
G Diskurs (zusammenhängender Text) (m)
F discours (m)
S discurso (m)
I discorso (m); conversazione (f)

943 *E* discourse constituent unit (dcu) (RECOGNITION)
G Diskursbestandteil (m)
F constituant de discours (m)
S constituyente de discurso (m)
I unità costituente di un discorso (f)

944 *E* discourse representation scheme (DRS) (RECOGNITION)
G Diskursdarstellungsschema (n)
F schéma de représentation de discours (m)
S esquema de representación de discurso (m)
I schema di rappresentazione di discorso (m)

945 *E* discourse segment (NLP)
G Diskurssegment (n)
F segment de discours (m)
S segmento de discurso (m)
I segmento di discorso (m)

946 *E* discourse understanding (RECOGNITION)
= comprehension of discourse
G Verstehen zusammenhängender (gesprochener) Texte (n)

F compréhension de discours (f)
S comprensión del discurso (f)
I comprensione di discorsi (f); comprensione del discorso (f)

947 *E* discourse unit (DU) (RECOGNITION)
G Diskurseinheit (f)
F unité de discours (f); élément de discours (m); partie de discours (f)
S unidad de discurso (f)
I unità di discorso (f)

948 *E* discrete words
→ isolated words

949 *E* discrete-words recognition system
→ isolated-words recognition system

950 *E* discrete-words understanding
→ isolated-words understanding

951 *E* discrimination
G Diskrimination (f); Unterscheidung (f)
F discrimination (f)
S discriminación (f)
I discriminazione (f)

952 *E* discrimination network (D net) (KNOWLEDGE)
G Diskriminationsnetz (n)
F réseau de discrimination (m)
S red de discriminación (f)
I rete di discriminazione (f)

953 *E* discrimination rule (EXPERT SYSTEMS)
G Diskriminationsregel (f)
F règle de discrimination (f)
S regla de discriminación (f)
I regola di discriminazione (f)

954 *E* discrimination strategy (EXPERT SYSTEMS)
G Diskriminationsstrategie (f)
F stratégie de discrimination (f)
S estrategia de discriminación (f)
I strategia di discriminazione (f)

955 *E* discrimination tree (EXPERT SYSTEMS)
G Diskriminationsbaum (m)
F arbre de discrimination (m)
S árbol de discriminación (m)
I albero di discriminazione (m)

956 *E* disjunction (*of conditions, involving an OR*) (LOGIC)
↔ conjunction
G Disjunktion (f); Adjunktion (f)
F disjonction (f)
S disyunción (f)
I disgiunzione (f)

957 *E* disjunctive generalization (LOGIC)
G disjunktive Generalisierung (f)
F généralisation par disjonction (f)
S generalización disyuntiva (f)
I generalizzazione disgiuntiva (f)

958 *E* disparity (IMAGE PROCESSING)
G Disparität (f); Unähnlichkeit (f)
F disparité (f)
S disparidad (f)
I disparità (f)

959 *E* disprove
→ refute

960 *E* disproving
→ refutation

961 *E* dissemination (*of knowledge etc.*)
G Verbreitung (f)
F dissémination (f)
S diseminación (f)
I disseminazione (f)

962 *E* distinctive feature (KNOWLEDGE)
G unterscheidendes Merkmal (n)
F trait distinctif (m)

S característica distintiva (f)
I caratteristica individuale (f)

963 E distributed AI
→ distributed artificial intelligence

964 E distributed AI system
G verteiltes KI-System (n)
F système d'intelligence artificielle réparti (m); système IA réparti (m)
S sistema de IA distribuido (m)
I sistema di intelligenza artificiale distribuito (m)

965 E distributed artificial intelligence
= distributed AI
G verteilte KI (f)
F intélligence artificielle répartie (f)
S inteligencia artificial distribuida (f)
I intelligenza artificiale distribuita (f)

966 E distributed parallel processing
= parallel distributed processing
→ connection science

967 E distributed problem solving (EXPERT SYSTEMS)
G verteilte Problemlösung (f)
F résolution de problèmes répartie (f)
S resolución distribuida de problemas (f)
I risoluzione distribuita dei problemi (f)

968 E divisive technique (*a clustering technique*) (KNOWLEDGE)
≠ agglomerative technique
G Aufteilungsverfahren (n)
F technique de division (f)
S técnica de división (f)
I tecnica divisoria (f)

969 E D net
→ discrimination network

970 E DOF
→ degree of freedom

971 E DOM
→ dynamic organization memory

972 E domain[1] (*of knowledge etc.*)
G Domäne (f); Bereich (m); Gebiet (n)
F domaine (m)
S dominio (m)
I dominio (m)

973 E domain[2]
→ application domain

974 E domain-closure assumption (DCA) (KNOWLEDGE)
G Annahme der Domänenabgeschlossenheit (f)
F hypothèse du domaine fermé (f)
S hipótesis del dominio cerrado (f)
I postulato del dominio chiuso (m)

975 E domain-dependent (KNOWLEDGE)
G domänenabhängig; bereichsabhängig
F dépendant du domaine
S dependiente del dominio
I dipendente dal dominio

976 E domain expert (KNOWLEDGE)
= expert
G Domänenexperte (m); Fachexperte (m); Fachbereichsexperte (m)
F expert de domaine (ED) (m)
S experto de dominio (m)
I esperto di dominio (m); esperto di un settore (m)

977 E domain expertise (KNOWLEDGE)
G Fachexpertenwissen (n)
F expertise du domaine (f)
S experiencia de dominio (f)
I esperienza di dominio (f)

978 E domain facts (KNOWLEDGE)

G Bereichsfakten (m pl)
F faits du domaine (m pl)
S factos de dominio (m pl)
I fatti del dominio (m pl)

979 *E* domain independence (KNOWLEDGE)
G Bereichsunabhängigkeit (f)
F indépendance de la domaine (f)
S independencia de dominio (f)
I indipendenza dal dominio (f)

980 *E* domain-independent (KNOWLEDGE)
G domänenunabhängig; bereichsunabhängig
F indépendant du domaine
S independiente del dominio
I indipendente dal dominio

981 *E* domain-independent knowledge
≠ domain-specific knowledge
G domänenunabhängiges Wissen (n)
F connaissance indépendante du domaine (f)
S conocimiento independiente de dominio (m)
I conoscenza indipendente dal dominio (f)

982 *E* domain-independent problem solving (EXPERT SYSTEMS)
G domänenunabhängiges Problemlösen (n)
F résolution indépendante du domaine (f)
S resolución de problemas independientemente de dominio (f)
I risoluzione di problemi indipendentemente dal dominio (f)

983 *E* domain-independent system (EXPERT SYSTEMS)
G domänenunabhängiges System (n)
F système indépendant du domaine (m)
S sistema independiente de dominio (m)
I sistema indipendente dal dominio (m)

984 *E* domain knowledge[1]
G Domänenwissen (n); Fachbereichswissen (n); Bereichswissen (n)
F connaissance du domaine (f)
S conocimiento sobre el dominio (m); conocimiento del dominio (m)
I conoscenza del dominio (f)

985 *E* domain knowledge[2]
→ domain-specific knowledge

986 *E* domain of discourse (LOGIC)
G Diskurswelt (f); Diskursbereich (m)
F domaine de discours (m)
S dominio de discurso (m)
I dominio del discorso (m); dominio della conversazione (m)

987 *E* domain of enquiry (*of an expert system*)
G Anfragebereich (m)
F domaine de consultation (m)
S dominio de consulta (m)
I dominio di indagine (m)

988 *E* domain of expertise (KNOWLEDGE)
= expertise domain; area of expertise
G Expertenwissensdomäne (f); Erfahrungsgebiet (eines Experten) (n)
F domaine d'expertise (m)
S dominio de experiencia (m); campo de experiencia (m)
I dominio di esperienza (m); campo di esperienza (m)

989 *E* domain problem solver (EXPERT SYSTEMS)
G domänenspezifischer Problemlöser (m)
F résolveur de problèmes d'une domaine (m)
S solucionador de problemas de un dominio (m)
I risolutore di problemi relativi a un dominio determinato (m)

990 *E* domain restriction (EXPERT SYSTEMS)
G Bereichseinschränkung (f)
F restriction de domaine (f)
S restricción de dominio (f)
I restrizione del dominio (f)

991 *E* domain-specific knowledge
= domain knowledge
≠ domain-independent knowledge
G domänenspezifisches Wissen (n); bereichsspezifisches Wissen (n)
F connaissance spécifique à un domaine (f)
S conocimiento específico del dominio (m); conocimiento sobre un dominio específico (m)
I conoscenza specifica del dominio (f)

992 *E* domestic robot
= robot in the home; household robot
G Heimroboter (m); Haushaltsroboter (m)
F robot domestique (m)
S robot doméstico (m)
I robot domestico (m)

993 *E* dot notation (*in LISP*) (PROGRAMMING)
G Punktschreibweise (f)
F notation à points (f)
S notación de puntos (f)
I notazione a punti (f)

994 *E* dot pattern analysis (IMAGE PROCESSING)
G Punktmusteranalyse (f)
F analyse d'un dessin de points (f)
S análisis de un pattern de puntos (m)
I analisi di un pattern di punti (f)

995 *E* draw conclusions
→ infer

996 *E* DRS
→ discourse representation scheme

997 *E* DSS
→ decision-support system

998 *E* DT
→ decision tree

999 *E* DU
→ discourse unit

1000 *E* dual semantics (*procedural and declarative*) (PROGRAMMING)
G duale Semantik (f)
F sémantique duale (f); sémantique mixte (f)
S semántica dual (f)
I semantica duale (f)

1001 *E* DUCS
→ dynamically updatable conceptual structure

1002 *E* DWIM
= do what I mean

1003 *E* dynamically updatable conceptual structure (DUCS) (NEURAL NETS)
G dynamisch aktualisierbare Begriffsstruktur (f)
F structure conceptuelle adaptable dynamiquement (f)
S estructura conceptual actualizable dinámicamente (f)

I struttura concettuale aggiornabile dinamicamente (f)

1004 *E* dynamic discourse model (DDM) (NLP)
G dynamisches Diskursmodell (n)
F modèle dynamique de discours (m)
S modelo dinámico de discurso (m)
I modello dinamico di discorso (m)

1005 *E* dynamic knowledge acquisition
G dynamischer Wissenserwerb (m)
F acquisition dynamique de connaissances (f)
S adquisición dinámica del conocimiento (f)
I acquisizione dinamica della conoscenza (f)

1006 *E* dynamic knowledge base
G dynamische Wissensbasis (f)
F base de connaissance(s) dynamique (f)
S base de conocimientos dinámica (f)
I base di conoscenza dinamica (f)

1007 *E* dynamic linking (*of variables etc.*) (PROGRAMMING)
G dynamische Verknüpfung (f)
F liaison dynamique (f)
S enlace dinámico (m)
I abbinamento dinamico (m)

1008 *E* dynamic logic
G dynamische Logik (f)
F logique dynamique (f)
S lógica dinámica (f)
I logica dinamica (f)

1009 *E* dynamic memory
G dynamischer Speicher (m)
F mémoire dynamique (f)
S memoria dinámica (f)
I memoria dinamica (f)

1010 *E* dynamic menu (EXPERT SYSTEMS)
G dynamisches Menü (n)
F menu dynamique (m)
S menú dinámico (m)
I menù dinamico (m)

1011 *E* dynamic object (KNOWLEDGE)
G dynamisches Objekt (n)
F objet dynamique (m)
S objeto dinámico (m)
I oggetto dinamico (m)

1012 *E* dynamic organization memory (DOM) (PROGRAMMING)
G dynamisch organisierter Speicher (m)
F mémoire à organisation dynamique (f)
S memoria de organización dinámica (f)
I memoria a organizzazione dinamica (f)

1013 *E* dynamic planning (EXPERT SYSTEMS)
G dynamische Planung (f)
F planification dynamique (f)
S planificación dinámica (f)
I planning dinamico (m); pianificazione dinamica (f)

1014 *E* dynamic programming
G dynamische Programmierung (f)
F programmation dynamique (f)
S programación dinámica (f)
I programmazione dinamica (f)

1015 *E* dynamic rule inheritance (EXPERT SYSTEMS)
G dynamische Regelvererbung (f)
F héritage dynamique de règles (m)
S herencia dinámica de reglas (f)
I ereditarietà dinamica di regole (f)

1016 *E* dynamic rule set (EXPERT SYSTEMS)
G dynamischer Regelsatz (m)
F jeu de règles dynamique (m)
S conjunto de reglas dinámico (m)
I pacchetto di regole dinamico (m)

E

1017 *E* eager evaluation (*of results*) (EXPERT SYSTEMS)
= immediate evaluation
≠ lazy evaluation
G Sofortauswertung (f)
F évaluation immédiate (f)
S evaluación inmediata (f)
I valutazione immediata (f)

1018 *E* EBL
→ explanation-based learning

1019 *E* EBP
→ error back propagation

1020 *E* ECAI
= European Conference on Artificial Intelligence

1021 *E* ECCAI
= European Coordinating Committee for Artificial Intelligence

1022 *E* edge[1] (*of an image*)
G Kontur (f); Kante (f)
F contour (m)
S borde (m); contorno (m)
I margine (f); bordo (m); confine (m)

1023 *E* edge[2]
→ arc[1]

1024 *E* edge description (IMAGE PROCESSING)
G Kantenbeschreibung (f)
F description de contours (f)
S descripción de puntos de borde (f)
I descrizione dei margini (f)

1025 *E* edge detection (IMAGE PROCESSING)
= outline detection
G Konturenermittlung (f); Konturenerkennung (f); Kantenfinden (n); Kantensuche (f)
F détection de contours (f)
S detección de puntos de borde (f); detección de contornos (f)
I riconoscimento dei margini (di un oggetto) (m); rilevamento di contorni (m)

1026 *E* edge detector (IMAGE PROCESSING)
G Kantendetektor (m)
F détecteur de contours (m)
S detector automático de contornos (m)
I rilevatore di margini (m)

1027 *E* edge interpretation (*in image understanding*)
G Kanteninterpretation (f)
F interprétation de contours (f)
S interpretación de bordes (f)
I interpretazione dei margini (f)

1028 *E* edge point (IMAGE PROCESSING)
G Kantenpunkt (m)
F point de contour (m)
S punto de borde (m); punto de contorno (m)
I punto dei margini (m)

1029 *E* edges
→ boundaries[1]

1030 *E* educational expert system
G Expertensystem für Unterrichtszwecke (n)
F système expert d'EAO (m)
S sistema experto educativo (m)
I sistema esperto per l'insegnamento (m)

1031 *E* effect variation (IMAGE PROCESSING)
G Effektvariation (f)
F variation d'effet (f)
S variación de efecto (f)
I variazione d'effetto (f)

1032 *E* EIS
→ electronic imaging system

1033 *E* electronic imaging system (EIS)
G elektronisches Bilderkennungssystem (n)
F imagerie électronique (f)
S sistema electrónico de reconocimiento de imágenes (m)
I sistema elettronico di riconoscimento delle immagini (m)

1034 *E* element (ELT)
G Element (n)
F élément (m)
S elemento (m)
I elemento (m)

1035 *E* elementary logic
→ propositional logic

1036 *E* elementary statement (LOGIC)
G Elementaraussage (f); Primaussage (f)
F proposition élémentaire (f)
S proposición elemental (f)
I proposizione elementare (f)

1037 *E* elimination rule (EXPERT SYSTEMS)
G Eliminierungsregel (f)
F règle éliminatoire (f)
S regla de eliminación (f)
I regola di eliminazione (f)

1038 *E* ellipsis (LINGUISTICS)
G Ellipse (f); Auslassung (f)
F ellipse (f)
S elipsis (f)
I ellissi (f)

1039 *E* ELT
→ element

1040 *E* embed (*knowledge etc.*)
G einpflanzen
F implanter
S incorporar
I immettere

1041 *E* embedded system (PROGRAMMING)
G eingebettetes System (n)
F système intégré (dans un autre système) (m)
S sistema integrado (m)
I sistema integrato (m)

1042 *E* EMM
→ extended Markov model

1043 *E* empirical approach (LOGIC)
= empirical method
G empirische Methode (f); empirisches Verfahren (n)
F méthode empirique (f)
S método empírico (m)
I metodo empirico (m)

1044 *E* empirical evidence (LOGIC)
G empirische Evidenz (f)
F évidence empirique (f)
S evidencia empírica (f)
I evidenza empirica (f)

1045 *E* empirical inference (LOGIC)
G empirische Schlußfolgerung (f)
F inférence empirique (f)
S inferencia empírica (f)
I inferenza empirica (f)

1046 *E* empirical method
→ empirical approach

1047 *E* empiricism (LOGIC)
G Empirismus (m)
F empirisme (m)
S empirismo (m)
I empirismo (m)

1048 *E* empiricist (LOGIC)
G Empiriker (m)
F empiriste (m)
S empírico (m)
I empirista (m)

1049 *E* empty clause (LOGIC)
G leere Klausel (f); Leerklausel (f)
F clause vide (f)
S cláusula vacía (f)
I clausola vuota (f)

1050 *E* empty list (PROGRAMMING)
G leere Liste (f)
F liste vide (f)
S lista vacía (f)
I lista vuota (f)

1051 *E* emulate (PROGRAMMING)
G emulieren
F émuler
S emular
I emulare

1052 *E* emulation (PROGRAMMING)
G Emulation (f)
F émulation (f)
S emulación (f)
I emulazione (f)

1053 *E* end effector (*e.g. gripper of a robot*)
→ manipulator

1054 *E* end node
→ terminal node

1055 *E* endorsement (*of a hypothesis etc.*) (EXPERT SYSTEMS)
G Bestätigung (f)
F confirmation (f)
S confirmación (f)
I endorsement (m); conferma (f)

1056 *E* ends analysis (EXPERT SYSTEMS)
G Zielanalyse (f)
F analyse des buts (f)
S análisis de los objetivos (m)
I analisi degli obiettivi (f)

1057 *E* enhancement (IMAGE PROCESSING)
G Verbesserung (der Erkennbarkeit) (f)
F amélioration (f)
S mejoramiento (m); intensificación (de imágenes) (f)
I miglioramento (m)

1058 *E* ENNS
= European Neural Network Society

1059 *E* enrolment (*inclusion of a new speaker*) (RECOGNITION)
G Lernen der Sprechweise (n); Trainieren (eines Erkennungssystems) (n)
F entraînement (m)
S entrenamiento (m)
I apprendimento delle peculiarità di un locutore (m)

1060 *E* entail (LOGIC)
G implizieren (nach sich ziehen)
F impliquer
S implicar; entrañar
I implicare

1061 *E* entailment
→ implication

1062 *E* entity (KNOWLEDGE)
G Entität (f); Entity (f)
F entité (f)
S entidad (f)
I entità (f)

1063 *E* entity/relationship diagram (KNOWLEDGE)
= ER diagram
G Entity-Relationship-Darstellung (f)
F diagramme entité/relation (m)
S diagrama entidad/relación (m)
I diagramma entità-relazione (m)

1064 *E* entity type (KNOWLEDGE)
= object type
G Objekttyp (m); Entitytyp (m)
F type d'objet (m)
S tipo de objeto (m)
I tipo di oggetto (m)

1065 *E* entropy (THEORY)
G Entropie (f)
F entropie (f)
S entropía (f)
I entropia (f)

1066 *E* entry
→ filler

1067 *E* enumeration (PROGRAMMING)
G Aufzählung (f); Enumeration (f)
F énumération (f)
S enumeración (f)
I enumerazione (f)

1068 *E* environmental knowledge
G Umgebungswissen (n)
F connaissances sur l'environnement (f pl)
S conocimiento relativo al entorno (circundante) (m)
I conoscenza sull'ambiente (f)

1069 *E* episode (RECOGNITION)
G Episode (f)
F épisode (m)
S episodio (m)
I episodio (m)

1070 *E* episodic memory (THEORY)
≠ semantic memory
G Episodengedächtnis (n); episodisches Gedächtnis (n)
F mémoire épisodique (f)
S memoria episódica (f)
I memoria episodica (f)

1071 *E* epistemic (THEORY)
≠ heuristic[1]
G epistemisch
F épistémique
S epistémico
I epistemico

1072 *E* epistemic logic
G epistemische Logik (f)
F logique épistémique (f)
S lógica epistémica (f)
I logica epistemica (f)

1073 *E* epistemological (THEORY)
G epistemologisch; erkenntnistheoretisch
F épistémologique
S epistemológico
I epistemologico

1074 *E* epistemological theory (LOGIC)
G Erkenntnistheorie (f)
F théorie épistémologique (f)
S teoría epistemológica (f)
I teoria epistemologica (f)

1075 *E* epistemologist (LOGIC)
G Epistemologe (m)
F épistémologiste (m)
S epistemólogo (m)
I epistemologo (m)

1076 *E* epistemology (THEORY)
G Epistemologie (f); Erkenntnislehre (f)
F épistémologie (f) (théorie de la connaissance)
S epistemología (f)
I epistemologia (f)

1077 *E* EQ
→ equality

1078 *E* equal-cost search (EXPERT SYSTEMS)
G Gleiche-Kosten-Suche (f)
F recherche sur la base de l'égalité des coûts (f)
S búsqueda de gastos iguales (f)
I ricerca sulla base dei costi uguali (f)

1079 *E* equality (EQ) (LOGIC)
G Gleichheit (f) (GL)
F égalité (f)
S igualdad (f)
I uguaglianza (f); eguaglianza (f)

1080 *E* equality clause (*of the form: $term_1 = term_2$*) (LOGIC)
G Gleichheitsklausel (f)
F clause d'égalité (f)
S cláusula de igualdad (f)
I clausola di uguaglianza (f); clausola di eguaglianza (f)

1081 *E* equality relation (LOGIC)
G Gleichheitsrelation (f)
F relation d'égalité (f)
S relación de igualdad (f)
I relazione di uguaglianza (f); relazione di eguaglianza (f)

1082 *E* equality theory (LOGIC)
G Gleichheitstheorie (f)
F théorie de l'égalité (f)
S teoría de igualdad (f)
I teoria dell'uguaglianza (f); teoria dell'eguaglianza (f)

1083 *E* equipotentiality (LOGIC)
G Equipotentialität (f)
F équipotentialité (f)
S equipotencialidad (f)
I equipotenzialità (f)

1084 *E* ER diagram
→ entity/relationship diagram

1085 *E* error back propagation[1] (EBP) (EXPERT SYSTEMS)
G Fehlerfortpflanzung in Rückwärtsrichtung (f)
F propagation des erreurs vers l'arrière (f)
S retropropagación de errores (f)
I retropropagazione dell'errore (f)

1086 *E* error back propagation[2]
→ back-propagation

1087 *E* error detection and correction (PROGRAMMING)
G Fehlererkennung und -behebung (f)
F détection et correction des erreurs (f)
S detección y corrección de errores (f)
I rilevazione e correzione di errori (f)

1088 *E* error-driven system (EXPERT SYSTEMS)
G fehlergesteuertes System (n)
F système dirigé par les erreurs (m)
S sistema guiado por errores (m)
I sistema guidato dagli errori (m)

1089 *E* error estimation (EXPERT SYSTEMS)
G Fehlerabschätzung (f)
F évaluation des erreurs (f)
S evaluación de los errores (f)
I stima degli errori (f)

1090 *E* error probability (EXPERT SYSTEMS)
G Fehlerwahrscheinlichkeit (f)
F probabilité d'erreurs (f)
S probabilidad de errores (f)
I probabilità di errori (f)

1091 *E* ES
→ expert system

1092 *E* ESP
= extended self-contained PROLOG

1093 *E* ESS
→ expert support system

1094 *E* ES software
→ expert system software

1095 *E* E-system
→ expert system

1096 *E* evaluate
G bewerten; evaluieren
F évaluer
S evaluar
I valutare

1097 *E* evaluation (LOGIC)
G Evaluierung (f); Bewertung (f)
F évaluation (f)
S evaluación (f); valoración (f)
I valutazione (f)

1098 *E* evaluation function (LOGIC)
G Bewertungsfunktion (f); Evaluierungsfunktion (f)
F fonction d'évaluation (f)
S función de evaluación (f); función evaluativa (f)
I funzione di valutazione (f)

1099 *E* event
G Ereignis (n)
F événement (m)
S acontecimiento (m); suceso (m)
I evento (m); avvenimento (m)

1100 *E* event-driven (EXPERT SYSTEMS)
G ereignisgesteuert
F dirigé par les événements
S guiado por acontecimientos
I guidato dagli eventi

1101 *E* event manager (EXPERT SYSTEMS)
G Event Manager (m)
F gestionnaire d'événements (m)
S gestor de acontecimientos (m)
I gestore degli eventi (m)

1102 *E* event-oriented (EXPERT SYSTEMS)
G ereignisorientiert
F orienté événements
S orientado acontecimientos
I orientato agli eventi

1103 *E* events memory (EXPERT SYSTEMS)
G Ereignisspeicher (m)
F mémoire événementielle (f)
S memoria de acontecimientos (f)
I memoria degli eventi (f)

1104 *E* everyday conversation (RECOGNITION)
G Alltagsunterhaltung (f)
F conversation ordinaire (f)
S conversación cotidiana (f); discurso diario (m)
I conversazione di ogni giorno (f)

1105 *E* everyday knowledge
→ commonsense knowledge; general knowledge

1106 *E* evidence (LOGIC)
G Evidenz (f); Hinweis (m)
F évidence (f)
S evidencia (f)
I evidenza (f)

1107 *E* evidence theory (LOGIC)
= theory of evidence
G Evidenztheorie (f)
F théorie de l'évidence (f)
S teoría de la evidencia (f)
I teoria dell'evidenza (f)

1108 *E* evidential reasoning (LOGIC)
G Evidenzschließen (n); evidenzorientiertes Inferieren (n)
F raisonnement basé sur évidence (m)
S razonamiento evidencial (m)
I ragionamento sulla base dell'evidenza (m)

1109 *E* exact logic (*two-valued logic, true or false*)
≠ inexact logic
G exakte Logik (f)
F logique exacte (f)
S lógica exacta (f)
I logica esatta (f)

1110 *E* example-based (LEARNING)
G beispielgesteuert
F à partir d'exemples; à base d'exemples
S a partir de muestras; a partir de ejemplos
I sulla base di esempi

1111 *E* example-driven learning
G beispielgesteuertes Lernen (n)
F apprentissage à partir d'exemples (m)
S aprendizaje a partir de muestras (APM) (m)
I apprendimento per esempi (m)

1112 *E* example-driven system
→ induction system

1113 *E* example-oriented (LEARNING)
G beispielorientiert
F orienté aux exemples
S orientado a ejemplos
I orientato verso gli esempi

1114 *E* example selection (LEARNING)
G Beispielauswahl (f)
F sélection d'exemples (f)
S selección de muestras (f)
I selezione di esempi (f)

1115 *E* example space
→ sample space

1116 *E* exception (*from a rule etc.*)
G Ausnahme (f)
F exception (f)
S excepción (f)
I eccezione (f)

1117 *E* exception-based (EXPERT SYSTEMS)
G ausnahmengesteuert
F basé sur les exceptions
S dirigido por excepciones
I guidato dalle eccezioni

1118 *E* exchange frame (NLP)
G Austausch-Frame (m)
F cadre d'échange (m)
S frame de cambio (m)
I frame di scambio (m); quadro di scambio (m)

1119 *E* exclusive rule (EXPERT SYSTEMS)
G ausschließende Regel (f)
F règle exclusive (f)
S regla exclusiva (f)
I regola esclusiva (f)

1120 *E* exclusive situations (GAMES)
G Exklusivsituationen (f pl); ausschließende Situationen (f pl)
F situations exclusives (f pl)
S situaciones exclusivas (f pl)
I situazioni di esclusione (f pl)

1121 *E* execution[1] (*of a rule*) (EXPERT SYSTEMS)
G Ausführung (f)
F exécution (f)
S ejecución (f)
I esecuzione (f)

1122 *E* execution[2]
→ firing

1123 *E* execution-driven reasoning (EXPERT SYSTEMS)
G ausführungsgesteuertes Inferieren (n)
F raisonnement dirigé par l'exécution (m)
S razonamiento guiado por la ejecución (m)
I ragionamento guidato dall'esecuzione (m)
G heuristisches Suchverfahren (n)

1124 *E* exhaustive search (*that considers all possibilities*) (EXPERT SYSTEMS)
= massive search
G erschöpfende Suche (f); umfassende Suche (f)
F recherche exhaustive (f)
S búsqueda exhaustiva (f); procedimiento exhaustivo de búsqueda (m)
I ricerca esaustiva (f)

1125 *E* existentially quantified variable (LOGIC)
≠ universally quantified variable
G existenzquantifizierte Variable (f)
F variable quantifiée existentiellement (f)
S variable cuantificada existencialmente (f)
I variabile quantificata esistenzialmente (f)

1126 *E* existential quantifier (LOGIC)
≠ universal quantifier
G Existenzquantor (m); Seinsquantor (m); Partikularisator (m)
F quantificateur existentiel (m)
S cuantificador existencial (m)
I quantificatore esistenziale (m)

1127 *E* exotic logics
→ non-classical logic

1128 *E* expand (*a node etc.*) (LOGIC)
G expandieren; erweitern
F développer
S expandir; alargar; desarrollar
I espandere

1129 *E* expanded graph
G expandierter Graph (m)
F graphe développé (m)
S grafo desarrollado (m)
I grafo espanso (m)

1130 *E* expanded node (*with all successor nodes generated*) (LOGIC)
G expandierter Knoten (m); erweiterter Knoten (m)
F nœud développé (m)
S nodo expandido (m)
I nodo espanso (m)

1131 *E* expanded tree (LOGIC)
G expandierter Baum (m)
F arbre développé (m)
S árbol desarrollado (m)
I albero espanso (m)

1132 *E* expansion (*of a node*) (LOGIC)
G Expansion (f); Expandieren (n); Erweiterung (f)
F expansion (f); développement (m)
S expansión (f); desarrollo (m)
I espansione (f)

1133 *E* expansion of a tree (LOGIC)
G Expandieren eines (Such)Baums (n); Entfaltung eines Baums (f); Baumentwicklung (f)
F expansion d'un arbre (f)
S expansión de un árbol (f); desarrollo del árbol (m)
I espansione di un'albero (f)

1134 *E* expectation
G Erwartung (f)
F attente (f); expectative (f)
S expectativa (f)
I aspettativa (f); attesa (f)

1135 *E* expectation-based
→ expectation-driven

1136 *E* expectation-driven (*reasoning etc.*) (EXPERT SYSTEMS)
= expectation-based
G erwartungsgetrieben; erwartungsgesteuert
F dirigé par les attentes
S dirigido por las expectativas

I guidato dall'attesa (di certi eventi); guidato dalle aspettative

1137 *E* expectation-driven filtering (EXPERT SYSTEMS)
G erwartungsgesteuertes Filtern (n)
F filtrage à génération d'attentes (m)
S filtraje dirigido por las expectativas (m)
I filtraggio basato sulle aspettative (m)

1138 *E* expectation-driven parsing (NLP)
G erwartungsgesteuertes Parsing (n)
F analyse dirigée par les expectatives (f)
S análisis dirigido por las expectativas (m)
I parsing guidato dall'attesa (m); analisi guidata dalle aspettative (f)

1139 *E* expected value (EXPERT SYSTEMS)
G erwarteter Wert (m)
F valeur expectée (f)
S valor atendido (m)
I valore atteso (m)

1140 *E* experiential knowledge
↔ deep knowledge
G Erfahrungswissen (n); Erfahrungsschatz (m)
F connaissance pratique (f); savoir expérientiel (m)
S conocimiento experimentado (m); conocimiento experimental (m)
I conoscenza perita (f)

1141 *E* experientially based learning system
G auf Erfahrung basierendes Lernsystem (n)
F système d'apprentissage basé sur l'expérience (m)
S sistema de aprendizaje basado en experiencia (m)
I sistema di apprendimento basato su sperimentazione (m)

1142 *E* experimental applications
G Testanwendungen (f pl); Versuchsanwendungen (f pl)
F applications expérimentales (f pl)
S aplicaciones experimentales (f pl)
I applicazioni sperimentali (f pl)

1143 *E* experimental expert system
G experimentelles Expertensystem (n)
F système expert expérimental (m)
S sistema experto experimental (m)
I sistema esperto sperimentale (m)

1144 *E* expert^1
→ human expert
G Experte (m)
F expert (m)
S experto (m); persona experta (f)
I esperto (m); perito (f)

1145 *E* expert^2 (*of a specific domain*)
→ domain expert

1146 *E* expert advice (KNOWLEDGE)
G Ratschlag eines Experten (m); Expertenrat (m)
F conseil d'expert (m)
S consejo perito (m)
I consiglio di un esperto (m)

1147 *E* expert domain (KNOWLEDGE)
G Expertendomäne (f)
F domaine expert (m)
S dominio de experto (m)
I dominio di un esperto (m)

1148 *E* expertise (KNOWLEDGE)
G Expertise (f); Expertenwissen (n); spezielles Fachwissen (n); Expertentum (n)
F expertise (f); compétence (f)
S maestría (f); experiencia (acumulada) (f); pericia del experto (f)

I esperienza (specifica) (f); expertise (f)

1149 *E* expertise acquisition (KNOWLEDGE)
G Aneignung von Expertenwissen (f)
F acquisition de compétence (f); recueil d'expertise (m)
S adquisición de maestría (f)
I acquisizione di esperienza (f)

1150 *E* expertise domain
→ domain of expertise

1151 *E* expertise transfer (KNOWLEDGE)
G Transfer von Expertise (m)
F transfert d'expertise (m)
S transferencia de maestría (f)
I trasferimento di esperienza (m)

1152 *E* expert judgement
G Expertenurteil (n); Beurteilung durch Experten (f)
F jugement d'expert (m)
S juicio de expertos (m)
I giudizio di un esperto (m)

1153 *E* expert knowledge
G Expertenwissen (n)
F connaissance experte (f); connaissance de l'expert (f)
S conocimiento de un experto (m); conocimiento experto (m); conocimientos expertos (m pl)
I conoscenza di un esperto (f)

1154 *E* expert-level reasoning (LOGIC)
G Inferieren auf Expertenniveau (n)
F raisonnement sur le niveau de l'expert (m)
S razonamiento a un nivel de experto (m)
I ragionamento al livello esperto (m); ragionamento a livello di esperto (m)

1155 *E* expert reasoning (LOGIC)
G expertenmäßiges Schlüsseziehen (n)
F raisonnement expert (m)
S razonamiento experto (m)
I ragionamento esperto (m)

1156 *E* expert software
→ expert system software

1157 *E* expert support system (ESS)
G Expertenunterstützungssystem (n)
F système de support d'expert (m)
S sistema de soporte de expertos (m)
I sistema di supporto esperti (m)

1158 *E* expert system (ES; XPS)
= E-system
G Expertensystem (ES) (n)
F système expert (SE) (m) (pl: systèmes experts)
S sistema experto (SE) (m) (pl: sistemas expertos)
I sistema esperto (m) (pl: sistemi esperti)

1159 *E* expert system architecture
G Architektur eines Expertensystems (f)
F architecture d'un système expert (f)
S arquitectura de los sistemas expertos (f)
I architettura di un sistema esperto (f)

1160 *E* expert-system-based
G auf einem Expertensystem beruhend; expertensystemgestützt
F basé sur un système expert
S basado en sistemas expertos
I basato su sistemi esperti

1161 *E* expert system builder
G Hersteller von Expertensystemen (m); Expertensystemhersteller (m)

F constructeur de systèmes experts (m); producteur de systèmes experts (m)
S constructor de sistemas expertos (m)
I costruttore di sistemi esperti (m)

1162 *E* expert system building
= building of expert systems
G Erstellen von Expertensystemen (n); Expertensystemerstellung (f)
F construction de systèmes experts (f)
S construcción de sistemas expertos (f)
I costruzione di sistemi esperti (f)

1163 *E* expert system building tool
G Entwicklungswerkzeug für Expertensysteme (n)
F outil de construction de systèmes experts (m); outil de développement de systèmes experts (m)
S software de ayuda a la construcción de sistemas expertos (m)
I strumento per costruire sistemi esperti (m)

1164 *E* expert system design
G Design von Expertensystemen (n)
F projet de systèmes experts (m)
S diseño de sistemas expertos (m)
I disegno di sistemi esperti (m)

1165 *E* expert system designer
→ expert system developer

1166 *E* expert system developer
= expert system designer
G Expertensystementwickler (m)
F développeur de systèmes experts (m)
S desarrollador de sistemas expertos (m)
I sviluppatore di sistemi esperti (m)

1167 *E* expert system development
= development of expert systems
G Entwicklung von Expertensystemen (f); Expertensystementwicklung (f); ES-Entwicklung (f)
F développement de systèmes experts (m)
S desarrollo de sistemas expertos (m)
I sviluppo di sistemi esperti (m)

1168 *E* expert system domain
G Domäne eines Expertensystems (f)
F domaine d'un système expert (m)
S dominio de un sistema experto (m)
I dominio di un sistema esperto (m)

1169 *E* expert system generator
G Expertensystemgenerator (m)
F générateur de systèmes experts (GSE) (m)
S generador de sistemas expertos (m)
I generatore di sistemi esperti (m)

1170 *E* expert system maintenance
G Wartung von Expertensystemen (f); ES-Wartung (f)
F entretien de systèmes experts (m); maintenance de systèmes experts (f)
S manutención de sistemas expertos (f); mantenimiento de un sistema experto (m)
I manutenzione di un sistema esperto (f)

1171 *E* expert system programming
G Programmieren von Expertensystemen (n); ES-Programmierung (f)
F programmation de systèmes experts (f)

S programación de sistemas expertos (f)
I programmazione di sistemi esperti (f)

1172 *E* expert system shell
= shell; system shell
G Shell (eines Expertensystems) (f); Rahmen-Expertensystem (n); Expertensystem-Shell (f); Rahmensystem (für ES) (n)
F noyau (d'un système expert) (m); système essentiel (m); coquille (vide) (f); système expert vide (ou nu) (m); système expert coquille (m)
S esqueleto de un sistema experto (m)
I nucleo del sistema esperto (m); shell (f)

1173 *E* expert system software
= expert software; ES software
G Expertensystemsoftware (f); ES-Software (f)
F logiciel pour systèmes experts (m)
S software para sistemas expertos (m)
I software per sistemi esperti (m)

1174 *E* expert system tool (PROGRAMMING)
G Expertensystemtool (n)
F outil pour systèmes experts (m)
S herramientas para sistemas expertos (f pl)
I tool per sistemi esperti (m); strumento per sistemi esperti (m)

1175 *E* explanation (EXPERT SYSTEMS)
→ mid-run explanation
G Erklärung (f)
F explication (f)
S explicación (f)
I spiegazione (f)

1176 *E* explanation-based learning (EBL)
G erklärungsgestütztes Lernen (n)
F apprentissage par explications (m)
S aprendizaje basado en explicaciones (m)
I apprendimento basato su spiegazioni (m)

1177 *E* explanation capability (EXPERT SYSTEMS)
= explanatory capability
G Erklärungfähigkeit (f)
F capacité d'explication(s) (f); capacité d'expliquer le raisonnement (f); autoexplication (f)
S capacidad para explicar el razonamiento (f)
I abilità di dare spiegazioni (f); capacità di costruire spiegazioni (f)

1178 *E* explanation component
→ explanation subsystem

1179 *E* explanation facility[1] (EXPERT SYSTEMS)
G Erklärungsmöglichkeit (f)
F possibilité d'explication (du raisonnement) (f)
S facilidades de explicación (f pl); posibilidad de generar explicaciones (f)
I possibilità di spiegazioni (f)

1180 *E* explanation facility[2]
→ explanation subsystem

1181 *E* explanation interface (EXPERT SYSTEMS)
G Erklärungsschnittstelle (f)
F interface d'explication (f)
S interfaz de explicación (f)
I interfaccia per le spiegazioni (f)

1182 *E* explanation subsystem (EXPERT SYSTEMS)

= explanation component
→ explanation facility
G Erklärungskomponente (f); Erklärungsteil (m)
F subsystème d'explication (m); module d'explication (m)
S subsistema explicativo (m); subsistema de explicación (m); programa explicativo (m)
I sotto-sistema di spiegazione (m); modulo esplicativo (m)

1183 *E* explanatory capability
→ explanation capability

1184 *E* explanatory text (EXPERT SYSTEMS)
G erklärender Text (m)
F texte explicatif (m)
S texto explicativo (m)
I testo esplicativo (m); testo di spiegazione (m)

1185 *E* explicit knowledge
G explizites Wissen (n)
F connaissance explicite (f)
S conocimiento explícito (m)
I conoscenza esplicita (f)

1186 *E* exploration model (PROGRAMMING)
G Explorationsmodell (n)
F modèle d'exploration (m)
S modelo de exploración (m)
I modello di esplorazione (m)

1187 *E* exponential search (LOGIC)
G exponentielle Suche (f)
F recherche exponentielle (f)
S búsqueda exponencial (f)
I ricerca esponenziale (f)

1188 *E* expression (LOGIC)
G Ausdruck (m)
F expression (f)
S expresión (f)
I espressione (f)

1189 *E* extended grammar (LINGUISTICS)
G erweiterte Grammatik (f)
F grammaire étendue (f)
S gramática extendida (f)
I grammatica estesa (f)

1190 *E* extended Horn clause (LOGIC)
G erweiterte Horn-Klausel (f)
F clause de Horn étendue (f)
S cláusula de Horn extendida (f)
I clausola tipo Horn estesa (f)

1191 *E* extended Markov model (EMM) (RECOGNITION)
G erweitertes Markoffmodell (EMM) (n)
F modèle de Markov étendu (m)
S modelo de Markov extendido (m)
I modello di Markov esteso (m)

1192 *E* extension (*of a concept*) (LINGUISTICS)
≠ intension
G Extension (f)
F extension (f)
S extensión (f)
I estensione (f)

1193 *E* extract (*knowledge etc.*)
G extrahieren
F extraire
S extraer
I estrarre

1194 *E* extraction of knowledge
→ knowledge extraction

1195 *E* extrapolation rule (LOGIC)
G Extrapolationsregel (f)
F règle d'extrapolation (f)
S regla de extrapolación (f)
I regola di estrapolazione (f)

F

1196 *E* facet (*of a slot*) (KNOWLEDGE)
G Facette (f)
F facette (f)
S facet (m)
I faccetta (f)

1197 *E* facet theory
G Facettentheorie (f)
F théorie des facettes (f)
S teoría de facetas (f)
I teoria delle faccette (f)

1198 *E* fact (LOGIC)
G Faktum (n); Fakt (m)
F fait (m)
S hecho (m)
I fatto (m)

1199 *E* fact base (KNOWLEDGE)
= facts base; factual base; factographic data base
G Faktenbasis (f)
F base de faits (BF) (f); base factuelle (f)
S base factual (f)
I base di fatti (f)

1200 *E* factographic data base
→ fact base

1201 *E* factor of belief (LOGIC)
G Glaubwürdigkeitsfaktor (m)
F facteur de croyance (m)
S factor de confianza (m); factor de credibilidad (m)
I fattore di convinzione (m)

1202 *E* factorization (LOGIC)
G Faktorisierung (f)
F factorisation (f)
S factorización (f)
I fattorizzazione (f)

1203 *E* fact retrieval
→ facts retrieval

1204 *E* facts base
→ fact base

1205 *E* facts-based (KNOWLEDGE)
G faktenbasiert; auf Fakten beruhend
F basé sur des faits
S basado en los hechos
I basato sui fatti

1206 *E* facts-oriented reasoning (LOGIC)
G faktenorientiertes Schließen (n)
F raisonnement guidé par les faits (m)
S razonamiento orientado a hechos (m)
I ragionamento orientato ai fatti (m)

1207 *E* facts representation (KNOWLEDGE)
G Faktenrepräsentation (f); Faktendarstellung (f)
F représentation de faits (f)
S representación de los hechos (f)
I rappresentazione di fatti (f)

1208 *E* facts retrieval (KNOWLEDGE)
= fact retrieval
G Faktenretrieval (n)
F recherche de faits (f)
S búsqueda de factores (f)
I ricerca di fatti (f)

1209 *E* factual (LOGIC)
G Fakten…; faktisch

F factuel
S factual
I fattuale

1210 E factual base
→ fact base

1211 E factual clause (LOGIC)
G Faktenklausel (f)
F clause factuelle (f)
S cláusula del tipo hecho (f)
I clausola fattuale (f)

1212 E factual information (KNOWLEDGE)
G Fakteninformation (f)
F information factuelle (f)
S información factual (f)
I informazione sui fatti (f)

1213 E factual knowledge
G Faktenwissen (n)
F connaissance factuelle (f)
S conocimiento factual (m)
I conoscenza fattuale (f)

1214 E false (LOGIC)
≠ true
G falsch
F faux, fausse
S falso
I falso

1215 E falsehood
→ falsity

1216 E falsity (LOGIC)
= falsehood
≠ truth
G Falschheit (f)
F fausseté (f)
S falsedad (f)
I falsità (f)

1217 E father (node) (LOGIC)
G Vater (Vorgängerknoten) (m)
F nœud père (m); père (m)
S nodo padre (m); padre (m)
I padre (nodo) (m)

1218 E fault diagnosis (EXPERT SYSTEMS)
G Fehlerdiagnose (f)
F diagnostic de défauts (m); diagnostic de pannes (m)
S diagnóstico de averías (m)
I diagnosi di guasti (f); individuazione dell'origine di guasti (f)

1219 E fault finding
= fault localization
G Lokalisierung von Fehlern (f)
F localisation de défauts (f)
S localización de averías (f)
I localizzazione di guasti (f)

1220 E fault isolation expert system (FIES)
→ fault isolation system

1221 E fault isolation system (FIS) (EXPERT SYSTEMS)
= fault isolation expert system (FIES)
G Fehlerisolierungssystem (n)
F système de diagnostic de pannes (m)
S sistema de diagnóstico de averías (m); localizador de averías (m)
I sistema di isolamento di guasti (m)

1222 E fault localization
→ fault finding

1223 E feasibility analysis (PROGRAMMING)
G Durchführbarkeitsanalyse (f)
F analyse de faisabilité (f)
S análisis de factibilidad (m)
I analisi di fattibilità (f)

1224 E feature (KNOWLEDGE)
G Merkmal (n)
F trait (distinctif) (m)
S característica (f)
I attributo (m); caratteristica (peculiare) (f)

1225 *E* feature analysis (IMAGE PROCESSING)
≠ template matching
G Merkmalsanalyse (f)
F analyse des traits distinctifs (f)
S análisis de características (m)
I analisi delle caratteristiche (f)

1226 *E* feature description (NLP)
G Merkmalsbeschreibung (f)
F description de traits (f)
S descripción de catacterísticas (f)
I descrizione degli attributi (f)

1227 *E* feature detection (IMAGE PROCESSING)
G Merkmalsfindung (f)
F détection de traits distinctifs (f)
S detección de características (f)
I rilevamento di caratteristiche peculiari (m)

1228 *E* feature extraction (IMAGE PROCESSING)
G Merkmalsextraktion (f)
F extraction de traits (f)
S extracción de características (f)
I estrazione delle caratteristiche (f)

1229 *E* feature quantifying (IMAGE PROCESSING)
G Merkmalsquantifizierung (f)
F quantification de traits (f)
S cuantificación de características (f)
I quantificazione delle caratteristiche (f)

1230 *E* feature recognition
G Merkmalserkennung (f)
F reconnaissance de traits (f)
S reconocimiento de características (m)
I riconoscimento delle caratteristiche (m)

1231 *E* feature representation (KNOWLEDGE)
G Merkmalsrepräsentation (f)
F représentation des traits distinctifs (f)
S representación de características (f)
I rappresentazione delle caratteristiche (f)

1232 *E* feature set
→ set of features

1233 *E* feature space (LEARNING)
G Merkmalsraum (m)
F espace de traits distinctifs (m)
S espacio de características (m)
I spazio degli attributi (m)

1234 *E* feedback loop (EXPERT SYSTEMS)
G Rückkopplungsschleife (f)
F boucle de rétro-alimentation (f)
S enlace de retroalimentación (m)
I ciclo di rialimentazione (m)

1235 *E* FGC
→ fifth-generation computer

1236 *E* field of knowledge
G Wissensgebiet (n)
F champ de connaissances (m)
S campo de conocimiento (m)
I campo di conoscimento (m)

1237 *E* FIES
→ fault isolation expert system

1238 *E* fifth-generation computer (FGC)
= 5G computer
G Rechner der fünften Generation (m)
F ordinateur de 5e génération (m)
S ordenador de la quinta generación (m); ordenador de la 5G (m)
I elaboratore della quinta generazione (m)

1239 *E* fifth-generation language (5GL) (PROGRAMMING)

G Sprache der fünften Generation (f)
F langage de la 5e génération (m)
S lenguaje de quinta generación (m); lenguaje 5G (m)
I linguaggio della quinta generazione (m)

1240 E filler (*of a slot*) (KNOWLEDGE)
= entry; value
G Filler (m); Eintrag (m) ; Wert (m)
F valeur (f)
S valor (m)
I valore (m)

1241 E filtering of rules
→ rule filtering

1242 E final goal (EXPERT SYSTEMS)
G Endziel (n)
F but final (m)
S objetivo final (m)
I obiettivo finale (m)

1243 E final state (EXPERT SYSTEMS)
G Endzustand (m)
F état final (m)
S estado final (m)
I stato finale (m)

1244 E finite set (MATHS)
G endliche Menge (f)
F ensemble fini (m)
S conjunto finito (m)
I insieme finito (m)

1245 E finite state automaton (FSA) (LOGIC)
= finite state machine
G endlicher Automat (EA) (m); Endlich-Zustand-Automat (m)
F automate fini (m); machine à état fini (f)
S autómata de estado finito (m)
I automa a stati finiti (m); macchina a stati finiti (f)

1246 E finite state grammar (NLP)
= regular grammar; type 3 grammar
G Grammatik mit endlich vielen Zuständen (f)
F grammaire d'états finis (f)
S gramática de estado finito (f)
I grammatica a stati finiti (f)

1247 E finite state machine
→ finite state automaton

1248 E finite state network (LOGIC)
G Netz mit endlich vielen Zuständen (n)
F réseau d'états finis (m)
S red de estados finitos (f)
I rete dei stati finiti (f)

1249 E fire[1] (*a rule; transitive verb*) (EXPERT SYSTEMS)
G anwenden; ausführen; feuern
F invoquer; déclencher
S disparar
I attivare

1250 E fire[2] (*of a rule; intransitive verb*) (EXPERT SYSTEMS)
G feuern
F être déclenché
S dispararse
I sparare

1251 E firing (*of a rule*) (EXPERT SYSTEMS)
= execution
G Anwendung (f); Ausführung (f); Feuern (n)
F déclenchement (m); invocation (f)
S activación (f); disparo (m)
I attivazione (f); sparo (m)

1252 E firing conditions (*for a rule*) (EXPERT SYSTEMS)
G Bedingungen für das Feuern einer Regel (f pl)
F conditions de déclenchement (f pl)
S condiciones de disparo (f pl)

I condizioni di sparo (f pl)

1253 *E* first-generation expert system
G Expertensystem der ersten Generation (n)
F système expert de 1ère génération (m)
S sistema experto de primera generación (m)
I sistema esperto della prima generazione (m)

1254 *E* first-order logic (FOL)
↔ second-order logic
G Logik erster Stufe (f)
F logique du premier ordre (f); logique d'ordre 1 (f)
S lógica de primer orden (f)
I logica del primo ordine (f)

1255 *E* first-order predicate (LOGIC)
G Prädikat erster Stufe (n)
F prédicat du premier ordre (m)
S predicado de primer orden (m)
I predicato del primo ordine (m)

1256 *E* first-order predicate calculus (FOPC) (LOGIC)
G Prädikatenkalkül erster Stufe (m)
F calcul des prédicats du premier ordre (m)
S cálculo de predicados de primer orden (m)
I calcolo dei predicati del primo ordine (m)

1257 *E* first-order predicate logic (FOPL)
G Prädikatenlogik erster Stufe (f); Prädikatenlogik der ersten Stufe (f)
F logique des prédicats du premier ordre (f)
S lógica de predicados de primer orden (f)
I logica dei predicati del primo ordine (f)

1258 *E* first-order relation (LOGIC)
G Relation erster Ordnung (f)
F relation du premier ordre (f)
S relación de primer orden (f)
I relazione del primo ordine (f)

1259 *E* FIS
→ fault isolation system

1260 *E* 5G computer
→ fifth-generation computer

1261 *E* 5GL
→ fifth-generation language

1262 *E* flexible manufacturing system (FMS)
G flexibles Produktionssteuerungssystem (n); flexibles Fertigungssystem (FFS) (n)
F système souple de fabrication (m)
S sistema flexible de fabricación (m)
I sistema flessibile di fabbricazione (m)

1263 *E* flow of control (EXPERT SYSTEMS)
= control flow
G Steuerungsfluß (m)
F flux de contrôle (m); débit de contrôle (m)
S flujo de control (m)
I flusso di controllo (m)

1264 *E* flow of execution (*of a program*)
G Ablauf (m)
F flux d'exécution (m)
S flujo de ejecución (m)
I flusso di esecuzione (m); flusso di scorrimento (m)

1265 *E* flow of reasoning (LOGIC)
G Inferenzfluß (m)
F flux de raisonnement (m)
S flujo de razonamiento (m)
I flusso di ragionamento (m)

1266 *E* flowsheet (*of a knowledge base*)
G Flowsheet (n)
F diagramme de flux (m)
S diagrama de flujo (m)
I diagramma di flusso (m)

1267 *E* fluent speech (RECOGNITION)
= running speech
↔ continuous speech
G flüssige Rede (f); fließende Rede (f)
F parole spontanée (f)
S diálogo fluido (m)
I discorso parlato continuo (m)

1268 *E* FMS
→ flexible manufacturing system

1269 *E* focal attention (RECOGNITION)
G fokale Aufmerksamkeit (f)
F attention focale (f)
S atención focal (f)
I attenzione focale (f)

1270 *E* focus[1] (*verb*) (LOGIC)
G fokussieren
F focaliser
S enfocar; focalizar; centrar la atención en
I focalizzare

1271 *E* focus[2] (*of a conversation*) (NLP)
G Thema (einer Konversation) (n); Fokus (m); inhaltlicher Schwerpunkt (m)
F foyer (m)
S foco (m); elemento focal (m)
I soggetto (di una conversazione) (m); concetto cruciale (m)

1272 *E* focus of attention (RECOGNITION)
G Zentrum der Aufmerksamkeit (n)
F centre d'attention (m)
S centro de atención (m)
I focalizzazione dell'attenzione (f)

1273 *E* focus-of-attention reasoning (EXPERT SYSTEMS)
G Schließen nach dem Brennpunkt der Aufmerksamkeit (n)
F méthode de focus of attention (f)
S razonamiento por centros de atención (m)
I ragionamento con focalizzazione dell'attenzione (m)

1274 *E* focused reasoning (LOGIC)
= goal-oriented reasoning
G fokussiertes Schließen (n)
F raisonnement focalisé (m)
S razonamiento enfocado (m)
I ragionamento focalizzato (m)

1275 *E* focusing strategy (EXPERT SYSTEMS)
G Fokussierungsstrategie (f)
F stratégie de focalisation (f); stratégie de centrage (f)
S estrategia de enfoque (f)
I strategia di focalizzazione (f)

1276 *E* FOL
→ first-order logic

1277 *E* FOPC
→ first-order predicate calculus

1278 *E* FOPL
→ first-order predicate logic

1279 *E* forecast[1] (*noun*) (EXPERT SYSTEMS)
G Vorhersage (f)
F prévision (f); pronostic (m)
S previsión (f)
I previsione (f)

1280 *E* forecast[2] (*verb*)
→ predict

1281 *E* forecasting
→ prediction

1282 *E* forecasting ability (EXPERT SYSTEMS)
G Vorhersagefähigkeit (f)

F capacité de prévision (f)
S capacidad de predicción (f)
I capacità previsionale (f)

1283 *E* 'for-every' statement (LOGIC)
G Allaussage (f) (von Typ: für alle *x* gilt *y*)
F proposition 'pour tous' (f)
S proposición 'para todos los' (f)
I proposizione 'per ogni' (f)

1284 *E* formal grammar (NLP)
G formale Grammatik (f)
F grammaire formelle (f)
S gramática formal (f)
I grammatica formale (f)

1285 *E* formal inference
→ formal reasoning

1286 *E* formalization (KNOWLEDGE)
G Formalisierung (f)
F formalisation (f)
S formalización (f)
I formalizzazione (f)

1287 *E* formal language (*having a limited number of rules*) (NLP)
G formale Sprache (f)
F langage formel (m)
S lenguaje formal (m)
I linguaggio formale (m)

1288 *E* formal logic
G formale Logik (f)
F logique formelle (f)
S lógica formal (f)
I logica formale (f)

1289 *E* formal reasoning (LOGIC)
= formal inference
G formales Schlüsseziehen (n)
F raisonnement formel (m)
S razonamiento formal (m)
I ragionamento formale (m)

1290 *E* formal truth (LOGIC)
G formale Wahrheit (f)
F vérité formelle (f)
S verdad formal (f)
I verità formale (f)

1291 *E* formant (*noun*) (RECOGNITION)
G Formant (m)
F formant (m)
S formante (m)
I formante (m o f)

1292 *E* formant analysis (RECOGNITION)
G Formantenanalyse (f)
F analyse des formants (f)
S análisis de los formantes (m)
I analisi dei formanti (f)

1293 *E* formant synthesis (RECOGNITION)
G Formantensynthese (f); Formantsynthese (f)
F synthèse par formants (f)
S síntesis de los formantes (f)
I sintesi delle formanti (f)

1294 *E* forward-acting rule (EXPERT SYSTEMS)
= forward (application) rule; forward-chaining rule
G Vorwärtsregel (f); vorwärts wirkende Regel (f)
F règle vers l'avant (f)
S regla hacia adelante (f)
I regola in avanti (f)

1295 *E* forward application rule
→ forward-acting rule

1296 *E* forward–backward algorithm (RECOGNITION)
= Baum–Welch algorithm
G Baum–Welch-Algorithmus (m)
F algorithme de Baum–Welch (m)
S algoritmo de Baum–Welch (m)
I algoritmo di Baum–Welch (m)

1297 *E* forward-chained (LOGIC)
G vorwärtsverkettet; vorwärtsverkettend
F enchaîné vers l'avant

S encadenado hacia adelante
I concatenato in avanti

1298 *E* forward chaining (LOGIC)
= bottom-up chaining
G Vorwärtsverkettung (f)
F chaînage avant (m); chaînage en avant (m)
S encadenamiento hacia adelante (m)
I concatenamento in avanti (m); concatenazione diretta (f); anteconcatenazione (f)

1299 *E* forward-chaining algorithm (LOGIC)
G Vorwärtsverkettungsalgorithmus (m)
F algorithme de chaînage avant (m)
S algoritmo de encadenamiento hacia adelante (m)
I algoritmo di forward chaining (m)

1300 *E* forward-chaining interpreter (PROGRAMMING)
G vorwärtsverkettender Interpreter (m)
F interpréteur en chaînage avant (m); interpréteur vers l'avant (m)
S intérprete de encadenamiento hacia adelante (m)
I interprete tipo forward chaining (m)

1301 *E* forward-chaining rule
→ forward-acting rule

1302 *E* forward-chaining strategy (EXPERT SYSTEMS)
G Vorwärtsverkettungsstrategie (f)
F stratégie de chaînage avant (f); stratégie en avant (f)
S estrategia de encadenamiento hacia adelante (f)
I strategia forward chaining (f)

1303 *E* forward planning (EXPERT SYSTEMS)
G Vorwärtsplanen (n)
F planification vers l'avant (f)
S planificación hacia adelante (f)
I pianificazione in avanti (f)

1304 *E* forward pruning (LOGIC)
≠ backward pruning
G Abschneiden in Vorwärtsrichtung (n)
F coupe vers l'avant (f)
S poda hacia adelante (f)
I potatura in avanti (f)

1305 *E* forward reasoning (EXPERT SYSTEMS)
≠ backward reasoning
G Vorwärtsschließen (n); Vorwärtsableitung (f)
F raisonnement vers l'avant (m)
S razonamiento hacia adelante (m)
I ragionamento in avanti (m)

1306 *E* forward-reasoning system (EXPERT SYSTEMS)
G vorwärtsgesteuertes System (n)
F système de raisonnement vers l'avant (m)
S sistema de razonamiento hacia adelante (m)
I sistema di ragionamento in avanti (m)

1307 *E* forward rule
→ forward-acting rule

1308 *E* forward search (EXPERT SYSTEMS)
≠ backward search
G Vorwärtssuche (f)
F recherche vers l'avant (f)
S búsqueda hacia adelante (f)
I ricerca in avanti (f)

1309 *E* frame (*noun*) (KNOWLEDGE)
= object; object frame; unit
G Frame (m); Schema (n)

F cadre (sémantique) (m); cadre de référence (m); objet (stéréotypé) (m); schéma (m)
S frame (m); estructura (f); cuadro (m); marco (de representación) (m); objeto (m); unidad (f)
I frame (m); quadro di contestualizzazione (m); cornice (f)

1310 *E* frame-based (*systems, methods, etc.*) (KNOWLEDGE)
G frame-basiert
F basé sur frames; à base de frames
S basado en frames; basado en esquemas
I frame-based; basato su frame

1311 *E* frame class (KNOWLEDGE)
G Frameklasse (f)
F classe de frame (f)
S clase de frame (f)
I classe di frame (f)

1312 *E* frame concept (KNOWLEDGE)
G Frame-Konzept (n)
F concept de frame (m)
S concepto de frame (m)
I concetto di frame (m)

1313 *E* frame hierarchy (KNOWLEDGE)
G Frame-Hierarchie (f)
F hiérarchie des cadres (f)
S jerarquía de frames (f)
I gerarchia dei frame (f)

1314 *E* frame problem (EXPERT SYSTEMS)
G Frame-Problem (n); Wissensrahmenproblem (n); Rahmenproblem (n)
F problème de cadre (m)
S problema del marco de representación (m)
I problema del contesto (m)

1315 *E* frame recognition (KNOWLEDGE)
G Frame-Erkennung (f)
F reconnaissance de frames (f)
S reconocimiento de frames (m)
I riconoscimento dei frame (m)

1316 *E* frame representation (KNOWLEDGE)
G Frame-Darstellung (f)
F représentation sous forme de frame (f)
S representación de tipo frame (f)
I rappresentazione tipo frame (f); rappresentazione dei frame (f)

1317 *E* frame representation language (KNOWLEDGE)
G Frame-Darstellungssprache (f)
F langage de représentation de frames (m)
S lenguaje de representación de frames (m)
I linguaggio per la rappresentazione dei frame (m)

1318 *E* frame theory
G Frame-Theorie (f)
F théorie des frames (f)
S teoría de los frames (f)
I teoria dei frame (f)

1319 *E* frame value (LOGIC)
G Frame-Wert (m)
F valeur de frame (f)
S valor de frame (m)
I valore del frame (m)

1320 *E* Franz LISP (*LISP version mainly for UNIX machines*) (PROGRAMMING)
G Franz LISP
F Franz LISP
S Franz LISP
I Franz LISP

1321 *E* free discourse (RECOGNITION)
G freie Rede (f)
F discours libre (m); parole spontanée (f)
S discurso libre (m)
I libero discorso (m)

1322 *E* free logic
G freie Logik (f)
F logique libre (f)
S lógica libre (f)
I logica libera (f)

1323 *E* free variable (PROGRAMMING)
= unbound variable
≠ bound variable
G freie Variable (f)
F variable libre (f); variable non quantifiable (f)
S variable libre (f)
I variabile libera (f)

1324 *E* fricative (consonant) (RECOGNITION)
G Reibelaut (m); Frikativlaut (m)
F fricative (f)
S consonante fricativa (f)
I fricativa (f)

1325 *E* FRL (*the first Frame Representation Language*) (PROGRAMMING)
G FRL
F FRL
S FRL
I FRL

1326 *E* FSA
→ finite state automaton

1327 *E* FUG
→ functional unification grammar

1328 *E* fulfil (*a condition*) (LOGIC)
= suffice
G erfüllen (eine Bedingung); genügen (einer Bedingung)
F satisfaire à
S cumplir; satisfacer
I soddisfare

1329 *E* full-width search (EXPERT SYSTEMS)
G Suche über die gesamte Breite (f)
F recherche de toute largeur (f)
S búsqueda de largura completa (f)
I ricerca in tutta la ampiezza (f)

1330 *E* functional dependency (LOGIC)
G funktionelle Abhängigkeit (f)
F dépendance fonctionnelle (f)
S dependencia funcional (f)
I dipendenza funzionale (f)

1331 *E* functional programming
G funktionale Programmierung (f)
F programmation fonctionnelle (f)
S programación funcional (f)
I programmazione funzionale (f)

1332 *E* functional relation (LOGIC)
G funktionale Relation (f)
F relation fonctionnelle (f)
S relación funcional (f)
I relazione funzionale (f)

1333 *E* functional unification grammar (FUG) (NLP)
G funktionale Unifikationsgrammatik (FUG) (f)
F grammaire fonctionnelle d'unification (f)
S gramática funcional de unificación (f)
I grammatica funzionale di unificazione (f)

1334 *E* function graph (LOGIC)
G Funktionsgraph (m)
F graphe d'une fonction (m)
S grafo de función (m)
I grafo di funzione (m)

1335 *E* function symbol
→ functor

1336 *E* functor (PROGRAMMING)
= function symbol
G Funktor (m)
F symbole de fonction (m)
S functor (m)
I funtore (m)

1337 *E* fuzzy (LOGIC)
G unscharf; vage; verschwommen
F flou
S difuso
I fuzzy (adj); sfumato

1338 *E* fuzzy algorithm (LOGIC)
G unscharfer Algorithmus (m)
F algorithme flou (m)
S algoritmo difuso (m)
I algoritmo fuzzy (m)

1339 *E* fuzzy conditions (LOGIC)
G unscharfe Bedingungen (f pl)
F conditions floues (f pl)
S condiciones difusas (f pl)
I condizioni sfumate (f pl)

1340 *E* fuzzy inference (LOGIC)
G unscharfer Schluß (m)
F inférence floue (f)
S inferencia difusa (f)
I inferenza sfumata (f)

1341 *E* fuzzy knowledge
G diffuses Wissen (n); vages Wissen (n)
F connaissances floues (f pl)
S conocimiento difuso (m)
I conoscenza sfumata (f)

1342 *E* fuzzy logic
G unscharfe Logik (f); verschwommene Logik (f); Fuzzy Logic (f)
F logique floue (f); logique de l'incertain (f)
S lógica difusa (f)
I fuzzy logic (f); logica fuzzy (f); logica sfumata (f); logica approssimata (f)

1343 *E* fuzzy predicate (LOGIC)
G Fuzzy-Prädikat (n)
F prédicat flou (m)
S predicado difuso (m)
I predicato sfumato (m)

1344 *E* fuzzy probability (LOGIC)
G Fuzzy-Wahrscheinlichkeit (f)
F probabilité floue (f)
S probabilidad difusa (f)
I probabilità sfumata (f)

1345 *E* fuzzy reasoning (EXPERT SYSTEMS)
G Fuzzy-Schließen (n)
F raisonnement flou (m)
S razonamiento difuso (m)
I ragionamento fuzzy (m)

1346 *E* fuzzy rule (EXPERT SYSTEMS)
G Fuzzy-Regel (f)
F règle floue (f)
S regla difusa (f)
I regola sfumata (f)

1347 *E* fuzzy set (MATHS)
G unscharfe Menge (f); nicht genau definierte Menge (f); Fuzzymenge (f)
F ensemble flou (m)
S conjunto difuso (m); conjunto borroso (m)
I insieme fuzzy (m); insieme sfumato (m)

1348 *E* fuzzy sets theory
= theory of fuzzy sets
G Theorie der unscharfen (oder Fuzzy-)Mengen (f); unscharfe Mengenlehre (f); Fuzzy-Set-Theorie (f)
F théorie des ensembles flous (f)
S teoría de conjuntos fuzzy (f)
I teoria degli insiemi sfumati (f)

1349 *E* fuzzy subset (MATHS)
G unscharfe Untermenge (f); Fuzzy-Teilmenge (f)
F sous-ensemble flou (m)
S subconjunto difuso (m)
I sottoinsieme fuzzy (m)

1350 *E* fuzzy truth (EXPERT SYSTEMS)
G Fuzzy-Wahrheit (f)

F vérité floue (f)
S verdad difusa (f)
I verità fuzzy (f)

1351 *E* fuzzy value (LOGIC)
G Fuzzy-Wert (m)
F valeur floue (f)
S valor difuso (m)
I valore fuzzy (m)

1352 *E* fuzzy variable (LOGIC)
G Fuzzy-Variable (f)
F variable floue (f)
S variable difusa (f)
I variabile fuzzy (f)

G

1353 *E* game-playing program
G Spielprogramm (n)
F programme de jeu (m)
S programa de juego (m)
I programma di gioco (m)

1354 *E* game theory
G Spieltheorie (f)
F théorie des jeux (f)
S teoría de juegos (f)
I teoria dei giochi (f)

1355 *E* game tree (*that contains all moves of a game*)
G Spielbaum (m)
F arbre de jeu (m)
S árbol del juego (m)
I albero di gioco (m)

1356 *E* GDB
→ global database[1]

1357 *E* generality (LOGIC)
G Allgemeinheit (f); Allgemeingültigkeit (f)
F généralité (f)
S generalidad (f)
I generalità (f)

1358 *E* generalization (LOGIC)
≠ refinement
G Generalisierung (im Gegensatz zum Verfeinern) (f); Verallgemeinerung (f)
F généralisation (f)
S generalización (f)
I generalizzazione (f)

1359 *E* generalization of language (NLP)
G Verallgemeinerung der Sprache (f)
F généralisation de la langue (f)
S generalización de lenguaje (f)
I generalizzazione del linguaggio (f)

1360 *E* generalization rule (LOGIC)
G Generalisierungsregel (f)
F règle de généralisation (f)
S regla de generalización (f)
I regola di generalizzazione (f)

1361 *E* generalized cylinder (IMAGE PROCESSING)
G generalisierter Zylinder (m)
F cylindre généralisé (m)
S cono generalizado (m)
I cilindro generalizzato (m)

1362 *E* generalized events (EXPERT SYSTEMS)
G generalisierte Ereignisse (n pl)
F événements généralisés (m pl)
S acontecimientos generalizados (m pl)
I eventi generalizzati (m pl)

1363 *E* generalized phrase structure grammar (GPSG) (NLP)
G generalisierte Phrasenstrukturgrammatik (f)
F grammaire généralisée de structure des phrases (f)
S gramática generalizada de estructura de frase (f)
I grammatica IC generalizzata (f)

1364 *E* generalized transition network (GTN) (NLP)
G generalisiertes Übergangsnetz (n)
F réseau de transition généralisé (m)

S red de transición generalizada (f)
I rete di transizione generalizzata (f)

1365 *E* generalized tree (LOGIC)
G verallgemeinerter Baum (m)
F arbre généralisé (m)
S árbol generalizado (m)
I albero generalizzato (m)

1366 *E* generalizer (*a logical operator*) (THEORY)
G Generalisator (m)
F généralisateur (m)
S generalizador (m)
I generalizzatore (m)

1367 *E* general knowledge
= everyday knowledge
G Allgemeinwissen (n); Alltagswissen (n); alltägliches Wissen (n)
F connaissance(s) générale(s) (f (pl)); connaissance fondamentale (f)
S conocimientos generales (m pl)
I conoscenza generale (f)

1368 *E* General Problem Solver (GPS) (EXPERT SYSTEMS)
G General Problem Solver (GPS) (m); Universal-Problemlöser (m); allgemeiner Problemlöser (m)
F résolveur de problèmes universels (m)
S Resolvente de Problemas Generales (GPS) (m); solucionador general de problemas (m)
I programma risolutore di tutti i problemi (m)

1369 *E* general problem solving (GPS) (EXPERT SYSTEMS)
G generelles Problemlösen (n)
F solution générale de problèmes (f)
S resolución general de problemas (f)
I risoluzione generale di problemi (f)

1370 *E* general-purpose heuristics (LOGIC)
G Mehrzweckheuristik (f)
F heuristique générale (f)
S heurística de uso general (f)
I euristica di uso generale (f)

1371 *E* general validity (LOGIC)
G Allgemeingültigkeit (f)
F validité générale (f)
S validez general (f)
I validità generale (f)

1372 *E* generate-and-test method (EXPERT SYSTEMS)
= generate-and-test strategy
G Methode des Generierens und Testens (f); Methode Erzeuge und Prüfe (f)
F méthode de production et de vérification (f)
S método de generar y comprobar (f)
I metodo generate-and-test (m); metodo generare e provare (m)

1373 *E* generate-and-test strategy
→ generate-and-test method

1374 *E* generated node (LOGIC)
G erzeugter Knoten (m); generierter Knoten (m)
F nœud généré (m)
S nodo generado (m)
I nodo generato (m)

1375 *E* generation (of a node) (LOGIC)
G Generierung (eines Knotens) (f)
F génération (d'un nœud) (f)
S generación (de un nodo) (f)
I generazione (di un nodo) (f)

1376 *E* generation of explanations (EXPERT SYSTEMS)
G Generierung von Erklärungen (f)
F génération des explications (f)
S generación de explicaciones (f)
I generazione di spiegazioni (f)

1377 *E* generation of plans
→ plan generation

1378 *E* generative grammar (LINGUISTICS)
G generative Grammatik (f)
F grammaire générative (f)
S gramática generativa (f)
I grammatica generativa (f)

1379 *E* generative transformational grammar (LINGUISTICS)
G generative Transformationsgrammatik (f)
F grammaire générative transformationnelle (f)
S gramática generativa transformacional (f)
I grammatica generativa trasformazionale (f)

1380 *E* generic concept (KNOWLEDGE)
G generischer Begriff (m); Gattungsbegriff (m)
F concept générique (m)
S concepto genérico (m)
I concetto generico (m)

1381 *E* generic task (EXPERT SYSTEMS)
G generische Aufgabe (f)
F tâche générique (f)
S tarea genérica (f)
I task generico (m)

1382 *E* genetic graph (LOGIC)
G genetischer Graph (m)
F graphe génétique (m)
S grafo genético (m)
I grafo genetico (m)

1383 *E* genetic net (NEURAL NETS)
G genetisches Netz (n)
F réseau génétique (m)
S red genética (f)
I rete genetica (f)

1384 *E* geometric pattern recognition (IMAGE PROCESSING)
G Erkennen geometrischer Muster (n)
F reconnaissance de figures géométriques (f)
S reconocimiento geométrico de formas (m)
I riconoscimento di pattern geometrici (m); riconoscimento di figure geometriche (m)

1385 *E* GHC
→ guarded Horn clause

1386 *E* giga logical inferences per second
→ GLIPS

1387 *E* GLIPS (EXPERT SYSTEMS)
= giga LIPS; giga logical inferences per second
→ logical inferences per second (LIPS)
G GLIPS (eine Milliarde logischer Inferenzen pro Sekunde)
F GLIPS
S GLIPS
I GLIPS

1388 *E* global database[1] (GDB) (KNOWLEDGE)
G globale Datenbank (f)
F base globale de données (f)
S base global de datos (f)
I base di dati globale (f)

1389 *E* global database[2]
→ production system

1390 *E* global feature (IMAGE PROCESSING)
G globales Merkmal (n)
F trait global (m)

S característica global (f)
I attributo globale (m)

1391 *E* global value (PROGRAMMING)
G globaler Wert (m)
F valeur globale (f)
S valor global (m)
I valore globale (m)

1392 *E* global variable (PROGRAMMING)
≠ local variable
G globale Variable (f)
F variable globale (f)
S variable global (f)
I variabile globale (f)

1393 *E* goal (EXPERT SYSTEMS)
= target; objective; aim
G Ziel (n); Zielsetzung (f)
F but (m)
S objetivo (m); meta (f)
I obiettivo (da raggiungere) (m); meta (f); scopo (m)

1394 *E* goal achievement (EXPERT SYSTEMS)
= reaching of the goal
G Erreichung des Ziels (f)
F atteinte de but (f); aboutissement (m)
S consecución de objetivos (f)
I raggiungimento di un obiettivo (m); conseguimento di un obiettivo (m)

1395 *E* goal ambivalence (EXPERT SYSTEMS)
G Zielambivalenz (f)
F ambivalence de buts (f); ambivalence de résolution (f)
S ambivalencia de objetivos (f)
I ambivalenza degli obiettivi (f)

1396 *E* goal-based (EXPERT SYSTEMS)
G zielbasierend
F basé sur buts
S basado en metas
I basato su obiettivi

1397 *E* goal condition
→ goal state

1398 *E* goal determination (EXPERT SYSTEMS)
G Bestimmung des Ziels (f)
F détermination du but (f)
S determinación del objetivo (f)
I determinazione dell'obiettivo (f)

1399 *E* goal-directed
→ goal-driven

1400 *E* goal-directed inference (LOGIC)
= goal-driven reasoning
↔ data-driven inference
G zielgesteuertes Schlüsseziehen (od. Schließen) (n); zielgerichtetes Inferieren (n)
F inférence dirigée par les buts (f); raisonnement guidé par les buts (m)
S inferencia guiada por objetivos (f)
I inferenza orientata agli obiettivi (f)

1401 *E* goal-directed input (EXPERT SYSTEMS)
G zielgesteuerte Eingabe (f)
F entrée dirigée par les buts (f); données guidées par les buts (f pl)
S entrada guiada por los objetivos (f)
I input orientato agli obiettivi (m)

1402 *E* goal-directed interpreter (PROGRAMMING)
G zielgesteuerter Interpreter (m)
F interpréteur guidé par les buts (m)
S intérprete guiado por objetivos (m)
I interprete orientato agli obiettivi (m)

1403 *E* goal directedness (EXPERT SYSTEMS)
G Zielorientierung (f)
F orientation buts (f)

S orientación a objetivos (f)
I orientamento agli obiettivi (m)

1404 E goal-directed search (EXPERT SYSTEMS)
= goal-driven search
G zielgesteuerte Suche (f)
F recherche guidée par les buts (f)
S búsqueda orientada a objetivos (f)
I ricerca orientata agli obiettivi (f)

1405 E goal-directed strategy (EXPERT SYSTEMS)
G zielgesteuerte Strategie (f)
F stratégie guidée par les buts (f)
S estrategia impulsada por objetivos (f)
I strategia orientata agli obiettivi (f)

1406 E goal-driven (EXPERT SYSTEMS)
= goal-directed; target-driven
≠ data-driven
G zielgesteuert; zielgerichtet
F guidé par les buts; dirigé par le cible
S dirigido a la meta; guiado por los objetivos; orientado al objetivo
I orientato a obiettivi; diretto a obiettivi

1407 E goal-driven reasoning
→ goal-directed inference

1408 E goal-driven search
→ goal-directed search

1409 E goal-driven system (EXPERT SYSTEMS)
G zielgesteuertes System (n)
F système guidé par les buts (m)
S sistema impulsado por objetivos (m)
I sistema guidato dagli obiettivi (m)

1410 E goal evaluation function (EXPERT SYSTEMS)
G Zielbewertungsfunktion (f)
F fonction d'évaluation des buts (f)
S función de valoración de objetivos (f)
I funzione di evaluazione degli obiettivi (f)

1411 E goal hierarchy (EXPERT SYSTEMS)
G Hierarchie der Ziele (f)
F hiérarchie des buts (f)
S jerarquía de metas (f)
I gerarchia di obiettivi (f)

1412 E goal node (LOGIC)
G Zielknoten (m)
F nœud-but (m)
S nodo de meta (m)
I nodo meta (m)

1413 E goal-oriented reasoning
→ focused reasoning

1414 E goal outline
→ goal structure

1415 E goal planning (EXPERT SYSTEMS)
G Zielplanung (f)
F planification de buts (f)
S planificación de objetivos (f)
I pianificazione degli obiettivi (f)

1416 E goal recognition (EXPERT SYSTEMS)
G Erkennung des Ziels (f); Zielerkennung (f)
F reconnaissance des buts (f)
S reconocimiento de objetivos (m)
I riconoscimento di obiettivi (m)

1417 E goal recognition function (EXPERT SYSTEMS)
G Zielerkennungsfunktion (f)
F fonction de reconnaissance des buts (f)
S función de reconocimiento de objetivos (f)
I funzione di riconoscimento degli obiettivi (f)

1418 *E* goal satisfaction (EXPERT SYSTEMS)
G Erfüllung der Zielvorstellung (f)
F satisfaction des buts (f)
S consecución de objetivos (f)
I raggiungimento degli obiettivi (m)

1419 *E* goal selection (EXPERT SYSTEMS)
G Wahl des Ziels (f); Zielauswahl (f)
F sélection de but (f)
S selección de metas (f)
I selezione di obiettivi (f)

1420 *E* goal state (EXPERT SYSTEMS)
= goal condition
G Zielzustand (m)
F état de but final (m)
S estado objetivo (m)
I stato obiettivo (m)

1421 *E* goal structure (EXPERT SYSTEMS)
= goal outline
G Zielstruktur (f)
F structure de buts (f)
S estructura de objetivos (f)
I struttura degli obiettivi (f)

1422 *E* goal subsumption (EXPERT SYSTEMS)
G Zielsubsumption (f)
F buts subsumés (m pl)
S objetivos presuntos (m pl)
I obiettivi assunti (m pl)

1423 *E* goal tree (EXPERT SYSTEMS)
G Zielbaum (m)
F arbre des buts (m)
S árbol de objetivos (m)
I albero degli obiettivi (m)

1424 *E* GPS
→ General Problem Solver; general problem solving

1425 *E* GPSG
→ generalized phrase structure grammar

1426 *E* gradient (LOGIC)
G Gradient (m)
F gradient (m)
S gradiente (m)
I gradiente (m)

1427 *E* gradient search (method) (EXPERT SYSTEMS)
G Gradientensuche (f); Suche nach dem Gradientenverfahren (f)
F méthode de recherche du gradient (f)
S método gradient search (m)
I metodo gradient search (m)

1428 *E* grammar analyser (NLP)
G Grammatikanalyseprogramm (n)
F analyseur de grammaire (m)
S analizador gramatical (m)
I analizzatore di grammatica (m)

1429 *E* grammar analysis (NLP)
G Grammatikanalyse (f)
F analyse grammaticale (f)
S análisis gramatical (m)
I analisi grammaticale (f); analisi di grammatica (f)

1430 *E* grammar-oriented (NLP)
G grammatikorientiert
F orienté grammaire
S orientado a la gramática
I orientato alla grammatica

1431 *E* grammar rule
→ grammatical rule

1432 *E* grammatical inference (LOGIC)
G grammatikalischer Schluß (m)
F inférence grammaticale (f)
S inferencia gramatical (f)
I inferenza grammaticale (f)

1433 *E* grammatical rule (LINGUISTICS)

= grammar rule
G Grammatikregel (f)
F règle grammaticale (f)
S regla de la gramática (f)
I regola grammaticale (f)

1434 *E* grammatical structure (NLP)
G grammatikalische Struktur (f)
F structure grammaticale (f)
S estructura gramatical (f)
I struttura grammaticale (f)

1435 *E* grandfather (*of a node*) (LOGIC)
= grandparent
G Großvater (m)
F grand-père (m)
S abuelo (m)
I nonno (m)

1436 *E* grandparent
→ grandfather

1437 *E* granularity (*of information etc.*) (KNOWLEDGE)
G Granularität (f); Feinheit (f); Detaillierung (f); Atomisierung (f)
F granularité (f)
S granularidad (f)
I granularità (f)

1438 *E* graph (LOGIC)
G Graph (m)
F graphe (m)
S grafo (m)
I grafo (m)

1439 *E* graph grammar (NLP)
G Graphgrammatik (f)
F grammaire de graphes (f)
S gramática de grafos (f)
I grammatica a grafi (f)

1440 *E* graph representation
G Graphendarstellung (f)
F représentation sous forme de graphe (f)
S representación por grafos (f)
I rappresentazione mediante grafi (f)

1441 *E* graph search (EXPERT SYSTEMS)
G Graphensuche (f); Graphensuchverfahren (n)
F recherche par graphes (f)
S búsqueda en grafos (f)
I ricerca tramite grafi (f)

1442 *E* graph theory
G Graphentheorie (f)
F théorie des graphes (f)
S teoría de grafos (f)
I teoria dei grafi (f)

1443 *E* graph transformation (PROGRAMMING)
G Graphtransformation (f)
F transformation de graphes (f)
S transformación de grafos (f)
I trasformazione di grafi (f)

1444 *E* graph traversal
→ tree traversal

1445 *E* grey scale modification (IMAGE PROCESSING)
G Modifizierung der Grauskala (f)
F modification de l'échelle des gris (f)
S modificación de escala de gris (f)
I modificazione della scala di grigi (f)

1446 *E* group theory
G Gruppentheorie (f)
F théorie des groupes (f)
S teoría de grupos (f)
I teoria dei gruppi (f)

1447 *E* GTN
→ generalized transition network

1448 *E* guarded clause (LOGIC)
G markierte Klausel (f)
F clause marquée (f)
S cláusula marcada (f)

I clausola che contiene una condizione di guardia (f)

1449 *E* guarded Horn clause (GHC) (PROGRAMMING)
G markierte Horn-Klausel (f)
F clause de Horn marquée (f)
S cláusula de Horn marcada (f)
I clausola GHC (clausola Horn con condizione di guardia) (f)

1450 *E* guided search
→ ordered search

H

1451 *E* half-synthetic voice (SYNTHESIS)
G halbsynthetische Stimme (f)
F voix semi-synthétique (f)
S voz semisintética (f)
I voce semi-sintetica (f)

1452 *E* half truth (LOGIC)
G Halbwahrheit (f)
F demi-vérité (f)
S media verdad (f)
I mezza verità (f)

1453 *E* HAMT
→ human-assisted machine translation

1454 *E* handwriting recognition (IMAGE PROCESSING)
G Handschrifterkennung (f)
F reconnaissance de l'écriture manuscrite (f)
S reconocimiento de caracteres escritos a mano (m)
I riconoscimento della scrittura a mano (m)

1455 *E* handwritten words recognition (IMAGE PROCESSING)
G Erkennung handschriftlicher Wörter (f)
F reconnaissance de mots manuscrits (f)
S reconocimiento de palabras escritas a mano (m)
I riconoscimento di parole scritte a mano (m)

1456 *E* has-a-part-of relation
→ has-a relation

1457 *E* has-a relation (KNOWLEDGE)
= has-a-part-of relation
≠ is-a relation
G Aggregationsbeziehung (f); Hat-Beziehung (f)
F relation 'possède' (f)
S relación tiene-un (f); enlace tiene-un (m)
I relazione ha-un (f)

1458 *E* hazard analysis
→ risk assessment

1459 *E* head (*of a clause, e.g. in PROLOG*) (PROGRAMMING)
G Kopf (m)
F tête (f)
S cabeza (f)
I testa (f)

1460 *E* head concept (KNOWLEDGE)
G Oberbegriff (m); übergeordneter Begriff (m)
F concept père (m)
S concepto principal (m)
I concetto principale (m)

1461 *E* Hearsay architecture (THEORY)
G Hearsay-Architektur (f)
F architecture Hearsay (f)
S arquitectura Hearsay (f)
I architettura Hearsay (f)

1462 *E* Herbrand universe (LOGIC)
G Herbrand-Universum (n); Herbrandsches Universum (n)
F univers de Herbrand (m)
S universo de Herbrand (m)
I universo di Herbrand (m)

1463 *E* hermeneutic (*adjective*) (NLP)
G hermeneutisch

F herméneutique
S hermenéutico
I ermeneutico

1464 *E* hermeneutics (*philosophy of text understanding*) (NLP)
G Hermeneutik (f)
F herméneutique (f)
S hermenéutica (f)
I ermeneutica (f)

1465 *E* heterarchy
G Heterarchie (f)
F hétérarchie (f)
S heterarquía (f)
I eterarchia (f)

1466 *E* heuristic[1] (*adjective*) (LOGIC)
≠ epistemic
G heuristisch
F heuristique
S heurístico
I euristico

1467 *E* heuristic[2] (*noun*)
→ heuristic rule

1468 *E* heuristic evaluation (GAMES)
G heuristische Evaluierung (f)
F évaluation heuristique (f)
S evaluación heurística (f)
I valutazione euristica (f)

1469 *E* heuristic information (LOGIC)
G heuristische Information (f)
F information heuristique (f)
S información heurística (f)
I informazione euristica (f)

1470 *E* heuristic knowledge
G heuristisches Wissen (n)
F connaissance heuristique (f)
S conocimiento heurístico (m)
I conoscenza euristica (f)

1471 *E* heuristic method (LOGIC)
G heuristisches Verfahren (n); heuristische Vorgehensweise (f)
F méthode heuristique (f)
S método heurístico (m)
I metodo euristico (m)

1472 *E* heuristic model (LOGIC)
≠ causal model
G heuristisches Modell (n)
F modèle heuristique (m)
S modelo heurístico (m)
I modello euristico (m)

1473 *E* heuristic problem solving (EXPERT SYSTEMS)
G heuristische Problemlösung (f)
F résolution heuristique de problèmes (f)
S resolución heurística de problemas (f)
I risoluzione euristica di problemi (f)

1474 *E* heuristic programming (HP)
≠ algorithmic programming
G heuristische Programmierung (f)
F programmation heuristique (f)
S programación heurística (f)
I programmazione euristica (f)

1475 *E* heuristic reasoning (LOGIC)
G heuristisches Inferieren (n)
F raisonnement heuristique (m)
S razonamiento heurístico (m)
I ragionamento euristico (m)

1476 *E* heuristic rule (EXPERT SYSTEMS)
= heuristic
G heuristische Regel (f)
F règle heuristique (f)
S regla heurística (f)
I regola euristica (f)

1477 *E* heuristics (LOGIC)
G Heuristik (f)
F heuristique (f)
S heurística (f)
I euristica (f)

1478 *E* heuristic search (LOGIC)

F recherche heuristique (f)
S búsqueda heurística (f)
I ricerca euristica (f)

1479 *E* hidden layer (NEURAL NETS)
G verborgene Schicht (f)
F couche cachée (f)
S capa oculta (f)
I strato nascosto (m)

1480 *E* hidden Markov model (HMM) (RECOGNITION)
G Hidden-Markoff-Modell (HMM) (n); verstecktes Markoffmodell (n)
F modèle de Markov caché (m); modèle HMM (m)
S modelo de Markov oculto (m)
I modello di Markov nascosto (m)

1481 *E* hidden unit (*in a neural network*)
G verdeckte Zelle (f)
F cellule cachée (f)
S objeto oculto (m)
I cellula nascosta (f)

1482 *E* hierarchical planner (EXPERT SYSTEMS)
G hierarchische Planungskomponente (f)
F planificateur hiérarchique (m)
S planificador jerárquico (m)
I pianificatore gerarchico (m)

1483 *E* hierarchical programming
→ top-down programming

1484 *E* hierarchization
G Hierarchisierung (f)
F hiérarchisation (f)
S jerarquización (f)
I gerarchizzazzione (f)

1485 *E* hierarchize
G hierarchisieren
F hiérarchiser
S jerarquizar
I gerarchizzare

1486 *E* hierarchy (KNOWLEDGE)
G Hierarchie (f)
F hiérarchie (f)
S jerarquía (f)
I gerarchia (f)

1487 *E* hierarchy level (KNOWLEDGE)
G Hierarchieebene (f)
F niveau d'hiérarchie (m)
S nivel de jerarquía (m)
I livello gerarchico (m)

1488 *E* higher-level class (KNOWLEDGE)
G Oberklasse (f)
F classe supérieure (f)
S clase de mayor nivel (f); clase de nivel superior (f)
I classe di un livello più alto (f)

1489 *E* higher-level concept
→ parent concept

1490 *E* higher-level frame
→ parent frame

1491 *E* higher-level knowledge structure
G höhere Wissensstruktur (f)
F structure évoluée des connaissances (f)
S estructura de conocimientos de alto nivel (f)
I struttura della conoscenza di un livello più alto (f)

1492 *E* high-level instructions (PROGRAMMING)
G höhere Instruktionen (f pl)
F instructions évoluées (f pl)
S instrucciones de alto nivel (f pl)
I istruzioni di alto livello (f pl)

1493 *E* high-level language (HLL) (PROGRAMMING)
= high order language; advanced language
G höhere Programmiersprache (f)

F langage évolué (m); langage de haut niveau (m)
S lenguaje de alto nivel (LAN) (m)
I linguaggio avanzato (di programmazione) (m)

1494 *E* high-level quantifier (LOGIC)
= superlogical quantifier
G Quantor höherer Ebene (m)
F quantificateur de haut niveau (m)
S cuantificador de alto nivel (m)
I quantificatore di alto livello (m)

1495 *E* high-level strategy (EXPERT SYSTEMS)
G höhere Strategie (f)
F stratégie de haut niveau (f)
S estrategia de alto nivel (f)
I strategia di alto livello (f)

1496 *E* high-level vision (IMAGE PROCESSING)
G höhere Bilderkennung (f)
F vision de haut-niveau (f)
S visión de alto nivel (f)
I visione di alto livello (f)

1497 *E* high order language
→ high-level language

1498 *E* high probability
G hohe Wahrscheinlichkeit (f)
F haute probabilité (f)
S alta probabilidad (f)
I alta probabilità (f)

1499 *E* hill climbing (EXPERT SYSTEMS)
G Bergsteigeverfahren (n); Hill Climbing (n)
F escalade (f)
S método de hill-climbing (m); procedimiento de escalada (m)
I hill-climbing (m)

1500 *E* hill-climbing search (EXPERT SYSTEMS)
G Suche nach dem Bergsteigeverfahren (f)
F recherche selon la stratégie escalade (f)
S búsqueda trepando a la cima (f)
I ricerca tipo hill-climbing (f)

1501 *E* HIP
→ human information processing

1502 *E* histogram flattening (IMAGE PROCESSING)
G Histogrammabflachung (f)
F lissage d'histogramme (m)
S alisamiento de histograma (m)
I smussamento di istogrammi (m)

1503 *E* history (*of a dialogue etc.*) (RECOGNITION)
G Historie (f)
F historique (du dialogue) (m)
S historia (f)
I storia (f)

1504 *E* history tree (KNOWLEDGE)
G Historienbaum (m)
F arbre d'histoires (m)
S árbol de historias (m)
I albero di storie (m)

1505 *E* HLL
→ high-level language

1506 *E* HMM
→ hidden Markov model

1507 *E* Hopfield net (NEURAL NETS)
G Hopfield-Netz (n)
F réseau de Hopfield (m)
S red de Hopfield (f)
I rete di Hopfield (f)

1508 *E* Horn clause (LOGIC)
G Horn-Klausel (f)
F clause de Horn (f)
S cláusula de Horn (f)
I formula tipo Horn clause (f); clausola di tipo Horn (o alla Horn) (f); Horn clause (f)

1509 *E* Horn clause logic
→ Horn logic

1510 *E* Horn logic
= Horn clause logic
G Horn-Logik (f)
F logique de Horn (f)
S lógica de Horn (f)
I logica di Horn (f)

1511 *E* household robot
→ domestic robot

1512 *E* how-explanation (EXPERT SYSTEMS)
G Wie-Erklärung (f)
F explication 'comment' (f)
S explicación 'como' (f)
I spiegazione 'come' (f)

1513 *E* HP
→ heuristic programming

1514 *E* HT
= hypothesis and test

1515 *E* human-assisted machine translation (HAMT)
G humanunterstützte maschinelle Übersetzung (f)
F traduction automatique assistée par l'homme (f)
S traducción automática asistida por el hombre (f)
I traduzione automatica con assistenza umana (f)

1516 *E* human brain
G menschliches Hirn (n); menschlicher Geist (m)
F cerveau humain (m)
S cerebro humano (m); mente humana (f)
I cervello umano (m); mente umana (f)

1517 *E* human expert
G Humanexperte (m)
F expert humain (m)
S experto humano (m)
I esperto umano (m)

1518 *E* human expertise
G menschliche Expertise (f)
F expertise humaine (f)
S experiencia humana (f); maestría humana (f)
I esperienza umana (f)

1519 *E* human information processing (HIP) (THEORY)
G Humaninformationsverarbeitung (f)
F traitement cognitif d'information (m)
S procesamiento humano de la información (m)
I elaborazione dell'informazione nel modo dell'uomo (f)

1520 *E* human intelligence
G menschliche Intelligenz (f)
F intelligence humaine (f)
S inteligencia humana (f)
I intelligenza umana (f)

1521 *E* human interface (EXPERT SYSTEMS)
G Humanschnittstelle (f)
F interface humaine (f)
S interfaz con el hombre (f)
I interfaccia con l'uomo (f)

1522 *E* human–machine communication
→ man–machine communication

1523 *E* human–machine interaction
→ man–machine interaction

1524 *E* human memory
G menschliches Gedächtnis (n)
F mémoire humaine (f)
S memoria humana (f)
I memoria umana (f)

1525 *E* human perception
G menschliche Wahrnehmung (f)
F perception humaine (f)
S percepción humana (f)
I percezione umana (f)

1526 *E* human problem solving
G humanes Problemlösen (n)
F résolution humaine de problèmes (f)
S resolución humana de problemas (f)
I risoluzione umana dei problemi (f)

1527 *E* human reasoning (*as opposed to machine reasoning*) (LOGIC)
G menschliches Schlüsseziehen (n); humanes Inferieren (n)
F raisonnement humain (m)
S razonamiento humano (m)
I ragionamento umano (m)

1528 *E* human speaker (RECOGNITION)
G humaner Sprecher (m)
F locuteur humain (m)
S locutor humano (m)
I locutore umano (m)

1529 *E* human speech recognition
G Erkennen menschlicher Sprache (n)
F reconnaissance du parler humain (f)
S reconocimiento del habla humana (m)
I riconoscimento del parlato umano (m)

1530 *E* human thinking
= thinking by humans
G menschliches Denken (n); humane Denkprozesse (m pl); Menschenverstand (m)
F pensée humaine (f)
S pensamiento humano (m)
I modo umano di pensare (m); attività mentale umana (f)

1531 *E* human vision
G menschliches Sehvermögen (n)
F vision humaine (f)
S visión humana (f)
I visione umana (f)

1532 *E* human visual system (IMAGE PROCESSING)
G menschliches Sehsystem (n)
F système visuel humain (m)
S sistema visual humano (SVH) (m)
I sistema visuale umano (m)

1533 *E* human vocal apparatus (RECOGNITION)
G menschlicher Sprechapparat (m)
F appareil vocal humain (m)
S aparato fonador humano (m)
I apparato vocale umano (m)

1534 *E* human voice
G menschliche Stimme (f)
F voix humaine (f)
S voz humana (f)
I voce umana (f)

1535 *E* hybrid control strategy (EXPERT SYSTEMS)
G hybride Kontrollstrategie (f); hybride Ablaufstrategie (f)
F stratégie hybride de contrôle (f)
S estrategia híbrida de control (f)
I strategia di controllo ibrida (f)

1536 *E* hybrid expert system (*that operates with several methods*)
G hybrides Expertensystem (n)
F système expert hybride (m)
S sistema experto híbrido (m)
I sistema esperto ibrido (m)

1537 *E* hybrid knowledge representation system (*e.g. rule and frame oriented*)
G hybrides Wissensrepräsentationssystem (n)

F système hybride de représentation des connaissances (m)
S sistema híbrido de representación de conocimientos (m)
I sistema ibrido di rappresentazione delle conoscenza (m)

1538 *E* hybrid model (EXPERT SYSTEMS)
G Hybridmodell (n)
F modèle hybride (m)
S modelo híbrido (m)
I modello ibrido (m)

1539 *E* hybrid tool (*for developing expert systems*) (PROGRAMMING)
G Hybridwerkzeug (n)
F outil hybride (m)
S herramienta híbrida (f)
I strumento ibrido (m)

1540 *E* hypercube (NEURAL NETS)
G Hyperkubus (m); Hyperwürfel (m)
F hypercube (m)
S hipercubo (m)
I ipercubo (m)

1541 *E* hyperedge (*of a hypergraph*) (LOGIC)
G Hyperkante (f)
F hyperarc (m)
S hiperarco (m)
I iperarco (m)

1542 *E* hypergraph (PROGRAMMING)
G Hypergraph (m)
F hypergraphe (m)
S hipergrafo (m)
I ipergrafo (m)

1543 *E* hyperplane (*in multidimensional models*) (NEURAL NETS)
G Hyperebene (f)
F hyperplan (m)
S hiperplano (m)
I iperpiano (m)

1544 *E* hypotheses list (EXPERT SYSTEMS)
G Hypothesenliste (f)
F liste des hypothèses (f)
S lista de hipótesis (f)
I elenco di ipotesi (possibili) (m)

1545 *E* hypotheses test (RECOGNITION)
= hypotheses verification
G Hypothesenprüfung (f); Hypothesenüberprüfung (f)
F vérification des hypothèses (f)
S test de hipótesis (m); prueba de hipótesis (f)
I test delle ipotesi (m); verifica delle ipotesi (f)

1546 *E* hypotheses verification
→ hypotheses test

1547 *E* hypothesis (*plural:* hypotheses) (LOGIC)
G Hypothese (f)
F hypothèse (f)
S hipótesis (f)
I ipotesi (f)

1548 *E* hypothesis candidate (RECOGNITION)
G Verdachtshypothese (f)
F candidat pour une hypothèse (m)
S candidato de hipótesis (m)
I candidato per una ipotesi (m)

1549 *E* hypothesis-driven (EXPERT SYSTEMS)
G hypothesengetrieben
F guidé par hypothèses
S guiado por hipótesis
I guidato da ipotesi

1550 *E* hypothesis evaluation (RECOGNITION)
G Hypothesenbewertung (f)
F évaluation des hypothèses (f)
S evaluación de hipótesis (f)
I valutazione delle ipotesi (f)

1551 *E* hypothesis generation (EXPERT SYSTEMS)
G Hypothesenbildung (f); Hypothesengenerierung (f); Hypothesenerzeugung (f)
F génération d'hypothèses (f)
S generación de hipótesis (f); planteamiento de una hipótesis (m)
I generazione delle ipotesi (f); attivazione delle ipotesi (f)

1552 *E* hypothesis generator (EXPERT SYSTEMS)
G Hypothesengenerator (m)
F générateur d'hypothèses (m)
S generador de hipótesis (m)
I generatore delle ipotesi (m)

1553 *E* hypothesis space (EXPERT SYSTEMS)
G Hypothesenraum (m)
F espace d'hypothèse (m)
S espacio de hipótesis (m)
I spazio di ipotesi (m)

1554 *E* hypothesize (LOGIC)
G eine Hypothese aufstellen
F émettre une hypothèse; hypothétiser
S proponer una hipótesis; hacer hipótesis
I ipotetizzare

1555 *E* hypothetical (LOGIC)
G hypothetisch
F hypothétique
S hipotético
I ipotetico

1556 *E* hypothetical reasoning (LOGIC)
G hypothetisches Inferieren (n)
F raisonnement hypothétique (m)
S razonamiento hipotético (m)
I ragionamento ipotetico (m)

1557 *E* hypothetical rule (LOGIC)
G hypothetische Regel (f)
F règle hypothétique (f)
S regla hipotética (f)
I regola ipotetica (f)

1558 *E* hypothetical world (EXPERT SYSTEMS)
G hypothetische Welt (f)
F monde hypothétique (m)
S mundo hipotético (m)
I mondo ipotetico (m)

I

1559 *E* ICAI
→ intelligent computer-aided instruction

1560 *E* IC grammar
→ phrase-structure grammar

1561 *E* if and only if (LOGIC)
= iff
G wenn und nur wenn
F si et seulement si
S si y solamente si
I se e solo se

1562 *E* 'if' clause (LOGIC)
↔ 'then' clause
G Wenn-Klausel (f)
F clause 'si' (f)
S cláusula si (f)
I clausola if (f); clausola se (f)

1563 *E* iff
→ if and only if

1564 *E* 'if' part
→ premise part

1565 *E* if … then (LOGIC)
G wenn … dann
F si … alors
S si … entonces
I se … allora

1566 *E* if–then clause (LOGIC)
G Wenn–Dann-Klausel (f)
F clause 'si–alors' (f)
S sentencia si–entonces (f)
I clausola if–then (f); clausola se–allora (f)

1567 *E* if–then reasoning (LOGIC)
G Wenn–Dann-Schluß (m)
F raisonnement si–alors (m); raisonnement déterministe (m)
S razonamiento si–entonces (m)
I ragionamento if–then (m)

1568 *E* if–then rule (LOGIC)
= production rule; condition–action rule
G Wenn–Dann-Regel (f); Produktionsregel (mit einem Wenn–Dann-Teil) (f)
F règle si–alors (f); règle de production (f); règle conditionnelle (f)
S regla si–entonces (f); regla IF–THEN (f)
I regola if–then (f)

1569 *E* IJCAI
= International Joint Conference on Artificial Intelligence

1570 *E* IJCNN
= International Joint Conference on Neural Networks

1571 *E* IKBS
= intelligent knowledge-based system

1572 *E* image analysis
= picture analysis
G Bildanalyse (f)
F analyse d'images (f)
S análisis de imágenes (m)
I analisi dell'immagine (f)

1573 *E* image comprehension
→ image understanding

1574 *E* image compression
G Bildkompression (f)
F compression de l'image (f)
S compresión de imagen (f)
I compressione dell'immagine (f)

1575 *E* image database
G Bilddatenbank (f)
F base de données d'images (f)
S base de datos de imágenes (f)
I base di dati contenente immagini (f)

1576 *E* image feature
= picture feature
G Bildmerkmal (n)
F caractéristique d'image (f)
S característica de imagen (f)
I caratteristica dell'immagine (f)

1577 *E* image interpretation
G Bildinterpretation (f)
F interprétation d'images (f)
S interpretación de imágenes (f)
I interpretazione di immagini (f)

1578 *E* image interpreter
G Bildinterpreter (m)
F interpréteur d'images (m)
S intérprete de imágenes (m)
I interprete dell'immagine (m)

1579 *E* image perception
G Bildperzeption (f); Bildwahrnehmung (f)
F perception de l'image (f)
S percepción de imagen (f)
I percezione dell'immagine (f)

1580 *E* image processing
= picture processing
G Bildverarbeitung (f)
F traitement d'images (m)
S procesamiento de imágenes (m); tratamiento de imágenes (m)
I elaborazione dell'immagine (f)

1581 *E* image processing system
→ image processor

1582 *E* image processor
= image processing system
G Bildverarbeitungssystem (n)
F système de traitement d'images (m); processeur d'images (m)
S sistema de procesamiento de imágenes (m)
I sistema di elaborazione dell'immagine (m)

1583 *E* image recognition
G Bilderkennen (n)
F reconnaissance d'images (f)
S reconocimiento de imágenes (m)
I riconoscimento delle immagini (m)

1584 *E* image recognition and understanding
G Bilderkennen und -verstehen (n)
F reconnaissance et compréhension d'images (f)
S reconocimiento (m) y comprensión (f) de imágenes (m)
I riconoscimento (m) e comprensione (f) di immagini (m)

1585 *E* image recognition system
G Bilderkennungssystem (n)
F système de reconnaissance d'images (m)
S sistema de reconocimiento de imágenes (m)
I sistema di riconoscimento di immagini (m)

1586 *E* image reconstruction
G Bildrekonstruktion (f)
F reconstruction d'image (f)
S reconstrucción de imagen (f)
I ricostruzione dell'immagine (f)

1587 *E* image retrieval
G Bildretrieval (n)
F recherche d'images (f)

S recuperación de imágenes (f)
I ritrovamento di immagini (m)

1588 *E* image segmentation
G Bildsegmentierung (f)
F segmentation d'image (f)
S segmentación de imagen (f)
I segmentazione dell'immagine (f)

1589 *E* image synthesis
G Bildsynthese (f)
F synthèse d'image (f)
S síntesis de imágenes (f)
I sintesi di immagini (f)

1590 *E* image understanding (IU) (*higher level than image recognition*)
= image comprehension
G Bildverstehen (n); Bildverständnis (n)
F compréhension d'images (f)
S comprensión de imágenes (f)
I comprensione di immagini (f)

1591 *E* image-understanding machine
G bildverstehende Maschine (f)
F machine de compréhension d'images (f)
S máquina de comprensión de imágenes (f)
I macchina di comprensione delle immagini (f)

1592 *E* image-understanding system (IUS)
G bildverstehendes System (n)
F système de compréhension d'images (m)
S sistema de comprensión de imágenes (m)
I sistema di comprensione di immagini (m)

1593 *E* IMM
→ inverted Markov model

1594 *E* immediate constituent grammar
→ phrase-structure grammar

1595 *E* immediate evaluation
→ eager evaluation

1596 *E* imperative language (PROGRAMMING)
G imperative Programmiersprache (f)
F langage impératif (m)
S lenguaje imperativo (m)
I linguaggio imperativo (m)

1597 *E* imperative programming
G imperatives Programmieren (n)
F programmation impérative (f)
S programación imperativa (f)
I programmazione imperativa (f)

1598 *E* imperfect knowledge
G unvollkommenes Wissen (n)
F connaissances imparfaites (f pl)
S conocimiento imperfecto (m)
I conoscenza imperfetta (f)

1599 *E* implementation (*of a system etc.*)
G Implementierung (f)
F implémentation (f)
S implementación (f)
I implementazione (f)

1600 *E* implementation environment (PROGRAMMING)
G Implementierungsumgebung (f); Einsatzumgebung (f)
F environnement d'implémentation (m)
S entorno de implementación (m)
I ambiente di implementazione (m)

1601 *E* implementation language (PROGRAMMING)
G Implementierungssprache (f)
F langage d'implémentation (m)
S lenguaje de implementación (m)
I linguaggio di implementazione (m)

1602 *E* implication (*symbol* :-) (LOGIC)
= entailment
G Implikation (f); (logische) Folge (f)
F implication (f)
S implicación (f)
I implicazione (f)

1603 *E* implicational expert system
G Implikationssystem (n)
F système expert basé sur implications (m)
S sistema experto basado en implicaciones (m)
I sistema esperto implicazionale (m)

1604 *E* implicational rule (*of the type: condition–action*) (KNOWLEDGE)
G Implikationsregel (f)
F règle d'implication (f)
S regla de implicación (f)
I regola di implicazione (f)

1605 *E* implicit graph (LOGIC)
G impliziter Graph (m)
F graphe implicite (m)
S grafo implícito (m)
I grafo implicito (m)

1606 *E* implicit knowledge
= tacit knowledge
G implizites Wissen (n)
F connaissance implicite (f)
S conocimiento implícito (m)
I conoscenza implicita (f)

1607 *E* improbable hypothesis (LOGIC)
G unwahrscheinliche Hypothese (f)
F hypothèse improbable (f)
S hipótesis improbable (f)
I ipotesi improbabile (f)

1608 *E* IMS
→ information management system

1609 *E* inactive state (EXPERT SYSTEMS)
G inaktiver Zustand (m); Zustand ohne Aktivität (m)
F état inactif (m)
S estado inactivo (m)
I stato inattivo (m)

1610 *E* incompatibility principle
G Inkompatibilitätsprinzip (n)
F principe d'incompatibilité (m)
S principio de incompatibilidad (m)
I principio di incompatibilità (m)

1611 *E* incomplete knowledge
G unvollständiges Wissen (n)
F connaissance incomplète (f)
S conocimiento incompleto (m)
I conoscenza incompleta (f)

1612 *E* incompleteness hypothesis (LOGIC)
G Hypothese der Unvollständigkeit (f)
F hypothèse d'incomplétude (f)
S hipótesis de incomplenitud (f)
I ipotesi dell'incompletezza (f)

1613 *E* incomplete search (EXPERT SYSTEMS)
G unvollständige Suche (f)
F recherche non complète (f)
S búsqueda no completa (f)
I ricerca non completa (f)

1614 *E* inconsistency (LOGIC)
G Inkonsistenz (f)
F inconsistance (f); incohérence (f)
S inconsistencia (f)
I incoerenza (f)

1615 *E* inconsistency-tolerant system (EXPERT SYSTEMS)
G inkonsistenztolerantes System (n)
F système tolérant les incohérences (m)
S sistema tolerante las inconsistencias (m)
I sistema tollerante incoerenze (m)

1616 *E* inconsistent (LOGIC)
G inkonsistent
F inconsistant; incohérent
S inconsistente
I incoerente

1617 *E* incremental learning
G stufenweises Lernen (n)
F apprentissage incrémental (m)
S aprendizaje incremental (m)
I apprendimento passo a passo (m)

1618 *E* in-depth understanding (*of a text etc.*) (NLP)
G eingehendes Verstehen (n)
F compréhension effective (f)
S comprensión profunda (f)
I comprensione profonda (f)

1619 *E* indeterminate (*adjective*) (LOGIC)
G indeterminiert; unbestimmt
F indéterminé
S indeterminado
I indeterminato

1620 *E* indirect graph
→ non-directed graph

1621 *E* induced knowledge
G induziertes Wissen (n); abgeleitetes Wissen (n)
F connaissance induite (f); connaissances dérivées (f pl)
S conocimiento inducido (m)
I conoscenza indotta (f)

1622 *E* induction (LOGIC)
↔ abduction
G Induktion (f)
F induction (f)
S inducción (f)
I induzione (f)

1623 *E* induction level (LOGIC)
G Induktionsgrad (m)
F niveau d'induction (m)
S nivel de inducción (m)
I livello di induzione (m)

1624 *E* induction method (LOGIC)
G Induktionsmethode (f)
F méthode d'induction (f)
S método de inducción (m)
I metodo di induzione (m); metodo induzionista (m)

1625 *E* induction system (KNOWLEDGE)
= example-driven system
G induktives System (n); beispielgesteuertes System (n)
F système d'induction (m)
S sistema de inducción (m); sistema guiado por ejemplos (m)
I sistema a induzione (m)

1626 *E* inductive (KNOWLEDGE)
G induktiv
F inductif
S inductivo
I induttivo

1627 *E* inductive inference (LOGIC)
G induktiver Schluß (m)
F inférence inductive (f)
S inferencia inductiva (f)
I inferenza induttiva (f)

1628 *E* inductive learning
= learning by induction
G induktives Lernen (n); Induktion (f)
F apprentissage inductif (m)
S aprendizaje inductivo (m); aprendizaje por inducción (m)
I apprendimento induttivo (m); apprendimento per induzione (m)

1629 *E* inductive logic
G induktive Logik (f)
F logique inductive (f)
S lógica inductiva (f)
I logica induttiva (f)

1630 *E* inductive machine (*that is capable of learning*) (THEORY)
G induktive Maschine (f)
F machine inductive (f)

S máquina inductiva (f)
I macchina induttiva (f)

1631 E inductive reasoning (LOGIC)
= reasoning by induction
G induktives Schließen (n)
F raisonnement inductif (m)
S razonamiento inductivo (m)
I ragionamento induttivo (m)

1632 E industrial expert system
G industrielles Expertensystem (n)
F système expert industriel (m)
S sistema experto industrial (m)
I sistema esperto industriale (m)

1633 E industrial robot (IR)
G Industrieroboter (m)
F robot industriel (m)
S robot industrial (m)
I robot industriale (m)

1634 E inequality relation (LOGIC)
G Ungleichheitsrelation (f)
F relation d'inégalité (f)
S relación de no igualdad (f); relación de desigualdad (f)
I relazione di non uguaglianza (f); relazione di ineguaglianza (f)

1635 E inexact (*knowledge etc.*)
= uncertain
G ungenau; inexakt; unsicher
F inexact
S inexacto
I inesatto

1636 E inexact inference (LOGIC)
G unsicherer Schluß (m)
F inférence inexacte (f)
S inferencia inexacta (f)
I inferenza inesatta (f)

1637 E inexact logic
≠ exact logic
G ungenaue Logik (f)
F logique inexacte (f)
S lógica inexacta (f)
I logica inesatta (f)

1638 E inexactness
G Ungenauigkeit (f)
F inexactitude (f)
S inexactitud (f)
I inesattezza (f)

1639 E inexact reasoning (LOGIC)
G ungenaues Inferieren (n); nicht-exaktes Schließen (n)
F raisonnement inexact (m); raisonnement imprécis (m)
S razonamiento inexacto (m)
I ragionamento inesatto (m)

1640 E infer (LOGIC)
= make inferences; reason; draw conclusions
G inferieren; schlußfolgern; schließen; Schlüsse ziehen
F tirer des inférences; inférer
S realizar inferencias; inferir; hacer inferencias; extraer conclusiones
I inferire; trarre conclusioni

1641 E inference[1] (LOGIC)
G Inferenz (f); Schlußfolgerung (f); Schluß (m); Rückschluß (m)
F inférence (f)
S inferencia (f)
I inferenza (f)

1642 E inference[2]
→ reasoning

1643 E inference algorithm
→ reasoning algorithm

1644 E inference by analogy (LOGIC)
G Analogieschluß (m)
F inférence par analogie (f)
S inferencia por analogía (f)
I inferenza per analogia (f)

1645 E inference chain (LOGIC)
= line of reasoning

G Inferenzkette (f); Schlußkette (f); Ableitungskette (f); Kette von Schlüssen (f)
F chaîne d'inférence (f); chaîne de raisonnement (f); ligne de raisonnement (f)
S cadena de inferencia (f); línea de razonamiento (f)
I catena di inferenza (f); linea di ragionamento (f); filone di ragionamento (m)

1646 *E* inference engine (*of an expert system*)
= inference machine
G Inferenzmaschine (f); Abarbeitungskomponente (f); Inferenzkomponente (f); Inference Engine (f)
F moteur d'inférence (MI) (m); machine d'inférence (f); machine à inférence (f)
S motor de inferencia(s) (m); máquina de inferencia(s) (f)
I motore di inferenza (m); motore inferenziale (m)

1647 *E* inference function (EXPERT SYSTEMS)
G Inferenzfunktion (f)
F fonction d'inférence (f)
S función de inferencia (f)
I funzione di inferenza (f)

1648 *E* inference graph (LOGIC)
G Inferenzgraph (m)
F graphe d'inférence (m)
S grafo de inferencia (m)
I grafo di inferenza (m)

1649 *E* inference machine
→ inference engine

1650 *E* inference mechanism (*of an expert system*)
= reasoning component
G Inferenzmechanismus (m); Auswertemechanismus (m); Schlußfolg erungsmechanismus (m); Konklusionsteil (eines Systems) (m)
F mécanisme inférentiel (m)
S mecanismo de inferencia (m)
I meccanismo di inferenza (m)

1651 *E* inference method (LOGIC)
G Inferenzmethode (f)
F méthode inférentielle (f)
S método de inferencia (m)
I metodo di inferenza (m)

1652 *E* inference mode (LOGIC)
G Inferenzmodus (m)
F mode inférentiel (m); mode inférence (m)
S modo inferencial (m)
I modo inferenziale (m)

1653 *E* inference net (EXPERT SYSTEMS)
G Inferenznetz (n)
F réseau d'inférences (m)
S red inferencial (f); red de inferencias (f)
I rete inferenziale (f)

1654 *E* inference procedure (EXPERT SYSTEMS)
G Inferenzprozedur (f)
F procédure d'inférences (f)
S procedimiento de inferencia (m); procedimiento inferencial (m)
I procedura di inferenza (f)

1655 *E* inference process (LOGIC)
= inferencing; reasoning process
G Inferenzprozeß (m); Inferenzbildung (f) (Ziehen von Schlüssen)
F processus d'inférence (m); procédé de raisonnement (m)
S proceso de inferencia (m); proceso inferencial (m); ejecución de inferencias (f); proceso de razonamiento (m)
I processo di inferenza (m); processo di ragionamento (m)

1656 *E* inferencer (EXPERT SYSTEMS)
G Inferenzprogramm (n); Schlußfolgerungsprogramm (n)
F raisonneur (f)
S programa de razonamiento (m)
I programma di ragionamento (m)

1657 *E* inference rule (EXPERT SYSTEMS)
= rule of inference
G Inferenzregel (f)
F règle d'inférence (f)
S regla de inferencia (f)
I regola di inferenza (f)

1658 *E* inference software (EXPERT SYSTEMS)
G Inferenzsoftware (f)
F logiciel d'inférence (m)
S software de inferencia (m)
I software di inferenza (m)

1659 *E* inference strategy
→ reasoning strategy

1660 *E* inference system (EXPERT SYSTEMS)
= inferencing system
G Inferenzsystem (n); Schlußfolgerungssystem (n)
F système d'inférence (m)
S sistema de inferencia (m)
I sistema di inferenza (m)

1661 *E* inference technique (EXPERT SYSTEMS)
= inferencing technique
G Inferenztechnik (f); Inferiertechnik (f)
F technique d'inférence (f)
S técnica de inferencia (f)
I tecnica di inferenza (f)

1662 *E* inference tree (LOGIC)
= proof tree
G Inferenzbaum (m)
F arbre des inférences (m)
S árbol de inferencias (m)
I albero delle inferenze (m)

1663 *E* inferencing
→ inference process

1664 *E* inferencing capacity (*of a system*) (EXPERT SYSTEMS)
G Inferierkapazität (f)
F capacité d'inférences (f)
S capacidad de inferencia (f)
I capacità di trarre conclusioni (f)

1665 *E* inferencing system
→ inference system

1666 *E* inferencing technique
→ inference technique

1667 *E* inferential (LOGIC)
G inferentiell; Inferenz...
F inférentiel
S inferencial
I inferenziale

1668 *E* inferential knowledge
G Inferenzwissen (n)
F connaissance inférentielle (f); savoir ratiocinatif (m)
S conocimiento inferencial (m)
I conoscenza inferenziale (m)

1669 *E* inferential reasoning (LOGIC)
G Schlußfolgern (n)
F raisonnement inférentiel (m)
S razonamiento con inferencias (m)
I ragionamento mediante inferenze (m)

1670 *E* infinite set (MATHS)
G unendliche Menge (f)
F ensemble infini (m)
S conjunto infinito (m)
I insieme infinito (m)

1671 *E* infix notation (PROGRAMMING)
G Infixschreibweise (f)
F notation infixe (f)
S notación infixa (f)
I notazione infissa (f)

1672 *E* inflection (*of a word*) (NLP)
G Flexion (f); Beugung (f)
F flexion (f)
S flexión (f)
I flessione (f)

1673 *E* informal reasoning (LOGIC)
G informales Schließen (n)
F raisonnement informel (m)
S razonamiento informal (m)
I ragionamento informale (m)

1674 *E* information management system (IMS) (PROGRAMMING)
G Informationsverwaltungssystem (n)
F système de gestion de l'information (m)
S sistema de gestión de la información (m)
I sistema di gestione dell'informazione (m)

1675 *E* inherit (KNOWLEDGE)
G vererben; erben
F hériter
S heredar
I ereditare

1676 *E* inheritable (KNOWLEDGE)
G vererbbar
F héritable
S heredable
I ereditabile

1677 *E* inheritance (KNOWLEDGE)
G Vererbung (f)
F héritage (m); transmission (de propriétés etc.) (f)
S herencia (f)
I ereditarietà (f)

1678 *E* inheritance edge
→ inheritance link

1679 *E* inheritance graph (KNOWLEDGE)
G Vererbungsgraph (m)
F graphe d'héritage (m)
S grafo de herencia (m)
I grafo di ereditarietà (m)

1680 *E* inheritance hierarchy (KNOWLEDGE)
G Vererbungshierarchie (f)
F hiérarchie d'héritage (f)
S jerarquía de herencias (f)
I gerarchia di ereditarietà (f)

1681 *E* inheritance link (KNOWLEDGE)
= inheritance edge
G Vererbungskante (f)
F lien d'héritage (m)
S enlace de herencia (m)
I arco di ereditarietà (m)

1682 *E* inheritance mechanism (EXPERT SYSTEMS)
G Vererbungsmechanismus (m)
F mécanisme d'héritage (m)
S mecanismo de herencia (m); funciones de herencia (f pl)
I meccanismo di eredatarietà (m)

1683 *E* inheritance network (KNOWLEDGE)
G Vererbungsnetz (n)
F réseau d'héritage (m)
S red de herencia (f)
I rete di ereditarietà (f)

1684 *E* inheritance of properties
→ property inheritance

1685 *E* inheritance relations (KNOWLEDGE)
G Vererbungsbeziehungen (f pl)
F relations d'héritage (f pl); liens d'héritage (m pl)
S relaciones hereditarias (f pl)
I relazione ereditarie (f pl)

1686 *E* inherited (*properties etc.*) (KNOWLEDGE)
G vererbt
F hérité
S heredado

I ereditato

1687 *E* initial facts (EXPERT SYSTEMS)
G Ausgangsfakten (n pl)
F faits initiaux (m pl)
S hechos de partida (m pl); hechos iniciales (m pl)
I fatti iniziali (m pl)

1688 *E* initial hypothesis
→ starting hypothesis

1689 *E* initial node
→ starting node

1690 *E* initial problem state (EXPERT SYSTEMS)
G Anfangsproblemzustand (m)
F état du problème initial (m)
S estado inicial de problema (m)
I stato iniziale del problema (m)

1691 *E* initial situation (EXPERT SYSTEMS)
G Ausgangssituation (f)
F situation initiale (f)
S situación inicial (f)
I situazione iniziale (f)

1692 *E* initial state (EXPERT SYSTEMS)
G Anfangszustand (m); Ausgangszustand (m)
F état initial (m)
S estado inicial (m); situación inicial (f)
I stato iniziale (m)

1693 *E* initial state node
→ starting node

1694 *E* initial version
→ prototype version

1695 *E* INKA
→ interactive knowledge acquisition

1696 *E* INNS
= International Neural Network Society

1697 *E* input clause (LOGIC)
G Eingangsklausel (f)
F clause d'entrée (f)
S cláusula de entrada (f)
I clausola di input (f); clausola di entrata (f)

1698 *E* input conditions (LOGIC)
G Eingangsbedingungen (f pl)
F conditions d'entrée (f pl)
S condiciones de entrada (f pl)
I condizione di input (f pl); condizione di entrata (f pl)

1699 *E* input node (NEURAL NETS)
G Eingangsknoten (m)
F nœud d'entrée (m)
S nodo de entrada (m)
I nodo di entrata (m)

1700 *E* input phrase analysis (NLP)
G Analyse des Eingabesatzes (f)
F analyse de phrase d'entrée (f)
S análisis de la frase de entrada (m)
I analisi delle frasi di input (f); analisi delle frasi di entrata (f)

1701 *E* input predicate (LOGIC)
≠ output predicate
G Eingabeprädikat (n)
F prédicat d'entrée (m)
S predicado de entrada (m)
I predicato di input (m); predicato di entrata (m)

1702 *E* input text (MT)
G Eingabetext (m)
F texte d'entrée (m)
S texto de entrada (m)
I testo di input (m); testo di entrata (m)

1703 *E* instance (KNOWLEDGE)
G Instanz (f) (konkretes Objekt); Ausprägung (f)
F instance (f)

S concreción (f); ejemplar (objeto con valores especificados) (m); instancia (f)
I istanza (f)

1704 *E* instances space (EXPERT SYSTEMS)
G Instanzenraum (m)
F espace des instances (m)
S espacio de instancias (m)
I spazio delle istanze (m)

1705 *E* instances tree (KNOWLEDGE)
G Instanzenbaum (m)
F arbre des instances (m)
S árbol de instancias (m)
I albero delle istanze (m)

1706 *E* instance variable (KNOWLEDGE)
G Instanzvariable (f)
F variable d'instance (f)
S variable de instancia (f)
I variabile di istanza (f)

1707 *E* instantiate (*provide with instances*) (KNOWLEDGE)
G instantiieren; konkretisieren
F instancier
S ejemplarizar
I istanziare

1708 *E* instantiated object (KNOWLEDGE)
G instantiiertes Objekt (n)
F objet instancié (m)
S objeto ejemplarizado (m)
I oggetto istanziato (m)

1709 *E* instantiated tree (LOGIC)
G instantiierter Baum (m)
F schéma instancié (m)
S árbol ejemplarizado (m)
I albero istanziato (m)

1710 *E* instantiating
→ instantiation

1711 *E* instantiation (*the process of producing instances*) (LOGIC)
= instantiating
G Instantiierung (f); Instanzi(i)erung (f); Instanzerzeugung (f)
F instanciation (f)
S instanciación (f); ejemplarización (f)
I istanziazione (f)

1712 *E* instructional software (LEARNING)
G Lernsoftware (f)
F logiciel d'enseignement (m)
S software para enseñanza (m)
I software per l'insegnamento (m)

1713 *E* integrated expert system
G integriertes Expertensystem (n)
F système expert intégré (m)
S sistema experto integrado (m)
I sistema esperto integrato (m)

1714 *E* integrity constraint (EXPERT SYSTEMS)
G Integritätsbedingung (f)
F contrainte d'intégrité (f)
S restricción de integridad (f)
I vincolo dell'integrità (m)

1715 *E* intelligence
G Intelligenz (f)
F intelligence (f)
S inteligencia (f)
I intelligenza (f)

1716 *E* intelligence level
= level of intelligence; degree of intelligence
G Intelligenzgrad (m)
F niveau d'intelligence (m)
S nivel de inteligencia (m)
I livello di intelligenza (m); grado di intelligenza (m)

1717 *E* intelligence quotient (IQ)
G Intelligenzquotient (IQ) (m)
F quotient d'intelligence (QI) (m)
S cociente de inteligencia (m)
I quoziente di intelligenza (m)

1718 *E* intelligent assistant (PROGRAMMING)
G intelligentes Assistenzprogramm (n)
F assistant intelligent (m)
S asistente inteligente (m)
I assistente intelligente (m)

1719 *E* intelligent computer-aided instruction (ICAI) (LEARNING)
G ICAI (computerunterstützte intelligente Lehrsysteme) (n pl)
F enseignement intelligemment assisté par ordinateur (EIAO) (m); enseignement assisté par systèmes intelligents (m)
S enseñanza asistida por ordenador inteligente (EAOI) (f); instrucción intelligente asistida por ordenador (f)
I insegnamento assistito da un elaboratore intelligente (m)

1720 *E* intelligent database (KNOWLEDGE)
G intelligente Datenbasis (f)
F base de données intelligente (f)
S base de datos inteligente (f)
I base di dati intelligente (f)

1721 *E* intelligent interface (EXPERT SYSTEMS)
G intelligente Schnittstelle (f)
F interface intelligente (f)
S interfaz inteligente (f)
I interfaccia intelligente (f)

1722 *E* intelligent machine
G intelligente Maschine (f)
F machine savante (f)
S máquina inteligente (f)
I macchina intelligente (f)

1723 *E* intelligent management system (EXPERT SYSTEMS)
G intelligentes Managementsystem (n)
F système de gestion intelligent (m)
S sistema de gestión inteligente (m)
I sistema di gestione intelligente (m)

1724 *E* intelligent man–machine interface
G intelligente Mensch–Maschine-Schnittstelle (f)
F interface homme–machine intelligente (f)
S interfaz inteligente hombre–máquina (f)
I interfaccia intelligente uomo–macchina (f)

1725 *E* intelligent robot
G intelligenter Roboter (m)
F robot intelligent (m)
S robot inteligente (m)
I robot intelligente (m)

1726 *E* intelligent software
G intelligente Software (f)
F logiciel intelligent (m)
S software inteligente (m)
I software intelligente (m)

1727 *E* intelligent system (EXPERT SYSTEMS)
G intelligentes System (n)
F système intelligent (m)
S sistema inteligente (m)
I sistema intelligente (m)

1728 *E* intelligent teaching system
→ intelligent tutoring system

1729 *E* intelligent tutoring system (ITS) (EXPERT SYSTEMS)
= intelligent teaching system; AI teaching system
G intelligentes Lernprogramm (n); KI-Lernprogramm (n)
F système d'enseignement intelligent (m); didacticiel intelligent (m); tuteur intelligent (m)

S programa didáctico inteligente (m); sistema de tutoría inteligente (m); tutor inteligente (m)
I programma di insegnamento intelligente (m); sistema tutore intelligente (m)

1730 *E* intelligent workstation (EXPERT SYSTEMS)
G intelligenter Arbeitsplatz (m)
F poste de travail intelligent (m); station (bureautique etc.) intelligente (f)
S estación de trabajo inteligente (f)
I stazione di lavoro intelligente (f)

1731 *E* intensifier (NEURAL NETS)
= reinforcement
G Verstärker (m)
F renforcement (m)
S intensificador (m)
I rinforzo (m)

1732 *E* intension (*of a concept etc.*) (LINGUISTICS)
≠ extension
G Intension (f)
F intension (f)
S intensión (f)
I intensione (f)

1733 *E* intensional logic
G intensionale Logik (f)
F logique intensionale (f)
S lógica intensional (f)
I logica intensionale (f)

1734 *E* intensional operator (LOGIC)
G intensionaler Operator (m)
F opérateur intensional (m)
S operador intensional (m)
I operatore intensionale (m)

1735 *E* intentions memory (EXPERT SYSTEMS)
G Intentionengedächtnis (n)
F mémoire des intentions (f)
S memoria de intenciones (f)
I memoria intenzionale (f)

1736 *E* interaction (PROGRAMMING)
G Interaktion (f)
F interaction (f)
S interacción (f)
I interazione (f)

1737 *E* interactive capacity (EXPERT SYSTEMS)
G Dialogfähigkeit (f)
F capacité interactive (f)
S capacidad interactiva (f)
I capacità interattiva (f)

1738 *E* interactive component (EXPERT SYSTEMS)
G Dialogkomponente (f)
F composante interactive (f)
S componente interactivo (m)
I componente interattiva (m)

1739 *E* interactive knowledge acquisition (INKA)
G interaktiver Wissenserwerb (m)
F acquisition interactive des connaissances (f)
S adquisición interactiva de conocimientos (f)
I acquisizione interattiva della conoscenza (f)

1740 *E* interactive learning
→ learning by interaction

1741 *E* interactive system (PROGRAMMING)
G interaktives System (n)
F système interactif (m)
S sistema interactivo (m)
I sistema interattivo (m)

1742 *E* interconnected
G miteinander verknüpft
F interconnecté
S interconectado
I interconnesso

1743 *E* interconnecting arc
→ branch

1744 *E* interconnection (NEURAL NETS)
G Verknüpfung (f)
F interconnexion (f)
S interconexión (f)
I interconnessione (f)

1745 *E* interconnection graph (LOGIC)
G Verknüpfungsgraph (m)
F graphe d'interconnexion (m)
S grafo de interconexión (m)
I grafo di interconnessione (m)

1746 *E* interconnections per second (IPS) (*a measure of performance*) (NEURAL NETS)
G Verknüpfungen pro Sekunde (f pl)
F interconnexions par seconde (f pl)
S interconexiones por segundo (f pl)
I interconnessioni al secondo (f pl)

1747 *E* interconnection weights (NEURAL NETS)
G Verknüpfungsgewichte (n pl)
F poids d'interconnexion (m pl)
S pesos de interconexión (m pl)
I pesi di interconnessione (m pl)

1748 *E* interface (*between systems*)
G Schnittstelle (f)
F interface (f)
S interfaz (f)
I interfaccia (f)

1749 *E* interior node (*with predecessors and successors*) (KNOWLEDGE)
G innerer Knoten (m)
F nœud intérieur (m)
S nodo interior (m)
I nodo interiore (m)

1750 *E* InterLISP (*one of many LISP versions*) (PROGRAMMING)
G InterLISP
F InterLISP
S InterLISP
I InterLISP

1751 *E* interlocutor (NLP)
G Dialogpartner (m)
F interlocuteur (m)
S interlocutor (m)
I interlocutore (m)

1752 *E* intermediate goal (EXPERT SYSTEMS)
G Zwischenziel (n)
F but intermédiaire (m)
S objetivo intermedio (m)
I obiettivo intermedio (m)

1753 *E* intermediate node (LOGIC)
G Zwischenknoten (m)
F nœud intermédiaire (m)
S nodo intermedio (m)
I nodo intermedio (m)

1754 *E* intermediate result
G Zwischenergebnis (n)
F résultat intermédiaire (m)
S resultado intermedio (m)
I risultato intermedio (m)

1755 *E* intermediate state
G Zwischenstadium (n)
F état intermédiaire (m)
S estado intermedio (m)
I stato intermedio (m)

1756 *E* internal representation (PROGRAMMING)
G interne Darstellung (f)
F représentation interne (f)
S representación interna (f)
I rappresentazione interna (f)

1757 *E* interpretation procedure (IMAGE PROCESSING)
G Interpretationsprozedur (f)
F procédure interprétative (f)
S procedimiento de interpretación (m)

I procedura di interpretazione (f)

1758 *E* interpretation system (EXPERT SYSTEMS)
G Interpretationssystem (n)
F système d'interprétation (m)
S sistema de interpretación (m)
I sistema di interpretazione (m)

1759 *E* interpreted language (PROGRAMMING)
G interpretierte Sprache (f)
F langage interprété (m)
S lenguaje interpretado (m)
I linguaggio interpretato (m)

1760 *E* interpreter
→ rule interpreter

1761 *E* intonation (RECOGNITION)
G Intonation (f)
F intonation (f)
S entonación (f)
I intonazione (f)

1762 *E* intrinsic characteristic (LOGIC)
G intrinsische Eigenschaft (f)
F propriété intrinsèque (f)
S carácter intrínsico (m)
I carattere intrinsico (m)

1763 *E* intrinsic image
G wahres Bild (n)
F image intrinsèque (f)
S imagen intrínseca (f)
I immagine intrisica (f)

1764 *E* intuitionistic logic
G intuitionistische Logik (f)
F logique intuitionniste (f)
S lógica intuicionista (f)
I logica intuizionistica (f)

1765 *E* inversion (*of a rule*) (EXPERT SYSTEMS)
G Umkehrung (f)
F inversion (f)
S inversión (f)
I inversione (f)

1766 *E* inverted Markov model (IMM) (RECOGNITION)
G invertiertes Markoffmodell (IMM) (n)
F modèle de Markov inversé (m)
S modelo de Markov invertido (m)
I modello di Markov invertito (m)

1767 *E* IPL-II (*one of the first AI languages*) (PROGRAMMING)
= Information Processing Language
G IPL-II
F IPL-II
S IPL-II
I IPL-II

1768 *E* IPS
→ interconnections per second

1769 *E* IQ
→ intelligence quotient

1770 *E* IR[1]
→ industrial robot

1771 *E* IR[2]
= information retrieval

1772 *E* irreversibility
G Nicht-Umkehrbarkeit (f)
F irréversibilité (f)
S no reversibilidad (f)
I irreversibilità (f)

1773 *E* irrevocable (EXPERT SYSTEMS)
G unwiderruflich; nicht widerrufbar
F irrévocable
S irrevocable
I irrevocabile

1774 *E* irrevocable control regime (EXPERT SYSTEMS)
G unwiderrufliche Steuerung (f)
F régime de contrôle irrévocable (m)

S estrategia de control irrevocable (f)
I strategia di controllo irrevocabile (f)

1775 *E* is-a hierarchy (KNOWLEDGE)
G 'Ist-ein'-Hierarchie (f)
F hiérarchie sorte-de (f)
S jerarquía es-un (f)
I gerarchia -un (f)

1776 *E* is-a-kind-of relation
→ is-a relation

1777 *E* is-a link (KNOWLEDGE)
G Zugehörigkeitsfunktion (f); 'Teilklasse von' (f)
F lien sorte-de (m)
S enlace es-un (m)
I funzione di appartenenza (f)

1778 *E* is-a-part-of relation
→ partitive relation

1779 *E* is-a relation (KNOWLEDGE)
= is-a-kind-of relation; AKO (a kind of) relation
≠ has-a relation
G Generalisierungsbeziehung (f); Ist-Ein-Beziehung (f); Zugehörigkeitsbeziehung (f)
F relation 'est-un(e)' (f)
S relación es-un (f)
I relazione -un (f); relazione di appartenenza (f)

1780 *E* island of reliability (NLP)
G Zuverlässigkeitsinsel (f)
F îlot de fiabilité (m); îlot le mieux reconnu (m)
S isla de fiabilidad (f); islote de fiabilidad (m)
I isola di affidabilità (f)

1781 *E* island-driven strategy (NLP)
= island strategy
G Island-Strategie (f)
F stratégie d'îlot (f)
S estrategia basada en islas (f)
I strategie delle isole (f)

1782 *E* island parsing (NLP)
G Insel-Parsing (n)
F analyse par îlots (f); parsing par îlots (m)
S parsing por islas (m)
I parsing mediante isole (m); analisi mediante isole (f)

1783 *E* island strategy
→ island-driven strategy

1784 *E* isolated characters (RECOGNITION)
G Einzelzeichen (n pl)
F caractères isolés (m pl)
S caracteres aislados (m pl)
I caratteri singoli (m pl)

1785 *E* isolated words (RECOGNITION)
= discrete words; unconnected speech
G einzelne Wörter (isoliert gesprochen) (n pl)
F mots isolés (m pl); paroles discrètes (f pl)
S palabras aisladas (f pl); palabras sueltas (f pl); palabras individuales (f pl); palabras pronunciadas aisladamente (f pl)
I parole singole (f pl)

1786 *E* isolated-words recognition
≠ continuous-speech recognition; connected-speech recognition
G Erkennen einzelner Wörter (isoliert gesprochen) (n); Einzelworterkennung (f)
F reconnaissance de mots isolés (f); reconnaissance de la parole discrète (f)
S reconocimiento de palabras aisladas (RPA) (m); reconocimiento de palabras distintas (m)

I riconoscimento di parole singole (m)

1787 *E* isolated-words recognition system
= discrete-words recognition system
G System zum Erkennen einzelner Wörter (n); Einzelworterkennungssystem (n)
F système de reconnaissance de mots isolés (m)
S sistema de reconocimiento de palabras aisladas (m)
I sistema di riconoscimento di parole singole (m)

1788 *E* isolated-words understanding (RECOGNITION)
= discrete-words understanding
G Verstehen einzelner Wörter (n)
F compréhension de mots isolés (f)
S comprensión de palabras aisladas (f)
I comprensione di parole singole (f)

1789 *E* isomorphism
G Isomorphismus (m)
F isomorphisme (m)
S isomorfismo (m)
I isomorfismo (m)

1790 *E* iterative deepening (*of the search*) (EXPERT SYSTEMS)
G iteratives Vertiefen (n)
F profondissement itératif (m)
S profundización iterativa (f)
I approfondimento iterativo (m)

1791 *E* iterative search (EXPERT SYSTEMS)
G iterative Suche (f)
F recherche itérative (f)
S búsqueda iterativa (f)
I ricerca iterativa (f)

1792 *E* ITS
→ intelligent tutoring system

1793 *E* IU
→ image understanding

1794 *E* IUS
→ image-understanding system

J

1795 *E* job list
→ agenda

1796 *E* justification (*of a decision*) (EXPERT SYSTEMS)
G Begründung (f)
F justification (f)
S justificación (f)
I giustificazione (f)

1797 *E* justification-based (*system etc.*) (EXPERT SYSTEMS)
≠ assumption-based
G begründungsgestützt
F basé sur justifications
S basado en justificaciones
I basato sulla giustificazione

1798 *E* justification facility (EXPERT SYSTEMS)
G Begründungskomponente (f)
F module de justification (m)
S componente de justificación (m)
I componente di giustificazione (m)

K

1799 *E* KAS
→ knowledge acquisition system

1800 *E* KB
→ knowledge base

1801 *E* KBM
→ knowledge-based machine

1802 *E* KE
→ knowledge engineering

1803 *E* KEE
= knowledge engineering environment

1804 *E* kernel language (KL) (PROGRAMMING)
G KL (Kernsprache) (f)
F langage KL (m)
S lenguaje núcleo (m)
I linguaggio KL (m)

1805 *E* kernel sentence (LINGUISTICS)
G Kernsatz (m)
F proposition nucléaire (f)
S frase núcleo (f)
I frase centrale (f)

1806 *E* keyword matching (NLP)
G Vergleich mit Schlüsselwortschablonen (m)
F comparaison de mots-clé (f)
S comparación de palabras clave (f)
I reazione standard a fronte di certe parole chiave (f)

1807 *E* keyword recognition (KWR)
= wordspotting
G Schlüsselwortdetektion (f)
F détection de mots-clé (f)
S reconocimiento de las palabras clave (m)
I rilevamento della parola chiave (m)

1808 *E* KH
→ knowledge handling

1809 *E* kilo logical inferences per second
→ KLIPS

1810 *E* kind
→ type

1811 *E* KIPS
= knowledge information processing system
→ knowledge processing system

1812 *E* KL
→ kernel language

1813 *E* KL (one and two)
→ Knowledge Language (one and two)

1814 *E* KLIPS (EXPERT SYSTEMS)
= kilo logical inferences per second
→ logical inferences per second (LIPS)
G KLIPS
F KLIPS
S KLIPS
I KLIPS

1815 *E* KL-ONE (*an AI programming language*)
G KL-ONE
F KL-ONE
S KL-ONE
I KL-ONE

1816 *E* KNOBS
→ knowledge-based system

1817 *E* knowledge
G Wissen (n)
F connaissance(s) (f (pl)); savoir (m)
S conocimiento(s) (m (pl)); saber (m)
I conoscenza (f)

1818 *E* knowledge accumulation
G Wissensanhäufung (f); Wissensakkumulation (f)
F accumulation de connaissance(s) (f)
S acumulación de conocimientos (f)
I accumulazione di conoscenza (f)

1819 *E* knowledge acquisition
G Wissenserwerb (m); Wissensaufnahme (f); Wissensakquisition (f)
F acquisition de la connaissance (f); acquisition des connaissances (f)
S adquisición de conocimientos (f); adquisición del conocimiento (f)
I acquisizione della conoscenza (f); acquisizione di conoscenze (f)

1820 *E* knowledge acquisition aid
→ knowledge acquisition tool

1821 *E* knowledge acquisition component (EXPERT SYSTEMS)
= knowledge acquisition facility
G Wissenserwerb(s)komponente (f); Wissenserwerbssystem (n); Akquisitionskomponente (f)
F module d'aide à l'acquisition des connaissances (m)
S módulo de adquisición de conocimiento (m)
I componente di acquisizione di conoscenza (m)

1822 *E* knowledge acquisition facility
→ knowledge acquisition component

1823 *E* knowledge acquisition program (EXPERT SYSTEMS)
G Wissenserwerb(s)programm (n)
F programme d'acquisition des connaissances (m)
S programa de adquisición de conocimientos (m)
I programma di acquisizione di conoscenza (m)

1824 *E* knowledge acquisition system (KAS) (EXPERT SYSTEMS)
G Wissenserwerb(s)system (n)
F système d'acquisition de connaissances (m)
S sistema de adquisición de conocimiento (m)
I sistema di acquisizione di conoscenza (m)

1825 *E* knowledge acquisition tool
= knowledge acquisition aid
G Hilfe für den Wissenserwerb (f)
F outil d'acquisition de connaissances (m); aide à l'acquisition de connaissances (f)
S ayuda a la adquisición del conocimiento (f)
I aiuto all'acquisizione di conoscenza (m)

1826 *E* knowledge base (KB)
G Wissensbasis (Faktenbasis + Regelbasis) (WB) (f)
F base de connaissance(s) (BC) (f)
S base de conocimientos (BC) (f); cuerpo de conocimiento (m)
I base di conoscenza (f)

1827 *E* knowledge base construction
G Aufbau einer Wissensbank (m)
F établissement d'une base de connaissances (m)

S construcción de bases de conocimientos (f)
I costruzione di una base di conoscenza (f)

1828 *E* knowledge-based (EXPERT SYSTEMS)
G wissensbasiert
F basé sur connaissance
S basado en conocimientos
I basato su conoscenza

1829 *E* knowledge-based expert system
= knowledge system
G wissensbasiertes Expertensystem (n)
F système expert basé sur connaissance (m)
S sistema experto basado en conocimientos (m)
I sistema esperto basato su conoscenza (m)

1830 *E* knowledge-based machine (KBM) (EXPERT SYSTEMS)
G wissensbasierte Maschine (f)
F machine à base de connaissances (f); machine-base de connaissances (f)
S máquina basada en conocimientos (f)
I macchina basata sulla conoscenza (f)

1831 *E* knowledge-based machine translation
G wissensbasierte maschinelle Übersetzung (f)
F traduction automatique à base de connaissances (f)
S traducción automática basada en conocimientos (f)
I traduzione automatica basata sulla conoscenza (f)

1832 *E* knowledge-based processing (EXPERT SYSTEMS)
G wissensbasierte Verarbeitung (f)
F traitement basé sur connaissances (m)
S procesamiento basado en conocimientos (m)
I elaborazione basata sulla conoscenza (f)

1833 *E* knowledge-based system (KNOBS) (EXPERT SYSTEMS)
= knowledge system
G wissensbasiertes System (WBS) (n)
F système à base de connaissances (SBC) (m); système basé sur connaissance (m)
S sistema basado en conocimientos (SBC) (m)
I sistema basato su conoscenza (m)

1834 *E* knowledge base editor
G Wissensbasiseditor (m)
F éditeur de la base de connaissances (m)
S editor de la base de conocimientos (m)
I editore di base di conoscenza (m)

1835 *E* knowledge base expansion (EXPERT SYSTEMS)
G Erweiterung der Wissensbasis (f)
F expansion de la base de connaissances (f)
S expansión de la base de conocimientos (f)
I espansione della base di conoscenza (f)

1836 *E* knowledge base maintenance (EXPERT SYSTEMS)
G Wartung der Wissensbasis (f); Wissenpflege (f)
F entretien de la base de connaissances (m)
S manutención de la base de conocimientos (f)
I mantenimento della base di conoscenza (m)

1837 *E* knowledge base management
G Verwaltung einer Wissensbasis (f)
F gestion de base de connaissances (f)
S gestión de la base de conocimientos (f)
I gestione della base di conoscenza (f)

1838 *E* knowledge base management system
G Wissensbasisverwaltungssystem (n)
F système de gestion de bases de connaissances (m)
S sistema de gestión de la base de conocimientos (m); gestor de conocimientos (m)
I sistema di gestione delle base di conoscenza (m)

1839 *E* knowledge basis
G Wissensbasis (Basis für das Wissen) (f)
F base pour les connaissances (f)
S base para el conocimiento (f)
I base per la conoscenza (f)

1840 *E* knowledge chip
G Wissenschip (m)
F puce savante (f)
S pastilla de conocimiento (f)
I chip di conoscenza (m)

1841 *E* knowledge chunk
→ chunk (of knowledge)

1842 *E* knowledge compilation
G Wissenskompilation (f); Wissenserfassung (f)
F compilation de connaissances (f)
S compilación de conocimientos (f)
I compilazione di conoscenze (f)

1843 *E* knowledge depth
= depth of knowledge
G Wissenstiefe (f)
F profondeur de connaissance (f)
S profundidad de conocimiento (f)
I profondità di conoscenza (f)

1844 *E* knowledge domain
= domain (of knowledge)
G Wissensdomäne (f); Wissensgebiet (n)
F domaine de connaissances (m); domaine (d'expertise) (m)
S dominio de conocimiento (m); dominio del saber (m); parcela de conocimientos (f); campo del saber (m)
I dominio di conoscenza (m); settore di conoscenze (m)

1845 *E* knowledge-driven (EXPERT SYSTEMS)
G wissensgetrieben
F dirigé par connaissance
S guiado por conocimiento
I guidato dalla conoscenza

1846 *E* knowledge elicitation
G Wissenserhebung (f); Erhebung des Wissens (f)
F récupération de l'expertise (f); élicitation des connaissances (f); acquisition des connaissances (f)
S obtención de conocimiento (f); extracción de conocimientos (f)
I ottenimento della conoscenza (m)

1847 *E* knowledge engineer
G Wissensingenieur (m); Knowledge Engineer (m)
F ingénieur de la connaissance (m); (ingénieur) cogniticien (m)
S ingeniero de conocimientos (m); ingeniero del conocimiento (m)
I ingegnere della conoscenza (m)

1848 *E* knowledge engineering (KE)
G Knowledge Engineering (n); Wissenstechnik (f); Wissensengineering (n); Wissensingenieurwesen (n)

F ingénierie de la connaissance (f); génie de la connaissance (m); génie cognitif (cognitique) (m)
S ingeniería del conocimiento (f); ingeniería de conocimientos (f)
I ingegneria della conoscenza (f)

1849 *E* knowledge engineering techniques
G Knowledge-Engineering-Verfahren (n); Wissenstechnik (f)
F méthodes de génie cognitif (f pl)
S técnicas de ingeniería de conocimiento (f pl)
I tecniche di ingegneria di conoscenza (f pl)

1850 *E* knowledge extension
G Wissenserweiterung (f)
F extension de la connaissance (f)
S ampliación de conocimientos (f)
I estensione della conoscenza (f)

1851 *E* knowledge extraction
= extraction of knowledge
G Wissensgewinnung (f); Wissensextraktion (f)
F extraction de la connaissance (f)
S extracción de los conocimientos (f)
I estrazione di conoscenza (f)

1852 *E* knowledge handling (KH)
G Umgang mit dem Wissen (m)
F traitement de la connaissance (m); gestion de la connaissance (f)
S manejo de conocimiento(s) (m); manipulación del conocimiento (f)
I manipolazione della conoscenza (f)

1853 *E* knowledge hierarchy
G Wissenshierarchie (f)
F hiérarchie de la connaissance (f)
S jerarquía de conocimiento (f)
I gerarchia di conoscenza (f)

1854 *E* knowledge import
G Wissensimport (m)
F importation de connaissances (f)
S importación de conocimientos (f)
I importazione di conoscenze (f)

1855 *E* knowledge information processing system (KIPS)
→ knowledge processing system

1856 *E* knowledge-intensive (*system etc.*) (EXPERT SYSTEMS)
G wissensintensiv
F à grande complexité de connaissances; à forte concentration d'expertise
S de gran concentración de conocimiento
I che richiede una ampia conoscenza

1857 *E* Knowledge Language (one and two) (*both based on semantic networks*) (PROGRAMMING)
= KL (one and two)
G Wissensrepräsentationssprache KL (One oder Two) (f)
F langage KL (de représentation de connaissances) (m)
S lenguaje KL (m)
I linguaggio KL (di rappresentazione della conoscenza) (m)

1858 *E* knowledge level
= level of knowledge
G Wissensniveau (n); Wissensstufe (f)
F niveau de connaissance (m)
S nivel de conocimiento(s) (m)
I livello di conoscenza (m)

1859 *E* knowledge maintenance
G Wissenserhaltung (f)
F maintien des connaissances (m)
S manutención del conocimiento (f)
I mantenimento della conoscenza (m)

1860 *E* knowledge manager
G Wissensmanager (m); Knowledge Manager (m)
F directeur des connaissances (m)
S gestor de conocimiento (m)
I gestore della conoscenza (m)

1861 *E* knowledge model
G Wissensmodell (n)
F modèle de connaissance (m)
S modelo de conocimiento (m)
I modello di conoscenza (m)

1862 *E* knowledge organization
G Wissensorganisation (f)
F organisation de la connaissance (f)
S organización del conocimiento (f)
I organizzazione della conoscenza (f)

1863 *E* knowledge processing
G Wissensverarbeitung (f)
F traitement des connaissances (m)
S tratamiento del conocimiento (m); tratamiento del saber (m); procesamiento del conocimiento (m)
I trattamento delle conoscenze (m); elaborazione della conoscenza (f)

1864 *E* knowledge processing system
= knowledge information processing system (KIPS)
G wissensverarbeitendes System (n); Wissensverarbeitungssystem (n)
F système de traitement de la connaissance (m); système de traitement de connaissances (m)
S sistema de proceso del conocimiento (m)
I sistema di elaborazione della conoscenza (m); sistema di trattamento della conoscenza (m)

1865 *E* knowledge representation (KR)
G Wissensrepräsentation (KR) (f); Wissensdarstellung (f)
F représentation des connaissances (f)
S representación del conocimiento (f)
I rappresentazione della conoscenza (f)

1866 *E* knowledge representation language (KRL) (PROGRAMMING)
G Wissensrepräsentationssprache (f); KR-Sprache (f)
F langage de représentation des connaissances (m); langage KR (m)
S lenguaje de representación del conocimiento (m)
I linguaggio di rappresentazione della conoscenza (m)

1867 *E* knowledge representation system
G Wissensrepräsentationssystem (n)
F système de représentation de connaissance (m)
S sistema de representación del conocimiento (m); esquema de representación del conocimiento (m)
I sistema di rappresentazione della conoscenza (m)

1868 *E* knowledge representation theory
G Theorie von der Wissensdarstellung (f); Wissensrepräsentationstheorie (f)
F théorie de représentation de connaissance (f)
S teoría de representación del conocimiento (f)
I teoria di rappresentazione della conoscenza (f)

1869 *E* knowledge server (EXPERT SYSTEMS)
G Wissensserver (m)
F serveur de connaissance (m)

S servidor de conocimiento (m)
I server di conoscenza (m)

1870 *E* knowledge source (KS)
G Wissensquelle (f)
F source de connaissance(s) (SC) (f)
S fuente de conocimientos (FC) (f)
I fonte di conoscenza (f); sorgente di conoscenza (f)

1871 *E* knowledge spectrum
G Wissensspektrum (n)
F spectre de connaissances (m)
S espectro de conocimientos (m)
I spettro di conoscenza (m)

1872 *E* knowledge storage
G Wissensspeicherung (f)
F stockage des connaissances (m)
S almacenamiento de conocimientos (m)
I immagazzinamento della conoscenza (m)

1873 *E* knowledge structure
G Wissensstruktur (f)
F structure de savoir (f)
S estructura de conocimiento (f)
I struttura della conoscenza (f)

1874 *E* knowledge structure level
G Niveau der Wissensstruktur (n)
F niveau de la structure des connaissances (m)
S nivel de la estructura de conocimiento (m)
I livello della struttura della conoscenza (m)

1875 *E* knowledge system[1]
G Wissenssystem (WS) (n)
F système de connaissances (m)
S sistema de conocimiento(s) (m)
I sistema di conoscenze (m)

1876 *E* knowledge system[2]
→ knowledge-based expert system; knowledge-based system

1877 *E* knowledge system control (EXPERT SYSTEMS)
G Wissenssystemsteuerung (f)
F stratégie d'utilisation des connaissances (f)
S control de un sistema de conocimiento (m)
I controllo del sistema di conoscenza (m)

1878 *E* knowledge technology
G Wissenstechnologie (f)
F technologie de la connaissance (f)
S tecnología del conocimiento (f)
I tecnologia della conoscenza (f)

1879 *E* knowledge transfer
G Wissenstransfer (m)
F transfert de connaissance (m); transfert de l'expertise (m); transfert du savoir (m)
S transferencia de conocimientos (f); traslación del conocimiento (f)
I trasferimento di conoscenza (m)

1880 *E* knowledge updating
G Wissensaktualisierung (f)
F mise-à-jour des connaissances (f)
S actualización del conocimiento (f)
I aggiornamento della conoscenza (m)

1881 *E* KR
→ knowledge representation

1882 *E* KRL
→ knowledge representation language

1883 *E* KS
→ knowledge source

1884 *E* KSL
= knowledge specification language

1885 *E* KWR
→ keyword recognition

L

1886 *E* lambda calculus (MATHS)
G Lambda-Kalkül (n)
F λ-calcul (m)
S lambda cálculo (m)
I lambda calcolo (m)

1887 *E* lambda expression (MATHS)
G Lambda-Ausdruck (m)
F expression lambda (f)
S expresión lambda (f)
I lambda espressione (f)

1888 *E* language acquisition system (LAS) (NLP)
G Spracherwerbsystem (n)
F système d'acquisition de langue (m)
S sistema de adquisición de lenguaje (m)
I sistema di acquisizione di linguaggio (m)

1889 *E* language comprehension
→ language understanding

1890 *E* language handling (NLP)
G Behandlung der Sprache (f)
F traitement de langues (m)
S tratamiento de lenguaje (m)
I trattamento del linguaggio (m)

1891 *E* language processing (NLP)
G Sprachverarbeitung (f)
F traitement de langues (m)
S procesamiento de lenguaje (m)
I elaborazione del linguaggio (f)

1892 *E* language processing system (NLP)
G sprachverarbeitendes System (n); Sprachverarbeitungssystem (n)
F système de traitement de langues (m)
S sistema de procesamiento de lenguaje (m)
I sistema di elaborazione del linguaggio (m)

1893 *E* language translation (MT)
G Sprachübersetzung (f)
F traduction de langues (f)
S traducción de lenguajes (f)
I traduzione di lingue (f)

1894 *E* language translator (MT)
G Sprachübersetzer (m)
F traducteur de langues (m)
S traductor de lenguajes (m)
I traduttore di lingue (m)

1895 *E* language understanding (NLP)
= language comprehension
G Sprachverstehen (n)
F compréhension du langage (f)
S comprensión de lenguaje (f)
I comprensione del linguaggio (f)

1896 *E* language-understanding program (NLP)
G sprachverstehendes Programm (n)
F programme de compréhension du langage (m)
S programa de comprensión de lenguaje (m); programa entendedor de languaje (m)
I programma di comprensione del linguaggio (m)

1897 *E* language-understanding system (NLP)
G sprachverstehendes System (n)

F système de compréhension du langage (m)
S sistema de comprensión de lenguaje (m)
I sistema di comprensione del linguaggio (m)

1898 *E* Laplacian equation (MATHS)
G Laplacesche Gleichung (f)
F équation laplacienne (f)
S ecuación Laplaciana (f) ; laplaciano (m)
I equazione di Laplace (f)

1899 *E* LAS
→ language acquisition system

1900 *E* layered network (NEURAL NETS)
G geschichtetes Netz (n)
F réseau à couches (m)
S red de capas (f)
I rete a strati (f)

1901 *E* lazy evaluation (*of results*) (PROGRAMMING)
= delayed evaluation
≠ eager evaluation
G langsame Auswertung (f)
F évaluation retardée (f)
S evaluación lenta (f)
I valutazione ritardata (f)

1902 *E* leaf (*of a tree; final node without successors*) (LOGIC)
G Blatt (n)
F feuille (f) (sommet sans successeur)
S hoja (f)
I foglio (m)

1903 *E* leaf node
→ terminal node

1904 *E* learning
G Lernen (n)
F apprentissage (m)
S aprendizaje (m)
I apprendimento (m)

1905 *E* learning aid
G Lernhilfe (f)
F aide à l'apprentissage (f)
S ayuda de aprendizaje (f)
I aiuto all'apprendimento (m)

1906 *E* learning algorithm (NEURAL NETS)
G Lernalgorithmus (m)
F algorithme d'apprentissage (m)
S algoritmo de aprendizaje (m)
I algoritmo di apprendimento (m)

1907 *E* learning by analogy
G Lernen durch Analogie (n); analoges Lernen (n)
F apprentissage par analogie (m); apprentissage analogique (m)
S aprendizaje por analogía (m) ; aprendizaje analógico (m)
I apprendimento per analogia (m); apprendimento analogico (m)

1908 *E* learning by comparison
G Lernen durch Vergleichen (n)
F apprentissage par comparaison (m)
S aprendizaje por comparación (m)
I apprendimento per confronto (m)

1909 *E* learning by deduction
→ deductive learning

1910 *E* learning by doing
G Lernen durch Tun (n)
F apprentissage par réalisation (m)
S aprendizaje haciendo (m)
I apprendimento non supervisionato (m)

1911 *E* learning by experience
G Lernen durch Erfahrung (n)
F apprentissage par expérience (m)
S aprendizaje por experiencia (m)
I apprendimento per esperienza (m)

1912 *E* learning by induction
→ inductive learning

1913 *E* learning by interaction
= interactive learning
G Lernen durch Interaktion (n)
F apprentissage par interaction (m)
S aprendizaje por interacción (m)
I apprendimento per interazione (m)

1914 *E* learning by observation
→ learning from observation

1915 *E* learning capacity
G Lernfähigkeit (f)
F capacité d'apprentissage (f)
S capacidad de aprendizaje (f); posibilidad de aprendizaje (f)
I capacità di apprendimento (f)

1916 *E* learning expert system
G Lernexpertensystem (n)
F système expert d'apprentissage (m)
S sistema experto de aprendizaje (m)
I sistema esperto per l'apprendimento (m)

1917 *E* learning from examples
= case-based learning
↔ concept learning
G Lernen aus Beispielen (n)
F apprentissage par exemples (m)
S aprendizaje por ejemplos (m)
I apprendimento tramite esempi (m); apprendimento supervisionato (m)

1918 *E* learning from observation
= learning by observation; unsupervised learning
G Lernen durch Beobachten (n)
F apprentissage par observation (m)
S aprendizaje por observación (m)
I apprendimento tramite osservazione (m)

1919 *E* learning model
G Lernmodell (n)
F modèle d'apprentissage (m)
S modelo de aprendizaje (m)
I modello di apprendimento (m)

1920 *E* learning of concepts
→ concept learning

1921 *E* learning of rules (EXPERT SYSTEMS)
= rule learning
G Lernen von Regeln (n)
F apprentissage de règles (m)
S aprendizaje de reglas (m)
I apprendimento di regole (m)

1922 *E* learning procedure (EXPERT SYSTEMS)
G Lernprozedur (f)
F procédure d'apprentissage (f)
S procedimiento de aprendizaje (m)
I procedura di apprendimento (f)

1923 *E* learning process (EXPERT SYSTEMS)
G Lernprozeß (m)
F processus d'apprentissage (m)
S proceso de aprendizaje (m)
I processo di apprendimento (m)

1924 *E* learning program
G Lernprogramm (n)
F programme d'apprentissage (PA) (m)
S programa de aprendizaje (m)
I programma apprenditore (m)

1925 *E* learning rule (EXPERT SYSTEMS)
G Lernregel (f)
F règle d'apprentissage (f)
S regla de aprendizaje (f); regla de enseñanza (f)
I regola di apprendimento (f)

1926 *E* learning system (NEURAL NETS)
G lernendes System (n); selbstlernendes System (n)

F système d'apprentissage (m); système à auto-apprentissage (m)
S sistema de aprendizaje (m)
I sistema di apprendimento (m)

1927 *E* learning theory
G Lerntheorie (f)
F théorie d'apprentissage (f)
S teoría de aprendizaje (f)
I teoria dell'apprendimento (f)

1928 *E* learning with a teacher
→ supervised learning

1929 *E* least-commitment strategy (EXPERT SYSTEMS)
G Strategie der geringsten Festlegung (f)
F stratégie de moindre engagement (f)
S estrategia de la mínima obligación (f)
I strategia least-commitment (f); strategia dell'obbligo minimo (f)

1930 *E* least-compromise strategy (EXPERT SYSTEMS)
G Strategie des kleinsten Kompromisses (f)
F stratégie du compromis minimum (f)
S estrategia del mínimo compromiso (f)
I strategia del compromesso minimo (f)

1931 *E* least mean squares rule
→ delta rule

1932 *E* left-hand side (LHS) (*of a rule*) (LOGIC)
= antecedent
↔ right-hand side
G linke Seite (f); Bedingungsteil (m)
F partie gauche (f); membre gauche (d'une règle) (m); situation (d'une règle) (f)
S lado izquierdo (m); elementos antecedentes (de una regla) (m pl)
I parte sinistra (se ...) (f); lato sinistro (m); antecedente (m)

1933 *E* letter recognition (IMAGE PROCESSING)
G Buchstabenerkennung (f)
F reconnaissance de lettres (f)
S reconocimiento de letras (m)
I riconoscimento di lettere (m)

1934 *E* level (*e.g. of hierarchy*) (KNOWLEDGE)
G Stufe (f)
F niveau (m)
S nivel (m)
I livello (m)

1935 *E* level of abstraction
→ abstraction level

1936 *E* level of greyness (IMAGE PROCESSING)
G Grauwert (m)
F niveau de gris (m)
S nivel de gris (m)
I livello di grigio (m)

1937 *E* level of intelligence
→ intelligence level

1938 *E* level of knowledge
→ knowledge level

1939 *E* lexical ambiguity (NLP)
G lexikalische Ambiguität (f)
F ambiguïté lexicale (f)
S ambigüedad lexical (f)
I ambiguità lessicale (f)

1940 *E* lexical analysis (NLP)
G lexikalische Analyse (f)
F analyse lexicale (f)
S análisis lexical (m)
I analisi lessicale (m)

1941 *E* lexical decomposition (NLP)

G lexikalische Dekomposition (f); lexikalische Zerlegung (f)
F décomposition lexicale (f)
S descomposición lexical (f)
I scomposizione lessicale (f)

1942 *E* lexical transfer (MT)
G Lexikontransfer (m)
F transfert lexical (m)
S transferencia lexical (f)
I trasferimento lessicale (f)

1943 *E* lexical variable (*in LISP*) (PROGRAMMING)
G lexikalische Variable (f)
F variable lexicale (f)
S variable lexical (f)
I variabile lessicale (f)

1944 *E* lexicon (KNOWLEDGE)
G Lexikon (n)
F lexique (m)
S léxico (m)
I lessico (m)

1945 *E* lexicon-driven (MT)
G lexikongesteuert
F guidé par le lexique
S controlado por léxico
I controllato da un lessico

1946 *E* LHS
→ left-hand side

1947 *E* likelihood (*a non-mathematical probability*) (LOGIC)
→ probability
G Wahrscheinlichkeit (f); Möglichkeit (f); Likelihood (f)
F vraisemblance (f)
S verosimilidad (f)
I attendibilità (f)

1948 *E* likelihood ratio (LR) (LOGIC)
G Wahrscheinlichkeitsquote (f)
F taux de vraisemblance (m)
S razón de verosimilitud (f)
I tasso di probabilità (m); rapporto di verosimiglianza (m)

1949 *E* linear backtracking (EXPERT SYSTEMS)
G lineares Backtracking (n)
F retour arrière linéaire (m); recul linéaire (m)
S retroceso lineal (m)
I backtracking lineare (m); ritorno all'indietro lineare (m)

1950 *E* linear prediction coding
→ linear predictive coding

1951 *E* linear predictive coding (LPC) (RECOGNITION)
= linear prediction coding
G lineare Vorhersagecodierung (f); LPC-Verfahren (n)
F codage prédictif linéaire (m); codage LPC (m)
S codificación de predicción lineal (f); codificación LPC (f); codificación predictiva lineal (f)
I codifica in assunzione di linearità (f)

1952 *E* linear resolution (LOGIC)
G lineare Resolution (f)
F résolution linéaire (f)
S resolución lineal (f)
I risoluzione lineare (f)

1953 *E* line of reasoning
→ inference chain

1954 *E* linguistic analysis (NLP)
G linguistische Analyse (f)
F analyse linguistique (f)
S análisis lingüístico (m)
I analisi linguistica (m)

1955 *E* link[1] (*between nodes in a semantic network*) (KNOWLEDGE)
= arc
G Verbindung (f)
F connexion (f)

S enlace (m)
I connessione (f)

1956 *E* link[2]
→ arc[1]

1957 *E* LIPS
→ logical inferences per second

1958 *E* LISP (*list processing language*) (PROGRAMMING)
G LISP
F LISP; langage LISP (m)
S LISP (lenguaje de programación)
I LISP

1959 *E* LISP dialect (PROGRAMMING)
G LISP-Dialekt (m)
F dialecte LISP (m); dialecte lispien (m); jargon Lisp (m)
S dialecto de LISP (m)
I dialetto del LISP (m)

1960 *E* LISP machine
G LISP-Maschine (f)
F machine LISP (f)
S máquina LISP (f)
I macchina LISP (f)

1961 *E* LISP program
G LISP-Programm (n)
F programme LISP (m)
S programa en LISP (m)
I programma scritto in LISP (m); programma in LISP (m); programma LISP (m)

1962 *E* LISP programmer
G LISP-Programmierer (m)
F lispien (m)
S programador de LISP (m)
I programmatore LISP (m)

1963 *E* LISP/PROLOG machine
G LISP/PROLOG-Maschine (f)
F machine mixte LISP/PROLOG (f)
S máquina LISP/PROLOG (f)
I macchina LISP/PROLOG (f)

1964 *E* LISP syntax (PROGRAMMING)
G LISP-Syntax (f)
F syntaxe lispienne (f)
S sintaxis de LISP (f)
I sintassi di LISP (f)

1965 *E* list of conditions (LOGIC)
= signal list
G Bedingungsliste (f)
F liste d'opérations conditionnelles (f); liste conditionnelle (f)
S lista de condiciones (f)
I elenco di condizioni (m)

1966 *E* list of constraints
→ constraints list

1967 *E* list processing (PROGRAMMING)
G Listenverarbeitung (f)
F traitement de listes (m)
S manipulación de listas (f)
I trattamento di liste (m)

1968 *E* list processing language (PROGRAMMING)
G Listenverarbeitungssprache (f)
F langage de traitement de listes (m)
S lenguaje de procesamiento de listas (m)
I linguaggio di trattamento di liste (m)

1969 *E* literal (*noun*) (LOGIC)
G Literal (n)
F littéral (m) (*plural*: littéraux)
S literal (m)
I literal (m)

1970 *E* local features (KNOWLEDGE)
G lokale Merkmale (n pl)
F traits locaux (m pl)
S atributos locales (m pl)
I caratteristiche locali (m pl)

1971 *E* local variable (PROGRAMMING)

≠ global variable
G lokale Variable (f)
F variable locale (f)
S variable local (f)
I variabile locale (f)

1972 *E* logic
G Logik (f)
F logique (f)
S lógica (f)
I logica (f)

1973 *E* logical approach
G logisches Verfahren (n)
F méthode logique (f)
S método lógico (m)
I approccio logico (m)

1974 *E* logical argument
G logisches Argument (n)
F argument logique (m)
S argumento lógico (m)
I argomento logico (m)

1975 *E* logical assertion
= logic statement
G logische Aussage (f)
F proposition logique (f)
S aserción lógica (f); proposición lógica (f)
I asserzione logica (f); proposizione logica (f)

1976 *E* logical calculus
G Logikkalkül (n)
F calcul logique (m)
S cálculo lógico (m)
I calcolo logico (m)

1977 *E* logical connective (*types: and, or, not*)
= logical operator
G logisches Verknüpfungssymbol (n); logisches Konnektiv (n)
F opérateur logique (m)
S operador lógico (m); conectivo lógico (m)
I connettivo logico (m)

1978 *E* logical empiricism
G logischer Empirismus (m)
F empirisme logique (m)
S empirismo lógico (m)
I empirismo logico (m)

1979 *E* logical expression
G logischer Ausdruck (m)
F expression logique (f)
S expresión lógica (f)
I espressione logica (f)

1980 *E* logical implication
G logische Implikation (f)
F implication logique (f)
S implicación lógica (f)
I implicazione logica (f)

1981 *E* logical inference (*on the basis of if–then rules*) (EXPERT SYSTEMS)
G logisches Schlüsseziehen (n)
F inférence logique (f)
S inferencia lógica (f)
I inferenza logica (f)

1982 *E* logical inferences per second (LIPS) (*a measure of performance of AI systems*) (EXPERT SYSTEMS)
G logische Schlüsse pro Sekunde (m pl)
F inférences logiques par seconde (ILPS) (f pl)
S inferencias lógicas por segundo (f pl)
I inferenze logiche al secondo (f pl)

1983 *E* logical operator
→ logical connective

1984 *E* logical quantifier
G logischer Quantifikator (m)
F quantificateur logique (m)
S cuantificador lógico (m)
I quantificatore logico (m)

1985 *E* logical representation scheme (LRS) (KNOWLEDGE)
G logisches Repräsentationsschema (LRS) (n)
F schéma logique de représentation (m)
S esquema lógico de representación (m)
I schema logico di rappresentazione (m)

1986 *E* logical truth
G logische Wahrheit (f)
F vérité logique (f)
S verdad lógica (f)
I verità logica (f)

1987 *E* logical value (PROGRAMMING)
G logischer Wert (m)
F valeur logique (f)
S valor lógico (m)
I valore logico (m)

1988 *E* logic-based method
G auf Logik beruhende Methode (f)
F méthode basée sur la logique (f)
S método basado en la lógica (m)
I metodo basato sulla logica (m)

1989 *E* logic-based system
G auf Logik basierendes System (n)
F système basé sur la logique (m)
S sistema basado en la lógica (m)
I sistema basato sulla logica (m)

1990 *E* logician
G Logiker (m)
F logicien (m)
S lógico (m)
I logico (m)

1991 *E* logic of beliefs
→ belief logic

1992 *E* logic of states
→ state logic

1993 *E* logic of time
→ temporal logic

1994 *E* logic processor
G Logikprozessor (m)
F processeur logique (m)
S procesador lógico (m)
I processore logico (m)

1995 *E* logic programming
G logisches Programmieren (n)
F programmation logique (f)
S programación lógica (f)
I programmazione logica (f)

1996 *E* logic representation (PROGRAMMING)
G logische Darstellung (f)
F représentation logique (f)
S representación lógica (f)
I rappresentazione logica (f)

1997 *E* logic simulation (PROGRAMMING)
G logische Simulation (f)
F simulation logique (f)
S simulación lógica (f)
I simulazione logica (f)

1998 *E* logic statement
→ logical assertion

1999 *E* logic theory machine
→ LT machine

2000 *E* logic tree
G Logikbaum (m)
F arbre logique (m)
S árbol lógico (m)
I albero logico (m)

2001 *E* long-term memory (LTM) (THEORY)
≠ short-term memory
G Langzeitspeicher (bei einem Expertensystem) (m); Langzeitgedächtnis (beim Menschen) (n)
F mémoire à long terme (MLT) (f)
S memoria a largo plazo (f)
I memoria a lungo termine (f)

2002 *E* look-up table (PROGRAMMING)
G Look-Up-Tabelle (f)
F table de consultation (f)
S tabla para buscar (f)
I tabella di consulta (f)

2003 *E* lower bound (IMAGE PROCESSING)
G untere Grenze (f)
F limite inférieure (f)
S límite inferior (m)
I limite inferiore (m)

2004 *E* lower-level concept
→ child concept

2005 *E* low-level language (PROGRAMMING)
G niedere Programmiersprache (f)
F langage de bas niveau (m)
S lenguaje de bajo nivel (m)
I linguaggio di basso livello (m)

2006 *E* low-level processing
G Verarbeitung auf niedriger Ebene (f)
F traitement bas-niveau (m)
S procesamiento de bajo nivel (m)
I processamento di basso livello (m)

2007 *E* low probability (LOGIC)
G geringe Wahrscheinlichkeit (f)
F probabilité basse (f)
S probabilidad baja (f)
I bassa probabilità (f)

2008 *E* LPC
→ linear predictive coding

2009 *E* LR
→ likelihood ratio

2010 *E* LRS
→ logical representation scheme

2011 *E* LTM
→ long-term memory

2012 *E* LT machine (*an early theorem prover*) (THEORY)
= logic theory machine
G LT-Maschine (f)
F machine LT (f)
S máquina LT (f)
I macchina LT (f)

M

2013 *E* machine-assisted human translation (MAHT) (NLP)
G maschinenunterstützte Humanübersetzung (f)
F traduction par l'homme assistée par ordinateur (f)
S traducción humana asistida por ordenador (f)
I traduzione umana assistita da elaboratore (f)

2014 *E* machine-assisted translation (MAT) (NLP)
= computer-assisted translation (CAT)
G maschinenunterstütztes Übersetzen (n)
F traduction assistée par ordinateur (f)
S traducción asistida por ordenador (f)
I traduzione assistita dall'elaboratore (f)

2015 *E* machine cognition[1] (THEORY)
G maschinelles Erkennen (n)
F cognition par machine (f)
S cognición por máquina (f)
I cognizione tramite macchina (f)

2016 *E* machine cognition[2]
→ artificial cognition

2017 *E* machine intelligence[1] (THEORY)
= computer intelligence
G maschinelle Intelligenz (f)
F intelligence par machine (f); intelligence par ordinateur (f); intelligence machine (f)
S inteligencia de máquina (f); inteligencia de ordenador (f)
I intelligenza della macchina (f); intelligenza da elaboratore (f)

2018 *E* machine intelligence[2] (*rare for* artificial intelligence)

2019 *E* machine language (PROGRAMMING)
G Maschinensprache (f)
F langage machine (m)
S lenguaje de máquina (m)
I linguaggio macchina (m)

2020 *E* machine learning
G naschinelles Lernen (n); Maschinenlernen (n)
F apprentissage-machine (m); apprentissage par machine (m)
S aprendizaje por máquina (m); aprendizaje en máquinas (m)
I apprendimento effettuato dall'elaboratore (m)

2021 *E* machine-oriented logic
G maschinenorientierte Logik (f)
F logique-machine (f)
S lógica orientada a la máquina (f)
I logica orientata alla macchina (f)

2022 *E* machine perception
→ artificial perception

2023 *E* machine reasoning (*as opposed to human reasoning*) (THEORY)
G maschinelles Inferieren (n)
F raisonnement par machine (m)
S razonamiento por máquina (m)
I ragionamento da una macchina (m)

2024 *E* machine reasoning system (EXPERT SYSTEMS)
G maschinelles Inferenzsystem (n)
F système de raisonnement par machine (m)
S sistema de razonamiento por máquina (m)
I sistema di ragionamento da macchina (m)

2025 *E* machine thinking (THEORY)
G maschinelles Denken (n)
F pensée par machine (f)
S pensamiento de máquina (m)
I pensamento da una macchina (m)

2026 *E* machine translation (MT)
= translation by machine
G Maschinenübersetzung (MÜ) (f); maschinelle Übersetzung (f)
F traduction automatique (f)
S traducción automática (TA) (f)
I traduzione automatica (f)

2027 *E* machine-understandable language (PROGRAMMING)
G maschinenverstehbare Sprache (f)
F langage compréhensible par l'ordinateur (m)
S lenguaje comprensible por máquina (m)
I linguaggio comprensibile dalla macchina (m)

2028 *E* machine vision (*not identical with computer vision*) (IMAGE PROCESSING)
↔ robot vision
G maschinelles Sehen (für Inspektionszwecke etc.) (n)
F vision artificielle (par machine) (f)
S visión artificial (por máquina) (f)
I visione artificiale (da macchina) (f)

2029 *E* MacLISP (*a LISP dialect*) (PROGRAMMING)
G MacLISP
F MacLISP
S MacLISP
I MacLISP

2030 *E* macrodecision (EXPERT SYSTEMS)
G Makroentscheidung (f)
F macrodécision (f)
S macrodecisión (f)
I macrodecisione (f)

2031 *E* macrooperator (*composed of single operators*) (PROGRAMMING)
G Makrooperator (m)
F macro-opérateur (m)
S macrooperador (m)
I macrooperatore (m)

2032 *E* MAHT
→ machine-assisted human translation

2033 *E* make inferences
→ infer

2034 *E* manipulator (ROBOTICS)
= end effector
G Manipulator (m)
F manipulateur (m)
S manipulador (m)
I manipolatore (m)

2035 *E* man–machine communication (EXPERT SYSTEMS)
= human–machine communication
G Mensch–Maschine-Kommunikation (f)
F communication homme–machine (f)
S comunicación hombre–máquina (f)
I comunicazione uomo–macchina (f)

2036 *E* man–machine interaction (EXPERT SYSTEMS)
= human–machine interaction

G Interaktion zwischen Mensch und Maschine (f)
F interaction homme–machine (f)
S interacción hombre–máquina (f)
I interazione uomo–macchina (f)

2037 *E* man–machine interface (MMI) (PROGRAMMING)
G Mensch–Maschine-Schnittstelle (f)
F interface homme–machine (f)
S interfaz hombre–máquina (f); interfaz persona–máquina (f); interfaz con el hombre (f)
I interfaccia uomo–macchina (f)

2038 *E* many-valued logic
→ multivalued logic

2039 *E* map (*e.g. of elements of a set; verb*)
G mappen; abbilden
F mapper
S mapear
I mappare

2040 *E* mapping (*e.g. of elements of a set*) (THEORY)
G Mapping (n); Abbildung (f)
F mappage (m)
S mapping (m)
I mappamento (m); mappatura (f)

2041 *E* marker (KNOWLEDGE)
G Markierung (f); Marker (m)
F marque (f); marqueur (m)
S marca (f)
I marca (f)

2042 *E* marker propagation (KNOWLEDGE)
G Markerpropagierung (f)
F propagation de marqueurs (f)
S propagación de marcas (f)
I propagazione di marche (f)

2043 *E* Markov chain (THEORY)
G Markoffsche Kette (f); Markoffkette (f); Markoffmodell (n)
F chaîne de Markov (f)
S cadena de Markov (f); modelo de Markov (m)
I catena di Markov (f)

2044 *E* mask matching (IMAGE PROCESSING)
G Maskenvergleich (m)
F appariement de masques (m)
S unificación de máscaras (f)
I confronto di maschere (f)

2045 *E* massively parallel processing (MPP)
G Massenparallelverarbeitung (f); massive Parallelität (f)
F traitement massivement parallèle (m)
S tratamiento paralelo de masa (m)
I parallelismo di massa (m)

2046 *E* massive search
→ exhaustive search

2047 *E* MAT
→ machine-assisted translation

2048 *E* match[1] (*noun*)
G Übereinstimmung (f); Match (m)
F correspondance (f)
S correspondencia (f)
I somiglianza (f)

2049 *E* match[2] (*patterns; verb*) (IMAGE PROCESSING)
G vergleichen; matchen
F apparier
S buscar correspondencias
I confrontare

2050 *E* match algorithm (RECOGNITION)
= matching algorithm
G Vergleichsalgorithmus (m)
F algorithme d'appariement (m)

S algoritmo de comparación (m); algoritmo de filtro (m)
I algoritmo di confronto (m)

2051 E matched filtering
→ template matching

2052 E match–execute cycle
→ recognize–act cycle

2053 E matching (*for recognition purposes*) (IMAGE PROCESSING)
G Vergleichen (n); Matchen (n)
F mise en correspondance (f)
S unificación (f)
I confronto (m)

2054 E matching algorithm
→ match algorithm

2055 E matching criterion (IMAGE PROCESSING)
G Vergleichskriterium (n)
F critère de correspondance (m)
S criterio de unificación (m)
I criterio di confronto (m)

2056 E mathematical induction (LOGIC)
G mathematische Induktion (f)
F induction mathématique (f)
S inducción matemática (f)
I induzione matematica (f)

2057 E mathematical logic
G mathematische Logik (f)
F logique mathématique (f)
S lógica matemática (f)
I logica matematica (f)

2058 E mathematical probability (LOGIC)
G mathematische Wahrscheinlichkeit (f)
F probabilité mathématique (f)
S probabilidad matemática (f)
I probabilità matematica (f)

2059 E mathematical reasoning (LOGIC)
G mathematisches Inferieren (n)
F raisonnement mathématique (m)
S razonamiento matemático (m)
I ragionamento matematico (m)

2060 E maximum probability (LOGIC)
G maximale Wahrscheinlichkeit (f)
F probabilité maximale (f)
S probabilidad máxima (f)
I probabilità massima (f)

2061 E maximum search depth (EXPERT SYSTEMS)
= depth bound
G maximale Suchtiefe (f); Maximaltiefe (f)
F profondeur limite (de recherche) (f); seuil de recherche en profondeur (m)
S profundidad máxima de búsqueda (f)
I profondità massima di ricerca (f)

2062 E MB
→ measure of belief

2063 E MCDM
→ multi-criteria decision making

2064 E MD
→ measure of disbelief

2065 E MEA
→ means–end analysis

2066 E meaning-based representation system
→ conceptual representation system

2067 E meaning representation (NLP)
G Bedeutungsdarstellung (f)
F représentation du sens (f)
S representación de sentido (f)
I rappresentazione del significato (f)

2068 E meaning-representation language (MRL) (NLP)

G Sprache zur Bedeutungsdarstellung (f); MR-Sprache (f)
F langage pour la représentation du sens (m)
S lenguaje de representación de sentido (m)
I linguaggio per la rappresentazione del significato (m)

2069 *E* meaning–text model (MT model) (NLP)
G Bedeutungs–Text-Modell (n)
F modèle sens–texte (m)
S modelo sentido–texto (m)
I modello significato–testo (m)

2070 *E* means–end analysis (MEA) (*a problem solution technique*) (EXPERT SYSTEMS)
= means–end method
G Means–End-Analyse (f); Mittel–Zweck-Analyse (f)
F méthode des fins et des moyens (f); analyse fins–moyens (f)
S análisis de los medios en relación a los fines (m)
I analisi tipo means–end (m); analisi dei mezzi e dei fini (m)

2071 *E* means–end method
→ means–end analysis

2072 *E* means–ends strategy (EXPERT SYSTEMS)
G Mittel–Zweck-Strategie (f)
F stratégie de fins et de moyens (f)
S estrategía de los medios y de los fines (f)
I strategia dei mezzi e dei fini (f)

2073 *E* measurement of intelligence
G Intelligenzmaß (n)
F mesure d'intelligence (f)
S medida de inteligencia (f)
I misurazione della intelligenza (f)

2074 *E* measure of belief (MB) (LOGIC)
G Maß der Glaubwürdigkeit (n); Glaubensmaß (n)
F mesure de croyance (f)
S medida de confianza (f); medida de credibilidad (f)
I misura di credibilità (f)

2075 *E* measure of disbelief (MD)
G Maß des Zweifels (n)
F mesure de doute (f)
S medida de duda (f)
I misura di dubbio (f)

2076 *E* medical advice system (EXPERT SYSTEMS)
G medizinisches Beratungssystem (n)
F système de diagnostic médical (m)
S sistema de diagnóstico médico (m)
I sistema di diagnostica medica (m)

2077 *E* medical diagnosis (EXPERT SYSTEMS)
G medizinische Diagnose (f)
F diagnostic médical (m)
S diagnóstico médico (m)
I diagnosi medica (m)

2078 *E* medical expert system
G medizinisches Expertensystem (n)
F système expert médical (m)
S sistema experto para aplicaciones médicas (m)
I sistema esperto medico (m)

2079 *E* member (*of a class etc.*) (MATHS)
G Mitglied (n)
F membre (m)
S miembro (m)
I membro (m)

2080 *E* memory-aiding techniques
→ mnemonic techniques

2081 *E* Memory Organization Packet (MOP) (KNOWLEDGE)
G Speicherorganisationspaket (n)
F système d'organisation de la mémoire (m); système MOP (m)
S paquete de organización de memoria (m)
I pacchetto di organizzazione della memoria (m)

2082 *E* mental image (THEORY)
G geistiges Bild (n)
F image mentale (f)
S imagen mental (f)
I immagine mentale (f)

2083 *E* mental model (EXPERT SYSTEMS)
G mentales Modell (n); Vorstellungsmodell (n)
F modèle mental (m)
S modelo mental (m)
I modello mentale (m)

2084 *E* mental operation (THEORY)
G geistige Operation (f)
F opération mentale (f)
S operación mental (f)
I operazione mentale (f)

2085 *E* mental representation (THEORY)
G mentale Darstellung (f)
F représentation mentale (f)
S representación mental (f)
I rappresentazione mentale (f)

2086 *E* menu-based natural language (NLMenu)
G menübasierte natürliche Sprache (f)
F langage naturel basé sur menu (m)
S lenguaje natural basado en menu (m)
I linguaggio naturale basato su menu (m)

2087 *E* menu-based natural language interface
= NLMenu interface
G menübasierte natürlichsprachliche Schnittstelle (f)
F interface en langage naturel à base de menus (f)
S interfaz de lenguaje natural basado en menu (f)
I interfaccia in linguaggio naturale basata su menu (f)

2088 *E* menu-based user interface (EXPERT SYSTEMS)
G menügestützte Benutzeroberfläche (f)
F interface utilisateur à base de menus (f)
S interfaz con el usuario basado en menu (f)
I interfaccia con l'utilizzatore basata su menu (f)

2089 *E* message passing (PROGRAMMING)
G Senden (und Empfangen) von Meldungen (n); Kommunikation (f)
F envoi de messages (m)
S envío de mensajes de uno a otro (m)
I passaggio di messaggi (m)

2090 *E* message understanding (RECOGNITION)
G Verstehen von Nachrichten (n)
F compréhension de messages (f)
S comprensión de mensajes (f)
I comprensione di messaggi (f)

2091 *E* metagrammar (NLP)
G Metagrammatik (f)
F métagrammaire (f)
S metagramática (f)
I metagrammatica (f)

2092 *E* metaheuristic rule (LOGIC)
G metaheuristische Regel (f)

F règle méta-heuristique (f)
S regla metaheurística (f)
I regola meta-euristica (f)

2093 *E* metaheuristics (LOGIC)
G Metaheuristik (f)
F métaheuristique (f)
S metaheurística (f)
I meta-euristica (f)

2094 *E* metainference (LOGIC)
= metalevel inference
G Metainferenz (f)
F métainférence (f)
S meta-inferencia (f)
I meta-inferenza (f)

2095 *E* metaknowledge
= metalevel knowledge
G Metawissen (n)
F métaconnaissance (f); savoir-faire (m)
S metaconocimiento (f)
I meta-conoscenza (f)

2096 *E* metalanguage (PROGRAMMING)
G Metasprache (f)
F métalangage (m)
S metalenguaje (m)
I metalinguaggio (m)

2097 *E* metalevel (LOGIC)
G Metaebene (f)
F métaniveau (m)
S metanivel (m)
I metalivello (m)

2098 *E* metalevel inference
→ metainference

2099 *E* metalevel knowledge
→ metaknowledge

2100 *E* metalevel reasoning (LOGIC)
≠ problem-level reasoning
G Metaebeneninferenz (f); Inferieren auf Metaebene (n)
F raisonnement de méta-niveau (m)
S razonamiento de meta-nivel (m)
I ragionamento di meta-livello (m)

2101 *E* metalevel rule
→ metarule

2102 *E* metalogical programming
G metalogische Programmierung (f)
F programmation métalogique (f)
S programación metalógica (f)
I programmazione metalogica (f)

2103 *E* metalogical reasoning (EXPERT SYSTEMS)
G metalogisches Schließen (n)
F raisonnement métalogique (m)
S razonamiento metalógico (m)
I ragionamento metalogico (m)

2104 *E* metaplanning (EXPERT SYSTEMS)
G Meta-Planen (n)
F méta-planning (m)
S metaplanificación (f)
I meta-pianificazione (f)

2105 *E* metareasoning (EXPERT SYSTEMS)
G Metainferieren (n)
F métaraisonnement (m)
S metarrazonamiento (m)
I metaragionamento (m)

2106 *E* metarule (EXPERT SYSTEMS)
= metalevel rule
G Metaregel (f)
F métarègle (f)
S metarregla (f)
I metaregola (f)

2107 *E* metascience
G Metawissenschaft (f)
F métascience (f)
S metaciencia (f)
I metascienza (f)

2108 *E* metatheorem (LOGIC)
G Metatheorem (n)
F métathéorème (m)
S metateorema (m)

I metateorema (m)

2109 *E* method of reasoning
→ reasoning method

2110 *E* MGU
→ most general unifier

2111 *E* microdecision (EXPERT SYSTEMS)
G Mikroentscheidung (f)
F microdécision (f)
S microdecisión (f)
I microdecisione (f)

2112 *E* micro-expert system
G Mikroexpertensystem (n)
F microsystème expert (m)
S microsistema experto (m)
I microsistema esperto (m)

2113 *E* microfeature (KNOWLEDGE)
G Mikromerkmal (n)
F micro-trait (m)
S micro-característico (m)
I micro-attributo (m)

2114 *E* mid-run explanation (EXPERT SYSTEMS)
= online explanation
G Erklärung während des Ablaufs (f); Runtime-Erklärung (f); Online-Erläuterung (f)
F explication mid-run (pendant l'exécution) (f); explication en ligne (f)
S explicación en curso de ejecución (f)
I spiegazione durante l'esecuzione (f)

2115 *E* mid-run explanation feature (EXPERT SYSTEMS)
G Runtime-Erklärungskomponente (f)
F module d'explication pendant l'exécution (m)
S módulo de explicación en curso de ejecución (m)
I modulo di spiegazione durante l'esecuzione (m)

2116 *E* millions of inferences per second (MIPS) (EXPERT SYSTEMS)
G Million Inferenzen pro Sekunde (f)
F millions d'inférences par seconde (m pl)
S millones de inferencias por segundo (m pl)
I milioni di inferenze al secondo (m pl)

2117 *E* millions of logical inferences per second (MLIPS) (EXPERT SYSTEMS)
G Million logischer Inferenzen pro Sekunde (f)
F millions d'inférences logiques par seconde (m pl)
S millones de inferencias lógicas por segundo (m pl)
I milioni di inferenze logiche al secondo (m pl)

2118 *E* minimaxing
→ minimax method

2119 *E* minimax method (GAMES)
= minimax procedure; minimax strategy; minimaxing; minimax principle
G Minimax-Strategie (f); Minimax-Verfahren (n)
F méthode minimax (f); procédure min–max (f)
S procedimiento minimax (minimizar–maximizar) (m); mini–maximizac (f)
I metodo min–max (m)

2120 *E* minimax principle
→ minimax method

2121 *E* minimax procedure
→ minimax method

2122 *E* minimax strategy
→ minimax method

2123 *E* minimax tree (GAMES)
G Minimax-Baum (m)
F arbre min–max (m)
S árbol minimax (m)
I albero min–max (m)

2124 *E* minimum cost strategy (EXPERT SYSTEMS)
G Strategie des geringsten Aufwands (f); kostenminimale Strategie (f); Parsimonitätsprinzip (n)
F stratégie des coûts minimales (f)
S estrategia de coste mínimo (f)
I strategia del costo minimo (f); strategia meno costosa (f)

2125 *E* minimum probability (LOGIC)
G Mindestwahrscheinlichkeit (f)
F probabilité minimum (f)
S probabilidad mínima (f)
I probabilità minima (f)

2126 *E* minimum-risk strategy (EXPERT SYSTEMS)
G Strategie des geringsten Risikos (f)
F stratégie du risque minimal (f)
S estrategia de mínimo riesgo (f)
I strategia del rischio minimo (f)

2127 *E* minimum search depth (EXPERT SYSTEMS)
G Mindestsuchtiefe (f)
F profondeur minimum de recherche (f)
S profundidad mínima de búsqueda (f)
I profondità minima di ricerca (f)

2128 *E* MIPS
→ millions of inferences per second

2129 *E* misclassification (KNOWLEDGE)
G Fehlklassifizierung (f)
F classification erronée (f)
S clasificación errónea (f)
I classificazione sbagliata (f)

2130 *E* misrecognition (IMAGE PROCESSING)
G Fehlerkennung (f)
F reconnaissance erronée (f)
S reconocimiento erróneo (m)
I riconoscimento sbagliato (m)

2131 *E* mixed chaining (*forward and backward*) (PROGRAMMING)
= mixed-mode chaining
G gemischte Verkettung (f)
F chaînage mixte (m)
S encadenamiento mixto (m)
I concatenamento misto (m)

2132 *E* mixed-mode chaining
→ mixed chaining

2133 *E* mixed representation (KNOWLEDGE)
G gemischte Darstellung (f)
F représentation mixte (f)
S representación mixta (f)
I rappresentazione mista (f)

2134 *E* mixed strategy (*forward and backward*) (EXPERT SYSTEMS)
G gemischte Strategie (f)
F stratégie mixte (f)
S estrategia mixta (atrás-adelante) (f)
I strategia mista (f)

2135 *E* MLIPS
→ millions of logical inferences per second

2136 *E* MMI
→ man–machine interface

2137 *E* mnemonic (*adjective*) (KNOWLEDGE)
G mnemotechnisch; mnemonisch
F mnémonique

S mnemónico
I mnemonico

2138 *E* mnemonic techniques (KNOWLEDGE)
= memory-aiding techniques
G gedächtnisunterstützende Verfahren (n pl)
F techniques mnémoniques (f pl)
S técnicas mnemónicas (f pl)
I tecniche mnemoniche (f pl)

2139 *E* modal logic
G Modallogik (f); modale Logik (f)
F logique modale (f)
S lógica modal (f)
I logica modale (f)

2140 *E* modal operator (LOGIC)
G modaler Operator (m)
F opérateur modal (m)
S operador modal (m)
I operatore modale (m)

2141 *E* model-based (*vision etc.*) (IMAGE PROCESSING)
G auf einem Modell basierend; modellgestützt
F à base de modèles
S basado en modelos
I basato su modello

2142 *E* model-based diagnosis (EXPERT SYSTEMS)
G modellgestützte Diagnose (f)
F diagnose à base de modèles (f)
S diagnóstico basado en modelos (m)
I diagnosi guidata da modelli (m)

2143 *E* model-based understanding (NLP)
G modellgestütztes Verstehen (n)
F compréhension basée sur modèles (f)
S comprensión basada en modelos (f)
I comprensione basata su modelli (f)

2144 *E* model-directed problem resolution (EXPERT SYSTEMS)
G Modellsteuerung (bei der Problemlösung) (f)
F résolution guidée par modèles (f)
S solución dirigida por modelos (f)
I soluzione guidata da modelli (f)

2145 *E* model-directed search (EXPERT SYSTEMS)
= model-driven search
G von einem Modell ausgehende Suche (f); modellorientierte Suche (f)
F recherche guidée par modèle(s) (f)
S búsqueda dirigida por modelo (f); búsqueda modélica (f)
I ricerca orientata a un modello (f)

2146 *E* model-driven search
→ model-directed search

2147 *E* model-driven system (EXPERT SYSTEMS)
≠ data-driven system
G modellgetriebenes System (n); modellgesteuertes System (n)
F système guidé par modèle(s) (m)
S sistema guiado por modelo (m)
I sistema model-driven (m); sistema guidato da modelli (m)

2148 *E* modelling (LOGIC)
G Modellierung (f); Modellbildung (f)
F modélisation (f)
S modelización (f); modelación (f)
I modellazione (f); modellizzazione (f)

2149 *E* modelling capability (EXPERT SYSTEMS)
G Modellierungsfähigkeit (f)
F capacité de modélisation (f)
S capacidad de modelización (f)
I capacità di modellazione (f)

2150 *E* model matching (IMAGE PROCESSING)
G Modellvergleich (m)
F appariement de modèles (m)
S unificación de modelos (f)
I abbinamento di modelli (m)

2151 *E* model neural network
G modellhaftes neuronales Netz (n); Neuronennetzmodell (n)
F modèle de réseau neuronal (m)
S modelo de red neural (m)
I modello di rete neuronale (m)

2152 *E* model recognition (IMAGE PROCESSING)
G Modellerkennung (f)
F reconnaissance de modèles (f)
S reconocimiento de modelos (m)
I riconoscimento di modelli (m)

2153 *E* model theory
G Modelltheorie (f)
F théorie des modèles (f)
S teoría de modelos (f)
I teoria dei modelli (f)

2154 *E* modular programming
→ bottom-up programming

2155 *E* modus ponens rule (LOGIC)
= MP rule; rule of entailment
G Modus-Ponens-Regel (f)
F règle du modus ponens (f)
S regla de inferencia modus ponens (f)
I regola di modus ponens (f)

2156 *E* modus tollens rule (LOGIC)
G Modus-Tollens-Regel (f)
F règle du modus tollens (f)
S regla de resolución por refutación (f); regla de modus tollens (f)
I regola di modus tollens (f)

2157 *E* monotonic logic
≠ non-monotonic logic
G monotone Logik (f)
F logique monotone (f)
S lógica monótona (f); lógica monotónica (f)
I logica monotonica (f)

2158 *E* monotonic reasoning (LOGIC)
≠ non-monotonic reasoning
G monotones Schließen (n)
F raisonnement monotone (m)
S razonamiento monótono (m); razonamiento monotónico (m)
I ragionamento monotonico (m)

2159 *E* MOP
→ Memory Organization Packet

2160 *E* morpheme boundary (RECOGNITION)
G Morphemgrenze (f)
F frontière de morphème (f)
S límite de morfema (m)
I limite del morfema (m)

2161 *E* morphological rules (LINGUISTICS)
G morpohologische Regeln (f pl)
F règles morphologiques (f pl)
S reglas morfológicas (f pl)
I regole morfologiche (f pl)

2162 *E* most general unifier (MGU) (LOGIC)
G allgemeinster Unifikator (m)
F plus général unifieur (m)
S unificador más general (m)
I unificatore più generale (m)

2163 *E* most promising hypothesis (LOGIC)
G meistversprechende Hypothese (f)
F hypothèse plus promettante (f)
S hipótesis más prometedora (f)
I ipotesi più promettente (f)

2164 *E* motion analysis (*in object recognition*) (IMAGE PROCESSING)

G Bewegungsanalyse (f)
F analyse de mouvement (f)
S análisis de movimiento (m)
I analisi del movimento (m)

2165 *E* motion pattern (IMAGE PROCESSING)
G Bewegungsmuster (n)
F modèle de mouvement (m)
S pattern de movimiento (m)
I pattern di movimento (m); modello di movimento (m)

2166 *E* movement rules (IMAGE PROCESSING)
G Bewegungsregeln (f pl)
F règles de mouvement (f pl)
S reglas de movimiento (f pl)
I regole di movimento (f pl)

2167 *E* moving-objects classification (IMAGE PROCESSING)
G Klassifizierung sich bewegender Objekte (f)
F classification d'objets en mouvement (f)
S clasificación de objetos en movimiento (f)
I classificazione di oggetti in movimento (f)

2168 *E* MPP
→ massively parallel processing

2169 *E* MP rule
→ modus ponens rule

2170 *E* MRL
→ meaning-representation language

2171 *E* MT
→ machine translation

2172 *E* MT model
→ meaning–text model

2173 *E* multi-criteria decision making (MCDM) (EXPERT SYSTEMS)
G Treffen von Entscheidungen auf Grund mehrerer Kriterien (n)
F prise de décisions à critères multiples (f); prise de décisions multicritères (f)
S toma de decisiones multicriterio (f)
I presa di decisioni secondo criteri multipli (f)

2174 *E* multicriterion technique (EXPERT SYSTEMS)
G multivariate Methode (f)
F technique à critères multiples (f)
S técnica multicriterio (f)
I tecnica a criteri multipli (f)

2175 *E* multidirectional search (EXPERT SYSTEMS)
≠ unidirectional search
G Suche in mehreren Richtungen (f)
F recherche multidirectionnelle (f)
S búsqueda multidireccional (f)
I ricerca multidirezionale (f); ricerca in più direzioni (f)

2176 *E* multiexpert system
G Expertensystem in mehreren Disziplinen (n); Multiexpertensystem (n)
F système multiexpert(s) (m)
S sistema multiexperto (m); multisistemas expertos (m pl)
I sistema multiesperto (m); sistema esperto multivalente (m)

2177 *E* multihypothesis variable (LOGIC)
G Mehrhypothesenvariable (f)
F variable à plusieurs hypothèses (f)
S variable de multiples hipótesis (f)
I variabile a più ipotesi (f)

2178 *E* multilayer(ed) (*neural net etc.; adjective*)
G mehrschichtig
F multi-couches
S multicapas
I a più strati; multistrato

2179 *E* multilingual interface (EXPERT SYSTEMS)
G mehrsprachige Schnittstelle (f)
F interface en plusieurs langues (f)
S interfaz en varias lenguas (f)
I interfaccia multilingue (f)

2180 *E* multilingual text synthesis (NLP)
G mehrsprachige Textsynthese (f)
F synthèse de textes multilingues (f)
S síntesis de textos multilingües (f)
I sintesi di testi multilingue (f)

2181 *E* multimodal dialogue (EXPERT SYSTEMS)
G multimodaler Dialog (m)
F dialogue multimodal (m)
S diálogo en varios modos (m)
I dialogo a più modi (m)

2182 *E* multipass algorithm (PROGRAMMING)
G mehrfach zu durchlaufender Algorithmus (m)
F algorithme de plusieurs passages (m)
S algoritmo de multiples pasos (m)
I algoritmo a più passaggi (m)

2183 *E* multiple hierarchy (KNOWLEDGE)
G Mehrfachhierarchie (f)
F hiérarchie multiple (f)
S jerarquía múltiple (f)
I gerarchie multiple (f)

2184 *E* multiple inheritance (KNOWLEDGE)
≠ simple inheritance
G Mehrfachvererbung (f); multiple Vererbung (f)
F héritage multiple (m)
S herencia múltiple (f)
I ereditarietà multipla (f)

2185 *E* multiple-path reasoning (LOGIC)
G Inferieren über mehrere Pfade
F raisonnement par chemins multiples
S razonamiento por múltiples líneas (independientes)
I ragionamento attraverso più vie

2186 *E* multiple planning (EXPERT SYSTEMS)
G Mehrfachplanung (f)
F planification multiple (f)
S planificación múltiple (f)
I planning multiplo (f)

2187 *E* multiple rule (EXPERT SYSTEMS)
G Mehrfachregel (f)
F règle multiple (f)
S regla múltiple (f)
I regola multipla (f)

2188 *E* multisensors (IMAGE PROCESSING)
G Mehrfachsensoren (m pl)
F multicapteurs (m pl)
S sensores múltiples (m pl)
I sensori multipli (m pl)

2189 *E* multispeaker recognition
G Erkennen mehrerer Sprecher (n); Erkennen bei mehreren Sprechern (n)
F reconnaissance multilocuteur (f)
S reconocimiento multilocutor (m)
I riconoscimento nel caso di più locutori (m)

2190 *E* multispeaker system (NLP)
G Mehrsprechersystem (n)
F système multilocuteurs (m)
S sistema multilocutores (m)
I sistema a più locutori (m); sistema multilocutori (m)

2191 *E* multistage decision (EXPERT SYSTEMS)
G Entscheidung in mehreren Stufen (f)
F décision en plusieurs phases (f)
S decisión multifase (f)
I decisione multifase (f)

2192 *E* multistep logical inference (EXPERT SYSTEMS)
G mehrschrittiges logisches Schließen (n)
F inférence logique à plusieurs pas (f)
S inferencia lógica de múltiples pasos (f)
I inferenza logica a più passi (f)

2193 *E* multistep problem (EXPERT SYSTEMS)
G mehrschrittiges Problem (n)
F problème de plusieurs pas (m)
S problema de pasos múltiples (m)
I problema a più passi (m)

2194 *E* multivalued attribute (KNOWLEDGE)
G mehrwertiges Attribut (n)
F attribut à valeurs multiples (m); attribut multivalué (m)
S atributo multivalorado (m)
I attributo a più valori (m)

2195 *E* multivalued logic (*inexact logic*)
= many-valued logic; polyvalent logics
G mehrwertige Logik (f)
F logique multivaluée (f); logique à plusieurs valeurs (f); logique multivalente (f)
S lógica multivaluada (f)
I logica a molti valori (f)

2196 *E* multivariate (*analysis etc.*) (LOGIC)
G multivariat
F multivarié
S multivariado
I multivariato

2197 *E* mutation (*of a rule*) (EXPERT SYSTEMS)
G Abwandlung (f)
F mutation (f)
S mutación (f)
I mutazione (f)

2198 *E* mutually exclusive (*conditions etc.*) (LOGIC)
G sich gegenseitig ausschließend; mit wechselseitigem Ausschluß
F mutuellement exclusif
S mutuamente exclusivo
I mutualmente esclusivi

N

2199 *E* narrative analysis (RECOGNITION)
G Textanalyse (f)
F analyse narrative (f)
S análisis del texto (m)
I analisi del testo narrativo (m)

2200 *E* narrative grammar (NLP)
G narrative Grammatik (f)
F grammaire narrative (f)
S gramática narrativa (f)
I grammatica narrativa (f)

2201 *E* narrative text (NLP)
G erzählender Text (m)
F texte narratif (m)
S texto narrativo (m)
I testo narrativo (m)

2202 *E* natural deduction (LOGIC)
G natürliches Schließen (n); Sequenzenkalkül (n)
F déduction naturelle (f)
S deducción natural (f)
I deduzione naturale (f)

2203 *E* natural deduction system (LOGIC)
G natürliches Deduktionssystem (n)
F système de déduction naturelle (m)
S sistema de deducción natural (m)
I sistema di deduzione naturale (m)

2204 *E* natural intelligence (NI)
G natürliche Intelligenz (f)
F intelligence naturelle (f)
S inteligencia natural (f)
I intelligenza naturale (f)

2205 *E* natural-language (*adjective*)
G natürlichsprachlich; natürlichsprachig
F en langage naturel
S de lenguaje natural
I del linguaggio naturale

2206 *E* natural language (NL)
G natürliche Sprache (f)
F langage naturel (m)
S lenguaje natural (LN) (m); idioma natural (m)
I linguaggio naturale (m)

2207 *E* natural-language analysis
= analysis of natural language
G Analyse natürlicher Sprache (f)
F analyse du langage naturel (f)
S análisis del lenguaje natural (m)
I analisi del linguaggio naturale (m)

2208 *E* natural-language capability
G Fähigkeit, mit natürlicher Sprache zu arbeiten (f)
F capacité de langage naturel (f)
S capacidad de lenguaje natural (f)
I capacità di linguaggio naturale (f)

2209 *E* natural-language dialogue
G Dialog in natürlicher Sprache (m); natürlichsprachlicher Dialog (m)
F dialogue en langage naturel (m)
S diálogo en lenguaje natural (m)
I dialogo in linguaggio naturale (m)

2210 *E* natural-language front end
→ natural-language interface

2211 *E* natural-language generation
G Generierung natürlicher Sprache (f)

F génération de langage naturel (f)
S generación de lenguaje natural (f)
I generazione di linguaggio naturale (f)

2212 *E* natural-language interface (NLI) (PROGRAMMING)
= natural-language front end
G natürlichsprachliche Schnittstelle (f)
F interface en langage naturel (f)
S interfaz de lenguaje natural (f)
I interfaccia in linguaggio naturale (f)

2213 *E* natural-language interpreter (EXPERT SYSTEMS)
G Interpreter für natürliche Sprache (m)
F interpréteur de langage naturel (m)
S intérprete de lenguaje natural (m)
I interprete di linguaggio naturale (m)

2214 *E* natural-language processing (NLP)
G Verarbeitung natürlicher Sprache (f); natürliche Sprachverarbeitung (f)
F traitement des langues naturelles (TLN) (m)
S procesamiento del lenguaje natural (m); tratamiento del lenguaje natural (m)
I elaborazione del linguaggio naturale (m)

2215 *E* natural-language processing systems
= NLP systems
G Systeme für natürliche Sprachverarbeitung (n pl)
F systèmes de traitement des langues naturelles (m pl)
S sistemas de procesamiento del lenguaje natural (m pl)
I sistemi di elaborazione del linguaggio naturale (m pl)

2216 *E* natural-language query system (EXPERT SYSTEMS)
G natürlichsprachliches Abfragesystem (n)
F système d'interrogation en langue naturelle (m)
S sistema de consulta en lenguaje natural (m)
I sistema di interrogazione in linguaggio naturale (m)

2217 *E* natural-language system (EXPERT SYSTEMS)
= NL system
G natürlichsprachliches System (n)
F système en langage naturel (m)
S sistema de lenguaje natural (m)
I sistema in linguaggio naturale (m)

2218 *E* natural-language understanding (NLU) (RECOGNITION)
G Verstehen natürlicher Sprache (n)
F compréhension de langages naturels (f)
S comprensión de lenguaje natural (f)
I comprensione del linguaggio naturale (f)

2219 *E* NE
→ non-equality

2220 *E* nearest-neighbour classifier (RECOGNITION)
G Nächster-Nachbar-Klassifikator (m)
F classificateur 'des plus proches voisins' (m)
S clasificador de vecino más próximo (m)
I classificatore tipo il più vicino (m)

2221 *E* nearest-neighbour search (LOGIC)

G Suche nach dem nächsten Nachbarn (f)
F recherche du plus proche voisin (f)
S búsqueda del vecino más próximo (f)
I ricerca del vicino più prossimo (f)

2222 E necessary condition (LOGIC)
G notwendige Bedingung (f)
F condition nécessaire (f)
S condición necesária (f)
I condizione necessaria (f)

2223 E negate (*a statement etc.*) (LOGIC)
G negieren; verneinen
F nier
S negar
I negare

2224 E negation (LOGIC)
G Negation (f); Verneinung (f)
F négation (f)
S negación (f)
I negazione (f)

2225 E negative clause (LOGIC)
G negative Klausel (f)
F clause négative (f)
S cláusula negativa (f)
I clausola negativa (f)

2226 E negative example (LEARNING)
G Negativbeispiel (n); negatives Beispiel (n)
F exemple négatif (m)
S ejemplo negativo (m)
I esempio negativo (m)

2227 E nest (*predicates etc.*) (LOGIC)
G schachteln
F imbriquer
S anidar
I imbricare

2228 E nested query (EXPERT SYSTEMS)
G verschachtelte Anfrage (f)
F interrogation imbriquée (f)
S interrogación anidada (f)
I interrogazione a più livelli (f)

2229 E network chaining (LOGIC)
G Netzverkettung (f)
F chaînage de réseaux (m)
S encadenamiento de redes (m)
I concatenamento di reti (m)

2230 E network of rules (EXPERT SYSTEMS)
G Regelnetz (n)
F réseau de règles (m)
S red de reglas (f)
I rete di regole (f)

2231 E network path (EXPERT SYSTEMS)
G Netzpfad (m)
F chemin d'un réseau (m)
S camino de red (m)
I cammino in una rete (m)

2232 E network search (EXPERT SYSTEMS)
= search over a network
G Suche über ein Netz (f)
F recherche dans un réseau (f)
S búsqueda en red (f)
I ricerca in una rete (f)

2233 E neural
= neuronal
G neural; neuronal
F neuronal
S neuronal
I neuronale; neurale

2234 E neural chip
G Neurochip (m)
F puce neuronale (f)
S pastilla neuronal (f)
I chip neuronale (m)

2235 E neural computer
→ neurocomputer

2236 E neural computing
→ neurocomputing

2237 *E* neural hardware
G neuronale Hardware (f)
F matériel neuronal (m)
S hardware neuronal (m)
I hardware neuronale (m)

2238 *E* neural logic
G Neuronenlogik (f)
F logique neuronale (f)
S lógica neuronal (f)
I logica neuronale (f)

2239 *E* neural net (*properly speaking:* artificial neural net)
= neural network
G neurales Netz (n); neurales Netzwerk (n); neuronales Netz (n)
F réseau neuronal (m); réseau de neurones (m)
S red neuronal (f)
I rete neurale (f); rete neuronale (artificiale) (f)

2240 *E* neural network
→ neural net

2241 *E* neural network approach (NLP)
G Methode der neuronalen Netze (f)
F approche neuro-physiologique (f)
S método de redes neuronales (m)
I modellazione degli stati neurali (m)

2242 *E* neural network model
= connectionist model
G Modell eines neuronalen Netzes (n); Netzmodell (n); KNN-Modell (n)
F modèle de réseau neuronal (m)
S modelo de red neuronal (m)
I modello di rete neuronale (m)

2243 *E* neural network technology
G Technologie der neuronalen Netze (f)
F technologie des réseaux neuronaux (f)
S tecnología de las redes neuronales (f)
I tecnologia delle reti neuronali (f)

2244 *E* neurocomputer
= neural computer; neuronal computer
G Neuronenrechner (m); Neurocomputer (m)
F ordinateur neuronal (m)
S ordenador neuronal (m)
I calcolatore neuronale (m)

2245 *E* neurocomputing
= neural computing
G Neuroinformatik (f)
F informatique neuronale (f)
S informática neuronal (f)
I calcolo neuronale (f)

2246 *E* neuron
G Neuron (n) (*plural*: Neurone, Neuronen)
F neurone (m)
S neurona (f)
I neurone (cellula nervosa) (m)

2247 *E* neuronal
→ neural

2248 *E* neuronal computer
→ neurocomputer

2249 *E* neuronal interconnection
→ synapse

2250 *E* NI
→ natural intelligence

2251 *E* NL
→ natural language

2252 *E* NLI
→ natural-language interface

2253 *E* NLMenu
→ menu-based natural language

2254 *E* NLMenu interface
→ menu-based natural language interface

2255 *E* NLP
→ natural-language processing

2256 *E* NLP systems
→ natural-language processing systems

2257 *E* NL system
→ natural-language system

2258 *E* NLU
→ natural-language understanding

2259 *E* NML
→ non-monotonic logic

2260 *E* no-backtrack facility (EXPERT SYSTEMS)
= cut
G Mechanismus ohne Backtracking (m)
F mécanisme sans possibilité de retour arrière (m)
S mecanismo sin vueltas atrás (m)
I mecanismo senza possibilità di backtracking (m); mecanismo senza possibilità di ritorno all'indietro (m)

2261 *E* no-backtrack predicate (LOGIC)
G Prädikat 'kein Backtracking' (n)
F prédicat 'pas de retour arrière' (m)
S predicado 'sin vuelta atrás' (m)
I predicato 'senza backtracking' (m); predicato 'senza ritorno all'indietro'

2262 *E* node (*in a graph*) (LOGIC)
G Knoten (m)
F nœud (m); sommet (m)
S nodo (m)
I nodo (m)

2263 *E* node of a tree (KNOWLEDGE)
G Knoten eines Baums (m)
F nœud d'un arbre (m)
S nodo de árbol (m)
I nodo di un albero (m)

2264 *E* nominal phrase
→ noun phrase

2265 *E* non-adaptive system
G nichtadaptives System (n)
F système non-adaptatif (m)
S sistema no adaptativo (m)
I sistema non adattivo (m)

2266 *E* non-algorithmic (MATHS)
G nichtalgorithmisch
F non-algorithmique
S no algorítmico
I non-algoritmico

2267 *E* non-classical logic
= non-standard logic; deviant logics; exotic logics
G nichtklassische Logik (f); unkonventionelle Logik (f)
F logique non conventionnelle (f)
S lógica no clásica (f); lógica no convencional (f)
I logica non classica (f); logica non convenzionale (f); logica non standard (f)

2268 *E* non-determinism (THEORY)
G Nichtdeterminismus (m)
F non-déterminisme (m)
S non-determinismo (m)
I non determinismo (m)

2269 *E* non-deterministic (*algorithm etc.*) (THEORY)
G nicht-deterministisch
F non-déterministe
S non-determinista
I non-deterministico

2270 *E* non-directed graph (LOGIC)

= non-oriented graph; undirected graph; indirect graph
G ungerichteter Graph (m); nicht gerichteter Graph (m)
F graphe non orienté (m); graphe non dirigé (m)
S grafo no orientado (m)
I grafo non orientato (m)

2271 *E* non-equality (NE) (MATHS)
G Ungleichheit (f)
F non-égalité (f)
S desigualdad (f)
I non-equalità (f)

2272 *E* non-exhaustive search (EXPERT SYSTEMS)
G nicht bis in die Tiefe gehende Suche (f)
F recherche incomplète (f)
S búsqueda no completa (f)
I ricerca non-esaustiva (f)

2273 *E* non-heuristic (LOGIC)
G nicht heuristisch
F non-heuristique
S no heurístico
I non euristico

2274 *E* non-linear system
G nichtlineares System (n)
F système non-linéaire (m)
S sistema no lineal (m)
I sistema non lineare (m)

2275 *E* non-logical reasoning (LOGIC)
G nichtlogisches Inferieren (n)
F raisonnement non-logique (m)
S razonamiento no lógico (m)
I ragionamento non logico (m)

2276 *E* non-monotonicity (LOGIC)
G Nichtmonotonität (f)
F non-monotonie (f); non-monotinicité (f)
S no monotonicidad (f)
I non-monotonia (f)

2277 *E* non-monotonic logic (NML)
≠ monotonic logic
G nichtmonotone Logik (f)
F logique non monotone (f)
S lógica no monótona (f); lógica no monotónica (f)
I logica non monotonica (f)

2278 *E* non-monotonic reasoning (LOGIC)
≠ monotonic reasoning
G nichtmonotones Schließen (n)
F raisonnement non monotone (m)
S razonamiento no monotónico (m)
I ragionamento non monotonico (m)

2279 *E* non-oriented graph
→ non-directed graph

2280 *E* non-probabilistic method (LOGIC)
G nichtprobabilistische Methode (f)
F méthode non probabilistique (f)
S método no probabilístico (m)
I metodo non-probabilistico (m)

2281 *E* non-procedural (*language etc.*) (PROGRAMMING)
G nichtprozedural
F non-procédural
S no procedural
I non-procedurale

2282 *E* non-standard logic
→ non-classical logic

2283 *E* non-structured environment
→ unstructured environment

2284 *E* non-terminal node (LOGIC)
G Nicht-Endknoten (m)
F nœud non terminal (m)
S nodo no terminal (m)
I nodo non-terminale (m)

2285 *E* non-visual perception (IMAGE PROCESSING)
G nichtvisuelle Wahrnehmung (f)
F perception non visuelle (f)

S percepción no visual (f)
I percezione non visiva (f)

2286 *E* non-von machine (*short for non-Von-Neumann*)
→ parallel processor

2287 *E* notation (PROGRAMMING)
G Notation (f)
F notation (f)
S notación (f)
I notazione (f)

2288 *E* notion (KNOWLEDGE)
G Notion (f)
F notion (f)
S noción (f)
I nozione (f)

2289 *E* noun phrase (NP) (LINGUISTICS)
= nominal phrase
G Nominalphrase (NP) (f)
F phrase nominale (f)
S frase nominal (f)
I frase nominale (f)

2290 *E* NP
→ noun phrase

2291 *E* number of facts
G Faktenzahl (f)
F nombre de faits (NF) (m)
S número de factos (m)
I numero di fatti (m)

2292 *E* number of rules (EXPERT SYSTEMS)
G Regelanzahl (f)
F nombre de règles (NR) (m)
S número de reglas (m)
I numero di regole (m)

2293 *E* Nyquist frequency (RECOGNITION)
G Nyquistfrequenz (f)
F fréquence de Nyquist (f)
S frecuencia de Nyquist (f)
I frequenza di Nyquist (f)

O

2294 *E* OAV triplet
→ object–attribute–value triplet

2295 *E* object[1] (KNOWLEDGE)
G Objekt (n)
F objet (m)
S objeto (m)
I oggetto (m)

2296 *E* object[2]
→ frame

2297 *E* object attribute (KNOWLEDGE)
G Objektattribut (n)
F attribut d'objet (m)
S atributo de objetos (m)
I attributo di un oggetto (m)

2298 *E* object–attribute–value triplet (KNOWLEDGE)
= OAV triplet
↔ context–parameter–value triplet
G Faktentripel (Objekt, Attribut und Wert) (n); Objekt–Attribut–Wert-Tripel (n); OAV-Schema (n)
F triplet objet–attribut–valeur (m); triplet OAV (m)
S tripla objeto–atributo–valor (f); tripla OAV (f)
I tripla OAV (oggetto–attributi–valori) (f)

2299 *E* object-centred (*representation etc.*) (KNOWLEDGE)
G objektzentriert
F centré autour des objets; centré-objet
S centrado entorno a los objetos
I centrato intorno agli oggetti

2300 *E* object class (KNOWLEDGE)
G Objektklasse (f)
F classe d'objets (f)
S clase de objeto (f)
I classe di oggetto (f)

2301 *E* object description (KNOWLEDGE)
G Objektbeschreibung (f)
F description de l'objet (f)
S descripción de objetos (f)
I descrizione del oggetto (f)

2302 *E* object evaluation function (EXPERT SYSTEMS)
G Objektbewertungsfunktion (f)
F fonction d'évaluation d'objet (f)
S función de evaluación de objetos (f)
I funzione di evaluazione degli oggetti (f)

2303 *E* object frame
→ frame

2304 *E* object hierarchy (KNOWLEDGE)
G Objekthierarchie (f)
F hiérarchie d'objets (f)
S jerarquía de objetos (f)
I gerarchia di oggetti (f)

2305 *E* object identification (IMAGE PROCESSING)
G Objektidentifizierung (f)
F identification d'objets (f)
S identificación del objeto (f)
I identificazioni di oggetti (f)

2306 *E* object identity (OI) (KNOWLEDGE)
G Objektidentität (OI) (f)
F identité de l'objet (f)

S identidad de objeto (f)
I identità dell'oggetto (f)

2307 *E* objective
→ goal

2308 *E* object knowledge
G Objektwissen (n)
F connaissances sur l'objet (f pl)
S conocimiento sobre objetos (m)
I conoscenza su oggetti (m)

2309 *E* object level (KNOWLEDGE)
G Objektebene (f)
F niveau de l'objet (m)
S nivel de objeto (m)
I livello dell'oggetto (m)

2310 *E* object machine (PROGRAMMING)
G Objektmaschine (f)
F machine objets (f)
S máquina objeto (f)
I macchina-oggetto (f)

2311 *E* object manipulation (KNOWLEDGE)
G Objektmanipulation (f)
F manipulation des objets (f)
S manipulación de objetos (f)
I manipolazione del oggetto (f)

2312 *E* object of discourse (LOGIC)
G Diskursobjekt (n)
F objet de discours (m)
S objeto de discurso (m)
I oggetto del discorso (m)

2313 *E* object-oriented (KNOWLEDGE)
G objektorientiert
F orienté aux objets
S orientado a los objetos
I orientato agli oggetti

2314 *E* object-oriented knowledge
G objektorientiertes Wissen (n); Objektwissen (n)
F connaissance orientée à l'objet (f)
S conocimiento orientado a objetos (m)
I conoscenza orientata all'oggetto (f)

2315 *E* object-oriented knowledge representation
G objektorientierte Wissensdarstellung (f)
F représentation des connaissances orientée à l'objet (f)
S representación de conocimientos orientada a objetos (f)
I rappresentazione della conoscenza orientata agli oggetti (f)

2316 *E* object-oriented (programming) language
G objektorientierte Sprache (f)
F langage orienté objets (LOO) (m); langage objets (m)
S lenguaje dirigido a objetos (m); lenguaje orientado a objeto (m)
I linguaggio orientato all'oggetto (m)

2317 *E* object-oriented programming (OOP)
G objektorientierte Programmierung (f)
F programmation à base d'objets (f); programmation orientée objets (POO) (f)
S programación orientada a objetos (f)
I programmazione orientata all'oggetto (f); programmazione per oggetti (f)

2318 *E* object-oriented representation (KNOWLEDGE)
G objektorientierte Darstellung (f)
F représentation à base d'objets (f)
S representación orientada a objetos (f)
I rappresentazione orientata all'oggetto (f)

2319 *E* object recognition (IMAGE PROCESSING)
G Erkennen von Objekten (n); Objekterkennung (f)
F reconnaissance d'objet(s) (f)
S reconocimiento de objetos (m)
I riconoscimento di oggetti (m)

2320 *E* object recognition program (IMAGE PROCESSING)
G Objekterkennungsprogramm (n)
F programme de reconnaissance d'objets (m)
S programa de reconocimiento de objetos (m)
I programma di riconoscimento di oggetti (m)

2321 *E* object recognition system (IMAGE PROCESSING)
G Objekterkennungssystem (n)
F système de reconnaissance d'objets (m)
S sistema de reconocimiento de objetos (m)
I sistema di riconoscimento di oggetti (m)

2322 *E* object space (EXPERT SYSTEMS)
G Objektraum (m)
F espace objets (m)
S espacio de objetos (m)
I spazio oggetti (m)

2323 *E* object state (EXPERT SYSTEMS)
G Objektzustand (m)
F état d'objets (m)
S estado objeto (m)
I stato oggetto (m)

2324 *E* object template (IMAGE PROCESSING)
G Objektschablone (f)
F modèle d'objets (m)
S modelo de objeto (m)
I modello di oggetto (m)

2325 *E* object tree (LOGIC)
G Objektbaum (m)
F arbre d'objets (m)
S árbol de objetos (m)
I albero degli oggetti (m)

2326 *E* object type
→ entity type

2327 *E* object variable (LOGIC)
G Objektvariable (f)
F variable d'objet (f)
S variable de objeto (f)
I variabile di oggetto (f)

2328 *E* occurrence (LINGUISTICS)
G Vorkommen (n); Auftreten (n)
F occurrence (f)
S ocurrencia (f)
I occorrenza (f)

2329 *E* OI
→ object identity

2330 *E* online explanation
→ mid-run explanation

2331 *E* OOP
→ object-oriented programming

2332 *E* opaque reference (LOGIC)
G undurchsichtiger Bezug (m)
F référence opaque (f)
S referencia opaca (f)
I riferimento opaco (f)

2333 *E* open list (*of generated but not yet expanded nodes*) (LOGIC)
G Open-Liste (f)
F liste ouverte (f)
S lista abierta (f)
I lista aperta (f)

2334 *E* operating environment
G Einsatzumgebung (f)
F environnement d'exploitation (m); environnement opérationnel (m)
S entorno operativo (m)

I ambiento operativo (m)

2335 *E* operational semantics (KNOWLEDGE)
G Operationssemantik (f)
F sémantique opérationnelle (f)
S semántica operacional (f)
I semantica operazionale (f)

2336 *E* optical flow (IMAGE PROCESSING)
G optischer Fluß (m)
F flux optique (m)
S flujo óptico (m)
I flusso ottico (m)

2337 *E* optimal path (LOGIC)
G optimaler Weg (m)
F chemin optimal (m)
S camino óptimo (m)
I cammino ottimale (m)

2338 *E* optimal solution (LOGIC)
= optimum solution
G optimale Lösung (f)
F solution optimale (f)
S solución óptima (f)
I soluzione ottimale (f)

2339 *E* optimal-solution graph (LOGIC)
G Graph für optimale Lösung (m)
F graphe de solution optimale (m)
S grafo de soluciones óptimas (m)
I grafo delle soluzioni ottimali (m)

2340 *E* optimization (PROGRAMMING)
G Optimierung (f)
F optimisation (f)
S optimización (f)
I ottimizzazione (f)

2341 *E* optimization net (PROGRAMMING)
G Optimierungsnetz (n)
F réseau d'optimisation (m)
S red de optimización (f)
I rete ottimizzatrice (f)

2342 *E* optimization procedure (PROGRAMMING)
G Optimierungsprozeß (m)
F procédure d'optimisation (f)
S procedimiento de optimización (m)
I procedura di ottimizzazione (f)

2343 *E* optimum solution
→ optimal solution

2344 *E* optional rule (EXPERT SYSTEMS)
G optionale Regel (f)
F règle facultative (f)
S regla opcional (f)
I regola facoltativa (f)

2345 *E* oral data input
→ voice input

2346 *E* ordered resolution (LOGIC)
G geordnete Resolution (f)
F résolution ordonnée (f)
S resolución ordenada (f)
I risoluzione ordinata (f)

2347 *E* ordered search (LOGIC)
= guided search
G organisiertes Suchverfahren (n); geordnete Suche (f)
F recherche ordonnée (f); recherche guidée (f)
S búsqueda ordenada (f)
I ricerca ordinata (f)

2348 *E* ordered tree (LOGIC)
G geordneter Baum (m)
F arbre ordonné (m)
S árbol ordenado (m)
I albero ordinato (m)

2349 *E* order of complexity (PROGRAMMING)
G Komplexitätsgrad (m)
F degré de complexité (m)
S grado de complexidad (m)
I grado di complessità (m)

2350 *E* OR expansion (LOGIC)
G ODER-Expansion (f)

F expansion OU (f)
S expansión OR (f)
I espansione OR (f)

2351 *E* oriented edge
→ directed arc

2352 *E* oriented graph
→ directed graph

2353 *E* original problem (LOGIC)
G Ausgangsproblem (n)
F problème d'origine (m)
S problema de origen (m)
I problema originario (m)

2354 *E* origin tag (OT) (KNOWLEDGE)
G Ursprungs-Tag (m)
F marque d'origine (f)
S marca de origen (f)
I tag di origine (m)

2355 *E* OR node (LOGIC)
↔ AND node
G ODER-Knoten (m); OR-Knoten (m)
F nœud OU (m)
S nodo OR (m)
I nodo OR (m)

2356 *E* OR relation (PROGRAMMING)
G ODER-Beziehung (f); Disjunktion (f)
F relation OU (f)
S relación OR (f)
I rapporto disgiuntivo (OR) (m)

2357 *E* OT
→ origin tag

2358 *E* outgoing arc (LOGIC)
G abgehende Kante (f)
F arc sortant (m)
S arco de salida (m)
I arco uscente (m)

2359 *E* outgoing node
→ output node

2360 *E* outline detection
→ edge detection

2361 *E* output node (LOGIC)
= outgoing node
G Ausgangsknoten (m)
F nœud de sortie (m); nœud sortant (m)
S nodo de salida (m)
I nodo di uscita (m); nodo uscente (m)

2362 *E* output predicate (LOGIC)
≠ input predicate
G Ausgabeprädikat (n)
F prédicat de sortie (m)
S predicado de salida (m)
I predicato di uscita (m)

P

2363 *E* P
→ predicate

2364 *E* PA
→ procedural attachment

2365 *E* pair of nodes (LOGIC)
G Knotenpaar (n)
F paire de nœuds (f)
S par de nodos (m)
I coppia di nodi (f)

2366 *E* paradigm (LOGIC)
G Paradigma (n); Grundmuster (n)
F paradigme (m)
S paradigma (m)
I paradigma (m)

2367 *E* paradigm of search
→ search paradigm

2368 *E* parallel distributed processing (PDP)
→ connection science

2369 *E* parallel inference (LOGIC)
G Parallelschluß (m)
F inférence parallèle (f); inférence en parallèle (f)
S inferencia paralela (f)
I inferenza parallela (f)

2370 *E* parallel inference machine (PIM) (EXPERT SYSTEMS)
G parallele Inferenzmaschine (PIM) (f)
F machine d'inférence en parallèle (f)
S máquina de inferencia en paralelo (f)
I macchina ad inferenza parallela (f)

2371 *E* parallel planning (EXPERT SYSTEMS)
G Parallelplanung (f)
F planification parallèle (f)
S planificación paralela (f)
I planning parallelo (m); pianificazione parallela (f)

2372 *E* parallel processing
G Parallelverarbeitung (f)
F traitement en parallèle (m)
S procesamiento en paralelo (m); paralelismo (m)
I trattamento in parallelo (m); parallelismo (m)

2373 *E* parallel processor
= non-von machine
G Parallelverarbeitungrechner (m); Non-Von-Rechner (mit Parallelarchitektur) (m)
F processeur parallèle (m); machine parallèle (f)
S procesador paralelo (m)
I elaboratore a processamento in parallelo (m)

2374 *E* parameter learning
G Lernen von Parametern (n)
F apprentissage de paramètres (m)
S aprendizaje de parámetros (m)
I apprendimento di parametri (m)

2375 *E* parametric (PROGRAMMING)
G parametrisch
F paramétrique
S paramétrico
I parametrico

2376 *E* parametric representation (SYNTHESIS)
G parametrische Darstellung (f)
F représentation paramétrique (f)
S representación paramétrica (f)
I rappresentazione parametrica (f)

2377 *E* paramodulation (*a deduction rule in predicate logic*)
G Paramodulation (f)
F paramodulation (f)
S paramodulación (f)
I paramodulazione (f)

2378 *E* parent (node)
→ ancestor (node)

2379 *E* parent clause (LOGIC)
G Elternklausel (f)
F clause parente (f)
S cláusula padre (f)
I clausola genitore (f)

2380 *E* parent concept (KNOWLEDGE)
= higher-level concept
≠ child concept
G Oberbegriff (m)
F concept parent (m)
S concepto padre (m)
I concetto genitore (m)

2381 *E* parent frame (KNOWLEDGE)
= higher-level frame
G hierarchisch übergeordneter Frame (m)
F cadre parent (m)
S frame padre (m)
I frame genitore (m); quadro genitore (m)

2382 *E* parent node (LOGIC)
G Elternknoten (m); Vorgängerknoten (m)
F nœud parent (m)
S nodo padre (m)
I nodo genitore (m)

2383 *E* parents (*predecessors*) (LOGIC)
G Eltern (pl)
F parents (m pl)
S padres (m pl)
I genitori (m pl)

2384 *E* parse (*verb*) (NLP)
G parsen
F analyser (syntaxiquement)
S analizar (sintácticamente)
I analizzare (sintatticamente)

2385 *E* parser (*syntactic analyser*) (NLP)
G Parser (m)
F analyseur (syntaxique) (m); parseur (m)
S analizador sintáctico (m)
I parser (m)

2386 *E* parse tree (NLP)
= parsing tree
G Parse Tree (m); Parsing-Baum (m); Ableitungsbaum (m); Satzstrukturbaum (m)
F arbre syntaxique (m)
S árbol de parsing (m)
I albero di parse (m)

2387 *E* parsing (NLP)
G Parsing (n)
F analyse (syntaxique) (f)
S análisis sintáctico (m); parsing (m)
I analisi sintattica (f); parsing (m)

2388 *E* parsing speed (NLP)
G Parsinggeschwindigkeit (f)
F vélocité d'analyse (f)
S velocidad de parsing (f)
I velocità di parsing (f)

2389 *E* parsing tree
→ parse tree

2390 *E* partial graph (LOGIC)
G partieller Graph (m)
F graphe partiel (m)
S grafo parcial (m)
I grafo parziale (m)

2391 *E* partial solution (EXPERT SYSTEMS)
G Teillösung (f)
F solution partielle (f)
S solución parcial (f)
I soluzione parziale (f)

2392 *E* partial speaker dependence (RECOGNITION)
G teilweise Sprecherabhängigkeit (f)
F dépendance partielle du locuteur (f)
S dependencia parcial del locutor (f)
I dipendenza parziale dal locutore (f)

2393 *E* partial term (NLP)
G Teilterm (m)
F terme partiel (m)
S término parcial (m)
I termine parziale (m)

2394 *E* partition
G Partition (Teilbereich) (f)
F partition (f)
S partición (f)
I partizione (f)

2395 *E* partitioned semantic network (LOGIC)
G partitioniertes semantisches Netz (n)
F réseau sémantique partitionné (m)
S red semántica particionada (f)
I rete semantica partizionata (f)

2396 *E* partitioning (*of semantic networks*) (NLP)
G Partitionieren (n); Aufteilen (n)
F partitionnement (m)
S particionamiento (m)
I partizionamento (di reti semantiche) (m)

2397 *E* partitive relation (LOGIC)
= part-of relation; is-a-part-of relation
G partitive Relation (f); Partitionsbeziehung (f); Teilmengenbeziehung (f)
F relation partitive (f); relation fait-partie-de (f)
S relación parte de (f); relación de pertinencia (a una clase etc.) (f)
I relazione partitiva (f)

2398 *E* part-of relation
→ partitive relation

2399 *E* part–whole description (KNOWLEDGE)
G Teil–Ganzes-Beschreibung (f)
F description part–total (f)
S descripción parte–total (f)
I descrizione del tipo parte–insieme (f)

2400 *E* passive blackboard (EXPERT SYSTEMS)
≠ active blackboard
G passives Blackboard (n)
F tableau noir passif (m)
S pizarra pasiva (f)
I blackboard passiva (f); lavagna passiva (f)

2401 *E* path (LOGIC)
= pathway
G Weg (m); Pfad (m)
F chemin (m); parcours (m)
S ruta (f); camino (m)
I cammino (m); percorso (m)

2402 *E* path constraint (LOGIC)
G Pfadrestriktion (f)
F contrainte de parcours (f)
S restricción de camino (f)
I restrizione di percorso (f)

2403 *E* path-dependent (LOGIC)
G wegabhängig
F dépendant du parcours
S dependiente de la ruta
I dipendente dal cammino

2404 *E* path finding (EXPERT SYSTEMS)
G Suche nach einer Vorgehensweise (f)
F recherche d'un parcours (f)
S búsqueda de una ruta (f)
I ricerca di un percorso (f)

2405 *E* path-independent (LOGIC)
G wegunabhängig
F indépendant du parcours
S independiente de la ruta
I indipendente dal cammino

2406 *E* path planning (EXPERT SYSTEMS)
G Planung der Vorgehensweise (f)
F planification du parcours (f)
S planificación de la ruta (f)
I pianificazione del cammino da seguire (f)

2407 *E* pathway
→ path

2408 *E* pattern (IMAGE PROCESSING)
G Pattern (n); Muster (n)
F forme (f); modèle (m); patron (m)
S plantilla (f); pattern (m); patrón (m); modelo (m); forma (f)
I pattern (da riconoscere) (m); modello (m)

2409 *E* pattern analysis (IMAGE PROCESSING)
G Musteranalyse (f)
F analyse de formes (f)
S análisis de patrones (m)
I analisi di pattern (f); analisi di modelli (f)

2410 *E* pattern classification (IMAGE PROCESSING)
G Musterklassifizierung (f)
F classification de formes (f)
S clasificación de patrones (f)
I classificazione di pattern (f); classificazione di modelli (f)

2411 *E* pattern completion (THEORY)
G Mustervervollständigung (f)
F complètement de modèles (m)
S completamiento de patrones (m)
I completamento di pattern (m); completamento di modelli (m)

2412 *E* pattern-directed (EXPERT SYSTEMS)
G mustergesteuert
F dirigé par modèle(s); dirigé par filtres
S activado bajo circunstancias determinadas; dirigido por patrones
I guidato da pattern; guidato da modelli

2413 *E* pattern-directed inference system (PDIS) (EXPERT SYSTEMS)
G mustergesteuertes Inferenzsystem (n)
F système d'inférence dirigé par des filtres (m)
S sistema de inferencia dirigido por patrones (m)
I sistema di inferenza guidato da pattern (m); sistema di inferenza guidato da modelli (m)

2414 *E* pattern-directed retrieval (EXPERT SYSTEMS)
G mustergesteuertes Retrieval (n)
F recherche dirigée par modèles (f)
S búsqueda dirigida por patrones (f)
I ricerca guidata da modelli (f)

2415 *E* pattern discrimination (IMAGE PROCESSING)
G Unterscheidung von Patterns (f)
F discrimination de formes (f)
S discriminación de patrones (f)
I discriminazione di pattern (f); discriminazione di modelli (f)

2416 *E* pattern generation (IMAGE PROCESSING)
G Mustererzeugung (f)
F génération de modèles (f)

S generación de patrones (f)
I generazione di pattern (f); generazione di modelli (f)

2417 E pattern identification (IMAGE PROCESSING)
G Musteridentifizierung (f)
F identification de formes (f)
S identificación de patrones (f); identificación de modelos (f)
I identificazione di pattern (f); identificazione di modelli (f)

2418 E pattern matcher (IMAGE PROCESSING)
G Mustervergleichsprogramm (n)
F programme d'appariement (m)
S programa de pattern matching (m)
I sistema di accoppiamento delle forme (m)

2419 E pattern matching[1] (KNOWLEDGE)
G Mustervergleich (m); Pattern Matching (n); Musteranpassung (f)
F pattern matching (m); appariement (m); filtrage (m)
S pattern matching (m); selección de reglas aplicables (f)
I abbinamento di forme (m); pattern matching (m)

2420 E pattern matching[2] (NLP)
G Mustervergleich (m); Mustervergleichsmethode (f)
F appariement (m)
S pattern matching (m)
I accoppiamento (m)

2421 E pattern-matching algorithm (NLP)
G Mustervergleichsalgorithmus (m)
F algorithme d'appariement de modèles (m)
S algoritmo de pattern matching (m)
I algoritmo di pattern matching (m); algoritmo di accoppiamento (m)

2422 E pattern-matching speech recognition
G Spracherkennung aufgrund Mustervergleichs (f)
F analyse de parole par filtrage (f)
S reconocimiento del habla por pattern matching (m)
I riconoscimento del parlato mediante pattern matching (m)

2423 E pattern-oriented (NLP)
G musterorientiert
F orienté modèle
S orientado pattern
I orientato ai pattern

2424 E pattern recognition (PR) (IMAGE PROCESSING)
G Mustererkennung (f)
F reconnaissance de formes (RF) (f)
S reconocimiento de formas (m)
I riconoscimento di pattern (m); riconoscimento di forme (m)

2425 E pattern recognition program (IMAGE PROCESSING)
= pattern recognizer
G Mustererkennungsprogramm (n)
F reconnaisseur de formes (m)
S programa de reconocimiento de patrones (m)
I programma di riconoscimento di forme (m)

2426 E pattern recognition system (IMAGE PROCESSING)
G mustererkennendes System (n)
F système de reconnaissance de formes (m)
S sistema de reconocimiento de formas (m)
I sistema di riconoscimento di pattern (m)

2427 *E* pattern recognition technology (PRT) (IMAGE PROCESSING)
G Mustererkennungstechnologie (f)
F technologie de reconnaissance de formes (f)
S tecnología de reconocimiento de patrones (f)
I tecnologia del riconoscimento delle forme (f)

2428 *E* pattern recognizer
→ pattern recognition program

2429 *E* pattern representation (IMAGE PROCESSING)
G Musterdarstellung (f)
F représentation de modèles (f)
S representación de patrones (f)
I rappresentazione dei pattern (f); rappresentazione delle forme (f)

2430 *E* pattern searching (NLP)
= search for patterns
G Mustersuche (f); Patternsuche (f)
F recherche de formes (f)
S búsqueda de patterns (f)
I ricerca di pattern (f); ricerca di forme (f)

2431 *E* PD
→ problem domain

2432 *E* PDIS
→ pattern-directed inference system

2433 *E* PDL
→ picture description language

2434 *E* PDP
= parallel distributed processing
→ connection science

2435 *E* percentage recognition rate
G prozentuale Erkennungsrate (f)
F taux de reconnaissance pour cent (m)
S porcentaje de reconocimiento (m)
I percentuale di riconoscimento (m)

2436 *E* perception
G Wahrnehmung (f); Wahrnehmen (n); Perzeption (f)
F perception (f)
S percepción (f)
I percezione (f)

2437 *E* perception mechanism
G Wahrnehmungsmechanismus (m)
F mécanisme de perception (m)
S mecanismo de percepción (m)
I meccanismo di percezione (m)

2438 *E* perception system (IMAGE PROCESSING)
G Wahrnehmungssystem (n)
F système de perception (m)
S sistema de percepción (m)
I sistema di percezione (m)

2439 *E* Perceptron (*an early AI device*) (THEORY)
G Perzeptron (n)
F Perceptron (m)
S Perceptron (m)
I Perceptron (m)

2440 *E* perceptual (IMAGE PROCESSING)
G perzeptiv
F perceptif; de perception
S perceptual; perceptivo
I percettuale

2441 *E* permanent knowledge
≠ temporary knowledge
G ständiges Wissen (n)
F connaissance permanente (f)
S conocimiento permanente (m)
I conoscenza permanente (f)

2442 *E* personal robot
G Personal Roboter (m)
F robot personnel (m)
S robot personal (m)
I robot personale (m)

2443 *E* perspective (LOGIC)
G Perspektive (f); Blickwinkel (m)
F perspective (f)
S perspectiva (f)
I perspettiva (f)

2444 *E* Petri net (LOGIC)
G Petri-Netz (n)
F réseau de Petri (m)
S red de Petri (f)
I rete di Petri (f)

2445 *E* phoneme (LINGUISTICS)
G Phonem (n); Sprachlaut (m)
F phonème (m)
S fonema (m)
I fonema (m)

2446 *E* phoneme synthesis
G Phonemsynthese (f)
F synthèse de phonèmes (f)
S síntesis de fonemas (f)
I sintesi dei fonemi (f)

2447 *E* phonemic data (RECOGNITION)
G Phonemdaten (pl)
F données phonémiques (f pl)
S datos fonémicos (m pl)
I dati fonemici (m pl)

2448 *E* phonetic recognition (*of a word*)
G phonetisches Erkennen (n)
F reconnaissance phonétique (f)
S reconocimiento fonético (m)
I riconoscimento fonetico (m)

2449 *E* phonetic transcription (LINGUISTICS)
G phonetische Umschrift (f); Lautumschrift (f)
F transcription phonétique (f)
S transcripción fonética (f)
I trascrizione fonetica (f)

2450 *E* phonology (LINGUISTICS)
G Phonologie (f); Phonemik (f)
F phonologie (f)
S fonologia (f)
I fonologia (f)

2451 *E* phrasal lexicon (MT)
G Phrasenlexikon (n)
F lexique de phrases (m); lexique syntagmatique (m)
S léxico de frases (m)
I lessico di frasi (m)

2452 *E* phrase generation (NLP)
G Phrasengenerierung (f)
F génération de groupe grammatical (f); génération de phrase (f)
S generación de frases (f)
I generazione di frasi (f)

2453 *E* phrase marker (NLP)
G Phrasenmarker (m); P-Marker (m)
F marqueur de phrase (m)
S marcador de frase (m)
I marker di frase (m); marcatore di frase (m)

2454 *E* phrase-structure grammar (PSG) (NLP)
= immediate constituent grammar; IC grammar
G Phrasenstrukturgrammatik (f); IC-Grammatik (f)
F grammaire de structure de phrase (f)
S gramática de estructura de frase (f)
I grammatica IC (f)

2455 *E* phrase-structure rule (NLP)
G Phrasenstrukturregel (f)
F règle de structure de phrase (f)
S regla de estructura de frases (f)
I regola sulla struttura delle frasi (f)

2456 *E* phrase-structure tree (NLP)
G Phrasenstrukturbaum (m)
F arbre de structure de phrase (m)
S árbol de estructura de frases (m)

I albero delle strutture delle frasi (m)

2457 *E* physical constraints analysis (EXPERT SYSTEMS)
G Analyse der physikalischen Randbedingungen (f)
F analyse des contraintes physiques (f)
S análisis de restricciones físicas (m)
I analisi delle restrizioni fisici (f)

2458 *E* picture analysis
→ image analysis

2459 *E* picture description language (PDL) (PROGRAMMING)
G Bildbeschreibungssprache (f)
F langage de description d'images (m)
S lenguaje de descripción de imágenes (m)
I linguaggio di descrizione di immagini (m)

2460 *E* picture feature
→ image feature

2461 *E* picture processing
→ image processing

2462 *E* PIM
→ parallel inference machine

2463 *E* PIPS
= Pattern Information Processing System

2464 *E* pl
→ plausibility

2465 *E* PL
→ propositional logic

2466 *E* plan[1] (*noun*) (EXPERT SYSTEMS)
G Plan (m)
F plan (m)
S plano (m); plan (m)
I piano (m)

2467 *E* plan[2] (*verb*) (EXPERT SYSTEMS)
G planen
F planifier
S planificar
I pianificare

2468 *E* plan generation (EXPERT SYSTEMS)
= generation of plans
G Planerzeugung (f); Plangenerierung (f)
F génération de plans (f)
S generación de planos (f); construcción de planos (f)
I generazione di piani (f)

2469 *E* planner (EXPERT SYSTEMS)
G Planer (m)
F planificateur (m)
S planificador (m); componente de planificación (m)
I pianificatore (m); planner (m)

2470 *E* planning (EXPERT SYSTEMS)
G Planen (n)
F planification (f)
S planificación (f); planning (m)
I pianificazione (f); planning (m); definizione del piano di azione (f)

2471 *E* planning knowledge (EXPERT SYSTEMS)
G Planungswissen (n)
F connaissance de planification (f)
S conocimientos sobre planning (m pl); conocimiento de cómo planificar (m)
I conoscenza di pianificazione (f)

2472 *E* planning method (EXPERT SYSTEMS)
G Planungsmethode (f)
F méthode de planification (f)
S método de planificación (m)
I metodo di pianificazione (m)

2473 *E* planning paradigm (EXPERT SYSTEMS)
G Planungsparadigma (n)
F paradigme de planification (m)
S paradigma de planificación (m)
I paradigma di pianificazione (f)

2474 *E* planning problem (EXPERT SYSTEMS)
G Planungsproblem (n)
F problème de planification (m)
S problema de planificación (m)
I problema di pianificazione (m)

2475 *E* planning strategy (EXPERT SYSTEMS)
G Planungsstrategie (f)
F stratégie de planification (f)
S estrategia de planificación (f)
I strategia di planificazione (f)

2476 *E* planning system (EXPERT SYSTEMS)
G Planungssystem (n)
F système de planification (m)
S sistema de planificación (m); planificador (m)
I sistema di pianificazione (m); sistema pianificatore (m)

2477 *E* planning tool (PROGRAMMING)
G Planungswerkzeug (n)
F outil de planification (m)
S herramienta de planificación (f)
I tool di pianificazione (m); strumento di pianificazione (m)

2478 *E* plan recognition (NLP)
G Planerkennung (f)
F reconnaissance de plans (f)
S reconocimiento de planos (m)
I riconoscimento di piani (m)

2479 *E* plan understanding program (NLP)
G planverstehendes Programm (n)
F programme de compréhension de plans (m)
S programa de comprensión de planos (m)
I programma di comprensione di piani (m)

2480 *E* plateau problem (*in hill climbing*) (EXPERT SYSTEMS)
G Plateauproblem (n)
F problème de plateau (m)
S problema de meseta (m)
I problema dell'altopiano (m)

2481 *E* plausibility[1] (pl)
G Plausibilität (f)
F plausibilité (f)
S plausibilidad (f)
I plausibilità (f)

2482 *E* plausibility[2]
→ credibility

2483 *E* plausibility check (PROGRAMMING)
G Plausibilitätskontrolle (f)
F contrôle de plausibilité (m)
S control de plausibilidad (m)
I controllo di plausibilità (m)

2484 *E* plausibility pattern (EXPERT SYSTEMS)
G Plausibilitätsschema (n)
F modèle de vraisemblances (m)
S esquema de plausibilidades (m)
I pattern di plausibilità (m); modello di plausibilità

2485 *E* plausibility threshold (LOGIC)
G Plausibilitätsschwelle (f)
F seuil de vraisemblance (m)
S umbral de plausibilidad (m)
I soglia di plausibilità (f)

2486 *E* plausibility value (LOGIC)
G Plausibilitätswert (m)
F valeur de plausibilité (f)
S valor de plausibilidad (m)
I valore di plausibilità (m)

2487 *E* plausible (LOGIC)
G plausibel
F plausible
S plausible
I plausibile

2488 *E* plausible inference
→ plausible reasoning

2489 *E* plausible reasoning (LOGIC)
= plausible inference
G plausibles Schließen (n)
F raisonnement plausible (m)
S inferencia plausible (f); razonamiento plausible (m)
I ragionamento plausibile (m)

2490 *E* PNF
→ pre-nex form

2491 *E* PNN
→ probabilistic neural net

2492 *E* pointer variable (PROGRAMMING)
G Zeigervariable (f)
F variable du type pointeur (f)
S variable puntador (f)
I variabile tipo puntatore (f)

2493 *E* polyvalent logics
→ multivalued logic

2494 *E* portability (*of an expert system*)
G Portabilität (f)
F portabilité (f)
S portabilidad (f)
I portabilità (f)

2495 *E* position-independent (IMAGE PROCESSING)
G positionsunabhängig
F indépendant de la position
S independiente de la posición
I indipendente della posizione

2496 *E* positive example (LEARNING)
G Positivbeispiel (n)
F exemple positif (m)
S ejemplo positivo (m)
I esempio positivo (m)

2497 *E* possibilistic (LOGIC)
G possibilistisch
F possibiliste
S posibilístico
I possibilistico

2498 *E* possibility distribution (MATHS)
G Wahrscheinlichkeitsverteilung (f)
F distribution de la possibilité (f)
S distribución de posibilidad (f)
I distribuzione della possibilità (f)

2499 *E* possibility list (LOGIC)
G Liste der Möglichkeiten (f); Möglichkeitenkatalog (m)
F liste des possibilités (f)
S lista de posibilidades (f)
I lista delle possibilità (f)

2500 *E* possibility theory (THEORY)
G Possibilitätstheorie (f)
F théorie de possibilité (f)
S teoría de posibilidad (f)
I teoria della possibilità (f)

2501 *E* possible worlds (THEORY)
G mögliche Welten (f pl)
F mondes possibles (m pl)
S mundos posibles (m pl)
I mondi possibili (m pl); possibili mondi (m pl)

2502 *E* PR^1
→ pattern recognition

2503 *E* PR^2
→ problem reduction

2504 *E* pragmatic analysis (LOGIC)
G pragmatische Analyse (f)
F analyse pragmatique (f)
S análisis pragmático (m)
I analisi pragmatica (f)

2505 *E* pragmatics (LOGIC)

G Pragmatik (f)
F pragmatique (f)
S pragmática (f)
I pragmatica (f)

2506 E precedence rule (LOGIC)
G vorrangige Regel (f); Vorzugsregel (f)
F règle prioritaire (f)
S regla prioritaria (f); regla de precedencia (f)
I regola prioritaria (f)

2507 E precon
→ precondition

2508 E precondition (precon) (LOGIC)
G Vorbedingung (f)
F précondition (f); condition préalable (f)
S precondición (f)
I precondizione (f)

2509 E predecessor
→ ancestor (node)

2510 E predefinable (LOGIC)
G vorher definierbar
F prédéfinissable
S predefinible
I predefinibile

2511 E predefined predicate (LOGIC)
G vordefiniertes Prädikat (n)
F prédicat prédéfini (m)
S predicado predefinido (m)
I predicato predefinito (m)

2512 E predetermined (*values etc.*) (LOGIC)
G vorbestimmt
F prédéterminé
S predeterminado
I predeterminato

2513 E predicate (P) (*sometimes also called* verb) (LOGIC)
G Prädikat (n) (manchmal auch: Prädikator (m))
F prédicat (m)
S predicado (m)
I predicato (m)

2514 E predicate assignment (LOGIC)
G Prädikatzuweisung (f)
F allocation de prédicats (f)
S asignación de predicados (f)
I assegnazione di predicati (f)

2515 E predicate calculus[1] (LOGIC)
G Prädikatenkalkül (n)
F calcul des prédicats (m)
S cálculo de predicados (m)
I calcolo dei predicati (m)

2516 E predicate calculus[2]
→ predicate logic

2517 E predicate logic
→ first-order predicate logic; predicate calculus
G Prädikatenlogik (PL) (f); (adjective: prädikatenlogisch)
F logique des prédicats (f)
S lógica de predicados (f)
I logica dei predicati (f)

2518 E predicate logic programming
G prädikatenlogische Programmierung (f)
F programmation à logique des prédicats (f)
S programación con lógica de predicados (f)
I programmazione con logica a predicati (f)

2519 E predicate variable (LOGIC)
G Prädikatsvariable (f)
F variable de prédicat (f)
S variable de predicado (f)
I variabile di predicato (f)

2520 E predict
= forecast

G vorhersagen
F prédire
S predecir
I predire; fare predizioni

2521 *E* prediction
= forecasting
G Vorhersage (f); Prädiktion (f)
F prédiction (f)
S predicción (f)
I predizione (f)

2522 *E* prediction rule (EXPERT SYSTEMS)
G Vorhersageregel (f)
F règle prédictive (f)
S regla de predicción (f)
I regola di predizione (f)

2523 *E* prediction system (EXPERT SYSTEMS)
G Vorhersagesystem (n)
F système prédictif (m)
S sistema de predicción (m)
I sistema di predizione (m)

2524 *E* predictive (*reasoning etc.*) (LOGIC)
G prädiktiv; vorhersagend
F prédictif
S predictivo
I predittivo

2525 *E* predictive parser (NLP)
G prädiktiver Parser (m)
F analyseur prédictif (m)
S analizador predictivo (m)
I parser predittivo (m)

2526 *E* preference semantics (NLP)
G Präferenzsemantik (f)
F sémantique préférentielle (f)
S semántica preferencial (f)
I semantica preferenziale (f)

2527 *E* prefix notation (PROGRAMMING)
G Präfixschreibweise (f); Präfixnotation (f)
F notation avec préfixe (f)
S notación con prefijo (f)
I notazione con prefisso (f)

2528 *E* premise (LOGIC)
G Prämisse (f); Voraussetzung (f); Bedingung (f)
F prémisse (f); antécédent (m)
S premisa (f)
I premessa (f); presupposto (m)

2529 *E* premise part (*of a rule*) (LOGIC)
= 'if' part
≠ conclusion part
G Wenn-Teil (einer Regel) (m); Prämissenteil (m)
F partie de la prémisse (f)
S parte de premisa (f); parte si (f)
I parte premessa (f)

2530 *E* pre-nex form (PNF) (PROGRAMMING)
G Pränex-Form (f); pränexe Form (f)
F forme prénexe (f)
S forma prenex (f)
I forma prenessa (f)

2531 *E* preprocessing (*noun*)
G Vorverarbeitung (f)
F prétraitement (m)
S preproceso (m)
I pre-elaborazione (f); pre-trattamento (m)

2532 *E* preprogrammed input (RECOGNITION)
= canned input
G vorprogrammierte Eingabe (f)
F entrée préprogrammée (f)
S entrada preprogramada (f); entrada pregrabada (f)
I input preprogrammato (m); entrata preprogrammata (f)

2533 *E* presupposition (LOGIC)
G Präsupposition (f); Voraussetzung (f)
F présupposition (f)

S presuposición (f)
I presupposizione (f)

2534 *E* primal sketch (*of an image*)
G Primärskizze (f); erster Entwurf (m)
F esquisse (f); squelette d'accès (f)
S croquis (m)
I primal sketch (m); schizzo primativo (m)

2535 *E* primitive[1] (RECOGNITION)
G Grundelement (n)
F primitive (f); élément de base (m)
S primitiva (f)
I primitiva (f)

2536 *E* primitive[2]
→ basic concept

2537 *E* primitive act
G primitiver Akt (m)
F action primitive (f)
S acto primitivo (m)
I atto primitivo (m)

2538 *E* primitive conceptual structure (KNOWLEDGE)
G primitive Begriffsstruktur (f)
F schéma conceptuel élémentaire (m)
S estructura conceptual primitiva (f)
I struttura concettuale primitiva (f)

2539 *E* primitive descriptor (KNOWLEDGE)
G primitiver Deskriptor (m)
F descripteur élémentaire (m)
S descriptor primitivo (m)
I descrittore primitivo (m)

2540 *E* primitive function (PROGRAMMING)
G Primitivfunktion (f)
F fonction primitive (f)
S función primitiva (f)
I funzione primitiva (f)

2541 *E* primitive object (KNOWLEDGE)
G Primitivobjekt (n)
F objet primitif (m)
S objeto primitivo (m)
I oggetto primitivo (m)

2542 *E* primitive shape (IMAGE PROCESSING)
G Primitivform (f)
F forme primitive (f); forme élémentaire (f)
S forma primitiva (f); forma simple (f)
I forma primitiva (f)

2543 *E* prior belief (LOGIC)
G frühere Annahme (f)
F croyance précédente (f)
S confianza precedente (f)
I convinzione precedente (f)

2544 *E* priority queue (PROGRAMMING)
G Prioritätsschlange (f)
F file d'attente prioritaire (f)
S cola de prioridad (f)
I coda di priorità (f)

2545 *E* prior knowledge
= advance knowledge
G vorher existierendes Wissen (n); Vorwissen (n)
F connaissances précédentes (f pl)
S conocimientos precedentes (m pl); conocimiento anterior (m); conocimiento previo (m)
I conoscenze previe (f)

2546 *E* privileged node (LOGIC)
G privilegierter Knoten (m)
F nœud privilégié (m)
S nodo privilegiado (m)
I nodo privilegiato (m)

2547 *E* probabilistic (LOGIC)
G probabilistisch; wahrscheinlichkeitstheoretisch
F probabilistique
S probabilístico

I probabilistico

2548 E probabilistic decision rule (EXPERT SYSTEMS)
G probabilistische Entscheidungsregel (f)
F règle de décision probabilistique (f)
S regla de decisión probabilística (f)
I regola di decisione probabilistica (f)

2549 E probabilistic inference
→ probabilistic reasoning

2550 E probabilistic model (LOGIC)
G probabilistisches Modell (n)
F modèle probabilistique (m)
S modelo probabilístico (m)
I modello probabilistico (m)

2551 E probabilistic neural net (PNN)
G probabilistisches neuronales Netz (n)
F réseau neuronal probabilistique (m)
S red neuronal probabilística (f)
I rete neuronale probabilistico (f)

2552 E probabilistic reasoning (LOGIC)
= probabilistic inference
G probabilistisches Schließen (n)
F raisonnement probabilistique (m)
S razonamiento probabilístico (m)
I ragionamento probabilistico (m)

2553 E probabilistic theory (LOGIC)
G Wahrscheinlichkeitstheorie (f)
F théorie probabilistique (f); théorie des probabilités (f)
S teoría probabilística (f)
I teoria probabilistica (f)

2554 E probability (MATHS)
→ likelihood
↔ certainty
G Wahrscheinlichkeit (f)
F probabilité (f)
S probabilidad (f)
I probabilità (f)

2555 E probability calculus (MATHS)
G Wahrscheinlichkeitsrechnung (f)
F calcul des probabilités (m)
S cálculo de probabilidades (m)
I calcolo della probabilità (m)

2556 E probability propagation (EXPERT SYSTEMS)
G Wahrscheinlichkeitspropagierung (f)
F propagation de la probabilité (f)
S propagación de probabilidad (f)
I propagazione della probabilità (f)

2557 E problem
G Problem (n)
F problème (m)
S problema (m)
I problema (m)

2558 E problem class (EXPERT SYSTEMS)
G Problemklasse (f)
F classe de problème (f)
S clase de problemas (f)
I classe di problemi (f)

2559 E problem definition (EXPERT SYSTEMS)
G Problemdefinition (f)
F définition du problème (f)
S definición de problema (f)
I definizione del problema (f)

2560 E problem description (EXPERT SYSTEMS)
G Problembeschreibung (f)
F description du problème (f)
S descripción del problema (f)
I descrizione del problema (f)

2561 E problem domain (PD) (EXPERT SYSTEMS)
G Problemdomäne (f); Problembereich (m)

F domaine de problème (m)
S dominio de problema (m)
I dominio del problema (m); dominio problemico (m)

2562 *E* problem evaluation (EXPERT SYSTEMS)
G Problemabschätzung (f)
F évaluation du problème (f)
S evaluación de los problemas (f)
I valutazione del problema (f)

2563 *E* problem formulation (EXPERT SYSTEMS)
G Problemformulierung (f)
F formulation de problèmes (f)
S formulación del problema (f)
I formulazione del problema (f)

2564 *E* problem generator (EXPERT SYSTEMS)
G Problemgenerator (m)
F générateur de problème (m)
S generador de problemas (m)
I generatore di problemi (m)

2565 *E* problem identification (EXPERT SYSTEMS)
G Problemidentifizierung (f)
F identification du problème (f)
S identificación de problemas (f)
I identificazione del problema (f)

2566 *E* problem knowledge (EXPERT SYSTEMS)
G Problemwissen (n)
F connaissances sur le problème (f pl)
S conocimientos sobre el problema (m pl)
I conoscenze sul problema (f pl)

2567 *E* problem-level reasoning (LOGIC)
≠ metalevel reasoning
G Inferieren auf Problemebene (n)
F raisonnement au niveau du problème (m)
S razonamiento de nivel problema (m)
I ragionamento sul livello problema (m)

2568 *E* problem reduction (PR) (EXPERT SYSTEMS)
G Problemreduzierung (f)
F réduction du problème (f)
S reducción de problemas (f)
I riduzione dei problemi (f)

2569 *E* problem-reduction technique (EXPERT SYSTEMS)
G Problemreduzierungsverfahren (n)
F méthode de réduction des problèmes (f)
S técnia de reducción de problemas (f)
I tecnica di riduzione dei problemi (f)

2570 *E* problem representation (EXPERT SYSTEMS)
G Problemdarstellung (f)
F représentation du problème (f)
S representación de problemas (f); planteamiento de un problema (m)
I rappresentazione del problema (f)

2571 *E* problem representation space (EXPERT SYSTEMS)
G Problemdarstellungsraum (m)
F espace de représentation du problème (m)
S espacio de representación del problema (m)
I spazio di rappresentazione del problema (m)

2572 *E* problem search space
→ search space

2573 *E* problem solver (*part of the expert system shell*)
G Problemlöser (m); Problemlösungsmodul (n)
F résolveur de problèmes (m); composante de résolution de problèmes (f)
S solucionador de problemas (m); solventador de problemas (m)
I risolutore di problemi (m)

2574 *E* problem solving (EXPERT SYSTEMS)
G Problemlösen (n); Problemlösung (f); Problemlösungsvorgang (m)
F résolution de problèmes (f)
S resolución de problemas (f)
I soluzione del problema (f); soluzione di problemi (f)

2575 *E* problem-solving and inference software (EXPERT SYSTEMS)
G Problemlösungs- und Inferenzsoftware (f)
F logiciel d'inférence et de résolution de problèmes (m)
S software de resolución de problemas y de inferencia (m)
I software per inferenze e soluzione di problemi (m)

2576 *E* problem-solving capability (EXPERT SYSTEMS)
G Problemlösungsfähigkeit (f)
F capacité de résolution de problèmes (f); capacité de résoudre des problèmes (f)
S capacidad de resolución de problemas (f)
I capacità di risolvere problemi (f)

2577 *E* problem-solving component (EXPERT SYSTEMS)
G Problemlösungskomponente (f)
F module de résolution de problèmes (m); composante de résolution de problèmes (f)
S módulo de resolución de problemas (m)
I modulo di risoluzione dei problemi (m)

2578 *E* problem-solving cost (EXPERT SYSTEMS)
G Problemlösungskosten (pl)
F coût de résolution (m)
S coste de resolución de problemas (m)
I costi per la soluzione di problemi (m)

2579 *E* problem-solving knowledge (EXPERT SYSTEMS)
G Problemlösungswissen (n)
F connaissance de résolution de problèmes (f)
S conocimiento sobre la resolución de problemas (m)
I conoscenza di soluzione di problemi (m)

2580 *E* problem-solving mechanism (EXPERT SYSTEMS)
G Problemlösungsmechanismus (m)
F mécanisme de résolution de problèmes (m)
S mecanismo de resolución de problemas (m)
I meccanismo di soluzione di problemi (m)

2581 *E* problem-solving method (EXPERT SYSTEMS)
G Problemlösungsmethode (f)
F méthode de résolution de problèmes (f)
S técnica de resolución de problemas (f)
I tecnica di risolvere problemi (f)

2582 *E* problem-solving program (EXPERT SYSTEMS)
G Problemlösungsprogramm (n)
F programme de résolution de problèmes (m)

S programa de resolución de problemas (m)
I programma di risoluzione di problemi (m)

2583 E problem-solving strategy (EXPERT SYSTEMS)
G Problemlösungsstrategie (f)
F stratégie de résolution de problèmes (f)
S estrategia de resolución de problemas (f)
I strategia di risolvere problemi (f)

2584 E problem space (EXPERT SYSTEMS)
G Problemraum (m)
F espace de problème (m); zone de problème (f)
S espacio del problema (m)
I spazio problema (m)

2585 E problem-specific knowledge (EXPERT SYSTEMS)
G problemspezifisches Wissen (n)
F connaissance spécifique sur le problème (f)
S conocimiento específico del problema (m)
I conoscenza specifica per un problema (f)

2586 E problem state (EXPERT SYSTEMS)
G Problemzustand (m); Problemstatus (m)
F état de problème (m)
S estado del problema (m)
I stato problema (m)

2587 E procedural (*adjective*)
≠ declarative
G prozedural
F procédural
S procedimental; procedural
I procedurale

2588 E procedural attachment (PA) (PROGRAMMING)
↔ attached procedure
G prozedurale Ankopplung (f); prozedurale Auswertung (f); prozedurales Attachment (n)
F attachement procédural (m)
S acoplamiento procedimental (m); ligadura a procedimiento (f)
I accoppiamento procedurale (m)

2589 E procedural expert system
G prozedurales Expertensystem (n)
F système expert procédural (m)
S sistema experto procedimental (m)
I sistema esperto procedurale (m)

2590 E procedural knowledge
≠ declarative knowledge
G prozedurales Wissen (n)
F connaissance(s) procédurale(s) (f (pl))
S conocimiento acerca de procesos (m); conocimiento procedimental (m)
I conoscenza procedurale (f)

2591 E procedural language (PROGRAMMING)
G prozedurale Sprache (f)
F langage procédural (m)
S lenguaje procedimental (m)
I linguaggio procedurale (m)

2592 E procedural learning
G prozedurales Lernen (n)
F apprentissage procédural (m)
S aprendizaje procedimental (m)
I apprendimento procedurale (m)

2593 E procedural node (KNOWLEDGE)
G prozeduraler Knoten (m)
F nœud procédural (NP) (m)
S nodo procedimental (m)
I nodo procedurale (m)

2594 E procedural programming
≠ declarative programming
G prozedurale Programmierung (f)
F programmation procédurale (f)

S programación procedimental (f)
I programmazione procedurale (f); proceduralità (f)

2595 E procedural programming language
G prozedurale Programmiersprache (f)
F langage de programmation procédurale (m)
S lenguaje de programación procedimental (m)
I linguaggio di programmazione procedurale (m)

2596 E procedural representation (KNOWLEDGE)
≠ declarative representation
G prozedurale Repräsentation (f)
F représentation procédurale (f)
S representación procedimental (f)
I rappresentazione procedurale (f)

2597 E procedural semantic network (PSN) (KNOWLEDGE)
G prozedurales semantisches Netz (n)
F réseau sémantique procédural (m)
S red semántica procedimental (f)
I rete semantica procedurale (f)

2598 E procedural semantics (PROGRAMMING)
≠ declarative semantics
G prozedurale Semantik (f)
F sémantique procédurale (f)
S semántica procedimental (f)
I semantica procedurale (f)

2599 E procedure (*in PROLOG*) (PROGRAMMING)
G Prozedur (f)
F procédure (f)
S procedimiento (m)
I procedura (f)

2600 E procedure-oriented (PROGRAMMING)
G prozedurorientiert
F orienté procédures; procéduriel
S orientado a procedimientos
I orientato alle procedure

2601 E production memory
→ production rule memory

2602 E production rule[1] (EXPERT SYSTEMS)
G Produktionsregel (f); Produktion (f)
F règle de production (f)
S regla de producción (f)
I regola di produzione (f)

2603 E production rule[2]
→ if–then rule

2604 E production rule memory (EXPERT SYSTEMS)
= production memory
G Produktionsregelspeicher (m)
F mémoire des règles de production (f)
S memoria de las reglas de producción (f)
I memoria delle regole di produzione (f)

2605 E production rules programming
G Programmierung von Produktionsregeln (f)
F programmation en règles de production (f)
S programación con reglas de producción (f)
I programmazione con regole di produzione (f)

2606 E production rule system
→ production system

2607 E production system (PS) (EXPERT SYSTEMS)
= production rule system; global database
G Produktionssystem (n)

F système à règles de production (m)
S sistema de producción (SP) (m); conjunto de reglas de producción (m); sistema de control (m)
I sistema di produzione (m)

2608 E production system language (PROGRAMMING)
G Produktionssystemsprache (f)
F langage pour systèmes à règles de production (m)
S lenguaje de sistemas de producción (m)
I linguaggio di sistemi di produzione (m)

2609 E production system model (EXPERT SYSTEMS)
G Produktionssystemmodell (n)
F modèle d'un système à règles de production (m)
S modelo de sistema de producción (m)
I modello di un sistema di produzione (m)

2610 E prognostic system (EXPERT SYSTEMS)
G Prognosesystem (n); Vorhersagesystem (n)
F système prognostique (m)
S sistema prognóstico (m)
I sistema prognostico (m)

2611 E programmed learning
G programmiertes Lernen (n)
F apprentissage programmé (m)
S aprendizaje programado (AP) (m)
I apprendimento programmato (m)

2612 E programmer's apprentice
→ programming assistant

2613 E programmer's assistant
→ programming assistant

2614 E programming assistant
= programmer's assistant; programmer's apprentice
G Hilfssystem für Programmierer (n); PA-Lehrprogramm (n); Assistenzsystem (n)
F apprenti programmeur (m)
S programa asistente de programación (m); aprendiz de programador (m)
I programma assistente del programmatore (m)

2615 E programming environment
G Programmierumgebung (f)
F environnement de programmation (m); atelier logiciel (m)
S entorno de programación (EP) (m); ambiente de programación (m)
I ambiente di programmazione (m)

2616 E programming paradigm
G Programmierparadigma (n); Programmiersprachtyp (m)
F paradigme de programmation (m)
S paradigma de programación (m)
I paradigma di programmazione (m)

2617 E programming support
G Programmierhilfe (f)
F aide à la programmation (f)
S ayuda a la programación (f)
I aiuto alla programmazione (m)

2618 E program synthesis
G Programmsynthese (f)
F synthèse de programme (f)
S síntesis de programas (f); generación de programas (f)
I sintesi dei programmi (f)

2619 E program synthesis system (PSS)
G Programmsynthesesystem (n)
F système de synthèse de programmes (m)

S sistema de síntesis de programas (SSP) (m)
I sistema di sintesi di programmi (m)

2620 *E* PROLOG (*an AI programming language*)
G PROLOG
F PROLOG
S PROLOG
I PROLOG

2621 *E* PROLOG dialect (PROGRAMMING)
G PROLOG-Dialekt (m)
F dialecte de PROLOG (m); dialecte prologien (m)
S dialecto PROLOG (m)
I dialetto PROLOG (m)

2622 *E* promising (*solution etc.*)
G vielversprechend; aussichtsreich
F promettant; prometteur (-euse) (*adjective*)
S prometedor (-a) (*adjective*)
I promettente

2623 *E* pronunciation (LINGUISTICS)
G Aussprache (f)
F prononciation (f)
S pronunciación (f)
I pronuncia (f)

2624 *E* proof (LOGIC)
G Beweis (m)
F preuve (f)
S prueba (f)
I prova (f)

2625 *E* proof of a theorem (LOGIC)
G Theorembeweis (m)
F preuve d'un théorème (f)
S prueba de un teorema (f)
I prova di un teorema (f)

2626 *E* proof of correctness (LOGIC)
G Korrektheitsbeweis (m)
F preuve de correction (f)
S prueba de corrección (f)
I prova di correttezza (f)

2627 *E* proof path (LOGIC)
G Beweispfad (m)
F chemin de preuve (m)
S camino de prueba (m)
I cammino di prova (m)

2628 *E* proof procedure (LOGIC)
G Beweisprozedur (f)
F procédure de preuve (f)
S procedimiento de prueba (m)
I procedura di prova (f)

2629 *E* proof strategy (EXPERT SYSTEMS)
G Beweisfindungsstrategie (f)
F stratégie de preuve (f)
S estrategia de prueba (f)
I strategia di prova (f)

2630 *E* proof theory (LOGIC)
G Beweistheorie (f)
F théorie de preuve (f)
S teoría de prueba (f)
I teoria di prova (f)

2631 *E* proof tree
→ inference tree

2632 *E* prop
→ property

2633 *E* propagation
G Propagierung (f); Fortpflanzung (f); Fortschaltung (f)
F propagation (f)
S propagación (f)
I propagazione (f)

2634 *E* propagation rule (EXPERT SYSTEMS)
G Propagierungsregel (f)
F règle de propagation (f)
S regla de propagación (f)
I regola di propagazione (f)

2635 *E* property (prop) (*of an object*) (KNOWLEDGE)
G Eigenschaft (f)
F propriété (f)
S propiedad (f)
I proprietà (f)

2636 *E* property inheritance (KNOWLEDGE)
= inheritance of properties
G Eigenschaftsvererbung (f); Vererbung von Eigenschaften (f)
F héritage de propriétés (m)
S herencia de propiedades (f)
I ereditarietà di proprietà (f)

2637 *E* property list (KNOWLEDGE)
G Eigenschaftsliste (f)
F liste des propriétés (f)
S lista de propiedades (f)
I lista delle proprietà (f)

2638 *E* proposition (LOGIC)
G Aussage, logische (f); Proposition (f)
F proposition (f)
S afirmación proposicional (f); proposición (f); afirmación (f)
I proposizione (f)

2639 *E* propositional calculus (LOGIC)
G propositionaler Kalkül (m); Propositionskalkül (m); Aussagenkalkül (m)
F calcul propositionnel (m); calcul des propositions (m)
S cálculo proposicional (m)
I calcolo proposizionale (m)

2640 *E* propositional constraint (LOGIC)
G propositionale Einschränkung (f)
F contrainte propositionnelle (f)
S restricción proposicional (f)
I restrizione proposizionale (f)

2641 *E* propositional deduction (LOGIC)
G propositionale Deduktion (f)
F déduction propositionnelle (f)
S deducción proposicional (f)
I deduzione proposizionale (f)

2642 *E* propositional language (LINGUISTICS)
G propositionale Sprache (f)
F langage propositionnel (m)
S lenguaje proposicional (m)
I linguaggio proposizionale (m)

2643 *E* propositional logic (PL)
= elementary logic; sentential logic
G Aussagenlogik (f); Junktorenlogik (f)
F logique des propositions (f); logique propositionnelle (f); logique élémentaire (f)
S lógica proposicional (f)
I logica proposizionale (f)

2644 *E* propositional network (KNOWLEDGE)
G propositionales Netz (n)
F réseau propositionnel (m)
S red proposicional (f)
I rete proposizionale (f)

2645 *E* propositional representation (LOGIC)
≠ analogical representation
G Darstellung in Form einer Aussage (f); propositionale Darstellung (f)
F représentation propositionnelle (f)
S representación proposicional (f)
I rappresentazione proposizionale (f)

2646 *E* propositional variable (LOGIC)
G Aussagenvariable (f)
F variable propositionnelle (f)
S variable proposicional (f)
I variabile proposizionale (f)

2647 *E* prosodics, prosody (*intonation of spoken language*) (LINGUISTICS)
G Prosodie (f)

F prosodie (f) (*adjective*: prosodique)
S prosodia (f); cambio de entonación (m)
I prosodia (f)

2648 *E* prototype development (PROGRAMMING)
→ prototyping
G Prototypentwicklung (f)
F prototypage (m)
S prototipado (m)
I sviluppo di prototipi (m)

2649 *E* prototype version (*of a system*) (PROGRAMMING)
= initial version
G Prototypversion (f); Prototyp (m); Alpha-Version (f)
F version prototype (f)
S versión prototipo (f)
I versione prototipo (f)

2650 *E* prototyping
G Herstellung von Prototypen (f)
F prototypage (m)
S construcción de prototipos (f)
I prototipaggio (m)

2651 *E* provability
→ validity

2652 *E* provable
G beweisbar
F preuvable
S probable
I provabile

2653 *E* prove[1] (*a theorem etc.*) (LOGIC)
G beweisen
F prouver
S probar; demostrar
I provare

2654 *E* prove[2] (*a rule*) (EXPERT SYSTEMS)
G erfüllen
F prouver
S comprobar
I provare

2655 *E* proximity (IMAGE PROCESSING)
G Proximität (Nähe) (f)
F proximité (f)
S proximidad (f)
I prossimità (f); vicinanza (f)

2656 *E* PRT
→ pattern recognition technology

2657 *E* prune (LOGIC)
G abschneiden
F couper
S podar
I potare

2658 *E* prune a search tree (EXPERT SYSTEMS)
G einen Suchbaum verkleinern (durch Abschneiden von Ästen)
F couper un arbre de recherche
S podar un árbol de búsqueda
I potare un albero di ricerca

2659 *E* pruning (*of a tree*) (LOGIC)
= cutoff
G Abschneiden (n); Kappen (n); Beschneidung (f)
F procédure de coupe (d'arbre) (f); élagage (m)
S poda (f); eliminación (f)
I potatura (dell'albero di ricerca) (f); sfoltimento (m); tecnica di potatura (f)

2660 *E* pruning heuristics (EXPERT SYSTEMS)
G Abschneideheuristik (f)
F heuristique d'élagage (f)
S heurística de poda (f)
I euristica di potatura (f)

2661 *E* pruning method (EXPERT SYSTEMS)
G Abschneideverfahren (n); Beschneidungsverfahren (n)

F méthode d'élagage (f)
S método de poda (m)
I metodo di potatura (m)

2662 *E* PS
→ production system

2663 *E* pseudolanguage (SYNTHESIS)
G Pseudosprache (f)
F pseudolangage (m)
S seudolenguaje (m); pseudolenguaje (m)
I pseudolinguaggio (m)

2664 *E* PSG
→ phrase-structure grammar

2665 *E* PSL
= problem statement language

2666 *E* PSN
→ procedural semantic network

2667 *E* PSS
→ program synthesis system

2668 *E* pure first-order logic
G reine Logik erster Ordnung (f)
F logique de premier ordre pure (f)
S lógica pura de primer orden (f)
I logica pura di primo ordine (f)

2669 *E* pure logic
G reine Logik (f)
F logique pure (f)
S lógica pura (f)
I logica pura (f)

2670 *E* pure procedural system
G reines prozedurales System (n)
F système procédural pur (m)
S sistema procedimental puro (m)
I sistema procedurale puro (m)

2671 *E* putative (LOGIC)
G putativ; vorausgesetzt
F putatif
S putativo
I putativo

Q

2672 *E* Q
→ query

2673 *E* Q/A
→ question answering

2674 *E* Q/A system
→ question-answering system

2675 *E* QL
→ query language

2676 *E* qualitative reasoning (LOGIC)
G qualitatives Schließen (n)
F raisonnement qualitatif (m)
S razonamiento cualitativo (m)
I ragionamento qualitativo (m)

2677 *E* quantification
G Quantifizierung (f)
F quantification (f)
S cuantificación (f)
I quantificazione (f)

2678 *E* quantification theory
G Quantifizierungstheorie (f)
F théorie de quantification (f)
S teoría de cuantificación (f)
I teoria di quantificazione (f)

2679 *E* quantified variable (LOGIC)
G quantifizierte Variable (f)
F variable quantifiée (f)
S variable cuantificada (f)
I variabile quantificata (f)

2680 *E* quantifier (*types: universal and existential*) (LOGIC)
G Quantor (m)
F quantificateur (m); quantifieur (m)
S cuantificador (m)
I quantificatore (m)

2681 *E* quantity of knowledge
G Wissensmenge (f)
F quantité de connaissances (f)
S cantidad de conocimiento (f)
I quantità di conoscenza (f)

2682 *E* quantity space (EXPERT SYSTEMS)
G Mengenraum (m)
F espace de quantité (m)
S espacio de cuantidad (m)
I spazio di quantità (m)

2683 *E* query (Q) (*noun*) (EXPERT SYSTEMS)
= question
G Abfrage (f); Anfrage (f); Frage (f); Query (f)
F interrogation (f); requête (f)
S pregunta (f)
I interrogazione (f); domanda (f); query (f)

2684 *E* query analyser (EXPERT SYSTEMS)
G Fragenanalysator (m)
F analyseur à requêtes (m)
S analizador de preguntas (m)
I analizzatore delle interrogazioni (m)

2685 *E* query language (QL) (EXPERT SYSTEMS)
G Abfragesprache (f)
F langage d'interrogation (m)
S lenguaje de consulta (m)
I linguaggio query (m)

2686 *E* query mode (EXPERT SYSTEMS)

G Abfragemodus (m); Fragemodus (m)
F mode requête (m)
S modo pregunta (m)
I modo interrogazione (m)

2687 *E* query program (EXPERT SYSTEMS)
G Abfrageprogramm (n)
F programme d'interrogation (m)
S programa de consulta (m)
I programma di interrogazione (m)

2688 *E* query system (EXPERT SYSTEMS)
G Abfragesystem (n)
F système d'interrogation (m)
S sistema de consulta (m)
I sistema di interrogazione (m)

2689 *E* question
→ query

2690 *E* question answering (Q/A)
G Beantwortung von Fragen (f)
F réponse à des questions (f)
S respuesta a preguntas (f)
I risposta a delle domande (f)

2691 *E* question-answering system (EXPERT SYSTEMS)
= Q/A system
G Frage-Antwort-System (FAS) (n)
F système de questions–réponses (m)
S sistema de obtención automática de respuestas (m); sistema de pregunta–respuesta (m); sistema de llamada-respuesta (m)
I sistema domanda–risposta (m); sistema in grado di rispondere a domande (m)

2692 *E* question flow (EXPERT SYSTEMS)
G Fragenfluß (m)
F flux de questions (m)
S flujo de preguntas (m)
I flusso di domande (m)

R

2693 *E* R
→ relation

2694 *E* radix (node) (LOGIC)
G Wurzel (f) (Knoten)
F racine (f) (nœud)
S raíz (f) (nodo)
I radice (f) (nodo)

2695 *E* ramification (LOGIC)
G Verzweigung (f)
F ramification (f)
S ramificación (f)
I ramificazione (f)

2696 *E* random search (EXPERT SYSTEMS)
G Zufallssuche (f)
F recherche aléatoire (f)
S búsqueda aleatoria (f)
I ricerca aleatoria (f)

2697 *E* random tree (LOGIC)
G Zufallsbaum (m)
F arbre aléatoire (m)
S árbol aleatório (m)
I albero aleatorio (m)

2698 *E* rank (*noun*) (KNOWLEDGE)
G Rang (m)
F rang (m); statut (m)
S rango (m)
I rango (m)

2699 *E* ranking (*noun*) (LOGIC)
G Rangstufung (f); Rangbestimmung (f)
F classement (m)
S clasificación (f); cálculo de rangos (m)
I classificazione (f)

2700 *E* ranking method (LOGIC)
G Rangbestimmungsmethode (f)
F méthode de classement (f)
S método de clasificación (m)
I metodo di classificazione (m)

2701 *E* rapid prototyping (PROGRAMMING)
G Rapid Prototyping (schnelle Erstellung erster Versionen) (n)
F prototypage rapide (m)
S prototipado rápido (m)
I rapida prototipazione (m); creazione rapida di prototipi (m)

2702 *E* rational decision (LOGIC)
G rationale Entscheidung (f)
F décision rationnelle (f)
S decisión racional (f)
I decisione razionale (f)

2703 *E* rational tree (LOGIC)
G rationaler Baum (m)
F arbre rationnel (m)
S árbol racional (m)
I albero razionale (m)

2704 *E* RBS
→ rule-based system

2705 *E* reaching of the goal
→ goal achievement

2706 *E* real-time recognition (IMAGE PROCESSING)
G Echtzeiterkennung (f)
F reconnaissance en temps réel (f)
S reconocimiento en tiempo real (m)
I riconoscimento in tempo reale (m)

2707 *E* real world (KNOWLEDGE)
G reale Welt (f); Real-World (f)
F monde réel (m)
S mundo real (m)
I mondo reale (m)

2708 *E* real-world object (KNOWLEDGE)
G Objekt der realen Welt (n)
F objet du monde réel (m)
S objeto de mundo real (m)
I oggetto del mondo reale (m)

2709 *E* real-world problem (KNOWLEDGE)
G Problem der realen Welt (n); Real-World-Problem (n)
F problème du monde réel (m)
S problema de mundo real (m)
I problema del mondo reale (m)

2710 *E* reason[1] (*verb*) (LOGIC)
G schließen
F raisonner; effectuer du raisonnement
S razonar; raciocinar
I ragionare; compiere ragionamenti

2711 *E* reason[2] (*verb*)
→ infer

2712 *E* reasoner (EXPERT SYSTEMS)
G Schlußfolgerer (m); Schlußfolgerungskomponente (f)
F module de raisonnement (m)
S razonador (m)
I ragionatore (m)

2713 *E* reasoning (LOGIC)
= inference
G Schließen (n); Ziehen von Schlüssen (n); Inferieren (n)
F raisonnement (m)
S razonamiento (m); raciocinio (m)
I ragionamento (m)

2714 *E* reasoning algorithm (LOGIC)
= inference algorithm
G Inferenzalgorithmus (m)
F algorithme de raisonnement (m); algorithme d'inférence (m)
S algoritmo de razonamiento (m); algoritmo de inferencia (m)
I algoritmo di ragionamento (m); algoritmo di inferenza (m)

2715 *E* reasoning by analogy (LOGIC)
G analoges Schließen (n)
F raisonnement par analogie (m)
S razonamiento por analogía (m)
I ragionamento per analogia (m)

2716 *E* reasoning by deduction
→ deductive reasoning

2717 *E* reasoning by default
→ default reasoning

2718 *E* reasoning by examples (LOGIC)
G Inferieren aufgrund von Beispielen (n)
F raisonnement par exemples (m)
S razonamiento por ejemplos (m)
I ragionamento mediante esempi (m)

2719 *E* reasoning by induction
→ inductive reasoning

2720 *E* reasoning capability (*of a system*) (EXPERT SYSTEMS)
G Fähigkeit zum Schlüsseziehen (f)
F capacité de raisonnement (f)
S poder de razonamiento (m)
I capacità di ragionamento (f)

2721 *E* reasoning component
→ inference mechanism

2722 *E* reasoning method (EXPERT SYSTEMS)
= method of reasoning
G Methode des Schlüsseziehens (f)
F méthode de raisonnement (f); mode de raisonnement (m)
S método de razonamiento (m)
I metodo di ragionamento (m)

2723 *E* reasoning path (EXPERT SYSTEMS)
G Inferenzpfad (m)
F parcours de raisonnement (m)
S línea de razonamiento (f)
I cammino di ragionamento (m)

2724 *E* reasoning power (EXPERT SYSTEMS)
G Inferiervermögen (n); Schließvermögen (n)
F pouvoir de raisonnement (m); pouvoir de conclusion (m)
S potencia de razonamiento (f)
I potenza di ragionamento (f)

2725 *E* reasoning process
→ inference process

2726 *E* reasoning rule (EXPERT SYSTEMS)
= rule of reasoning
G Regel für das Schlüsseziehen (f)
F règle de raisonnement (f)
S regla de razonamiento (f)
I regola di ragionamento (f)

2727 *E* reasoning scheme (EXPERT SYSTEMS)
G Inferenzschema (n)
F schéma de raisonnement (m)
S esquema de razonamiento (m)
I schema di ragionamento (m)

2728 *E* reasoning step (EXPERT SYSTEMS)
G Schritt beim Schlüsseziehen (m)
F pas de raisonnement (m)
S paso de razonamiento (m)
I passo di ragionamento (m)

2729 *E* reasoning strategy (EXPERT SYSTEMS)
= inference strategy
G Inferenzstrategie (f)
F stratégie de raisonnement (f); stratégie d'inférence (f)
S estrategia de razonamiento (f); estrategia inferencial (f)
I strategia di ragionamento (f); strategia di inferenza (f)

2730 *E* reasoning with uncertainty
→ uncertain reasoning

2731 *E* reason maintenance system (RMS)
→ truth maintenance system

2732 *E* recognition
G Erkennung (f); Erkennen (n)
F reconnaissance (f)
S reconocimiento (m)
I riconoscimento (m)

2733 *E* recognition accuracy
G Erkenngenauigkeit (f)
F précision de reconnaissance (f)
S precisión de reconocimiento (f)
I accuratezza di riconoscimento (f)

2734 *E* recognition–action
→ recognize–act

2735 *E* recognition level (IMAGE PROCESSING)
G Erkennungsebene (f)
F niveau de reconnaissance (m)
S nivel de reconocimiento (m)
I livello di riconoscimento (m)

2736 *E* recognition of word strings
= word-sequence recognition

2737 *E* recognition ratio (IMAGE PROCESSING)
G Erkennungsrate (f); Erkennungsquote (f)
F taux de reconnaissance (m); pourcentage de reconnaissance (m); score de reconnaissance (m)
S tasa de reconocimiento (f)
I tasso di riconoscimento (m)

2738 *E* recognition rule (IMAGE PROCESSING)
G Erkennungsregel (f)
F règle de reconnaissance (f)
S regla de reconocimiento (f)
I regola di riconoscimento (f)

2739 *E* recognition strategy (IMAGE PROCESSING)
G Erkennungsstrategie (f)
F stratégie de reconnaissance (f)
S estrategia de reconocimiento (f)
I strategia di riconoscimento (f)

2740 *E* recognition system (IMAGE PROCESSING)
G Erkennungssystem (n)
F système de reconnaissance (m)
S sistema de reconocimiento (m)
I sistema di riconoscimento (m)

2741 *E* recognize–act
= recognition–action
G Bedingung–Handlung (f)
F situation–action (f)
S reconocimiento–acción (m)
I riconoscimento–azione (m)

2742 *E* recognize–act cycle (*in a production cycle*) (EXPERT SYSTEMS)
= match–execute cycle
G Erkennen–Handeln-Zyklus (m)
F cycle situation–action (m)
S ciclo de reconocimiento–acción (m)
I ciclo riconoscimento–azione (m)

2743 *E* recognizer (IMAGE PROCESSING)
G Erkennungskomponente (f)
F reconnaisseur (m)
S reconocedor (m)
I riconoscitore (m)

2744 *E* recursion (PROGRAMMING)
G Rekursion (f)
F récursion (f)
S recursión (f)
I ricorsione (f)

2745 *E* recursive (*function, search, etc.*) (PROGRAMMING)
G rekursiv
F récursive
S recursivo
I ricorsivo; ricorrente

2746 *E* recursive definition (KNOWLEDGE)
G rekursive Definition (f)
F définition récursive (f)
S definición recursiva (f)
I definizione ricorsiva (f)

2747 *E* recursive language (PROGRAMMING)
G rekursive Sprache (f)
F langage récursif (m)
S lenguaje recursivo (m)
I linguaggio ricorsivo (m)

2748 *E* recursive program
G rekursives Programm (n)
F programme récursif (m)
S programa recursivo (m)
I programma ricorsivo (m)

2749 *E* recursive transition network (RTN) (LOGIC)
G rekursives Übergangsnetzwerk (n)
F réseau de transition récursif (RTN) (m)
S red de transición recursiva (f)
I rete di transizione ricorrente (f)

2750 *E* reduced vocabulary (RECOGNITION)
G beschränktes Vokabular (n); beschränkter Wortschatz (m)
F vocabulaire réduit (m)
S vocabulario reducido (m); conjunto reducido de palabras (m)
I vocabolario ridotto (m)

2751 *E* reductio ad absurdum reasoning (*proof that the contrary is impossible*) (LOGIC)
G reductio-ad-absurdum-Schließen (n)
F raisonnement par l'absurde (m)

S razonamiento de reducción al absurdo (m)
I dimostrazione per assurdo (f)

2752 *E* reduction strategy (EXPERT SYSTEMS)
G Reduktionsstrategie (f)
F stratégie de réduction (f)
S estrategia de reducción (f)
I strategia di riduzione (f)

2753 *E* reference pattern (IMAGE PROCESSING)
G Bezugsmuster (n)
F modèle de référence (m)
S patrón de referencia (m)
I pattern di riferimento (m); modello di riferimento (m)

2754 *E* reference world (IMAGE PROCESSING)
G Bezugswelt (f)
F monde de référence (m)
S mundo de referencia (m)
I mondo di riferimento (m)

2755 *E* refinement (*of rules*) (EXPERT SYSTEMS)
≠ generalization
G Verfeinern (im Gegensatz zum Generalisieren) (n)
F affinement (m)
S refinación (de reglas) (f); refino (m)
I raffinamento (m)

2756 *E* refinement strategy (EXPERT SYSTEMS)
G Verfeinerungsstrategie (f)
F stratégie d'affinement (f)
S estrategia de refinamiento (f)
I strategia di raffinamento (f)

2757 *E* refutation (LOGIC)
= disproving
G Beweis des Gegenteils (m); Widerlegung (f); Refutation (f)
F réfutation (f)
S refutación (f)
I rifutazione (f)

2758 *E* refutation graph (LOGIC)
G Refutationsgraph (m)
F graphe de réfutation (m)
S grafo de refutación (m)
I grafo di rifutazione (m)

2759 *E* refutation procedure (LOGIC)
G Refutationsprozedur (f); Widerlegungsverfahren (n)
F procédure de réfutation (f)
S procedimiento de refutación (m)
I procedura di rifutazione (f)

2760 *E* refutation theorem (LOGIC)
G Widerlegungstheorem (n)
F théorème de réfutation (m)
S teorema de refutación (m)
I teorema di rifutazione (m)

2761 *E* refutation tree (LOGIC)
G Widerlegungsbaum (m)
F arbre de réfutation (m)
S árbol de refutación (m)
I albero di rifutazione (m)

2762 *E* refute (LOGIC)
= disprove
G widerlegen
F réfuter
S refutar
I rifutare

2763 *E* region analysis (IMAGE PROCESSING)
G Flächenanalyse (f)
F analyse régionale (f)
S análisis regional (m)
I analisi regionale (f)

2764 *E* region-based segmentation (*of an image; splitting and/or merging*)
G regionsbasierte Segmentierung (f)
F segmentation régionale (f)
S segmentación regional (f)

I segmentazione regionale (f)

2765 E region detection (IMAGE PROCESSING)
G Ermittlung von Regionen (f)
F détection de régions (f)
S detección de regiones (f)
I rilevamento di regioni (m)

2766 E region merging (IMAGE PROCESSING)
G Flächenverschmelzung (f)
F fusion de régions (f)
S fusión de regiones (f)
I fusione di regioni (f)

2767 E region method (IMAGE PROCESSING)
G Flächenanalyseverfahren (n)
F méthode des zones paramétrées (f)
S método de regiones (m)
I metodo delle regioni (m)

2768 E region splitting (IMAGE PROCESSING)
G Regionsaufspaltung (f)
F division en régions (f)
S división en regiones (f)
I divisione in regioni (f)

2769 E regular grammar
→ finite state grammar

2770 E reinforcement
= intensifier

2771 E relate (*objects*) (KNOWLEDGE)
G in Beziehung zueinander setzen
F mettre en relation
S relacionar
I porre in rapporto (tra loro)

2772 E relation (R) (KNOWLEDGE)
G Relation (f); Beziehung (f)
F relation (f)
S relación (f)
I relazione (f)

2773 E relational algebra (MATHS)
G relationale Algebra (f)
F algèbre relationnelle (f)
S álgebra relacional (f)
I algebra relazionale (f)

2774 E relational clause (*pattern: term 1* operator term 2) (LOGIC)
G Beziehungsklausel (f)
F clause relationnelle (f)
S cláusula relacional (f)
I clausola relazionale (f)

2775 E relational database (PROGRAMMING)
G relationale Datenbasis (f)
F base de données relationnelle (f)
S base de datos relacional (f)
I base di dati relazionale (f)

2776 E relational grammar (NLP)
G Relationsgrammatik (f)
F grammaire relationnelle (f)
S gramática relacional (f)
I grammatica relazionale (f)

2777 E relational model (KNOWLEDGE)
G relationales Modell (n)
F modèle relationnel (m)
S modelo relacional (m)
I modello relazionale (m)

2778 E relational node (LOGIC)
G Beziehungsknoten (m)
F nœud relationnel (m)
S nodo de relación (m)
I nodo di relazione (m)

2779 E relational operator (LOGIC)
= relation symbol
G Beziehungssymbol (n); Relationssymbol (n)
F opérateur relationnel (m)
S operador relacional (m)
I operatore relazionale (m)

2780 E relation graph (KNOWLEDGE)

G Beziehungsgraph (m); relationaler Graph (m)
F graphe de relations (m)
S grafo de relaciones (m)
I grafo delle relazioni (m)

2781 E relationship (*e.g. between objects*) (LOGIC)
G Beziehung (f)
F relation (f)
S relación (f)
I relazione (f)

2782 E relation symbol
→ relational operator

2783 E relative information loss (RIL) (RECOGNITION)
G relativer Informationsverlust (m)
F perte relative d'information (f)
S pérdida relativa de información (f)
I perdita relativa di informazione (f)

2784 E relative knowledge
→ context-dependent knowledge

2785 E relaxation (*of constraints etc.*) (LOGIC)
G Abschwächen (n)
F relâchement (m); relaxation (f)
S relajación (f)
I rilassamento (m)

2786 E relaxation algorithm (LOGIC)
G Abschwächungsalgorithmus (m)
F algorithme de relâchement (m)
S algoritmo de relajación (m)
I algoritmo di rilassamento (m)

2787 E representation (*of knowledge etc.*)
G Darstellung (f); Repräsentation (f)
F représentation (f)
S representación (f)
I rappresentazione (f)

2788 E representation language (*for knowledge etc.*)
G Darstellungssprache (f)
F langage de représentation (m)
S lenguaje de representación (m)
I linguaggio di rappresentazione (m)

2789 E representation level (KNOWLEDGE)
G Darstellungsebene (f)
F niveau de représentation (m)
S nivel de representación (m)
I livello di rappresentazione (m)

2790 E representation method (KNOWLEDGE)
G Darstellungsmethode (f)
F méthode de représentation (f)
S método de representación (m)
I metodo di rappresentazione (m)

2791 E representation system (*for knowledge etc.*) (KNOWLEDGE)
G Darstellungssystem (n)
F système de représentation (m)
S esquema de representación (m)
I sistema di rappresentazione (m)

2792 E representation world (KNOWLEDGE)
G Darstellungswelt (f)
F monde de représentation (m)
S mundo de representación (m)
I mondo di rappresentazione (m)

2793 E represented world (KNOWLEDGE)
G dargestellte Welt (f)
F monde représenté (m)
S mundo representado (m)
I mondo rappresentato (m)

2794 E research prototype (EXPERT SYSTEMS)
G Forschungsprototyp (m)
F prototype de recherche (m)
S prototipo de investigación (m)
I prototipo di ricerca (m)

2795 *E* residual problem
G Restproblem (n)
F problème résiduel (m)
S problema residual (m)
I problema residuale (m)

2796 *E* resolution (LOGIC)
G Resolution (f); Auflösung (f); Lösung (f)
F résolution (f)
S resolución (f)
I risoluzione (f)

2797 *E* resolution-based (*prover etc.*) (THEORY)
G resolutionsbasiert
F basé sur résolution
S basado en resoluciones
I basato su risoluzioni

2798 *E* resolution graph (LOGIC)
G Resolutionsgraph (m)
F graphe de résolution (m)
S grafo de resolución (m)
I grafo di risoluzione (m)

2799 *E* resolution method (LOGIC)
G Resolutionsmethode (f); Resolutionsverfahren (n)
F méthode de résolution (f)
S método de resolución (m)
I metodo di risoluzione (m)

2800 *E* resolution principle (LOGIC)
G Resolutionsprinzip (n)
F principe de résolution (m)
S estrategia de resolución (f)
I principio di risoluzione (m)

2801 *E* resolution refutation (LOGIC)
G Widerlegung durch Resolution (f); Resolutionswiderlegung (f)
F résolution avec réfutation (f)
S resolución con refutación (f)
I risoluzione attraverso refutazione (f)

2802 *E* resolution technique (EXPERT SYSTEMS)
G Lösungstechnik (f)
F technique de résolution (f)
S técnica de resolución (f)
I tecnica di risoluzione (f)

2803 *E* resolve (*problems etc.*)
→ solve

2804 *E* resolvent (LOGIC)
= resolvent clause
G Resolvente (f)
F clause résolvante (f); résolvant (m)
S resolvente (m)
I risolvente (f)

2805 *E* resolvent clause
→ resolvent

2806 *E* response clause (LOGIC)
G Antwortklausel (f)
F clause de réponse (f)
S cláusula de respuesta (f)
I clausola di risposta (f)

2807 *E* response frame (RECOGNITION)
G Antwortframe (m)
F cadre de réponse (m)
S trama respuesta (f)
I frame di risposta (m); quadro di risposta (m)

2808 *E* restricted chaining (PROGRAMMING)
G eingeschränkte Verkettung (f)
F chaînage restreint (m)
S encadenamiento restringido (m)
I concatenamento ristretto (m)

2809 *E* restricted domain (KNOWLEDGE)
= constrained domain
G beschränkte Domäne (f); eingeschränktes Gebiet (n)
F domaine restreint (m)
S dominio restringido (m); dominio limitado (m)

I dominio ristretto (m); dominio limitato (m)

2810 *E* restricted grammar (NLP)
G eingeschränkte Grammatik (f)
F grammaire restreinte (f)
S grámatica restringida (f); gramática limitada (f)
I grammatica ristretta (f)

2811 *E* restricted language (RECOGNITION)
G eingeschränkte Sprache (f)
F langage limité (m)
S lenguaje restringido (m)
I linguaggio ristretto (m)

2812 *E* restricted reasoning (LOGIC)
G eingeschränktes Inferieren (n)
F raisonnement restreint (m)
S razonamiento restringido (m); razonamiento sujeto a restricciones (m)
I ragionamento ristretto (m)

2813 *E* restricted search (EXPERT SYSTEMS)
G eingeschränkte Suche (f)
F recherche limitée (f)
S búsqueda limitada (f)
I ricerca limitata (f)

2814 *E* restricted-syntax language (NLP)
G Sprache mit eingeschränkter Syntax (f); Sprache mit restriktiver Syntax (f)
F langage à syntaxe limitée (m); langage à syntaxe contrôlée (m)
S lenguaje con sintaxis restringida (m)
I linguaggio con sintassi ristretta (m)

2815 *E* restricted vocabulary (RECOGNITION)
G eingeschränktes Vokabular (n); eingeschränkter Wortschatz (m)
F vocabulaire restreint (m); vocabulaire limité (m)
S vocabulario restringido (m)
I vocabolario ristretto (m)

2816 *E* restriction
G Einschränkung (f); Beschränkung (f); Restriktion (f)
F restriction (f)
S restricción (f)
I restrizione (f)

2817 *E* restriction strategy (EXPERT SYSTEMS)
G Restriktionsstrategie (f)
F stratégie de restriction (f)
S estrategia de restricción (f)
I strategia di restrizione (f)

2818 *E* restrictive grammar (NLP)
G Restriktionsgrammatik (f)
F grammaire de restriction (f)
S gramática restrictiva (f)
I grammatica restrittiva (f)

2819 *E* resynthesis
G Wiedersynthese (f); Neusynthese (f)
F resynthèse (f)
S resíntesis (f)
I risintesi (f)

2820 *E* reversability (*in propositional logic*)
G Reversibilität (f)
F reversibilité (f)
S reversibilidad (f)
I reversabilità (f)

2821 *E* revision of beliefs
→ belief revision

2822 *E* rewrite rule (LOGIC)
G Ersetzungsregel (f)
F règle de réécriture (f)
S regla de reescritura (f)
I regola di riscrittura (f)

2823 *E* rewriting (LOGIC)
G Ersetzung (f); Termersetzung (f)
F réécriture (f)
S reescritura (f)
I riscrittura (f)

2824 *E* RHS
→ right-hand side

2825 *E* right-hand side (RHS) (EXPERT SYSTEMS)
= consequent; consequence; action part
↔ left-hand side
G rechte Seite (f); Aktionsteil (m)
F partie droite (f); membre droit (d'une règle) (m); action (d'une règle) (f)
S lado derecho (m); elementos consecuentes (de una regla) (m pl)
I parte destra (allora ...) (f); lato destro (m); conseguente (m)

2826 *E* RIL
→ relative information loss

2827 *E* risk assessment (EXPERT SYSTEMS)
= hazard analysis
G Risikoabwägung (f); Gefahrenanalyse (f)
F évaluation de risques (f); analyse de risque (f)
S análisis de riesgos (m)
I analisi dei rischi (f)

2828 *E* RLL
= representation language language

2829 *E* RMS
= reason maintenance system
→ truth maintenance system

2830 *E* robot
= robot system
G Roboter (m)
F robot (m)
S robot (m); sistema robotizado (m)
I robot (m)

2831 *E* robotics
G Robotik (f)
F robotique (f)
S robótica (f)
I robotica (f)

2832 *E* robot in the home
→ domestic robot

2833 *E* robot system
→ robot

2834 *E* robot vision
↔ machine vision
G Sehen durch Roboter (n)
F vision par robots (f)
S visión por robot (f)
I visione da robot (f)

2835 *E* role[1] (EXPERT SYSTEMS)
G Rolle (f)
F rôle (m)
S papel (m)
I ruolo (m)

2836 *E* role[2] (*in a script*) (KNOWLEDGE)
G Person (f); Rolle (f)
F rôle (m)
S personaje (m)
I personaggio (m)

2837 *E* role instantiation (EXPERT SYSTEMS)
G Rolleninstantiierung (f)
F instanciation de rôle (f)
S instanciación de personajes (f)
I instanziamento di personaggi (m)

2838 *E* role merging (EXPERT SYSTEMS)
G Rollenverschmelzung (f)
F fusion de rôles (f)
S fusión de roles (f)
I fusione di ruoli (f)

2839 *E* root (*of a tree*) (LOGIC)

G Wurzel (f)
F racine (d'un arbre) (f)
S raíz (f)
I radice (f)

2840 *E* root node (*with no predecessors*) (KNOWLEDGE)
= top node
G Wurzelknoten (m); oberster Knoten (m); Spitzenknoten (m)
F nœud-racine (m); tête (f)
S nodo raíz (m)
I nodo radice (m)

2841 *E* rooted tree (PROGRAMMING)
G Baum mit Wurzel (m)
F arbre avec racine (m)
S árbol con raíz (m)
I albero con radice (m)

2842 *E* rote learning
G Auswendiglernen (n)
F apprentissage par cœur (m)
S aprendizaje rutinario (m)
I apprendimento passivo (m)

2843 *E* RTN
→ recursive transition network

2844 *E* rule
G Regel (f)
F règle (f)
S regla (f)
I regola (f)

2845 *E* rule acquisition (EXPERT SYSTEMS)
G Regelerwerb (m)
F acquisition de règles (f)
S adquisición de reglas (f)
I acquisizione di regole (f)

2846 *E* rule base (EXPERT SYSTEMS)
G Regelbasis (f)
F base de règles (f)
S base de reglas (f)
I base di regole (f)

2847 *E* rule-based (EXPERT SYSTEMS)
G regelbasiert; auf der Basis von Regeln; regelgestützt
F basé sur règles
S basado en reglas
I sulla base di regole; basato su regole

2848 *E* rule-based diagnosis (EXPERT SYSTEMS)
G regelbasierte Diagnose (f)
F diagnose à base de règles (f)
S diagnóstico basado en reglas (m)
I diagnosi basata su regole (f)

2849 *E* rule-based expert system
G regelbasiertes Expertensystem (n)
F système expert à base de règles (m)
S sistema experto basado en reglas (m)
I sistema esperto basato su regole (di inferenza) (m)

2850 *E* rule-based inference system (EXPERT SYSTEMS)
G regelbasiertes Inferenzsystem (n)
F système d'inférence basé sur règles (m)
S sistema de inferencia basada en reglas (f)
I sistema di inferenza basata su regole (f)

2851 *E* rule-based knowledge
G Regelwissen (n)
F connaissance à base de règles (f)
S conocimiento basado en reglas (m)
I conoscenza basata su regole (f)

2852 *E* rule-based method (EXPERT SYSTEMS)
G regelbasierte Methode (f)
F méthode à base de règles (f)
S metodo basado en reglas (m)
I metodo basato su regole (m)

2853 *E* rule-based program (EXPERT SYSTEMS)
G regelgesteuertes Programm (n)
F programme à base de règles (m)
S programa basado en reglas (m)
I programma basato su regole (m)

2854 *E* rule-based programming
G regelbasierte Programmierung (f)
F programmation à base de règles (f)
S programación basada en reglas (f)
I programmazione basata su regole (f)

2855 *E* rule-based representation (KNOWLEDGE)
G regelbasierte Darstellung (f)
F représentation sous forme de règles (f)
S representación basada en reglas (f)
I rappresentazione basata su regole (f)

2856 *E* rule-based strategy (EXPERT SYSTEMS)
G regelbasierte Strategie (f)
F stratégie à base de règles (f)
S estrategia basada en reglas (f)
I strategia basata su regole (f)

2857 *E* rule-based synthesis (RECOGNITION)
= synthesis by rule
G regelbasierte Synthese (f)
F synthèse sur la base de règles (f); synthèse par règles (f)
S síntesis por reglas (f); síntesis según reglas (f)
I sintesi mediante regole (f); sintesi a mezzo di regole (f); sintesi secondo regole (f)

2858 *E* rule-based system (RBS) (EXPERT SYSTEMS)
G regelgesteuertes System (n); regelbasiertes System (n)
F système à base de règles (SBR) (m)
S sistema basado en reglas (m)
I sistema basato su regole (m)

2859 *E* rule certainty (EXPERT SYSTEMS)
G Sicherheit einer Regel (f)
F certitude d'une règle (f)
S certidumbre de una regla (f)
I certezza di una regola (f)

2860 *E* rule class (EXPERT SYSTEMS)
G Regelklasse (f)
F classe de règles (f)
S clase de reglas (f)
I classe di regola (f)

2861 *E* rule cluster (EXPERT SYSTEMS)
G Regelkomplex (m)
F ensemble de règles (m); paquet de règles (m)
S conjunto de reglas (m)
I gruppo di regole (m)

2862 *E* rule compilation (EXPERT SYSTEMS)
G Zusammenstellung der Regeln (f)
F compilation de règles (f)
S compilación de reglas (f)
I compilazione di regole (f)

2863 *E* rule compiler (EXPERT SYSTEMS)
G Regelcompiler (m)
F compilateur des règles (m)
S compilador de reglas (m)
I compilatore delle regole (m)

2864 *E* rule definition (EXPERT SYSTEMS)
G Regeldefinition (f)
F définition des règles (f)
S definición de reglas (f)
I definizione di una regola (f)

2865 *E* rule editor (EXPERT SYSTEMS)
G Regeleditor (m)
F éditeur de règles (m)
S editor de reglas (m)
I editore di regole (m)

2866 *E* rule filtering (*the exclusion of certain rules*) (EXPERT SYSTEMS)
= filtering of rules
G Filtern von Regeln (n)
F filtrage des règles (m)
S filtraje de reglas (m); filtrado de reglas (m)
I filtraggio di regole (m)

2867 *E* rule interpretation (EXPERT SYSTEMS)
G Regelinterpretation (f)
F interprétation de règles (f)
S interpretación de reglas (f)
I interpretazione delle regole (f)

2868 *E* rule interpreter (EXPERT SYSTEMS)
= interpreter
G Regelinterpreter (m)
F interpréteur de règles (m)
S intérprete de reglas (m)
I interprete delle regole (m)

2869 *E* rule learning
→ learning of rules

2870 *E* rule memory (EXPERT SYSTEMS)
G Regelspeicher (m)
F mémoire de règles (f)
S memoria de reglas (f)
I memoria delle regole (f)

2871 *E* rule of entailment
→ modus ponens rule

2872 *E* rule of good judgement
→ rule of thumb

2873 *E* rule of inference
→ inference rule

2874 *E* rule of reasoning
→ reasoning rule

2875 *E* rule of thumb
= rule of good judgement
G Faustregel (f); 'Daumenregel' (f)
F règle de jugement (f)
S regla de buen juicio (f)
I regola del buon senso (f)

2876 *E* rule-oriented (*system etc.*) (EXPERT SYSTEMS)
G regelorientiert; regelbezogen
F orienté règles
S orientado en reglas
I orientato a regole

2877 *E* rule path (EXPERT SYSTEMS)
G Regelfolge (f)
F parcours de règles (m); chemin de règles (m)
S secuencia de reglas (f)
I sequenza delle regole (f)

2878 *E* rule representation (EXPERT SYSTEMS)
G Regeldarstellung (f)
F représentation de règles (f)
S representación de reglas (f)
I rappresentazione delle regole (f)

2879 *E* rule-representation language (EXPERT SYSTEMS)
G Sprache zur Regeldarstellung (f); Regeldarstellungssprache (f)
F langage d'interprétation de règles (m)
S lenguaje de representación de reglas (m)
I linguaggio per la rappresentazione di regole (m)

2880 *E* rule set
→ set of rules

2881 *E* rule space (EXPERT SYSTEMS)
G Regelraum (m)
F espace des règles (m)
S espacio de las reglas (m)
I spazio delle regole (m)

2882 *E* rule synthesis
≠ analysis/resynthesis
G Regelsynthese (f); Synthese nach Regeln (f)

F synthèse basée sur règles (f)
S síntesis por regla(s) (f)
I sintesi sulla base di regole (f)

2883 *E* rule system
→ system of rules

2884 *E* rule transformation (EXPERT SYSTEMS)
G Umsetzung einer Regel (f); Regelumsetzung (f)
F transformation d'une règle (f)
S transformación de una regla (de reglas) (f)
I trasformazione delle regole (f)

2885 *E* rule tree (EXPERT SYSTEMS)
G Regelbaum (m)
F arbre de règles (m)
S árbol de reglas (m)
I albero delle regole (m)

2886 *E* running speech
→ fluent speech

2887 *E* runtime environment (*e.g. of an expert system*) (PROGRAMMING)
G Runtime-Umgebung (f)
F environnement runtime (m)
S entorno a tiempo de ejecución (m)
I ambiente runtime (m)

2888 *E* runtime package
→ runtime version

2889 *E* runtime version (EXPERT SYSTEMS)
= runtime package
G Runtime-Version (f)
F version runtime (f); module utilisateur autonome (m)
S sistema para explotación (m)
I versione runtime (f)

S

2890 *E* SAISB
= Society for Artificial Intelligence and Simulation of Behavior

2891 *E* sample space (EXPERT SYSTEMS)
= example space
G Beispielraum (m)
F espace des exemples (m)
S espacio de ejemplos (m)
I spazio degli esempi (m)

2892 *E* sampling period (RECOGNITION)
G Abtastzeitraum (m)
F temps de balayage (m)
S período de muestreo (m)
I periodo di scansione (m)

2893 *E* satisfice procedure (EXPERT SYSTEMS)
G Erfüllungsprozedur (f)
F procédure non optimale (f)
S procedimiento de satifacción (m)
I procedura non ottimale (f)

2894 *E* SBL
→ similarity-based learning

2895 *E* SC
→ situation calculus

2896 *E* scale parameter (IMAGE PROCESSING)
G Skalierungsparameter (m)
F paramètre d'échelle (m)
S parámetro de escala (m)
I parametro di scalamento (m)

2897 *E* scenario (KNOWLEDGE)
G Szenario (n)
F scénario (m)
S escenario (m)
I scenario (m)

2898 *E* scene (*a sequence of actions in a script*) (KNOWLEDGE)
G Szene (f)
F scène (f); épisode (m); abrégé (m)
S escena (f)
I scena (f)

2899 *E* scene analysis (IMAGE PROCESSING)
G Szenenanalyse (f)
F analyse de scènes (f)
S análisis de escenas (m)
I analisi della scena (f)

2900 *E* scene analysis system (IMAGE PROCESSING)
G Szenenanalysesystem (n)
F système d'analyse des scènes (m)
S sistema de análisis de escenas (m)
I sistema di analisi delle scene (m)

2901 *E* scene data (IMAGE PROCESSING)
G Szenendaten (pl)
F données de scène (f pl)
S datos de la escena (m pl)
I dati di scena (f pl)

2902 *E* scene feature (IMAGE PROCESSING)
G Szenenmerkmal (n)
F caractéristique d'une scène (f)
S característica de una escena (f); aspecto particular de una escena (m)
I caratteristica di una scena (f)

2903 *E* scene interpretation (IMAGE PROCESSING)
G Szeneninterpretation (f)

F interprétation de scènes (f)
S interpretación de escenas (f)
I interpretazione di scene (f)

2904 *E* scene quantifying (IMAGE PROCESSING)
G Szenenquantifizierung (f)
F quantification de scène(s) (f)
S cuantificación de escena (f)
I quantificazione di scene (f)

2905 *E* scene recognition (IMAGE PROCESSING)
G Szenenerkennung (f)
F reconnaissance de scènes (f)
S reconocimiento de escenas (m)
I riconoscimento di scene (m)

2906 *E* scene understanding (IMAGE PROCESSING)
G Szenenverstehen (n)
F compréhension de scènes (f)
S comprensión de escenas (f)
I comprensione delle scene (f)

2907 *E* SCH
→ self-chaining rule

2908 *E* scheduler (*of an expert system*)
G Zeitplanungskomponente (f)
F module d'ordonnancement (m)
S módulo gestor (m)
I gestore (m)

2909 *E* scheduling (EXPERT SYSTEMS)
G Zeitplanung (f)
F ordonnancement (m)
S gestión (f)
I gestione (f)

2910 *E* schema (*plural:* schemata) (KNOWLEDGE)
= view
G Schema (n)
F schéma (m)
S esquema (m)
I schema (m)

2911 *E* scope (*of a variable etc.*) (PROGRAMMING)
G Bereich (m); Wertebereich (m); Geltungsbereich (m)
F portée (f)
S gama (f)
I scopo (m)

2912 *E* score (*noun*) (EXPERT SYSTEMS)
G Bewertung (f)
F évaluation (f); score (m)
S evaluación (f)
I valutazione (f)

2913 *E* scoring function (RECOGNITION)
G Bewertungsfunktion (f); Score-Funktion (f)
F fonction d'évaluation (f); fonction de score (f)
S función de evaluación (f)
I funzione di evaluazione (f)

2914 *E* script (KNOWLEDGE)
G Script (n)
F script (m); scénario (m)
S script (m); guión (m)
I script (m); schema comportamentale (m); copione (m)

2915 *E* script-based (KNOWLEDGE)
G scriptbasiert; auf Scripts basierend
F à base de scripts
S basado en scripts
I basato su scripts

2916 *E* script-based understanding (RECOGNITION)
G scriptbasiertes Verstehen (n)
F compréhension à base de scripts (f)
S comprensión basada en scripts (f)
I comprensione basata su scripts (f)

2917 *E* search (*for solutions etc.*) (EXPERT SYSTEMS)
G Suche (f)

F recherche (d'une solution etc.) (f)
S búsqueda (f)
I ricerca (di soluzioni ecc.) (f); search (f)

2918 *E* search algorithm (EXPERT SYSTEMS)
G Suchalgorithmus (m)
F algorithme de recherche (m)
S algoritmo de búsqueda (m)
I algoritmo di ricerca (m)

2919 *E* search-and-optimization technique (GAMES)
G Such- und Optimierungstechnik (f)
F technique de recherche et d'optimisation (f)
S técnica de búsqueda y optimización (f)
I tecnica di ricerca e ottimizazzione (f)

2920 *E* search beam (*in a beam search*) (EXPERT SYSTEMS)
G Suchbreite (f)
F largeur du faisceau (de recherche) (f)
S largura de búsqueda (f)
I larghezza della ricerca (f)

2921 *E* search cycle (EXPERT SYSTEMS)
G Suchzyklus (m)
F cycle de recherche (m)
S ciclo de búsqueda (m); ciclo de control (m)
I ciclo di ricerca (m)

2922 *E* search depth (EXPERT SYSTEMS)
G Suchtiefe (f); Penetranz (f)
F profondeur de recherche (f)
S profundidad de búsqueda (f)
I profondità della ricerca (f); penetranza (f)

2923 *E* search direction (EXPERT SYSTEMS)
G Suchrichtung (f)
F direction de la recherche (f)
S dirección de búsqueda (f)
I direzione della ricerca (f)

2924 *E* search for patterns
→ pattern searching

2925 *E* search graph (LOGIC)
G Suchgraph (m)
F graphe de recherche (m)
S grafo de búsqueda (m)
I grafo di ricerca (m)

2926 *E* search language (NLP)
G Suchsprache (f)
F langage de recherche (m)
S lenguaje de búsqueda (m)
I linguaggio di ricerca (m)

2927 *E* search method (EXPERT SYSTEMS)
G Suchmethode (f)
F méthode de recherche (f)
S método de búsqueda (m)
I metodo di ricerca (m)

2928 *E* search over a network
→ network search

2929 *E* search paradigm (EXPERT SYSTEMS)
= paradigm of search
G Suchparadigma (n)
F paradigme de recherche (m)
S paradigma de búsqueda (m)
I paradigma di ricerca (m)

2930 *E* search path (EXPERT SYSTEMS)
G Suchweg (m)
F chemin de recherche (m)
S camino a buscar (m); camino de búsqueda (m)
I cammino di ricerca (m)

2931 *E* search process (EXPERT SYSTEMS)
G Suchprozeß (m)
F procédé de recherche (m)
S proceso de búsqueda (m)
I processo di ricerca (m)

2932 *E* search reduction (EXPERT SYSTEMS)
G Reduzierung des Suchaufwands (f)
F réduction de la recherche (f)
S reducción de búsqueda (f)
I riduzione della ricerca (f)

2933 *E* search space (EXPERT SYSTEMS)
= problem search space
G Suchraum (m)
F espace de recherche (m); zone de recherche (f)
S espacio de búsqueda (m)
I spazio di ricerca (m)

2934 *E* search step (EXPERT SYSTEMS)
G Suchschritt (m)
F pas de recherche (m)
S paso de búsqueda (m)
I passo di ricerca (m)

2935 *E* search strategy (EXPERT SYSTEMS)
G Suchstrategie (f)
F stratégie de recherche (f)
S estrategia de búsqueda (f)
I strategia di ricerca (f)

2936 *E* search technique (EXPERT SYSTEMS)
G Suchtechnik (f)
F technique de recherche (f)
S técnica de búsqueda (f)
I tecnica di ricerca (f)

2937 *E* search time (EXPERT SYSTEMS)
G Suchzeit (f)
F temps de recherche (m)
S tiempo de búsqueda (m)
I tempo di ricerca (m)

2938 *E* search tree (EXPERT SYSTEMS)
G Suchbaum (m)
F arbre de recherche (m)
S árbol de búsqueda (m)
I albero di ricerca (m)

2939 *E* second-order logic
↔ first-order logic
G Logik zweiter Ordnung (f)
F logique de deuxième ordre (f); logique de second ordre (f); logique d'ordre 2 (f)
S lógica de segundo orden (f)
I logica di secondo ordine (f)

2940 *E* SEG
→ sequence of events generator

2941 *E* segment (*of speech*) (RECOGNITION)
= chunk
G Segment (n)
F segment (m)
S segmento (de habla) (m)
I segmento (m)

2942 *E* segmentation (*of images*) (IMAGE PROCESSING)
G Segmentierung (f)
F segmentation (f)
S segmentación (f)
I segmentazione (f)

2943 *E* select-best-of (LOGIC)
G die beste Alternative selektieren
F sélecter la meilleur alternative
S elegir la mejor alternativa
I scegliere l'alternative migliore

2944 *E* select function (EXPERT SYSTEMS)
G Selektionsfunktion (f)
F fonction de sélection (f)
S función de selección (f)
I funzione di selezione (f)

2945 *E* selection
G Auswahl (f); Selektion (f)
F sélection (f)
S selección (f)
I selezione (f); scelta (f)

2946 *E* selection criterion (NLP)
G Selektionskriterium (n)
F critère de sélection (m)

S criterio de selección (m)
I criterio di selezione (m)

2947 *E* selector (PROGRAMMING)
G Selektor (m)
F sélecteur (m)
S selector (m)
I selettore (m)

2948 *E* self-chaining rule (SCH) (EXPERT SYSTEMS)
G Selbstverkettungsregel (f)
F règle d'auto-enchaînement (f)
S regla de autoconcatenación (f)
I regola autoconcatenante (f)

2949 *E* self-identifying data
→ tagged data

2950 *E* self-improvement (NEURAL NETS)
G Selbstverbesserung (f)
F auto-amélioration (f)
S automejoramiento (m)
I automiglioramento (m)

2951 *E* self-knowledge
G Eigenwissen (n)
F connaissance de soi (f)
S conocimiento propio (m)
I conoscenza propria (f)

2952 *E* semantic (*adjective*) (NLP)
G semantisch
F sémantique
S semántico
I semantico

2953 *E* semantic analyser
→ semantic parser

2954 *E* semantic analysis (LINGUISTICS)
G semantische Analyse (f)
F analyse sémantique (f)
S análisis semántico (m)
I analisi semantica (f)

2955 *E* semantic ATN (KNOWLEDGE)
G semantisches ATN (n)
F réseau de transition augmenté sémantique (m)
S red ATN semántica (f)
I rete ATN semantica (f)

2956 *E* semantic attachment (NLP)
G semantische Auswertung (f)
F attachement sémantique (m)
S acoplamiento semántico (m)
I accoppiamento semantico (m)

2957 *E* semantic checking (NLP)
G Semantikprüfung (f)
F contrôle sémantique (m)
S verificación semántica (f)
I controllo semantico (m)

2958 *E* semantic closeness (*of knowledge elements*)
G semantische Nähe (f)
F proximité sémantique (f)
S verificación semántica (f)
I prossimità semantica (f)

2959 *E* semantic constituent (KNOWLEDGE)
G semantischer Bestandteil (m)
F composante sémantique (f)
S componente semántico (m)
I componente semantica (m)

2960 *E* semantic constraint (NLP)
G semantischer Constraint (m)
F contrainte sémantique (f)
S restricción semántica (f)
I vincolo semantico (m)

2961 *E* semantic dependency (NLP)
G semantische Abhängigkeit (f)
F dépendance sémantique (f)
S dependencia semántica (f)
I dipendenza semantica (f)

2962 *E* semantic distance (NLP)
G semantische Distanz (f)
F distance sémantique (f)
S distancia semántica (f)
I distanza semantica (f)

2963 *E* semantic entity (NLP)
G semantische Einheit (f)
F entité sémantique (f)
S entidad semántica (f)
I entità semantica (f)

2964 *E* semantic feature (NLP)
G semantische Eigenschaft (f)
F trait sémantique (m)
S rasgo semántico (m)
I caratteristica semantica (f)

2965 *E* semantic grammar (NLP)
G semantische Grammatik (f)
F grammaire sémantique (f)
S gramática semántica (f)
I grammatica semantica (f)

2966 *E* semantic information retrieval (SIR) (KNOWLEDGE)
G semantisches Informationsretrieval (n)
F recherche sémantique de l'information (f)
S búsqueda semántica de informaciones (f)
I reperimento semantico di informazioni (m)

2967 *E* semantic interpretation (NLP)
G semantische Interpretation (f)
F interprétation sémantique (f)
S interpretación semántica (f)
I interpretazione semantica (f)

2968 *E* semantic marker (KNOWLEDGE)
G semantische Markierung (f)
F marqueur sémantique (m)
S marca semántica (f); marcador semántico (m)
I marca semantica (f)

2969 *E* semantic memory (*an associative memory*) (KNOWLEDGE)
≠ episodic memory
G semantischer Speicher (m)
F mémoire sémantique (f)
S memoria semántica (f)
I memoria semantica (f)

2970 *E* semantic network (KNOWLEDGE)
G semantisches Netz (n); assoziatives Netz (n)
F réseau sémantique (m)
S red semántica (f)
I rete semantica (f)

2971 *E* semantic network node (KNOWLEDGE)
G Knoten eines semantischen Netzes (m)
F nœud de réseau sémantique (m)
S nodo de una red semántica (m)
I nodo di una rete semantica (m)

2972 *E* semantic parser (NLP)
= semantic analyser
G semantischer Parser (m)
F analyseur sémantique (m)
S analizador semántico (m)
I analizzatore semantico (m)

2973 *E* semantic parsing (NLP)
G semantisches Parsing (n)
F analyse sémantique (f)
S análisis semántico (m)
I parsing semantico (m); analisi semantica (f)

2974 *E* semantic pointer (KNOWLEDGE)
G semantischer Zeiger (m)
F pointeur sémantique (m)
S puntador semántico (m)
I puntatore semantico (m)

2975 *E* semantic primitives (NLP)
G semantische Primitiva (f pl)
F primitives sémantiques (f pl)
S primitivas semánticas (f pl)
I primitive semantiche (f pl)

2976 *E* semantic representation language (SRL) (KNOWLEDGE)
G semantische Darstellungssprache (f)

F langage de représentation sémantique (m)
S lenguaje de representación semántica (m)
I linguaggio di rappresentazione semantica (m)

2977 *E* semantic rule (NLP)
G Semantikregel (f)
F règle sémantiques (f)
S regla semántica (f)
I regola semantica (f)

2978 *E* semantics (LINGUISTICS)
G Semantik (f)
F sémantique (f)
S semántica (f)
I semantica (f)

2979 *E* semantic tree (KNOWLEDGE)
G semantischer Baum (m)
F arbre sémantique (m)
S árbol semántico (m)
I albero semantico (m)

2980 *E* semi-automatic reasoning (LOGIC)
G halbautomatisches Inferieren (n)
F raisonnement semi-automatique (m)
S razonamiento semi-automático (m)
I ragionamento semiautomatico (m)

2981 *E* semi-connected speech (*word groups separated by pauses*) (RECOGNITION)
G halbfließende Rede (f)
F parole semi-continue (f)
S discurso semi-continuo (m)
I parlato semiconnesso (m)

2982 *E* semi-exact (LOGIC)
G teilgenau
F semi-exact
S semi-exacto
I semi-esatto

2983 *E* semi-exact reasoning (*exact and inexact reasoning combined*) (LOGIC)
G teilgenaues Inferieren (n)
F raisonnement semi-exact (m)
S razonamiento semi-exacto (m)
I ragionamento semi-esatto (m)

2984 *E* semiexpert system
G Teilexpertensystem (n); Semiexpertensystem (n)
F système semi-expert (m)
S sistema semi-experto (m)
I sistema semi-esperto (m)

2985 *E* sensory information
G sensorische Information (f)
F information sensorielle (f)
S información sensorial (f)
I informazione sensoriale (f)

2986 *E* sentence analysis (NLP)
G Satzanalyse (f)
F analyse de phrases (f)
S análisis de frases (m)
I analisi di frasi (f)

2987 *E* sentence generation (NLP)
G Satzgenerierung (f)
F génération de phrases (f)
S composición de sentencias (f)
I generazione di frasi (f)

2988 *E* sentence generator (NLP)
G Satzgenerator (m)
F générateur de phrases (m)
S generador de frases (m)
I generatore di frasi (m)

2989 *E* sentence interpretation (NLP)
G Satzinterpretation (f)
F interprétation de phrases (f)
S interpretación de frases (f)
I interpretazione di frasi (f)

2990 *E* sentence recognition (NLP)
G Satzerkennung (f); Erkennen von Sätzen (n)

F reconnaissance de phrases (f)
S reconocimiento de frases (m)
I riconoscimento di frasi (m)

2991 E sentence understanding (NLP)
G Satzverstehen (n)
F compréhension de phrases (f)
S comprensión de frases (f)
I comprensione di frasi (f)

2992 E sentential constituent (LOGIC)
G Aussagenbestandteil (m)
F composante propositionnelle (f)
S componente proposicional (m)
I costituente proposizionale (m)

2993 E sentential logic
→ propositional logic

2994 E sequence of events generator (SEG) (EXPERT SYSTEMS)
G Ereignisfolgegenerator (m)
F générateur d'une séquence d'événements (m)
S generador de una secuencia de acontecimientos (m)
I generatore di una sequenza di eventi (m)

2995 E sequential constraint satisfaction (EXPERT SYSTEMS)
G sequentielle Erfüllung von Randbedingungen (f)
F satisfaction séquentielle des contraintes (f)
S satisfacción secuencial de restricciones (f)
I soddisfazione sequenziale dei vincoli (f)

2996 E sequential inference machine (SIM) (EXPERT SYSTEMS)
G sequentielle Inferenzmaschine (f)
F machine à inférence séquentielle (f)
S máquina de inferencia secuencial (f)
I macchina di inferenza sequenziale (f)

2997 E sequential learning
G sequentielles Lernen (n)
F apprentissage séquentiel (m)
S aprendizaje secuencial (m)
I apprendimento sequenziale (m)

2998 E session (*consultation of an expert system*)
G Sitzung (f)
F session (f)
S sesión (de consulta etc.) (f)
I sessione (f)

2999 E set (*noun*) (MATHS)
G Menge (f)
F ensemble (m)
S conjunto (m)
I insieme (m)

3000 E set of assertions (LOGIC)
G Aussagenmenge (f)
F ensemble d'assertions (m)
S conjunto de aserciones (m)
I insieme di asserzioni (m)

3001 E set of beliefs (EXPERT SYSTEMS)
G Überzeugungsmenge (f)
F ensemble de croyances (m)
S conjunto de confianzas (m)
I insieme di convinzioni (m)

3002 E set of clauses (LOGIC)
= clause set
G Klauselmenge (f); Klausenmenge (f); Komplex von Klauseln (m)
F ensemble de clauses (m)
S conjunto de cláusulas (m)
I insieme di clausole (m)

3003 E set of conditions (LOGIC)
G Komplex von Bedingungen (m)
F ensemble de conditions (m)
S conjunto de condiciones (m); colección de condiciones (f)

I insieme di condizioni (m)

3004 *E* set of constraints (EXPERT SYSTEMS)
G Menge von Constraints (f)
F ensemble de contraintes (m)
S conjunto de restricciones (m)
I insieme di vincoli (m)

3005 *E* set of events (EXPERT SYSTEMS)
G Ereignismenge (f)
F ensemble d'événements (m)
S conjunto de eventos (m)
I insieme di eventi (m)

3006 *E* set of expectations (LOGIC)
G Erwartungsmenge (f)
F ensemble d'expectatives (m)
S conjunto de expectativas (m)
I insieme di aspettative (m)

3007 *E* set of facts (LOGIC)
G Faktenkomplex (m)
F ensemble de faits (m)
S conjunto de factos (m)
I insieme di fatti (m)

3008 *E* set of features (KNOWLEDGE)
= feature set
G Merkmalsmenge (f)
F ensemble de traits caractéristiques (m)
S conjunto de características (m)
I insieme di caratteristiche (m)

3009 *E* set of hypotheses (LOGIC)
G Hypothesenmenge (f)
F ensemble des hypothèses (m)
S conjunto de hipótesis (m)
I insieme di ipotesi (m)

3010 *E* set of properties (KNOWLEDGE)
G Eigenschaftsmenge (f)
F ensemble de propriétés (m)
S conjunto de propiedades (m)
I insieme di proprietà (m)

3011 *E* set of relations (LOGIC)
G Beziehungsmenge (f)
F ensemble de relations (m)
S conjunto de relaciones (m)
I insieme di relazioni (m)

3012 *E* set of rules (EXPERT SYSTEMS)
= rule set; block of rules
G Regelsatz (m); Regelblock (m)
F jeu de règles (m); paquet de règles (m)
S conjunto de reglas (m); bloque de reglas (m); paquete de reglas (m)
I insieme di regole (m); pacchetto di regole (m); popolazione di regole (f); rule set (m)

3013 *E* set of statements (LOGIC)
G Komplex von Aussagen (m)
F ensemble de propositions (m)
S conjunto de proposiciones (m)
I insieme di proposizioni (m)

3014 *E* set of support
→ support set

3015 *E* set theory (MATHS)
= theory of sets
G Mengenlehre (f)
F théorie des ensembles (f)
S teoría de los conjuntos (f)
I insiemistica (f)

3016 *E* s-expr
→ symbolic expression

3017 *E* S-expression
→ symbolic expression

3018 *E* shallow knowledge
→ surface knowledge

3019 *E* shape analysis (IMAGE PROCESSING)
G Formanalyse (f); Gestaltanalyse (f)
F analyse de la forme (f)
S análisis de formas (m)

I analisi di forme (f)

3020 *E* shape identification (IMAGE PROCESSING)
G Formidentifikation (f)
F identification de la forme (f)
S identificación de formas (f)
I identificazione della forma (f)

3021 *E* shape recognition (IMAGE PROCESSING)
G Gestalterkennung (f); Formerkennung (f)
F reconnaissance de la forme (f)
S reconocimiento de forma (m)
I riconoscimento della forma (m)

3022 *E* shape representation (IMAGE PROCESSING)
G Formdarstellung (f)
F représentation des formes (f)
S representación de formas (f)
I rappresentazione di forme (f)

3023 *E* sharable knowledge
G teilbares Wissen (n)
F connaissances partageables (f pl)
S conocimiento compartible (m)
I conoscenza condivisibile (f)

3024 *E* shell (*of an expert system*)
→ expert system shell

3025 *E* shell program
G Shellprogramm (n)
F programme générique de développement (m); programme coquille (m)
S programa esqueleto (m)
I programma shell (m)

3026 *E* short constraint (EXPERT SYSTEMS)
G kurze Restriktion (f)
F contrainte courte (f)
S restricción corta (f)
I restrizione corta (f)

3027 *E* shortcut technique (PROGRAMMING)
G abgekürztes Verfahren (n)
F méthode simplifiée (f)
S método abreviado (m)
I metodo abbreviato (m)

3028 *E* shortest path (*to a solution etc.*) (EXPERT SYSTEMS)
G kürzester Weg (m)
F chemin plus court (m); plus court chemin (m)
S camino más corto (m)
I cammino più corto (m)

3029 *E* short-term memory (STM) (KNOWLEDGE)
≠ long-term memory
G Kurzzeitspeicher (bei einem Expertensystem) (m); Kurzzeitgedächtnis (beim Menschen) (n)
F mémoire à court terme (MCT) (f)
S memoria a corto plazo (f)
I memoria a breve termine (f)

3030 *E* short-term memory buffer (EXPERT SYSTEMS)
= context
G Arbeitsspeicher (m)
F mémoire de travail (f)
S memoria de trabajo (f)
I memoria di lavoro (f)

3031 *E* side condition (LOGIC)
G Nebenbedingung (f)
F condition marginale (f)
S condición marginal (f)
I condizione marginale (f)

3032 *E* side effect
G Nebenwirkung (f)
F effet latéral (m)
S efecto lateral (m)
I effetto laterale (m)

3033 *E* sideways chaining (*in addition to forward and backward*) (EXPERT SYSTEMS)
G Seitwärtsverkettung (f)
F enchaînement latéral (m)
S concatenación lateral (f)
I concatenazione laterale (f)

3034 *E* signal list
→ list of conditions

3035 *E* signal processing (RECOGNITION)
G Signalverarbeitung (f)
F traitement du signal (m)
S procesamiento de señales (m)
I processamento di segnali (m)

3036 *E* SIM
→ sequential inference machine

3037 *E* similarity-based learning (SBL)
G auf Ähnlichkeit basierendes Lernen (n)
F apprentissage par détection de similarités (ADS) (m)
S aprendizaje basado en similaridad (m)
I apprendimento mediante riconoscimento di similarità (m)

3038 *E* simple clause (*with only one predicate*) (LOGIC)
↔ compound clause
G einfache Klausel (f)
F clause simple (f)
S cláusula simple (f)
I clausola semplice (f)

3039 *E* simple inheritance (KNOWLEDGE)
≠ multiple inheritance
G Einfachvererbung (f)
F héritage simple (m)
S herencia simple (f)
I ereditarietà semplice (f)

3040 *E* simplification (*of rules*) (EXPERT SYSTEMS)
G Vereinfachung (f)
F simplification (f)
S simplificación (f)
I semplificazione (f)

3041 *E* simplification strategy (EXPERT SYSTEMS)
G Vereinfachungsstrategie (f)
F stratégie de simplification (f)
S estrategia de simplificación (f)
I strategia di semplificazione (f)

3042 *E* simplify (*a problem etc.*) (EXPERT SYSTEMS)
G vereinfachen
F simplifier
S simplificar
I semplificare

3043 *E* simulated annealing (NEURAL NETS)
G Simulated Annealing (n); simuliertes Tempern (n)
F recuit simulé (m)
S recocido simulado (m)
I ricottura simulata (m)

3044 *E* single-layer Perceptron (NEURAL NETS)
G einschichtiges Perceptron (n)
F Perceptron à une couche (m)
S Perceptron de una capa (m)
I Perceptron ad un strato solo (m)

3045 *E* single speaker (RECOGNITION)
G einzelner Sprecher (m); Einzelsprecher (m)
F locuteur unique (m); monolocuteur (m)
S único locutor (m)
I unico locutore (m); monolocutore (m)

3046 *E* single-speaker recognition
G Einzelsprechererkennung (f)
F reconnaissance monolocuteur (f)
S reconocimiento monolocutor (m)
I riconoscimento di un locutore solo (m)

3047 *E* single-speaker system (RECOGNITION)
G Einzelsprechersystem (n)
F système monolocuteur (m)
S sistema de locutor único (m)
I sistema a locutore unico (m); sistema monolocutore (m)

3048 *E* singularity
G Eigenständigkeit (f)
F singularité (f)
S singularidad (f)
I singolarità (f); unitarietà (f)

3049 *E* SIR
→ semantic information retrieval

3050 *E* situation–action rule (EXPERT SYSTEMS)
G Situations–Aktions-Regel (f)
F règle situation–action (f)
S regla situación–acción (f)
I regola situazione–azione (f)

3051 *E* situational
G situationsbezogen; situationsbedingt; situativ
F situationnel; en fonction des situations
S situacional
I situazionale

3052 *E* situational calculus
→ situation calculus

3053 *E* situational context (RECOGNITION)
G situativer Kontext (m)
F contexte situationnel (m)
S contexto situacional (m)
I contesto situazionale (m)

3054 *E* situational knowledge
G Situationswissen (n)
F connaissance situationnelle (f)
S conocimiento situacional (m)
I conoscenza situazionale (f)

3055 *E* situational memory (KNOWLEDGE)
G Situationsgedächtnis (n)
F mémoire situationnelle (f)
S memoria situacional (f)
I memoria situazionale (f)

3056 *E* situational variable (KNOWLEDGE)
G Situationsvariable (f)
F variable situationnelle (f)
S variable situacional (f)
I variabile situazionale (f)

3057 *E* situation calculus (SC) (KNOWLEDGE)
= situational calculus
G Situationskalkül (n)
F calcul situationnel (m)
S cálculo de situaciones (m)
I calcolo delle situazioni (m)

3058 *E* situation description (KNOWLEDGE)
G Situationsbeschreibung (f)
F description de la situation (f)
S descripción de una situación (f)
I descrizione di una situazione (f)

3059 *E* situation model (KNOWLEDGE)
G Situationsmodell (n)
F modèle de situation (m)
S modelo situacional (m); modelo de situación (m)
I modello situazionale (m)

3060 *E* situation recognition (KNOWLEDGE)
G Situationserkennung (f)
F reconnaissance de situations (f)
S reconocimiento de situaciones (m)
I riconoscimento di situazioni (m)

3061 *E* situation semantics (KNOWLEDGE)
G Situationssemantik (f)
F sémantique situationnelle (f)
S semántica situacional (f)

I semantica situazionale (f); semantica delle situazioni (f)

3062 *E* skeleton
→ sketch

3063 *E* sketch (IMAGE PROCESSING)
= skeleton
→ primal sketch
G Skelett (n); Rahmen (m)
F squelette (m)
S esqueleto (m); croquis (m)
I scheletro (m)

3064 *E* Skolem constant (MATHS)
G Skolemkonstante (f)
F constante de Skolem (f)
S constante de Skolem (f)
I costante di Skolem (f)

3065 *E* Skolem function (MATHS)
G Skolemfunktion (f)
F fonction de Skolem (f)
S función de Skolem (f)
I funzione di Skolem (f)

3066 *E* skolemization (*elimination of existential qualifiers*) (MATHS)
G Skolemisierung (f)
F représentation comme fonction de Skolem (f)
S skolemización (f)
I skolemizzazione (f)

3067 *E* slot (KNOWLEDGE)
= attribute
G Slot (eines Frame) (m); Frame-Slot (m); Element eines Frame (n); Abteil (n)
F tiroir (d'un frame) (m); aspect d'un objet (m); rubrique (f)
S slot (elemento de un cuadro) (m); slot de frame (m); ranura (componente de un objeto) (f); registro (de un marco) (m)
I slot (di un frame) (m); attributo di un frame (m); incastro (m); casella (f)

3068 *E* slot filler (KNOWLEDGE)
G Slot-Füller (m); Slot-Filler (m)
F élément de tiroir (m)
S elemento de relleno de slot (m)
I riempitore di posti (m)

3069 *E* slot name (KNOWLEDGE)
G Slot-Name (m)
F nom de tiroir (m)
S nombre de slot (m)
I nome dello slot (m)

3070 *E* slot value (KNOWLEDGE)
G Slot-Wert (m)
F valeur de tiroir (f)
S valor de slot (m)
I valore dello slot (m)

3071 *E* small knowledge system (EXPERT SYSTEMS)
G kleines Wissenssystem (n)
F petit système à base de connaissances (m); minisystème à base de connaissances (m)
S sistema de conocimiento pequeño (m)
I sistema piccolo basato su conoscenza (m)

3072 *E* smart tree (LOGIC)
G optimaler Suchbaum (m)
F arbre optimal (m)
S árbol optimal (m)
I albero ottimale (m)

3073 *E* smoothing (*of values etc.*) (IMAGE PROCESSING)
G Glättung (f); Glätten (n)
F lissage (m)
S alisamiento (m)
I smussamento (m)

3074 *E* software platform
G Softwareplattform (f)
F plateforme logicielle (f)
S plataforma de software (f)
I piattaforma di software (f)

3075 *E* solution
G Lösung (f)
F solution (f)
S solución (a un problema) (f)
I soluzione (f)

3076 *E* solution algorithm (PROGRAMMING)
G Lösungsalgorithmus (m)
F algorithme de solution (m)
S algoritmo de resolución (m)
I algoritmo di soluzione (m)

3077 *E* solution graph (PROGRAMMING)
G Lösungsgraph (m) (grafische Darstellung der Lösung)
F graphe de solution (m)
S grafo de soluciones (m)
I grafo delle soluzioni (m); grafo risolutivo (m)

3078 *E* solution method (LOGIC)
G Lösungsmethode (f)
F méthode de solution (f)
S método de solución (m)
I metodo di soluzione (m)

3079 *E* solution node (EXPERT SYSTEMS)
G Lösungsknoten (m)
F nœud-solution (m)
S nodo solución (m)
I nodo soluzione (m)

3080 *E* solution path (*from initial node to end node*) (EXPERT SYSTEMS)
G Lösungsweg (m); Lösungspfad (m)
F chemin de solution (m)
S camino solución (m); camino de solución (m)
I cammino di soluzione (m); cammino risolutivo (m); cammino che conduce alla soluzione (m)

3081 *E* solution space (EXPERT SYSTEMS)
G Lösungsraum (m)
F espace de solution (m)
S espacio de solución (m)
I spazio delle soluzioni (m)

3082 *E* solution strategy (EXPERT SYSTEMS)
G Lösungsstrategie (f)
F stratégie de solution (f)
S estrategia de solución (f)
I strategie di soluzione (f)

3083 *E* solution tree (EXPERT SYSTEMS)
G Lösungsbaum (m)
F arbre de solution (m)
S árbol de solución (m)
I albero di soluzioni (m)

3084 *E* solve (*problems etc.*)
= resolve
G lösen
F résoudre
S resolver
I risolvere

3085 *E* solving strategy
→ problem-solving strategy

3086 *E* sort[1] (*of data, in predicate logic*)
G Sorte (f)
F type (m)
S tipo (m)
I tipo (m)

3087 *E* sort[2] (*noun*)
→ type

3088 *E* sound (*rule etc.; adjective*)
G bewährt
F sain
S sano
I sano

3089 *E* sound synthesis (RECOGNITION)
G Klangsynthese (f)
F synthèse de son (f)
S síntesis de sonido (f)
I sintesi del suono (f)

3090 *E* source coding (RECOGNITION)

G Quellcodierung (f)
F codage source (m)
S codificación de fuente (f)
I codifica fonte (f)

3091 *E* source language (MT)
G Ausgangssprache (f)
F langage source (m)
S lenguaje fuente (m)
I linguaggio di origine (m)

3092 *E* source node (LOGIC)
G Ursprungsknoten (m)
F nœud source (m)
S nodo origen (m)
I nodo sorgente (m); nodo origine (n)

3093 *E* spanning tree (*in which all nodes are linked*) (LOGIC)
G Spannbaum (m)
F arbre recouvrant (m); arbre de recouvrement (m)
S árbol interconectado (m)
I albero interconnesso (m)

3094 *E* spatial knowledge (IMAGE PROCESSING)
G räumliches Wissen (n)
F connaissance spatiale (f)
S conocimiento espacial (m)
I conoscenza spaziale (f)

3095 *E* spatial planning (EXPERT SYSTEMS)
G räumliches Planen (n)
F planification spatiale (f)
S planificación espacial (f)
I pianificazione dello spazio (f)

3096 *E* spatial reasoning (EXPERT SYSTEMS)
G Inferieren im räumlichen Zusammenhang (n)
F raisonnement spatial (m)
S razonamiento espacial (m)
I ragionamento spaziale (m); ragionamento sullo spazio (m)

3097 *E* SPC
→ speech-processing chip

3098 *E* speaker (RECOGNITION)
G Sprecher (m)
F locuteur (m)
S locutor (m)
I locutore (m); parlatore (m)

3099 *E* speaker adaptation (RECOGNITION)
G Anpassung an den Sprecher (f)
F adaptation au locuteur (f)
S adaptación al locutor (f)
I adattamento al locutore (m)

3100 *E* speaker-adaptive (*system*) (RECOGNITION)
G sprecheradaptiv (an den Sprecher anpassungsfähig)
F qui s'adapte au locuteur
S de adaptación al locutor
I con adattamento al locutore

3101 *E* speaker-bound (*system*) (RECOGNITION)
G sprechergekoppelt (an den Sprecher gebunden)
F lié au locuteur
S acoplado al locutor
I legato al locutore

3102 *E* speaker dependence (RECOGNITION)
G Sprecherabhängigkeit (f)
F dépendance du locuteur (f)
S dependencia del locutor (f)
I dipendenza dal locutore (f)

3103 *E* speaker-dependent (RECOGNITION)
≠ speaker-independent
G sprecherabhängig
F dépendant du locuteur
S dependiente del locutor
I dipendente dal locutore

3104 *E* speaker-independent (RECOGNITION)
≠ speaker-dependent
G sprecherunabhängig
F indépendant du locuteur
S independiente del locutor
I indipendente dal locutore

3105 *E* speaker-independent recognition system
≠ speaker-trained recognition system
G sprecherunabhängiges Erkennungssystem (n)
F système de reconnaissance indépendant du locuteur (m); système multilocuteurs (m)
S sistema de reconocimiento independiente del locutor (m)
I sistema di riconoscimento indipendente dal locutore (m)

3106 *E* speaker-trained recognition system
= user-tuned recognition system
≠ speaker-independent recognition system
G sprechergeschultes Erkennungssystem (n)
F système de reconnaissance adapté au locuteur (m); système monolocuteur spécialisé (m)
S sistema de reconocimiento adaptado al locutor (m)
I sistema di riconoscimento adattato al locutore (m)

3107 *E* speaking style (RECOGNITION)
G Sprechweise (f)
F élocution (f); mode d'élocution (m)
S modo de hablar (m)
I modo di parlare (m)

3108 *E* specification language (PROGRAMMING)
G Spezifikationssprache (f)
F langage de spécification (m)
S lenguaje de especificación (m)
I linguaggio di specificazione (m)

3109 *E* specific domain (EXPERT SYSTEMS)
G spezifische Domäne (f)
F domaine spécifique (m)
S dominio específico (m)
I dominio specifico (m); settore specifico (m)

3110 *E* specific problem solver (EXPERT SYSTEMS)
G spezieller Problemlöser (m)
F résolveur de problèmes spécifiques (m)
S solucionador de problemas específicos (m)
I risolutore di problemi specifici (m)

3111 *E* spectrogram (*of voice*) (RECOGNITION)
G Spektrogramm (n)
F spectrogramme (m)
S espectrograma (m)
I spettrogramma (m)

3112 *E* speech (*continuous speech*) (RECOGNITION)
G Sprache (zusammenhängende Wörter oder Sätze) (f); Sprechsprache (f)
F parole (f)
S habla (f); lenguaje hablado (m)
I parlato (m)

3113 *E* speech act (RECOGNITION)
G sprachlicher Akt (m); Akt des Sprechens (m); Sprechakt (m)
F acte de parler (m); acte de parole (m)
S acto de hablar (m); acto verbal (m)
I atto di parlare (m)

3114 *E* speech activity (RECOGNITION)
= utterance

G sprachliche Aktivität (f)
F émission de parole (f)
S actividad de hablar (f)
I attività parlante (f)

3115 *E* speech analysis (RECOGNITION)
G Sprachanalyse (Analyse gesprochener Sprache) (f)
F analyse de la parole (f)
S análisis del habla (m)
I analisi del parlato (f)

3116 *E* speech generation (SYNTHESIS)
G Spracherzeugung (f)
F génération de la parole (f)
S generación de habla (f); generación de lenguaje hablado (f)
I generazione di linguaggio parlato (f); generazione del parlato (f)

3117 *E* speech output
→ voice output

3118 *E* speech pattern recognition
G Sprechmustererkennung (f)
F reconnaissance de formes sonores (p.e. des paroles) (f)
S reconocimiento de formas de habla (m)
I riconoscimento delle forme del parlato (m)

3119 *E* speech processing (RECOGNITION)
G Sprechdatenverarbeitung (f)
F traitement de la parole (m)
S procesamiento del habla (m)
I processamento del parlato (m)

3120 *E* speech-processing chip (SPC) (RECOGNITION)
↔ voice chip
G Sprachchip (m)
F puce de traitement de la parole (f)
S chip de habla (m)
I chip per l'elaborazione del parlato (m)

3121 *E* speech recognition (SR) (*without understanding the contents*)
= voice recognition
↔ word recognition
G Spracherkennung (f); Spracherkennen (n); Erkennen gesprochener Sprache (n)
F reconnaissance de la parole (f); reconnaissance vocale (f)
S reconocimiento de habla (m); reconocimiento del habla (m); reconocimiento de voz (m)
I riconoscimento della parola (m); riconoscimento della voce (m)

3122 *E* speech-recognition system
= voice-recognition system; continuous-speech recognizer
↔ word-recognition system
G Spracherkennungssystem (n)
F système de reconnaissance de la parole (m); système de reconnaissance vocale (m)
S sistema de reconocimiento del lenguaje hablado (m); sistema de reconocimiento de voz (m)
I sistema di riconoscimento della parola (o della voce) (m); sistema per il riconoscimento di parole o frasi (m)

3123 *E* speech signal
→ voice signal

3124 *E* speech synthesis
G Sprachsynthese (f)
F synthèse de la parole (f)
S síntesis de(l) habla (f)
I sintesi della parola (f)

3125 *E* speech understanding (SU) (*recognition and contents understanding*) (RECOGNITION)
G Sprachverstehen (gesprochene Sprache) (n)
F compréhension de la parole (CP) (f)

S comprensión del habla (f); entendimiento del habla (m)
I comprensione della parola (f); comprensione del linguaggio parlato (f)

3126 *E* speech understanding program (RECOGNITION)
G sprachverstehendes Programm (gesprochene Sprache) (n)
F programme de compréhension de la parole (m)
S programa de comprensión del habla (m)
I programma di comprensione della parola (m)

3127 *E* speech understanding research (SUR) (RECOGNITION)
G Sprachverstehensforschung (f)
F recherche de la compréhension de la parole (f)
S investigación de comprensión del habla (f)
I ricerca di comprensione della parola (f)

3128 *E* speech understanding system (SUS) (RECOGNITION)
G Sprachverstehsystem (gesprochene Sprache) (n); sprachverstehendes System (n)
F système de compréhension de la parole (m)
S sistema de comprensión del habla (m)
I sistema in grado di capire il linguaggio parlato (m)

3129 *E* speech wave analysis (RECOGNITION)
G Sprachsignalanalyse (f)
F analyse acoustique de la parole (f)
S análisis de las ondas sonoras (del habla) (m)
I analisi delle onde sonore (del parlato) (f)

3130 *E* spelling corrector (NLP)
G Orthografiekorrekturprogramm (n)
F correcteur d'orthographe (m)
S comprobador ortográfico (m)
I correttore ortografico (m)

3131 *E* split (*a problem into sub-problems*) (EXPERT SYSTEMS)
G zerlegen
F décomposer
S dividir
I dividere

3132 *E* spoken command
→ voice command

3133 *E* spoken dialogue (RECOGNITION)
G gesprochener Dialog (m)
F dialogue oral (m); dialogue vocal (m)
S diálogo hablado (m)
I dialogo parlato (m)

3134 *E* SR
→ speech recognition

3135 *E* S–R
→ stimulus–response

3136 *E* SRL
= schema representation language
→ semantic representation language

3137 *E* standalone expert system
G autonomes Expertensystem (n)
F système expert autonome (m)
S sistema experto autónomo (m)
I sistema esperto autonomo (m)

3138 *E* standard language (*for queries etc.*) (NLP)
G Standardsprache (f); Orthosprache (f)
F langage normalisé (m)
S lenguaje estándar (m)
I linguaggio standard (m)

3139 *E* standard logic
→ classical logic

3140 *E* starting clause (LOGIC)
= top clause
G Startklausel (f)
F clause de départ (f)
S cláusula de partida (f)
I clausola di partenza (f)

3141 *E* starting hypothesis (LOGIC)
= initial hypothesis
G Ausgangshypothese (f)
F hypothèse d'origine (f)
S hipótesis de partida (f)
I ipotesi di partenza (f)

3142 *E* starting node (LOGIC)
= start node; initial node; initial state node
G Startknoten (m); Anfangsknoten (m)
F nœud d'origine (m); nœud initial (m)
S nodo de partida (m); nodo inicial (m)
I nodo di partenza (m); nodo iniziale (m)

3143 *E* starting point (LOGIC)
G Ausgangspunkt (m)
F point de départ (m)
S punto de partida (m)
I punto di partenza (m)

3144 *E* start node
→ starting node

3145 *E* state change (LOGIC)
G Zustandswechsel (m)
F changement d'état (m)
S cambio de estado (m)
I cambiamento di stato (m)

3146 *E* state description (EXPERT SYSTEMS)
G Zustandsbeschreibung (f)
F description de l'état (f)
S descripción de estado (f)
I descrizione dello stato (f)

3147 *E* state descriptor (LOGIC)
G Zustandsdeskriptor (m)
F descripteur de l'état (m)
S descriptor de estado (m)
I descrittore di stato (m)

3148 *E* state graph (LOGIC)
G Zustandsgraph (m)
F graphe des états (m); graphe d'états (m)
S grafo de estados (m)
I grafo degli stati (m); diagramma di stato (m); grafo per la rappresentazione di stati (m)

3149 *E* state graph expansion
→ state tree expansion

3150 *E* state graph search (EXPERT SYSTEMS)
G Suche mittels Zustandsgraphen (f)
F recherche par graphe d'états (f)
S búsqueda mediante grafos de estado (f)
I ricerca mediante grafo degli stati (f)

3151 *E* state logic
= logic of states
G Zustandslogik (f)
F logique des états (f)
S lógica de los estados (f)
I logica degli stati (f)

3152 *E* statement (LOGIC)
G Aussage (f)
F proposition (f); énoncé (m)
S proposición (f)
I proposizione (f)

3153 *E* state problem (EXPERT SYSTEMS
G Zustandsproblem (n)
F problème d'état (m)
S problema de estado (m)

I problema riguardante lo stato (m)

3154 *E* state space (EXPERT SYSTEMS)
G Zustandsraum (m)
F espace des états (m); espace d'états (m)
S espacio de estados (m)
I spazio degli stati (m)

3155 *E* state space representation (EXPERT SYSTEMS)
G Zustandsraumrepräsentation (f)
F représentation de l'espace des états (f)
S representación de espacio de estados (f)
I rappresentazione dello spazio degli stati (f)

3156 *E* state transition (EXPERT SYSTEMS)
G Zustandsübergang (m); Zustandsüberführung (f)
F transition d'états (f)
S transición entre estados (f)
I transizione fra stati (f); cambiamento di stato (m)

3157 *E* state tree (LOGIC)
G Zustandsbaum (m)
F arbre des états (m)
S árbol de estados (m)
I albero degli stati (m)

3158 *E* state tree expansion (LOGIC)
= state graph expansion
G Expansion eines Zustandsgraphen (f)
F expansion de l'arbre des états (f)
S expansión de un árbol de estados (f)
I espansione di un grafo degli stati (f)

3159 *E* state variable (LOGIC)
G Zustandsvariable (f)
F variable d'état (f)
S variable de estado (f)
I variabile di stato (f)

3160 *E* static knowledge
G statisches Wissen (n)
F connaissance statique (f)
S conocimiento estático (m)
I conoscenza statica (f)

3161 *E* static object (KNOWLEDGE)
G statisches Objekt (n)
F objet statique (m)
S objeto estático (m)
I oggetto statico (m)

3162 *E* static set (MATHS)
G statische Menge (f)
F ensemble statique (m)
S conjunto estático (m)
I insieme statico (m)

3163 *E* stem (*of a word*) (LINGUISTICS)
G Stamm (m)
F racine (f)
S raíz (f)
I radice (f)

3164 *E* stereotyped events chain
→ stereotypical events chain

3165 *E* stereotyped knowledge
G stereotypes Wissen (n)
F connaissances stéréotypées (f pl)
S conocimiento estereotípico (m)
I conoscenza stereotipata (f)

3166 *E* stereotyped situation
→ stereotypical situation

3167 *E* stereotypical event (KNOWLEDGE)
G stereotypes Ereignis (n); immer wiederkehrendes Ereignis (n)
F événement stéréotypé (m); événement standard (m)
S acontecimiento estereotipado (m)
I avvenimento stereotipico (m)

3168 *E* stereotypical events chain (KNOWLEDGE)
= stereotyped events chain
G Kette stereotyper Ereignisse (f)

F suite standard d'événements (f)
S secuencia de acontecimientos estereotípicos (f)
I sequenza di eventi stereotipi (f)

3169 *E* stereotypical events chaining (KNOWLEDGE)
G Verkettung stereotyper Ereignisse (f)
F enchaînement d'événements stéréotypés (m)
S encadenamiento de acontecimientos estereotípicos (m)
I concatenamento di avvenimenti stereotipati (m)

3170 *E* stereotypical script (KNOWLEDGE)
G stereotypes Script (n)
F script stéréotypé (m)
S script estereotípico (m)
I script stereotipo (m)

3171 *E* stereotypical situation (KNOWLEDGE)
= stereotyped situation
G stereotype Situation (f); Klischeesituation (f)
F situation stéréotypée (f)
S situación estereotípica (f); situación estereotipada (f)
I situazione stereotipica (f)

3172 *E* stimulus frame (RECOGNITION)
G Reizframe (m)
F frame de stimulation (m)
S trama estímulo (f)
I frame di stimolo (m); quadro di stimolo (m)

3173 *E* stimulus–response (S–R) (NEURAL NETS)
G Stimulation–Reaktion (f)
F stimulation–réaction (f)
S éstimulo–reacción (f)
I stimolo–reazione (f)

3174 *E* STM
→ short-term memory

3175 *E* stochastic (*function, model, etc.*) (MATHS)
G stochastisch
F stochastique
S estocástico
I stocastico

3176 *E* story
G Geschichte (f); Erzählung (f); Story (f)
F histoire (f)
S historia (f); narración (f); relato (corto) (m)
I storia (f)

3177 *E* story analysis (RECOGNITION)
↔ story understanding
G Geschichtenanalyse (f)
F analyse d'histoires (f)
S análisis de historias (m)
I analisi di storie (f)

3178 *E* story understanding (RECOGNITION)
↔ story analysis
G Geschichtenverstehen (n)
F compréhension d'histoires (f)
S comprensión de narraciones (f)
I comprensione di storie (f)

3179 *E* stratagem (LOGIC)
G Strategem (n)
F stratagème (m)
S estratagema (m)
I strategemma (m)

3180 *E* strategic expert system
= control strategy system
G strategisches Expertensystem (n); Kontrollstrategiesystem (n)
F système expert en stratégie (m)
S sistema experto estratégico (m)
I sistema esperto strategico (m)

3181 *E* strategic knowledge
G strategisches Wissen (n)
F connaissance stratégique (f)
S conocimiento estratégico (m)
I conoscenza strategica (f)

3182 *E* strategic planning (EXPERT SYSTEMS)
G strategische Planung (f)
F planification stratégique (f)
S planificación estratégica (f)
I pianificazione strategica (f)

3183 *E* strategy
G Strategie (f)
F stratégie (f)
S estrategia (f)
I strategia (f)

3184 *E* strategy rule (EXPERT SYSTEMS)
G Strategieregel (f)
F règle stratégique (f); règle de stratégie (f)
S regla estratégica (f)
I regola strategica (f)

3185 *E* strategy space (EXPERT SYSTEMS)
G Strategienraum (m)
F espace stratégique (m); espace des stratégies (m)
S espacio estratégico (m)
I spazio strategico (m)

3186 *E* string of phonemes (RECOGNITION)
G Phonemkette (f)
F suite de phonèmes (f)
S cadena de fonemas (f)
I stringa di fonemi (f)

3187 *E* structural analysis (NLP)
G Strukturanalyse (f)
F analyse structurale (f)
S análisis estructural (m)
I analisi strutturale (f)

3188 *E* structural description (NLP)
G Strukturbeschreibung (f)
F description structurelle (f)
S descripción estructural (f)
I descrizione strutturale (f)

3189 *E* structural model (IMAGE PROCESSING)
= structural template
G Strukturmodell (n)
F modèle structural (m)
S modelo estructural (m)
I modello strutturale (m)

3190 *E* structural template
→ structural model

3191 *E* SU
→ speech understanding

3192 *E* subclass (KNOWLEDGE)
G Unterklasse (f)
F sous-classe (f)
S subclase (f)
I sottoclasse (f)

3193 *E* subconcept
→ child concept

3194 *E* subfield (KNOWLEDGE)
G Unterfeld (n); Teilfeld (n)
F sous-champ (m)
S subcampo (m)
I sottocampo (m)

3195 *E* subgoal (EXPERT SYSTEMS)
G Subziel (n); Teilziel (n); Unterziel (n)
F sous-but (m)
S subobjetivo (m); submeta (f)
I sotto-goal (m); sottobiettivo (m)

3196 *E* subgoal-driven search
→ subgoal search

3197 *E* subgoal generation (EXPERT SYSTEMS)
G Generierung von Subzielen (f)
F génération de sous-buts (f)
S generación de subobjetivos (f)

I generazione di sotto-goal (f)

3198 *E* subgoal search (EXPERT SYSTEMS)
= subgoal-driven search
G Suche nach Subzielen (f)
F recherche par sous-buts (f)
S búsqueda de subobjetivos (f)
I ricerca di sotto-goal (f)

3199 *E* subgraph (LOGIC)
G Untergraph (m); Teilgraph (m)
F sous-graphe (m)
S subgrafo (m)
I sottografo (m)

3200 *E* sublanguage (NLP)
G Fachsprache (f)
F sous-langage (m)
S sublenguaje (m)
I sottolinguaggio (m)

3201 *E* sublevel
G Unterebene (f)
F sous-niveau (m)
S subnivel (m)
I sottolivello (m)

3202 *E* sublink (KNOWLEDGE)
G Teilverknüpfung (f)
F lien partiel (m)
S sub-enlace (m)
I connessione parziale (f)

3203 *E* subnet (KNOWLEDGE)
G Teilnetz (n); Subnetz (n)
F sous-réseau (m)
S sub-red (f)
I sotto-rete (f)

3204 *E* suboptimal solution (EXPERT SYSTEMS)
G suboptimale Lösung (f)
F solution sous-optimale (f)
S solución sub-optimal (f)
I soluzione sub-ottimale (f)

3205 *E* subpattern (IMAGE PROCESSING)
G Teilmuster (n)
F sous-schéma (m)
S sub-pattern (m)
I sotto-pattern (m)

3206 *E* subplan
G Teilplan (m)
F sous-plan (m)
S sub-plano (m)
I parte di un piano (f)

3207 *E* subproblem (EXPERT SYSTEMS)
G Unterproblem (n); Teilproblem (n)
F sous-problème (m)
S subproblema (m)
I sottoproblema (m)

3208 *E* subproblem graph (EXPERT SYSTEMS)
G Teilproblemgraph (m)
F graphe de sous-problèmes (m)
S grafo de subproblemas (m)
I grafo dei sottoproblemi (m)

3209 *E* subset (MATHS)
G Untermenge (f)
F sous-ensemble (m)
S subconjunto (m)
I sotto-insieme (m)

3210 *E* subslot (KNOWLEDGE)
G Sub-Slot (m)
F sous-tiroir (m)
S subslot (m)
I sotto-slot (m)

3211 *E* subspace (EXPERT SYSTEMS)
G Teilraum (m)
F sous-espace (m)
S subespacio (m)
I sotto-spazio (m)

3212 *E* substitution
G Substitution (f); Ersetzen (n)
F substitution (f)
S sustitución (f)
I sostituzione (f)

3213 *E* substitutionary error rate (RECOGNITION)
G Anteil der Substitutionsfehler (m); Substitutionsfehlerrate (f)
F taux des erreurs de substitution (m)
S proporción de errores de substitución (f)
I tasso degli errori di sostituzione (m)

3214 *E* substring (PROGRAMMING)
G Substring (m); Teilstring (m)
F sous-chaîne (f)
S sub-stringa (f); subsecuencia (f)
I sottostringa (f)

3215 *E* subsumption (LOGIC)
= assumption
G Subsumierung (f); Subsumption (f); Annahme (f)
F supposition (f)
S suposición (f)
I assunzione (f)

3216 *E* subsystem
G Untersystem (n); Subsystem (n)
F sous-système (m)
S subsistema (m)
I sotto-sistema (m)

3217 *E* subtask
G Teilaufgabe (f)
F sous-tâche (f)
S subtarea (f)
I sotto-compito (m)

3218 *E* subterm (NLP)
G Unterterm (m)
F sous-terme (m)
S subtérmino (m)
I sottotermine (m)

3219 *E* subtree (EXPERT SYSTEMS)
G Unterbaum (m); Teilbaum (m)
F sous-arbre (m)
S subárbol (m)
I sotto-albero (m)

3220 *E* successor
→ descendant

3221 *E* successor node
→ descendant node

3222 *E* suffice (*verb*)
→ fulfil

3223 *E* sufficiency (LOGIC)
G Suffizienz (f); Hinlänglichkeit (f)
F suffisance (f)
S suficiencia (f)
I sufficienza (f)

3224 *E* sufficient condition (LOGIC)
G hinreichende Bedingung (f)
F condition suffisante (f)
S condición suficiente (f)
I condizione sufficiente (f)

3225 *E* superlogical quantifier
→ high-level quantifier

3226 *E* supervised learning
= learning with a teacher
≠ unsupervised learning
G überwachtes Lernen (n)
F apprentissage supervisé (m)
S aprendizaje controlado (m)
I apprendimento sorvegliato (m)

3227 *E* support hypothesis (LOGIC)
G stützende Hypothese (f); Stützhypothese (f)
F hypothèse de support (f)
S hipótesis de apoyo (f)
I ipotesi di supporto (f)

3228 *E* support set (LOGIC)
= set of support
G Stützmenge (f); Unterstützungsmenge (f)
F ensemble support (m)
S conjunto de apoio (m)
I insieme di appoggio (m)

3229 *E* SUR
→ speech understanding research

3230 *E* surface contour (IMAGE PROCESSING)
G Oberflächenkontur (f)
F contour de la surface (m)
S contorno de superfície (m)
I contorno della superficie (m)

3231 *E* surface knowledge
= shallow knowledge
≠ deep knowledge
G oberflächliches Wissen (n); Oberflächenwissen (n)
F connaissances de surface (f pl); connaissances peu profondes (f pl)
S conocimiento superficial (m)
I conoscenza di superficie (f)

3232 *E* surface structure (IMAGE PROCESSING)
G Oberflächenstruktur (f)
F structure de la surface (f)
S estructura de superficie (f)
I struttura della superficie (f)

3233 *E* surveillance system (EXPERT SYSTEMS)
G Überwachungssystem (n)
F système de surveillance (m); système de supervision (m)
S sistema de monitorización (m)
I sistema di sorvegliamento (m)

3234 *E* SUS
→ speech understanding system

3235 *E* syllogism (*an inference rule*) (LOGIC)
G Syllogismus (m)
F syllogisme (m)
S silogismo (m)
I sillogismo (m)

3236 *E* syllogistic (LOGIC)
G syllogistisch
F syllogistique
S silogístico
I sillogistico

3237 *E* symbolic expression (s-expr) (PROGRAMMING)
= S-expression
G symbolischer Ausdruck (m); S-Ausdruck (m)
F expression symbolique (f)
S expresión simbólica (f)
I espressione simbolica (f)

3238 *E* symbolic inference (LOGIC)
= symbolic reasoning
G symbolisches Schließen (n); symbolische Inferenz (f)
F inférence symbolique (f); raisonnement symbolique (m)
S inferencia simbólica (f)
I inferenza simbolica (f)

3239 *E* symbolic integration (PROGRAMMING)
G symbolische Integration (f)
F intégration symbolique (f)
S integración simbólica (f)
I integrazione simbolica (f)

3240 *E* symbolic knowledge
G symbolisches Wissen (n)
F connaissance symbolique (f)
S conocimiento simbólico (f)
I conoscenza simbolica (f)

3241 *E* symbolic language (PROGRAMMING)
G symbolische Sprache (f)
F langage symbolique (m)
S lenguaje simbólico (m)
I linguaggio simbolico (m)

3242 *E* symbolic learning
G symbolisches Lernen (n)
F apprentissage symbolique (m)
S aprendizaje simbólico (m)
I apprendimento simbolico (m)

3243 *E* symbolic logic
G symbolische Logik (f)
F logique symbolique (f)
S lógica simbólica (f)
I logica simbolica (f)

3244 *E* symbolic problem solving (EXPERT SYSTEMS)
G symbolische Problemlösung (f)
F résolution symbolique de problèmes (f)
S resolución simbólica de problemas (f)
I soluzione simbolica di problemi (f)

3245 *E* symbolic reasoning
→ symbolic inference

3246 *E* symbolic reference (PROGRAMMING)
G symbolischer Bezug (m)
F référence symbolique (f)
S referencia simbólica (f)
I riferimento simbolico (m)

3247 *E* symbolic representation (KNOWLEDGE)
G symbolische Darstellung (f)
F représentation symbolique (f)
S representación simbólica (f)
I rappresentazione simbolica (f)

3248 *E* symbolic structure (PROGRAMMING)
G symbolische Struktur (f)
F structure symbolique (f)
S estructura simbólica (f)
I struttura simbolica (f)

3249 *E* symbol-oriented language (PROGRAMMING)
G symbolorientierte Sprache (f)
F langage (de programmation) orienté symboles (m)
S lenguaje (de programación) orientado a símbolos (m)
I linguaggio (di programmazione) orientato ai simboli (m)

3250 *E* synapse (*connection between two neurons*)
= neuronal interconnection
G Synapse (f)
F synapse (f)
S sinapsis (f)
I sinapsi (f)

3251 *E* synaptic weight (NEURAL NETS)
G synaptisches Gewicht (n); Verbindungsgewicht (n)
F poids synaptique (m)
S peso sináptico (m)
I peso sinaptico (m)

3252 *E* syntactic, -al (NLP)
G syntaktisch
F syntaxique
S sintáctico
I sintattico

3253 *E* syntactic analysis (LINGUISTICS)
G Syntaxanalyse (f)
F analyse syntaxique (f)
S análisis sintáctico (m)
I analisi sintattica (f)

3254 *E* syntactic category (NLP)
G syntaktische Kategorie (f)
F catégorie syntaxique (f)
S categoria sintáctica (f)
I categoria sintattica (f)

3255 *E* syntactic parser (NLP)
= syntax parser
G Syntaxparser (m)
F analyseur syntaxique (m)
S analizador sintáctico (m)
I parser sintattico (m)

3256 *E* syntactic parsing (NLP)
= syntax parsing; syntax-based parsing
G Syntaxparsing (n)
F analyse syntaxique (f)

S análisis sintáctico (m)
I parsing sintattico (m); analisi sintattica (f)

3257 *E* syntactic pattern recognition (NLP)
G Syntaxmustererkennung (f)
F reconnaissance de formes syntaxiques (f)
S reconocimiento de formas sintácticas (RFS) (m)
I riconoscimento di pattern sintattici (m)

3258 *E* syntactic property (LINGUISTICS)
G syntaktische Eigenschaft (f)
F propriété syntaxique (f)
S propiedad sintáctica (f)
I proprietà sintattica (f)

3259 *E* syntactic tree (NLP)
= syntax tree
G Syntaxbaum (m)
F arbre syntaxique (m)
S árbol sintáctico (m)
I albero sintattico (m)

3260 *E* syntax (LINGUISTICS)
G Syntax (f)
F syntaxe (f)
S sintaxis (f)
I sintassi (f)

3261 *E* syntax-based parsing
→ syntactic parsing

3262 *E* syntax check (NLP)
G Syntaxprüfung (f)
F contrôle de syntaxe (m)
S verificación sintáctica (f)
I controllo sintattico (m)

3263 *E* syntax-directed parsing (NLP)
G syntaxorientiertes Parsing (n)
F analyse orientée syntaxe (f)
S parsing orientado en el sintaxis (m)
I parsing orientato alla sintassi (m); analisi orientata all sintassi (f)

3264 *E* syntax-driven editor (NLP)
G syntaxgesteuerter Editor (m)
F éditeur dirigé par syntaxe (m)
S editor dirigido por la sintaxis (EDS) (m)
I editore guidato dalla sintassi (m)

3265 *E* syntax-driven system (RECOGNITION)
G syntaxgesteuertes System (n)
F système guidé par la syntaxe (m)
S sistema dirigido por la sintaxis (m)
I sistema guidato dalla sintassi (m)

3266 *E* syntax parser
→ syntactic parser

3267 *E* syntax parsing
→ syntactic parsing

3268 *E* syntax tree
→ syntactic tree

3269 *E* synthesis by rule
→ rule-based synthesis

3270 *E* synthesized (*speech etc.*)
G synthetisch
F synthétisé
S sintetizado
I sintetizzato

3271 *E* synthetic speech
= artificial speech
G synthetische Sprache (f); künstlich erzeugte Sprache (f)
F parole synthétique (f); parole artificielle (f)
S habla sintética (f)
I parlato sintetico (m)

3272 *E* systemization (*of knowledge etc.*)
G Systematisierung (f)

F systématisation (f)
S sistematización (f)
I sistematizzazione (f)

3273 *E* system of rules (EXPERT SYSTEMS)
= rule system
G Regelsystem (System von Regeln) (n)
F système de règles (m)
S sistema de reglas (m)
I sistema di regole (m)

3274 *E* system shell
→ expert system shell

T

3275 *E* t
→ tree

3276 *E* tacit knowledge
→ implicit knowledge

3277 *E* tactical decision making (EXPERT SYSTEMS)
G taktische Entscheidungsfindung (f)
F prise tactique de décisions (f)
S toma táctica de decisiones (f)
I presa tattica di decisioni (f)

3278 *E* tactile perception (IMAGE PROCESSING)
= tactile sensing
G Wahrnehmung durch Berührung (f)
F perception tactile (f)
S percepción táctil (f)
I percezione tattile (f)

3279 *E* tactile sensing
→ tactile perception

3280 *E* tactile sensor
= touch sensor
G taktiler Sensor (m); Berührungssensor (m)
F capteur tactile (m)
S sensor táctil (m)
I sensore di tatto (m)

3281 *E* tactile systems
= touch systems
G berührungssensitive Systeme (n pl)
F systèmes tactiles (m pl)
S sistemas táctiles (m pl)
I sistemi sensibili al tatto (m pl)

3282 *E* tag[1] (*attribute added to an information*) (KNOWLEDGE)
G Etikett (n); Tag (m); Attribut (n)
F tag (m); marque (f); étiquette (f)
S tag (m); marca (f)
I etichetta (f); tag (m)

3283 *E* tag[2] (*objects; verb*) (KNOWLEDGE)
G attribuieren; typisieren
F étiqueter; diviser en types
S marcar
I marcare

3284 *E* tagged architecture (KNOWLEDGE)
G Tag-Architektur (f)
F architecture typée (f)
S arquitectura de marcas (f); arquitectura marcada (f)
I architettura tipo tagged (f); architettura etichettata (f)

3285 *E* tagged data (KNOWLEDGE)
= self-identifying data
G attribuierte Daten (n pl); typisierte Daten (n pl)
F données étiquetées (f pl)
S datos marcados (m pl)
I dati tipo tagged (m pl); dati etichettati (m pl)

3286 *E* tagged graph (KNOWLEDGE)
G mit Attributen versehener Graph (m)
F graphe attribué (m); graphe typifié (m)
S grafo con atributos (m); grafo etiquetado (m)
I grafo con attributi (m)

3287 *E* tagged memory (KNOWLEDGE)

G Speicher mit Tags (m); Tag-Speicher (m); attribuierter Speicher (m)
F mémoire typée (f)
S memoria de marcas (f)
I memoria tipo tagged (f); memoria etichettata (f)

3288 *E* tagged variable (PROGRAMMING)
G typisierte Variable (f)
F variable typée (f)
S variable marcada (f)
I variabile etichettata (f)

3289 *E* tagging (*noun*) (KNOWLEDGE)
G Markierung mit typisierender Information (f); Attribuierung (f)
F étiquetage (m)
S etiquetaje (m); etiquetado (m); marcaje (m)
I etichettamento (m)

3290 *E* talking software (SYNTHESIS)
G sprechende Software (f)
F logiciel sonore (m); logiciel à synthétiseur vocal (m)
S software hablante (m)
I software parlante (m)

3291 *E* target
→ goal

3292 *E* target clause (LOGIC)
G Zielklausel (f)
F clause cible (f)
S cláusula objetivo (f)
I clausola oggetto (f)

3293 *E* target-driven
→ goal-driven

3294 *E* target language (MT)
G Zielsprache (f)
F langage cible (m)
S lenguaje objeto (m)
I linguaggio di arrivo (m)

3295 *E* target node (LOGIC)
G Zielknoten (m)
F nœud de destination (m)
S nodo de llegada (m)
I nodo di arrivo (m)

3296 *E* target rule (EXPERT SYSTEMS)
G Zielregel (f)
F règle cible (f)
S regla objeto (f)
I regola di arrivo (f)

3297 *E* task
G Aufgabe (f)
F tâche (f)
S tarea (f)
I compito (m); azione (f)

3298 *E* task analysis (EXPERT SYSTEMS)
G Aufgabenanalyse (f)
F analyse des tâches (f)
S análisis de tareas (m)
I analisi delle azioni (f)

3299 *E* task decomposition (EXPERT SYSTEMS)
G Zerlegung der Aufgabe (f); Aufgabenzerlegung (f)
F décomposition de la tâche (f)
S descomposición de tarea (f)
I scomposizione del compito (f)

3300 *E* task domain (EXPERT SYSTEMS)
G Aufgabendomäne (f)
F domaine de la tâche (m)
S dominio de tarea (m)
I dominio dell'azione (m)

3301 *E* task knowledge (EXPERT SYSTEMS)
G aufgabenbezogenes Wissen (n)
F connaissance sur la tâche (f)
S conocimiento sobre la tarea (m)
I conoscenza sul compito specifico (f)

3302 *E* task-level language
→ task-oriented language

3303 *E* task-oriented (EXPERT SYSTEMS)
= task-specific
G aufgabenspezifisch; aufgabenorientiert
F orienté tâches
S orientado a las tareas
I orientato ai compiti

3304 *E* task-oriented language (PROGRAMMING)
= task-level language
G aufgabenorientierte Sprache (f)
F langage de programmation à tâches (m)
S lenguaje orientado a la(s) tarea(s) (m)
I linguaggio orientato al compito (m)

3305 *E* task planner (EXPERT SYSTEMS)
G Aufgabenplaner (m)
F planificateur de tâches (m); gestionnaire de tâches (m)
S planificador de tareas (m); sistema de planificación de tareas (m)
I pianificatore dei compiti (m); pianificatore delle azioni (m)

3306 *E* task planning (EXPERT SYSTEMS)
G Aufgabenplanung (f)
F planification de tâches (f)
S planificación de tareas (f)
I pianificazione dei compiti (f)

3307 *E* task scheduling (EXPERT SYSTEMS)
G Aufgabenverteilung (f)
F ordonnancement des tâches (OT) (m)
S planificación de tareas (f)
I smistamento dei compiti (m)

3308 *E* task space (EXPERT SYSTEMS)
G Aufgabenraum (m)
F espace de la tâche (m)
S espacio de tareas (m)
I spazio compiti (m)

3309 *E* task-specific
→ task-oriented

3310 *E* taxonomic (KNOWLEDGE)
G taxonomisch
F taxonomique
S taxonómico
I tassonomico

3311 *E* taxonomic knowledge (*of relations between facts and rules*)
G Taxonomiewissen (n)
F connaissance taxonomique (f)
S conocimiento taxonómico (m)
I conoscenza taxonomica (f)

3312 *E* taxonomic system (LOGIC)
≠ declarative system
G taxonomisches System (n)
F système taxonomique (m)
S sistema taxonómico (m)
I sistema taxonomico (m)

3313 *E* taxonomy (*hierarchical structure of concepts*) (KNOWLEDGE)
G Taxonomie (f)
F taxonomie (f)
S taxonomía (f)
I tassonomia (f)

3314 *E* TD
→ top down

3315 *E* teaching aid (LEARNING)
G Lehrhilfe (f)
F aide à l'enseignement (f)
S ayuda a la enseñanza (f)
I aiuto all'insegnamento (m)

3316 *E* technical sublanguage (NLP)
G technische Fachsprache (f)
F sous-langage technique (m)
S lenguaje técnico (m)
I linguaggio tecnico (m)

3317 *E* technology transfer (KNOWLEDGE)

G Technologietransfer (m)
F transfert(s) de technologie (m (pl))
S transferencia tecnológica (f)
I trasferimento di tecnologia (m)

3318 E template (IMAGE PROCESSING)
G Schablone (f); Standardvorlage (f)
F modèle (m); gabarit (m)
S árbol de primitivas (m); plantilla (de referencia) (f)
I modello (m); template (m)

3319 E template matching (IMAGE PROCESSING)
= matched filtering
≠ feature analysis
G Schablonenvergleich (m)
F appariement modèle–objet (m)
S comparación de plantillas (f); adaptación de plantillas (f)
I confronto di templates (m)

3320 E temporal constraint (IMAGE PROCESSING)
= time constraint
G zeitliche Beschränkung (f)
F contrainte temporelle (f)
S restricción de tiempo (f); restricción temporal (f)
I restrizione temporale (f)

3321 E temporal knowledge (*knowledge about time factors*)
G zeitliches Wissen (n)
F connaissance temporelle (f)
S conocimiento temporal (m)
I conoscenza temporale (f)

3322 E temporal logic
= logic of time
G Zeitlogik (f); temporale Logik (f)
F logique temporelle (f)
S lógica temporal (f)
I logica temporale (f)

3323 E temporal model
G temporales Modell (n)
F modèle temporel (m)
S modelo temporal (m)
I modello temporale (m)

3324 E temporal reasoning (EXPERT SYSTEMS)
G Inferieren über eine längere Zeitspanne hinweg (n)
F raisonnement temporel (m)
S razonamiento temporal (m)
I ragionamento temporale (m)

3325 E temporal relation (LOGIC)
G Zeitrelation (f)
F relation temporelle (f)
S relación temporal (f)
I relazione temporale (f)

3326 E temporary knowledge
≠ permanent knowledge
G temporäres Wissen (n)
F connaissance temporaire (f)
S conocimiento temporáneo (m); conocimiento temporario (m); conocimiento temporal (m)
I conoscenza temporaria (f)

3327 E term (*a constant, a variable, an expression*) (LOGIC)
G Term (m)
F terme (m)
S término (m)
I termine (m)

3328 E terminal node (*of a tree*) (KNOWLEDGE)
= end node; leaf node; tip node
G Endknoten (m); Blatt (n); Blattknoten (m); Terminalknoten (m)
F nœud terminal (m); nœud final (m); nœud-feuille (m)
S nodo terminal (m); nodo final (m); hoja (f)
I nodo terminale (m); nodo finale (m)

3329 *E* termination condition (PROGRAMMING)
G Endebedingung (f); Abbruchbedingung (f)
F conditions d'aboutissement (f pl)
S condición de terminación (f)
I condizione di terminazione (f)

3330 *E* texel
→ texture element

3331 *E* text analysis (NLP)
G Textanalyse (f)
F analyse de texte(s) (f); analyse textuelle (f)
S análisis de texto (m)
I analisi di testi (f)

3332 *E* text comprehension
→ text understanding

3333 *E* text recognition (NLP)
G Texterkennung (f)
F reconnaissance de textes (f)
S reconocimiento de textos (m)
I riconoscimento di testi (m)

3334 *E* text-to-speech conversion (SYNTHESIS)
G Text-nach-Sprache-Umsetzung (f)
F conversion texte–parole (f)
S transcripción texto–voz (f)
I conversione testo–voce (f)

3335 *E* text-to-speech synthesis
= TTS synthesis
G Text–Sprache-Synthese (f); konstruktive Synthese (f)
F synthèse texte–parole (f)
S síntesis texto–voz (f)
I sintesi testo–voce (f)

3336 *E* text understanding (NLP)
= text comprehension
G Textverstehen (n); Textverständnis (n)
F compréhension de textes (f)
S comprensión de textos (f)
I comprensione di testi (f)

3337 *E* text understanding machine (NLP)
G textverstehende Maschine (f)
F machine capable de comprendre les textes (f); interprète textuel (m)
S máquina capaz de comprender textos (f)
I macchina in grado di comprendere il significato di un testo (f)

3338 *E* texture (*of an object or image*) (IMAGE PROCESSING)
G Textur (f)
F texture (f)
S textura (f)
I tessitura (f)

3339 *E* texture analysis (IMAGE PROCESSING)
G Texturanalyse (f)
F analyse de texture (f)
S análisis de textura (m)
I analisi di tessitura (f)

3340 *E* texture element (IMAGE PROCESSING)
= texel
G Texel (n); Texturelement (n)
F élément de texture (m); texel (m)
S elemento de textura (m); texel (m)
I elemento di tessitura (m); texel (m)

3341 *E* TG
→ transformational grammar

3342 *E* 'then' clause (LOGIC)
↔ 'if' clause
G Dann-Klausel (f)
F clause 'alors' (f)
S cláusula entonces (f)
I clausola allora (f)

3343 *E* 'then' part
→ conclusion part

3344 *E* theorem (*a provable statement*) (LOGIC)
G Theorem (n)
F théorème (m)
S teorema (m)
I teorema (m)

3345 *E* theorem prover (PROGRAMMING)
= theorem-proving program
G automatischer Beweiser (m); Resolutionsbeweiser (m); theorembeweisendes Programm (n)
F démonstrateur (automatique) de théorèmes (m); programme de démonstration de théorèmes (m)
S solucionador de teoremas (lógicos) (m); demostrador automático (m); programa de demostración de teoremas (m)
I programma per la dimostrazione (automatica) di teoremi (m); algoritmo per la dimostrazione di teoremi (m)

3346 *E* theorem proving (LOGIC)
G Beweisverfahren (n); Theorembeweis (m)
F preuve de théorèmes (f); démonstration de théorèmes (f)
S demostración de teoremas (f)
I dimostrazione di teoremi (f)

3347 *E* theorem-proving program
→ theorem prover

3348 *E* theorem set (LOGIC)
G Theoremkomplex (m)
F ensemble de théorèmes (m)
S conjunto de teoremas (m)
I insieme di teoremi (m)

3349 *E* theoretical logic
G theoretische Logik (f)
F logique théorique (f)
S lógica teórica (LT) (f)
I logica teorica (f)

3350 *E* theory-driven
G theoriegetrieben
F dirigé par théories
S guiado por teorías
I basato su teorie

3351 *E* theory forming (LOGIC)
G Bilden von Theorien (n)
F formation de théories (f)
S formación de teorías (f)
I formazione di teorie (f)

3352 *E* theory of concepts
G Begriffstheorie (f)
F théorie conceptuelle (f)
S teoría conceptual (f)
I teoria concettuale (f)

3353 *E* theory of evidence
→ evidence theory

3354 *E* theory of fuzzy sets
→ fuzzy sets theory

3355 *E* theory of sets
→ set theory

3356 *E* thinking by humans
→ human thinking

3357 *E* thought process
G Denkprozeß (m)
F processus de pensée (m)
S procedimiento de pensamiento (m)
I processo di pensamento (m)

3358 *E* threshold
= threshold value
G Schwelle (f); Schwellenwert (m)
F seuil (m)
S umbral (m); valor umbral (m)
I soglia (f); valore soglia (m)

3359 *E* threshold value
→ threshold

3360 *E* time constraint
→ temporal constraint

3361 *E* time-dependent analysis (RECOGNITION)
G zeitabhängige Analyse (f)
F analyse dépendante du temps (f)
S análisis dependiente del tiempo (m)
I analisi dipendente dal tempo (f)

3362 *E* time-invariant
G zeitinvariant
F invariant dans le temps
S invariado en el tiempo
I invariantivo nel tempo

3363 *E* tip node
→ terminal node

3364 *E* TM
→ Turing machine

3365 *E* TMS
→ truth maintenance system

3366 *E* top clause
→ starting clause

3367 *E* top down (TD)
≠ bottom up
G top-down (von oben nach unten)
F descendant
S arriba-abajo; descendiente
I dall'alto verso il basso

3368 *E* top-down chaining
→ backward chaining

3369 *E* top-down interpreter (PROGRAMMING)
≠ bottom-up interpreter
G Top-Down-Interpreter (m)
F interpréteur descendant (m)
S intérprete top-down (m)
I interprete top-down (m)

3370 *E* top-down parser (NLP)
≠ bottom-up parser
G Top-Down-Parser (m)
F analyseur descendant (m)
S parser descendiente (m)
I parser tipo top-down (m)

3371 *E* top-down programming
= hierarchical programming
≠ bottom-up programming
G Top-Down-Programmierung (f)
F programmation descendante (f)
S programación top-down (f); programación arriba-abajo (f)
I programmazione top-down (f)

3372 *E* top-down reasoning[1] (LOGIC)
G absteigendes Schließen (n)
F raisonnement descendant (m)
S razonamiento top-down (m)
I ragionamento top-down (m)

3373 *E* top-down reasoning[2]
→ backward reasoning

3374 *E* top-down strategy (EXPERT SYSTEMS)
≠ bottom-up strategy
G Top-Down-Strategie (f)
F stratégie descendante (f)
S estrategia top-down (f)
I strategia top-down (f)

3375 *E* top node
→ root node

3376 *E* touch sensor
→ tactile sensor

3377 *E* touch systems
→ tactile systems

3378 *E* toy world
→ blocks world

3379 *E* traditional logic
→ classical logic

3380 *E* train (*a neural net; verb*)
G trainieren
F entraîner
S entrenar
I addestrare

3381 *E* trainability (*of a neural net*)
G Trainierbarkeit (f)
F capacité d'entraînement (f)
S capacidad de entrenamiento (f)
I capacità di addestramento (f)

3382 *E* training (*of a neural net*)
G Trainieren (n)
F entraînement (m)
S ejercicio (m); entrenamiento (m)
I addestramento (m)

3383 *E* training mode
→ training phase

3384 *E* training phase (NEURAL NETS)
= training mode
G Trainingsphase (f); Lernphase (f)
F phase d'entraînement (f)
S fase de ejercicio (f)
I fase di addestramento (f)

3385 *E* training rule (NEURAL NETS)
G Trainingsregel (f)
F règle d'entraînement (f)
S regla de entrenamiento (f)
I regola training rule (f)

3386 *E* training set (EXPERT SYSTEMS)
G Trainingsmenge (f)
F ensemble d'entraînement (m)
S conjunto de ejemplos (para entrenamiento) (m)
I insieme di esempi (che viene immesso in un sistema) (m); esempi utilizzati nell'addestramento (m pl)

3387 *E* transfer function (NEURAL NETS)
G Transferfunktion (f); Übertragungsfunktion (f)
F fonction de transfert (f)
S función de transferencia (f)
I funzione di trasferimento (f)

3388 *E* transfer grammar (MT)
G Transfergrammatik (f)
F grammaire de transfert (f)
S gramática de transferencia (f)
I grammatica di trasferimento (f)

3389 *E* transformational grammar (TG) (NLP)
G Transformationsgrammatik (TG) (f)
F grammaire transformationnelle (f)
S gramática transformacional (f)
I grammatica trasformazionale (f)

3390 *E* transformational rule
→ transformation rule

3391 *E* transformation rule (LINGUISTICS)
= transformational rule
G Transformationsregel (f)
F règle de transformation (f)
S regla de transformación (f)
I regola di trasformazione (f)

3392 *E* transition (*between states etc.*)
G Übergang (m); Transition (f)
F transition (f)
S transición (f)
I transizione (f)

3393 *E* transition diagram (NLP)
G Transitionsdiagramm (n)
F diagramme de transition (m)
S diagrama de transición (m); grafo de transiciones (m)
I diagramma di transizione (m)

3394 *E* transition net
→ transition network

3395 *E* transition network (KNOWLEDGE)
= transition net

G Übergangsnetzwerk (n)
F réseau de transition (m)
S red de transición (f)
I rete di transizione (f)

3396 *E* translation by machine
→ machine translation

3397 *E* translator's workstation (MT)
G Übersetzerarbeitsplatz (m)
F poste de travail pour traducteur (m)
S estación de trabajo para traductores (f)
I stazione di lavoro per traduttori (f)

3398 *E* travelling salesman problem (LOGIC)
G Problem des Handlungsreisenden (n); Handlungsreisendenproblem (n)
F problème du voyageur de commerce (m)
S problema del viajante de comercio (m)
I problema del commesso viaggiatore (m)

3399 *E* tree (t) (LOGIC)
G Baum (m)
F arbre (graphe connexe sans cycle) (m); arborescence (arbre muni d'une racine) (f)
S árbol (m)
I albero (m)

3400 *E* tree breadth (LOGIC)
G Breite des Baums (f); Baumbreite (f)
F largeur d'arborescence (f)
S largura de árbol (f)
I larghezza dell'albero (f)

3401 *E* tree cutoff
→ tree pruning

3402 *E* tree depth (LOGIC)
G Tiefe des Baums (f); Baumtiefe (f)
F profondeur d'arbre (f); profondeur d'arborescence (f)
S profundidad del árbol (f)
I profondità di un albero (f)

3403 *E* tree diagram (LOGIC)
G Baumdiagramm (n)
F diagramme d'arbre (m)
S diagrama de árbol (m)
I diagramma ad albero (m)

3404 *E* tree pruning (EXPERT SYSTEMS)
= tree cutoff
G Baumbeschneidung (f); Abschneiden von Ästen (n)
F coupe d'arbre (f)
S poda de árbol(es) (f)
I potatura dell'albero (f)

3405 *E* tree representation (LOGIC)
G Baumdarstellung (f)
F arborisation (f)
S grafo de árbol (m)
I rappresentazione ad albero (f)

3406 *E* tree search (LOGIC)
G Suche mittels Baum (f); Baumsuche (f)
F exploration d'arbre (f); recherche arborescente (f)
S búsqueda mediante árbol (f)
I ricerca mediante albero (f)

3407 *E* tree structure (LOGIC)
G Baumstruktur (f)
F structure arborescente (f); arborescence (f)
S estructura de árbol (f); estructura arborescente (f); estructura arbórea (f)
I struttura ad albero (f)

3408 *E* tree traversal (EXPERT SYSTEMS)
= graph traversal

G Baumtraversierung (f); Durchqueren eines Suchbaums (n)
F traversée d'un graphe (f)
S travesía de un grafo (f)
I percorso di un grafo (m)

3409 *E* trial-and-error principle (PROGRAMMING)
G Versuch-und-Irrtum-Prinzip (n)
F régime par tentatives (m)
S procedimiento de ensayo y error (m)
I ricerca per tentativi (f)

3410 *E* trigger[1] (*noun*) (EXPERT SYSTEMS)
G Auslöser (m)
F déclencheur (m)
S disparo (m)
I trigger (m); puntatore (m)

3411 *E* trigger[2] (*a rule; verb*) (EXPERT SYSTEMS)
G anstoßen; aktivieren; triggern
F déclencher
S actuar
I attivare

3412 *E* trigger condition (EXPERT SYSTEMS)
G auslösende Bedingung (f); Trigger-Bedingung (f)
F condition de déclenchement (f)
S condición de disparo (f)
I condizione di sparo (f)

3413 *E* trigger event
→ trigger
G Triggerereignis (n)
F événement de déclenchement (m)
S acontecimiento de disparo (m)
I evento di sparo (m)

3414 *E* triggering (*noun*) (EXPERT SYSTEMS)
G Auslösen (n)
F déclenchement (m)
S disparo (m)
I sparo (m)

3415 *E* triple
→ triplet

3416 *E* triplet (LOGIC)
= triple
G Tripel (n) (z.B. Objekt-, Attribut-, Wert-Tripel)
F triplet (m)
S tripleta (f); terna (f)
I triplo (m); terna (f); tripla (f)

3417 *E* true (LOGIC)
≠ false
G wahr
F vrai
S verdadero
I vero

3418 *E* true expert system
G echtes Expertensystem (n)
F système expert pur (m)
S sistema experto verdadero (m)
I sistema esperto vero (m)

3419 *E* truth (LOGIC)
≠ falsity
G Wahrheit (f)
F vérité (f)
S verdad (f); veracidad (f)
I verità (f)

3420 *E* truth content (LOGIC)
G Wahrheitsgehalt (einer Aussage) (m)
F contenu de vérité (m)
S contenido de verdad (m)
I contenuto di verità (m)

3421 *E* truth maintenance (EXPERT SYSTEMS)
= truth preserving
G Wahrheitserhaltung (f)
F maintenance de la vérité (f); conservation de la cohérence (f)
S mantenimiento de la verdad (m)

I mantenimento della verità (m)

3422 *E* truth maintenance system (TMS) (EXPERT SYSTEMS)
= reason maintenance system (RMS)
G System zur Verwaltung von richtigen Schlüssen (n); Wahrheitserhaltungssystem (f); Begründungsverwaltung (f)
F système de maintenance des vérités (m)
S sistema de mantenimiento de verdad (m)
I sistema di mantenimento della verità (m)

3423 *E* truth preserving
→ truth maintenance

3424 *E* truth table (LOGIC)
G Wahrheitstabelle (f)
F table de vérité (f)
S tabla de verdad (f)
I tabella di verità (f)

3425 *E* truth value (*0 is false, 100 is absolutely true*) (LOGIC)
G Wahrheitswert (m)
F valeur de vérité (f)
S valor de verdad (m)
I valore di verità (m)

3426 *E* truth value calculation (LOGIC)
G Wahrheitswertermittlung (f)
F calcul des valeurs de vérité (m)
S cálculo de los valores de verdad (m)
I calcolo dei valori di verità (m)

3427 *E* truth value propagation (EXPERT SYSTEMS)
G Wahrheitswertpropagierung (f)
F propagation des valeurs de vérité (f)
S propagación de valores de verdad (f)
I propagazione dei valori di verità (f)

3428 *E* TTS synthesis
→ text-to-speech synthesis

3429 *E* Turing machine (TM) (THEORY)
G Turing-Maschine (TM) (f)
F machine de Turing (f)
S máquina de Turing (f)
I macchina Turing (f)

3430 *E* Turing test (THEORY)
G Turing-Test (m)
F test de Turing (m)
S test de Turing (m)
I test di Turing (m)

3431 *E* tutor (***noun***) (LEARNING)
G Tutor (m)
F tuteur (pédagogique) (m)
S tutor (m)
I tutore (m)

3432 *E* tutoring system (LEARNING)
G Tutorsystem (n)
F système d'enseignement (m)
S sistema de tutoría (m); sistema tutor (m)
I sistema di insegnamento (m)

3433 *E* twins (*descendants of the same node*) (LOGIC)
G Zwillinge (m pl)
F jumeaux (m pl)
S gemelos (m pl)
I gemelli (m pl)

3434 *E* two-layer (*network etc.*) (NEURAL NETS)
G zweischichtig
F à deux couches
S de dos capas
I a due strati

3435 *E* two-step algorithm (PROGRAMMING)
G zweischrittiger Algorithmus (m

F algorithme à deux pas (m)
S algoritmo de dos pasos (m)
I algoritmo a due passi (m)

3436 *E* two-valued logic (*exact logic*)
G zweiwertige Logik (f)
F logique à deux valeurs (f)
S lógica de dos valores (f)
I logica a due valori (f)

3437 *E* type (*in a semantic network*) (KNOWLEDGE)
= sort; kind
G Typ (m); Objektklasse (f)
F type (m)
S type (m)
I tipo (m)

3438 *E* type 1 grammar
→ context-sensitive grammar

3439 *E* type 3 grammar
→ finite state grammar

U

3440 *E* U
→ universe

3441 *E* unbound variable
→ free variable

3442 *E* uncertain[1] (*value etc.; any truth value between 1 and 99*) (LOGIC)
G unsicher
F incertain
S incierto; inseguro
I incerto

3443 *E* uncertain[2]
→ inexact

3444 *E* uncertain environment (EXPERT SYSTEMS)
G unsichere Umgebung (f)
F environnement incertain (m)
S entorno incierto (m)
I ambiente incerto (m)

3445 *E* uncertain knowledge
G unsicheres Wissen (n)
F connaissance incertaine (f)
S conocimiento incierto (m)
I conoscenza incerta (f)

3446 *E* uncertain planning (EXPERT SYSTEMS)
G unsichere Planung (f)
F planification incertaine (f)
S planificación incierta (f)
I planning incerto (m); pianificazione incerta (f)

3447 *E* uncertain premise (LOGIC)
G unsichere Prämisse (f)
F prémisse incertaine (f)
S premisa incierta (f)
I premessa incerta (f)

3448 *E* uncertain reasoning (LOGIC)
= reasoning with uncertainty
G unsicheres Schlußfolgern (n)
F raisonnement incertain (m); raisonnement sous incertitude (m)
S razonamiento con incertidumbre (m)
I ragionamento inesatto (m)

3449 *E* uncertain rule (EXPERT SYSTEMS)
G unsichere Regel (f)
F règle incertaine (f)
S regla incierta (f)
I regola inesatta (f)

3450 *E* uncertainty (LOGIC)
G Unsicherheit (f); Unbestimmtheit (f)
F incertitude (f)
S incertidumbre (f)
I incertezza (f)

3451 *E* uncertainty assessment (EXPERT SYSTEMS)
= assessment of uncertainty
G Bewertung der Unsicherheit (f)
F évaluation de l'incertitude (f)
S estimación de la incertidumbre (f)
I valutazione della incertezza (f)

3452 *E* uncertainty factor (EXPERT SYSTEMS)
G Unsicherheitsfaktor (m)
F facteur d'incertitude (m)
S factor de incertidumbre (m)
I fattore di incertezza (m)

3453 *E* uncertainty management (EXPERT SYSTEMS)

G Unsicherheitsverwaltung (f)
F traitement de l'incertain (m); traitement de l'incertitude (m)
S gestión de incertidumbre (f)
I gestione dell'incertezza (f)

3454 E unconnected speech
→ isolated words

3455 E understandability (RECOGNITION)
G Verständlichkeit (f)
F compréhensibilité (f)
S comprensibilidad (f)
I comprensibilità (f)

3456 E understander (NLP)
= understanding system
G verstehendes System (n)
F système de compréhension (m)
S sistema de comprensión (m); módulo entendedor (m)
I sistema comprendente (m)

3457 E understanding (*of language etc.*) (NLP)
G Verstehen (n); Verständnis (n)
F compréhension (f)
S comprensión (f); entendimiento (m)
I comprensione (f)

3458 E understanding criterion (NLP)
G Verständniskriterium (n)
F critère de compréhension (m)
S criterio de compresión (m)
I criterio di comprensione (m)

3459 E understanding of meaning (RECOGNITION)
G Sinnverstehen (n)
F compréhension du sens (f)
S comprensión del significado (f)
I comprensione del significato (f)

3460 E understanding system
→ understander

3461 E undirected graph
→ non-directed graph

3462 E unidirectional search (EXPERT SYSTEMS)
≠ multidirectional search
G Suche in einer Richtung (f)
F recherche dans une seule direction (f); recherche unidirectionnelle (f)
S búsqueda unidireccional (f)
I ricerca in una direzione sola (f)

3463 E unification (*of variables etc.*) (LOGIC)
= consolidation
G Unifikation (f); Unifizierung (f)
F unification (f)
S unificación (f)
I unificazione (f)

3464 E unification algorithm (LOGIC)
G Unifikationsalgorithmus (m); Unifizierungsalgorithmus (m); Vereinheitlichungsalgorithmus (m)
F algorithme d'unification (m)
S algoritmo de unificación (m)
I algoritmo di unificazione (m)

3465 E unifier (LOGIC)
G Unifikator (m); Unifizierer (m)
F unifieur (m)
S unificador (m)
I unificatore (m)

3466 E uniform cost strategy (EXPERT SYSTEMS)
G Strategie der uniformen Kosten (f)
F stratégie des coûts uniformes (f)
S estrategia de costes uniformes (f)
I metodo del costo uniforme (m)

3467 E unify (LOGIC)
G unifizieren; vereinheitlichen
F unifier
S unificar

I unificare

3468 *E* uninstantiated variable (LOGIC)
G nicht-instantiierte Variable (f)
F variable non instantiée (f)
S variable no instanciada (f)
I variabile non instanziata (f)

3469 *E* union (MATHS)
G Vereinigung(smenge) (f)
F union (f)
S unión (f)
I unione (f)

3470 *E* unique name (LOGIC)
G eindeutiger Name (m)
F nom unique (m)
S nombre único (m)
I nome unico (m)

3471 *E* unit
→ frame

3472 *E* universal expert system
G universelles Expertensystem (n)
F système expert universel (m)
S sistema experto universal (m)
I sistema esperto universale (m)

3473 *E* universal grammar (NLP)
G Universalgrammatik (f)
F grammaire universelle (f)
S gramática universal (f)
I grammatica universale (f)

3474 *E* universal knowledge
→ world knowledge

3475 *E* universally quantified variable (LOGIC)
≠ existentially quantified variable
G allquantifizierte Variable (f)
F variable quantifiée universellement (f)
S variable cuantificada universalmente (f)
I variabile quantificata universalmente (f)

3476 *E* universal quantification (LOGIC)
G Allquantifizierung (f); Allquantifikation (f)
F quantification universelle (f)
S cuantificación universal (f)
I quantificazione universale (f)

3477 *E* universal quantifier (LOGIC)
≠ existential quantifier
G Allquantor (m); Generalisator (m)
F quantificateur universel (m)
S cuantificador universal (m)
I quantificatore universale (per-ogni) (m)

3478 *E* universal representation system (LOGIC)
G universelles Darstellungssystem (n)
F système de représentation universelle (m)
S sistema de representación universal (m)
I sistema di rappresentazione universale (m)

3479 *E* universe (U)
G Universum (n)
F univers (m)
S universo (m)
I universo (m)

3480 *E* universe of discourse (NLP)
G Diskurswelt (f)
F univers de discours (m)
S universo de discurso (m)
I universo del discorso (m)

3481 *E* unknown (LOGIC)
G unbekannt
F ignoré
S desconocido
I sconosciuto; ignoto; incognito (in matematica)

3482 *E* unordered set (MATHS)
G ungeordnete Menge (f)
F ensemble non ordonné (m)

S conjunto no ordenado (m)
I insieme non ordinato (m)

3483 *E* unordered tree (LOGIC)
G nicht geordneter Baum (m)
F arbre non ordonné (m)
S árbol no ordenado (m)
I albero non ordinato (m)

3484 *E* unrestricted continuous speech recognition (*highest level of speech recognition*)
G uneingeschränktes Erkennen gesprochener Sprache (n)
F reconnaissance multilocuteurs multiréférences (f)
S reconocimiento no limitado del habla (m)
I riconoscimento illimitato del parlato (m)

3485 *E* unstructured environment
= non-structured environment
G unstrukturierte Umgebung (f)
F environnement non structuré (m)
S entorno no estructurado (m)
I ambiente non strutturato (m)

3486 *E* unsupervised learning[1]
≠ supervised learning
G nicht überwachtes Lernen (n)
F apprentissage non surveillé (m)
S aprendizaje no controlado (m)
I apprendimento non sorvegliato (m); apprendimento non supervisionato (m)

3487 *E* unsupervised learning[2]
→ learning from observation

3488 *E* upper bound (IMAGE PROCESSING)
G obere Grenze (f)
F limite supérieure (f)
S límite superior (m)
I limite superiore (m)

3489 *E* user-defined condition (EXPERT SYSTEMS)
G vom Benutzer definierte Bedingung (f); benutzerdefinierte Bedingung (f)
F condition définie par l'utilisateur (f)
S condición definida por el usuario (f)
I condizione definita dall'utente (f)

3490 *E* user-defined predicate (EXPERT SYSTEMS)
G vom Benutzer definiertes Prädikat (n); benutzerdefiniertes Prädikat (n)
F prédicat défini par l'utilisateur (m)
S predicado definido por el usuario (m)
I predicato definito dall'utente (m)

3491 *E* user-friendly
G benutzerfreundlich
F convivial
S amistoso con el usuario; convivencial
I amichevole verso l'utilizzatore

3492 *E* user-friendly interface (EXPERT SYSTEMS)
G benutzerfreundliche Schnittstelle (f)
F interface amicale (f); interface agréable (f)
S interfaz amistosa con el usuario (f)
I interfaccia amichevole verso l'utilizzatore (f)

3493 *E* user interface (PROGRAMMING)
G Benutzeroberfläche (f); Benutzerschnittstelle (f); Benutzungsoberfläche (f)
F interface avec l'utilisateur (f); interface utilisateur (f)
S interfaz de usuario (f); interfaz de comunicación usuario–sistema (f)
I interfaccia dell'utente (f)

3494 *E* user language (EXPERT SYSTEMS)
G Benutzersprache (f)
F langage d'utilisateur (m)
S lenguaje de usuario (m)
I linguaggio dell'utente (m)

3495 *E* user model (*in an ICAI system*) (LEARNING)
G Benutzermodell (n); Partnermodell (n)
F modèle de l'utilisateur (m)
S modelo de usuario (m)
I modello dell'utente (m)

3496 *E* user-modifiable (PROGRAMMING)
G vom Benutzer veränderbar
F modifiable par l'utilisateur
S modificable por el usuario
I modificabile dall'utente

3497 *E* user-tuned recognition system
→ speaker-trained recognition system

3498 *E* utterance
→ speech activity

V

3499 *E* vague fact
G vage Tatsache (f)
F fait vague (m)
S hecho vago (m)
I fatto vago (m)

3500 *E* validation (*e.g. of a system*)
G Validierung (f)
F validation (f)
S validación (f)
I validazione (f)

3501 *E* validity
= provability
G Beweisbarkeit (f)
F validité (f)
S validez (f)
I validità (f)

3502 *E* validity factor
G Gültigkeitsfaktor (m)
F facteur de validité (m)
S factor de validez (m)
I fattore di validità (m)

3503 *E* value[1] (KNOWLEDGE)
G Wert (m)
F valeur (f)
S valor (m)
I valore (m)

3504 *E* value[2]
→ filler

3505 *E* value stack (PROGRAMMING)
G Wertespeicher (m)
F pile de valeurs (f)
S pila de valores (f)
I pila dei valori (f)

3506 *E* value system (LOGIC)
G Wertesystem (n)
F système de valeurs (m)
S sistema de valores (m)
I sistema di valori (m)

3507 *E* VAR
→ variable

3508 *E* variable (VAR) (*noun*) (PROGRAMMING)
G Variable (f)
F variable (f)
S variable (f)
I variabile (f)

3509 *E* variable binding
→ binding

3510 *E* variable-breadth search (EXPERT SYSTEMS)
G Suche über eine variable Breite (f)
F recherche de largeur variable (f)
S búsqueda de anchura variable (f)
I ricerca di larghezza variabile (f)

3511 *E* variable-precision logic
G Logik mit variabler Präzision (f)
F logique de précision variable (f)
S lógica de precisión variable (f)
I logica della precisione variabile (f)

3512 *E* variable rule (EXPERT SYSTEMS)
G variable Regel (f)
F règle variable (f)
S regla variable (f)
I regola variabile (f)

3513 *E* variable scope (PROGRAMMING)
G variabler Geltungsbereich (m)

F gamme variable (f)
S gama variable (f)
I scopo variabile (m)

3514 *E* variable–value pair (KNOWLEDGE)
G Variable–Wert-Paar (n)
F paire variable–valeur (f); couple variable–valeur (m); couple v–v (m)
S par variable–valor (m)
I coppia variabile–valore (f); legame variabile–valore (m)

3515 *E* Venn diagram (MATHS)
G Venn-Diagramm (n)
F diagramme de Venn (m)
S diagrama de Venn (m)
I diagramma di Venn (m)

3516 *E* verbal phrase (LINGUISTICS)
G Verbalphrase (VP) (f)
F phrase verbale (f)
S frase verbal (f)
I frase verbale (f)

3517 *E* version graph (EXPERT SYSTEMS)
G Versionsgraph (m)
F graphe de version (m)
S grafo de versión (m)
I grafo di versione (m)

3518 *E* version space (EXPERT SYSTEMS)
G Versionsraum (m)
F espace de version (m)
S espacio de versión (m)
I spazio di versione (m)

3519 *E* view[1] (*noun*)
→ belief space

3520 *E* view[2] (*noun*)
→ schema

3521 *E* viewer-centred representation (IMAGE PROCESSING)
G betrachterzentrierte Darstellung (f)
F représentation centrée autour du spectateur (f)
S representación centrada en torno al espectador (f)
I rappresentazione centrata intorno allo spettatore (f)

3522 *E* view model (IMAGE PROCESSING)
G Betrachtungsmodell (n)
F modèle de vision (m)
S modelo de visión (m)
I modello di visione (m)

3523 *E* virtual relation (LOGIC)
G virtuelle Beziehung (f)
F relation virtuelle (f)
S relación virtual (f)
I relazione virtuale (f)

3524 *E* vision (IMAGE PROCESSING)
G Sehen (n); Vision (f)
F vision (f)
S visión (f)
I visione (f)

3525 *E* vision system (IMAGE PROCESSING)
G Sehsystem (n)
F système de vision (m)
S sistema de visión (m)
I sistema visuale (m); sistema di visione (m)

3526 *E* vista
→ belief space

3527 *E* visual depth (IMAGE PROCESSING)
G Sehtiefe (f)
F profondeur visuelle (f)
S profundidad visual (f)
I profondità visuale (f)

3528 *E* visual information (IMAGE PROCESSING)
G visuelle Information (f)
F information visuelle (f)
S información visual (f)
I informazione visuale (f)

3529 *E* visual perception (IMAGE PROCESSING)
G visuelle Wahrnehmung (f)
F perception visuelle (f)
S percepción visual (f)
I percezione visiva (f)

3530 *E* visual processing (IMAGE PROCESSING)
G visuelle Verarbeitung (f)
F traitement visuel (m)
S procesamiento visual (m)
I elaborazione visiva (f)

3531 *E* visual recognition (*e.g. of words*) (IMAGE PROCESSING)
G visuelle Erkennung (f)
F reconnaissance visuelle (f)
S reconocimiento visual (m)
I riconoscimento visuale (m)

3532 *E* visual signal (IMAGE PROCESSING)
G visuelles Signal (n)
F signal visuel (m)
S señal visual (f)
I segnale visivo (m)

3533 *E* Viterbi algorithm (*in pattern recognition*)
G Viterbi-Algorithmus (m)
F algorithme de Viterbi (m)
S algoritmo de Viterbi (m)
I algoritmo di Viterbi (m)

3534 *E* vocabulary of concepts (EXPERT SYSTEMS)
G Begriffsvokabular (n)
F vocabulaire de concepts (m); vocabulaire notionnel (m)
S vocabulario de conceptos (m)
I vocabolario di concetti (m)

3535 *E* vocal chord (RECOGNITION)
G Stimmband (n)
F corde vocale (f)
S cuerda vocal (f)
I corda vocale (f)

3536 *E* voice-activated
→ voice-operated

3537 *E* voice chip (SYNTHESIS)
↔ speech-processing chip
G Sprachchip (m)
F puce de synthèse de la parole (f)
S chip de síntesis del habla (m)
I chip di sintesi del parlato (m)

3538 *E* voice command (RECOGNITION)
= spoken command
G gesprochener Befehl (m)
F commande vocale (f); commande verbale (f)
S comando vocal (m); instrucción hablada (f)
I comando vocale (m)

3539 *E* voice command language (RECOGNITION)
G Kommandosprache für gesprochene Befehle (f)
F langage de commande vocale (m)
S lenguaje para comandos vocales (m)
I linguaggio per comandi vocali (m)

3540 *E* voice command system (RECOGNITION)
G Kommandosystem (mit Sprache als Eingabe) (n)
F système à commande vocale (m)
S sistema de comandos vocales (m)
I sistema a comando vocale (m)

3541 *E* voice communication
G gesprochene Kommunikation (f); verbale Kommunikation (f)
F communication vocale (f); communication parlée (f)
S comunicación oral (f)
I comunicazione vocale (f)

3542 *E* voice input (RECOGNITION)
= oral data input

G Spracheingabe (Eingabe gesprochener Sprache) (f); gesprochene Eingabe (f)
F entrée vocale (f)
S entrada por voz (f); entrada de voz (f); entrada hablada (f)
I input vocale (m); entrata vocale (f)

3543 *E* voice-operated (RECOGNITION)
= voice-activated
G sprachgesteuert
F à commande verbale; à entrée vocale
S controlado por voz
I a comando vocale

3544 *E* voice-operated robot
G sprachgesteuerter Roboter (m)
F robot commandé à la voix (m)
S robot controlado por voz (m)
I robot a comando vocale (m)

3545 *E* voice-operated typewriter (RECOGNITION)
G Schreibmaschine mit Spracheingabe (f)
F machine à écrire à commande verbale (f)
S máquina de escribir controlada por voz (f)
I macchina da scrivere a comando vocale (f)

3546 *E* voice output (RECOGNITION)
= speech output
G Sprachausgabe (f); Ausgabe gesprochener Daten (f)
F sortie vocale (f)
S respuesta oral (por ordenador) (f); salida hablada (f)
I output vocale (m); uscita vocale (f)

3547 *E* voice processing (RECOGNITION)
G Sprachverarbeitung (gesprochene Sprache) (f)
F traitement de la voix (m)
S tratamiento de la voz (m)
I trattamento della voce (m)

3548 *E* voice processor (RECOGNITION)
G Sprachprozessor (m)
F processeur de la parole (m)
S procesador de habla (m)
I processore del parlato (m)

3549 *E* voice recognition
→ speech recognition

3550 *E* voice-recognition board
G Spracherkennungsplatine (f)
F carte de reconnaissance vocale (f)
S tarjeta de reconocimiento de voz (f)
I scheda di riconoscimento della voce (f)

3551 *E* voice-recognition system^1
G Stimmerkennungssystem (n)
F système de reconnaissance vocale (m)
S sistema de reconocimiento de voz (m); reconocedor de voz (m)
I sistema di riconoscimento della voce (m)

3552 *E* voice-recognition system^2
→ speech-recognition system

3553 *E* voice signal (RECOGNITION)
= speech signal
G Sprachsignal (n)
F signal vocal (m)
S señal de voz (f); señal de habla (f)
I segnale vocale (m)

3554 *E* volumetric description (*of an object*) (IMAGE PROCESSING)
G Volumenbeschreibung (f)
F description volumétrique (f)
S descripción volumétrica (f)
I descrizione volumetrica (f)

3555 *E* volumetric representation (IMAGE PROCESSING)

G Volumendarstellung (f)
F représentation volumétrique (f)
S representación volumétrica (f)
I rappresentazione volumetrica (f)

3556 *E* Von Neumann machine (*conventional, non-parallel computer*)
G Von-Neumann-Maschine (f)
F machine de Von Neumann (f)
S máquina tipo Von Neumann (f)
I macchina di Von Neumann (f)

W

3557 *E* Waltz filtering
→ Boolean constraint propagation

3558 *E* waveform coding (SYNTHESIS)
G Wellenformcodierung (f)
F codage de forme d'onde (m)
S codificación de forma de onda (f); síntesis de forma de onda (f)
I codifica della forma d'onda (f)

3559 *E* weak constraint (LOGIC)
G schwache Randbedingung (f)
F contrainte faible (f)
S restricción débil (f)
I vincolo debole (m)

3560 *E* weak method (*in problem solving*) (EXPERT SYSTEMS)
G schwaches Verfahren (n)
F méthode faible (f)
S método débil (m)
I metodo debole (m)

3561 *E* weight allocation (NEURAL NETS)
G Gewichtszuordnung (f)
F allocation de poids (f)
S asignación de peso (f)
I assegnazione dei pesi (f)

3562 *E* weighted (*adjective*) (LOGIC)
G gewichtet
F pondéré
S ponderado
I ponderato

3563 *E* weighted evidence (LOGIC)
G gewichtete Evidenz (f)
F évidence pondérée (f)
S evidencia ponderada (f)
I evidenza ponderata (f)

3564 *E* weighted graph (LOGIC)
G gewichteter Graph (m)
F graphe pondéré (m); graphe valué (m)
S grafo ponderado (m)
I grafo ponderato (m)

3565 *E* weighting (*of hypotheses etc.*) (LOGIC)
G Gewichtung (f); Gewichten (n); Wichtung (f); Wichten (n)
F pondération (f)
S ponderación (f)
I ponderazione (f)

3566 *E* weighting problem (LOGIC)
G Gewichtungsproblematik (f)
F problème de pondération (m)
S problema de ponderación (m)
I problema di ponderazione (m)

3567 *E* weight of a hypothesis (LOGIC)
G Gewicht einer Hypothese (n)
F poids d'une hypothèse (m)
S peso de una hipótesis (m)
I peso di una ipotesi (m)

3568 *E* well-defined (*problem etc.*) (LOGIC)
G wohldefiniert
F bien défini
S bien definido
I ben definito

3569 *E* well-formed formula (WFF) (LOGIC)
G wohlformulierte Formel (f)
F formule bien formée (fbf) (f)
S fórmula bien formada (f)
I formula ben formata (f)

3570 *E* well-formed proposition (WFP) (LOGIC)
G wohlformulierte Aussage (f)
F proposition bien formée (f)
S proposición bien formada (f)
I proposizione ben formata (f)

3571 *E* well-ordered set (MATHS)
G wohlgeordnete Menge (f)
F ensemble bien ordonné (m)
S conjunto bien ordenado (m)
I insieme ben ordinato (m)

3572 *E* WFF
→ well-formed formula

3573 *E* WFP
→ well-formed proposition

3574 *E* what if?
→ what will happen if?

3575 *E* what-if capability (EXPERT SYSTEMS)
G Fähigkeit zu Was-wäre-wenn-Folgerungen (f); Prognostizierungsfähigkeit (f)
F capacité de prévision (f)
S capacidad de previsión (f)
I capacità di previsione (f)

3576 *E* what will happen if? (WWHI)
= what if?
G was wäre wenn?
F prévision (f)
S previsión (f)
I previsione (gli effetti di una certa azione sul sistema) (f)

3577 *E* why-explanation (EXPERT SYSTEMS)
G 'Warum'-Erklärung (f)
F explication 'pourquoi?' (f)
S explicación 'porqué' (f)
I spiegazione 'perché' (f)

3578 *E* Widrow–Hoff rule
→ delta rule

3579 *E* 'winner takes all' strategy (NEURAL NETS)
= WTA strategy
G Winner-takes-all-Strategie (f)
F stratégie WTA (f)
S estrategia WTA (f)
I strategia WTA (nella quale un neurone rimane l'unico vincitore) (f)

3580 *E* WM
→ working memory

3581 *E* word boundaries (RECOGNITION)
G Wortgrenzen (f pl)
F frontières des mots (f pl); début et fin de mot (m)
S límites de las palabras (m pl)
I limiti delle parole (m pl)

3582 *E* word hypothesis (RECOGNITION)
G Worthypothese (f)
F hypothèse de mots (f)
S hipótesis de palabra (f)
I ipotesi di parole (f)

3583 *E* word hypothesis generation (RECOGNITION)
G Generierung von Worthypothesen (f); Worthypothesengenerierung (f)
F génération des hypothèses de mots (f)
S generación de hipótesis de palabra (f)
I generazione di ipotesi di parole (f)

3584 *E* word pattern (RECOGNITION)
G Wortmuster (n)
F modèle de mots (m)
S patrón de palabra (m)
I pattern di parole (m); modello di parole (m)

3585 *E* word perception (NLP)
G Wortwahrnehmung (f)
F perception des mots (f)

S percepción de palabras (f)
I percezione di parole (f)

3586 *E* word recognizer
≠ continuous-speech recognizer
G Worterkennungskomponente (f)
F reconnaisseur de mots (m)
S módulo de reconocimiento de palabras (m)
I modulo di riconoscimento di parole (m)

3587 *E* word recognition
↔ speech recognition
G Worterkennung (f)
F reconnaissance des mots (f)
S reconocimiento de palabras (m)
I riconoscimento delle parole (m)

3588 *E* word-recognition algorithm
G Worterkennungsalgorithmus (m)
F algorithme de reconnaissance des mots (m)
S algoritmo de reconocimiento de palabras (m)
I algoritmo di riconoscimento delle parole (m)

3589 *E* word-recognition system
↔ speech-recognition system
G Worterkennungssystem (n); Einzelworterkennungssystem (n)
F système de reconnaissance de paroles (isolées) (m)
S sistema de reconocimiento de palabras (m)
I sistema di riconoscimento di parole (singole) (m)

3590 *E* word-sequence recognition
= recognition of word strings
G Erkennung von Wortfolgen (f)
F reconnaissance de mots enchaînés (f)
S reconocimiento de cadenas de palabras (m)
I riconoscimento della sequenza delle parole (m); riconoscimento di stringhe di parole (m)

3591 *E* wordspotting
→ keyboard recognition

3592 *E* word string (RECOGNITION)
G Wortkette (f); Wortfolge (f)
F mots enchaînés (m pl)
S cadena de palabras (f)
I stringa di parole (f)

3593 *E* working hypothesis (EXPERT SYSTEMS)
G Arbeitshypothese (f)
F hypothèse valable (f)
S hipótesis de trabajo (f)
I ipotesi di lavoro (f)

3594 *E* working memory (WM) (EXPERT SYSTEMS)
G Arbeitsspeicher (m)
F mémoire de travail (f)
S memoria de trabajo (f)
I memoria di lavoro (f)

3595 *E* working space
→ workspace

3596 *E* workspace (EXPERT SYSTEMS)
= working space
G Arbeitsraum (m)
F espace de travail (m)
S espacio de trabajo (m)
I spazio di lavoro (m)

3597 *E* world (KNOWLEDGE)
→ hypothetical world
G Kontextumgebung (f); 'Welt' (f)
F monde (m)
S mundo (m)
I mondo (m)

3598 *E* world knowledge[1]
= universal knowledge
G Weltwissen (n)
F connaissance générale (f)

S conocimiento general (m)
I conoscenza generale (f)

3599 *E* world knowledge[2]
→ commonsense knowledge

3600 *E* world model (NLP)
G Weltmodell (n)
F modèle du monde (m)
S modelo de un mundo (m)
I modello di un mondo (m); modello del mondo (m)

3601 *E* worst-case hypothesis (LOGIC)
G Worst-Case-Hypothese (f)
F hypothèse au pire (f)
S hipótesis del caso más desfavorable (f); hipótesis de peor caso (f)
I ipotesi del peggiore dei casi (f)

3602 *E* worst-case result (THEORY)
G Worst-Case-Ergebnis (n)
F résultat au pire (m)
S resultado del caso más desfavorable (m)
I risultato nel peggiore dei casi (m)

3603 *E* WTA strategy
→ 'winner takes all' strategy

3604 *E* WWHI
→ what will happen if?

X

3605 *E* **XPS**
→ expert system

Z

3606 *E* zero-argument predicate (LOGIC)
G Nullargumentprädikat (n)
F prédicat avec zéro arguments (m)
S predicado de cero argumentos (m)
I predicato a zero argomenti (m)

3607 *E* zero-order inference engine (EXPERT SYSTEMS)
G Inferenzmaschine nullter Ordnung (f)
F moteur d'inférence à ordre zéro (m)
S máquina de inferencias de cero orden (f); máquina de inferencias de orden cero (f)
I macchina di inferenza di ordine zero (f)

3608 *E* zero-order logic
G Logik nullter Ordnung (f)
F logique à ordre zéro (f)
S lógica de cero orden (f); lógica de orden cero (f)
I logica di ordine zero (f)

3609 *E* ZetaLISP (*a version of LISP*) (PROGRAMMING)
G ZetaLISP
F ZetaLISP
S ZetaLISP
I ZetaLISP

INDEXES

DEUTSCH

FRANÇAIS

ESPAÑOL

ITALIANO